STEALING SECRETS,

TELLING LIES

STEALING SECRETS,

TELLING LIES

How Spies and Codebreakers Helped Shape the Twentieth Century

JAMES GANNON

Brassey's
Washington, D.C.

Library of Congress Cataloging-in-Publication Data

Gannon, James.
    Stealing secrets, telling lies : how spies and codebreakers helped shape the twentieth century / James Gannon.
       p. cm.
    Includes bibliographical references and index.
    ISBN 1-57488-367-4
    1. Espionage. 2. International relations. I. Title.

    JF1525.I6 G36 2001
    355.3'432—dc21

                                                00-069888

ISBN 1-57488-367-4   (alk. paper)

Photograph of Klaus Fuchs; U.S. vs. Ethel and Julius Rosenberg, and Morton Sobel, Criminal Case Number 114868; Records of U.S. Attorneys and Marshals, Office of the U.S. Attorney for the Southern Judicial District of New York; National Arrchives and Records Administration, Northeast Region, New York City.

Brassey's, Inc.
22841 Quicksilver Drive
Dulles, Virginia 20166

First Edition

10 9 8 7 6 5 4 3 2

To Kevin, Michael, and Amy

CONTENTS

The seed for this book was planted in the late eighties when an Asian friend then teaching political science at an American college urged me to consider producing a documentary on the extent to which an anti-Asian bias in the State Department made it impossible for the United States to avoid war with Japan. The idea intrigued me. I still remember clearly the Sunday morning of December 7, 1941, when I first heard of the Japanese attack on Pearl Harbor. I was a ten-year-old playing pickup football near my boyhood home in Spokane. It came as a shock nearly a half-century later, however, to learn the depth of my ignorance about World War II. As I read more about it, I began to zero in on the impact of codebreaking on the war's outcome. That subject, rather than what might or might not have triggered the war, became my passion.

One book led to another and another. The story of codebreaking during World War II took shape in my mind. Having spent much of my career as a television news producer, I was thinking of it as a series of documentaries, but those thoughts did not pan out. Along the way, I became intrigued with the story of the Pearl Harbor spy, Takeo Yoshikawa, and was struck by the impact of this casual, sybaritic, yet professional intelligence officer on a watershed event of the twentieth century, whereas the great American cryptological achievement in duplicating the Japanese diplomatic cipher machine, Purple, yielded no advance warning of the Pearl Harbor attack. I took time out to write an article, "The Spy Who Watched Pearl Harbor," for the December 1991 edition of *The American Legion Magazine,* which marked the fiftieth anniversary of the event that plunged America into history's bloodiest war. From that point, espionage found a place in my mind alongside codebreaking as another consequential form of secret information gathering.

My research broadened as my focus narrowed to the impact of intelligence gathering on some of the major turning points of the twentieth century. I now consider myself knowledgeable about the subject, although I make no claim to technical expertise or scholarship, nor am I a maven of historiography. I think of myself essentially as a reporter with a nose for a good story. This book, in my admittedly biased opinion, contains many good stories, carefully researched from multiple sources, bearing on events that shaped our lives. I wrote it because the subject matter interests me. I tried to do it in direct, simple prose without pretense or embellishment—going light on the arcane technical details of codebreaking while, at the same time, taking the reader inside cipher machines and key-recovery machines for a better understanding of this remarkable, history-making technology.

I owe thanks to my nephew's wife, Robin Woodson Gannon, for initially suggesting sometime in the mid- to late-nineties that I put my research to good use by writing a book. The thought might have occurred to me before, but I never took it seriously until then. My son, Kevin Gannon, reinforced the idea. I was fortunate to find an agent, Max Gartenberg, who specializes in the shadow world of intelligence and believed in my project. He offered constructive criticism that made this a better book. At the publishing house, Brassey's, Inc., the manuscript went through a gauntlet of perceptive editors. Don Jacobs suggested improvements in both substance and style. Terry Belanger read the copy with a sharp eye and zero tolerance for error. Finally, Jeanne Hickman smoothed out some of the rough edges. I am indebted to other authors for most of the basic research and for insights that contributed to my understanding of the subject. In particular, I wish to thank Mark Kramer, director of the Harvard University Project on Cold War Studies, for sharing his research on Col. Ryszard Kuklinski and recommending other useful sources for the story in Chapter 16. David Kahn deserves credit for whetting my appetite for codebreaking over dinner in a Long Island restaurant, although my mind was then on a documentary, not a book. Christopher Kasparek, translator for Polish authors Wladyslaw Kozaczuk and

Marian Rejewski, made valuable referrals relating to the Polish contribution to the solution of the Enigma cipher machine.

For their help in digging out certain archival material, I am grateful to the venerable John Taylor of the military history section at the National Archives and Records Administration in College Park, Maryland, and to researcher Mia Waller. I also wish to express my appreciation to the Military Academy at West Point for permission to use the academy library and to those dedicated reference librarians in the Rockland County, New York, system, who, in the course of their day-to-day responsibilities, located obscure or outdated books and periodicals without knowing anything of my project or asking why some crazy bookworm should want them. My thanks, in particular, to Ann Ludwig of the Rose Memorial Library in Stony Point, New York. In the end, I take full responsibility for any errors of commission or omission.

JAMES GANNON

Information, Please!

During the first month of World War I, while Germany was busy invading Belgium and France in the west, Russia lost the initiative on the eastern front by failing to protect its vital secrets. Two ill-prepared Russian armies invaded East Prussia and held a two-to-one advantage in manpower over the German defenders.[1] The First Army crossed the frontier north of the Masurian Lakes on August 17, 1914. Two days later, the Second Army followed south of the lakes. There was scant coordination between them. The goal was to crush the German Eighth Army in a classic pincer east of the Vistula River. By the end of the month, however, nothing remained of the pincer's lower claw after the Germans annihilated the Second Army in a gory killing field called Tannenberg.

The German Eighth Army, about the size of either Russian army, hoped to hold off the invaders by engaging them one army at a time. The Germans attacked the First Army on August 20, halted it temporarily, and then turned south to meet the advancing Second Army. They shifted one entire corps by rail from the German far left flank, where it faced the Russian First Army in the north, to the far right flank against the Russian Second Army in the south. They were uncertain, however, whether to leave a large blocking force of about

1

two and a half corps against the First Army or to go all out against the Second Army.

The issue was decided by the sorry state of Russian communications that left the invading armies short on wire for telephone connections and without adequate preparation in codes and ciphers for wireless transmissions. Overnight on August 25–26, the Russian First and Second Army headquarters broadcast their troops' marching orders by wireless in plain language, thus revealing to German eavesdroppers the location of Second Army units and their lines of attack and objectives for the day and also divulging information that the First Army would be on the move again but nowhere near the likely battlefield. Leaving only a light screening force in the north, the German Eighth Army brought full force to bear against the Russian Second Army in the south. During a three-day battle, the Germans turned both flanks to surround and demolish the Russian center. Even the Germans were astonished by the extent of their victory. Only about one in six Russian combatants escaped death or capture. Russia remained in the war another three years, but it did not seriously threaten Germany again.

Nations go to great lengths to gain the kind of information that the inept Tsarist armies gave away at Tannenberg, by using the time-honored tools of espionage and codebreaking to gather information secretly. At Tannenberg, in fact, the Germans already knew of the coming Russian pincer movement because they had bought the Tsar's strategic war plan from a Russian traitor a decade earlier. They were also equally prepared for any opportunities that presented themselves on the battlefield, with experienced codebreakers standing by to decrypt messages they fully expected to be guarded by codes and ciphers. As at Tannenberg, so at other decisive moments of the twentieth century, knowledge of the enemy's secrets can affect the course of history.

The stories in this book bear on the impact of espionage and codebreaking at historical turning points of the major conflicts, World Wars I and II and the Cold War, that dominated the century. During a century marked by wondrous changes in the lives of people and the affairs of nations, codebreaking evolved from the ancient art of pencil-and-paper puzzle solving to the science of cryptanalysis, which has used such instruments as electromechanical cipher machines and electronic computers. Celebrated codebreakers of the past were language experts. During the twentieth century, mathematicians rose to prominence—

Marian Rejewski, Alan Turing, and Gordon Welchman, whose names are associated with solving the German Enigma military cipher machine; the Maxwell H. A. ("Max") Newman team, which built the electronic Colossus to recover German teleprinter cipher keys; and the Frank B. Rowlett team, which broke the Japanese diplomatic cipher called Purple. From their fundamental contributions, the codebreakers at Bletchley Park in the English countryside about 50 miles northwest of London profoundly affected the outcome of World War II in Europe. During the war, the United States and Great Britain forged a secret codebreaking alliance to exchange cryptotechnology and worked together on a global scale in the recovery of secret German, Italian, and Japanese messages.

In the field of espionage, romantic freelance spies of the past were supplanted by a new generation of organized, tightly controlled agents directed from central bureaucracies. Soviet intelligence—though not always successful and sometimes pathetically unsuccessful—set the standard for systematic intelligence gathering by deep agent penetration of real or imagined adversaries. The KGB (Soviet security and intelligence service) once boasted that 1,240 agents and informers worldwide turned in 41,718 items of intelligence during World War II.[2] Large numbers of these agents operated in the United States and Great Britain, the Soviets' wartime partners against Nazi Germany. In their most stunning achievement, the Soviets stole vital information about America's deepest military secret, the atomic bomb (A-bomb). This information greatly accelerated the Soviet nuclear program, and the plutonium bomb exploded by the Soviet Union in 1949 was an "exact copy" of the first American A-bomb tested in the New Mexico desert in July 1945.[3] The Soviet blast shifted the postwar balance of power.

The techniques of the police state in combining terror and espionage in one agency complicates the business of sorting out productive Soviet achievements in information gathering. In Lenin's time and during the Stalinist purges of the thirties, the agency under different names carried out bloody campaigns against the Soviets' own people—"Terrors" with a capital T worthy of the ancient barbarians—which made it difficult to see beyond the frightful image they projected. During the interwar years, however, some very bright people, believing in communism as the all-embracing answer to global injustice, served the Soviet state by stealing the secrets of the capitalist world. The half-Russian, German-reared Richard Sorge (Hamburg University, Ph.D. in political science) and his scholarly Japanese colleague Hotsumi Ozaki used weapons no more lethal than pencils to take notes and typewriters to help them shape sentences.

They were Soviet moles working as journalists, Sorge from inside the German embassy in Tokyo and Ozaki from the inner circle of Japanese left-wing politics. England's esteemed Cambridge University—unwittingly, of course—produced some of the Soviet Union's best penetration agents. Kim Philby, Donald Maclean, Guy Burgess, Anthony Blunt, John Cairncross and Alan Nunn May, to name only the most famous, all gained access to Western secrets from the inside.

In the chapters that follow, eight stories, all or in part, relate to codebreaking and to the decisive battles that they affected, and eight relate to espionage. In some cases, as in the Polish solution of the Enigma, the D-Day deception, and Soviet intelligence at the battles of Moscow and Kursk, both spying and codebreaking played a part. They are stories behind the stories repeatedly told about events that changed the world.

High-impact undercover events are isolated from the purely sensational. The femme fatale Mata Hari is barely mentioned, but the lesser-known Hans-Thilo Schmidt is prominently covered. He was, in the words of an American expert on cryptology, "the spy who most affected World War II."[4] A well-situated German, Schmidt supplied information to French intelligence during the early thirties that helped to set the stage for the Polish solution of the Enigma—the basis for the British solution of the Enigma—which was one of the Allies' most powerful weapons of World War II (Chapter 2).

Other operatives are tied to other events that shaped the century. The communist idealist Richard Sorge and the mercenary Rudolf Roessler, the man called "Lucy," supplied information vital to the success of the Red Army in World War II (Chapters 8 and 9). The Cambridge mole Donald Maclean was possibly the most damaging spy ever to work against the interests of the United States (Chapter 12). Another mole, Klaus Fuchs, German by birth and British by naturalization, did more than any other known spy to help the Soviet Union build an atomic bomb (Chapter 13). Takeo Yoshikawa, a Japanese naval intelligence officer under diplomatic cover, watched Pearl Harbor in the months before the surprise Japanese attack of December 7, 1941, that catapulted America into World War II (Chapter 10). Soviet Col. Oleg Vladimirovich Penkovsky was a vital contributor to the American triumphs in the Cuban missile crisis in 1962 and the less memorable but equally important crisis over Berlin earlier that year during the administration of President John F. Kennedy (Chapter 15).

Polish Col. Ryszard Kuklinski, the U.S. Central Intelligence Agency's (CIA's) most important mole inside the Warsaw Pact during the 1970s, played a part in the downfall of the Soviet empire that began with the rise of Solidarity (Chapter 16). Both of these Soviet bloc men, disillusioned insiders, volunteered their services to the West.

Some of the great codebreakers of the twentieth century are virtually unknown to American readers. Marian Rejewski was a Polish mathematician who broke the Enigma seven years earlier than the more famous Alan Turing. Turing worked from Rejewski's groundbreaking achievement (Chapter 2). Just what Turing did is widely misunderstood fully six decades after the British solution of Enigma. He was a great thinker, deservedly honored as the first to conceptualize the electronic computer. He visualized a machine that would think and compute like a human. He called it the "Universal Turing Machine," but he never built one. His key-finding machine for the Enigma, based on Polish technology, was electromechanical. Later, a Bletchley Park team, headed by Maxwell H. A. Newman, built an electronic key-finding machine, the Colossus, to cope with a German teleprinter cipher. The Colossus is hailed as the first electronic computer. Its construction was entirely separate from the Enigma project, and Turing had little or nothing to do with it (Chapter 5). The American cryptanalyst Frank B. Rowlett worked in the shadow of his more famous mentor and civil service superior, William F. Friedman. If any one man can be called "the man who broke Purple," however, it is Rowlett, not Friedman. The fact is that no one man broke Purple; the Rowlett team did it (Chapter 6).

So important was the influence of these achievements that the history of World War II has had to be rewritten since the first startling revelations in the mid-seventies of Bletchley Park's wartime role. It stretches the imagination to think that men, far removed in time and distance, mulling over abstract mathematical formulas could help save the lives of merchant seamen in the North Atlantic, or help defeat the great German Field Marshal Erwin Rommel, or help ease the D-Day landing at Normandy. Remote as it might seem, the seminal work of Rejewski in 1932–33—together with the contributions of Turing and Welchman in 1939—played a part in the Allied victory over German U-boats in the Battle of the Atlantic (Chapter 3) and helped Gen. Sir Bernard Montgomery defeat Rommel at El Alamein in 1942 (Chapter 4). When one adds to the efforts of those three mathematicians the separate contributions of the Newman and Rowlett teams, the result is Bletchley Park's formidable array of codebreaking tools, which laid the groundwork for the magnificent D-Day deception that facilitated the Allied landing in Normandy on June 6, 1944 (Chapter 7). Without knowing it Bletchley Park even helped the Red Army defeat the Germans in history's largest tank battle at Kursk during the summer of 1943. The Soviet mole from Cambridge, John Cairncross, was on the inside at Bletchley as a language specialist, and he passed pertinent information to his Soviet control (Chapter 9).

Other great codebreaking feats stand apart from the arrival of the machine cipher. The British naval intelligence chief, Capt. William Reginald ("Blinker") Hall, used a decoded German telegram to lure America into war against Germany in World War I, thus tipping the balance of power in favor of the Western Allies (Chapter 1). Meredith Gardner was a linguistically gifted American codebreaker who, poring over difficult Soviet codes in deep secrecy inside the American government during the late forties, helped to unmask the atomic spies and a vast Soviet intelligence network in the United States (Chapter 14). Codebreaking also made an important impact on the Pacific War. The decisive Battle of Midway in June 1942, according to Adm. Chester W. Nimitz, Pacific Fleet commander, was an American victory of intelligence. U.S. Navy codebreakers at Pearl Harbor decrypted the entire Japanese battle plan several days prior to the fighting. The information was about as good as that given to the Germans at Tannenberg. Thanks to codebreaking, the Americans knew where to look for the Japanese carrier striking force, which, in its eagerness to deliver a decisive knockout blow to the American presence in the Western Pacific, never saw the American punch coming (Chapter 11).

The reader is invited to take these stories as interest dictates. Each chapter is meant to be self-contained and unrelated to the other chapters—and most are. But the full Bletchley Park story is too big to be thus confined; it requires an entire section—Part II, "The Cipher War," Chapters 2 through 7. Even the reader who has little interest in the mechanics of cipher and key-recovery machines will better appreciate the Allied victories in the North Atlantic (Chapter 3) and North Africa (Chapter 4) by a preliminary understanding of the Polish and British solutions of the Enigma (Chapter 2). In the same way, the Allies' grand deception for D-Day (Chapter 7) is brought into better focus by knowing the full extent of Bletchley Park's cryptanalytic capabilities, including the technology to break three major enemy machine ciphers: Enigma, the

German teleprinter cipher called Fish (Chapter 5), and the Japanese diplomatic cipher, Purple (Chapter 6).

Many familiar spies are not included in this book. The famous Americans John Walker and Aldrich Ames had no decisive impact on history. Walker, a Navy communications specialist, might have made a difference if there had been a Soviet-American nuclear war during the seventies. He sold information so sensitive—operating manuals and daily cipher keys—that the Soviets might have been able to cripple part of the American nuclear striking force. They knew, for example, where to find missile-launching nuclear submarines. As it turned out, Walker's treachery enabled the Soviets to decrypt more than a million naval, military, and diplomatic messages during the Cold War.[5]

Ames, the CIA official who provided the KGB with the names of American agents inside the Soviet Union, operated on an entirely different scale. His treachery posed no threat of wholesale annihilation. In a television interview, he once said of his actions, "No significant damage to our national security interests occurred. Tremendous damage was done to the agency's institutional framework, the agency's operations and, most importantly, to an awful lot of people."[6] By that, he recognized that the interests of the American people and the CIA did not necessarily coincide, and that the undercover "war within the Cold War" among rival intelligence bureaucracies took on an essentially parochial life of its own. To put it another way, the loss of an American spy in the Soviet Union would have been a setback for the CIA and a personal tragedy for the agent's family, but it did not threaten to bring on Armageddon.

Kim Philby, one of the most able and resourceful known spies of the century, operated in the same limited arena as Ames. Had his cover not been blown by the flight of Guy Burgess and Maclean in 1951, Philby might one day have become the chief of MI6, the British Secret Intelligence Service. At one time in the aftermath of World War II, he ran the Soviet desk in London. He recruited agents to spy for Britain inside the Soviet Union and then gave their identities to Soviet intelligence so they would be liquidated when they landed behind the Iron Curtain. In 1945, a Soviet intelligence official, Konstantin Volkov, tried to defect to the British in Turkey with information that would have exposed Philby. In London, Philby was among the first to hear about it and had the good fortune of being assigned to handle it. He passed word to his

Soviet control and stalled the defection until the hapless Volkov could be bundled onboard a Soviet plane and flown back to Moscow.

As MI6 liaison in Washington during the late forties, Philby looked over Meredith Gardner's shoulder to watch the American codebreaker narrow the list of possible Soviet spies who had operated within the British Embassy. Philby knew long before Gardner that the mole in question was his friend and fellow Cambridge alumnus Donald Maclean (Chapter 14). A high-ranking embassy official, Maclean had access to American atomic, military, and political secrets and revealed them to Soviet intelligence. Because Maclean helped the Soviet Union become an atomic power and gave away British and American secrets useful to Stalin at Yalta and during the Korean War, he, rather than Philby, is a focus for this book (Chapter 12).

To some people, it might seem wretched that snooping—to put it inelegantly—should play such a vital role in history. With security at stake, however, a nation ignores the secrets of other nations at its own peril. In 1929, President Herbert Hoover's new secretary of state, Henry L. Stimson, discontinued the American Black Chamber, a secret codebreaking operation funded jointly by the Army and the State Department, with the famous comment, "Gentlemen do not read each other's mail"—a commendable, high-minded sentiment. But, by 1940, after the Rowlett team broke Purple, Stimson, as President Roosevelt's secretary of war, was on the Magic distribution list and became an avid reader of decrypted Japanese diplomatic messages. He learned, among other things, that key Japanese embassies and consulates were havens for espionage. For that, Japan need not be condemned because, during the twenties, the American Black Chamber had eavesdropped in a most ungentlemanly fashion on Japanese diplomats. Undercover intelligence gathering is part of the fabric of history—always has been and always will be—whether it is espionage or codebreaking or some other form not yet imagined.

PART 1

THE GREAT
WAR

CHAPTER 1

Herr Zimmermann's
Fatal Blunder

It was called "the war to end all wars," but, by the beginning of 1917, frightened Europeans had come to think of it as the war to end civilization. What the lofty generals believed would be a short war, measured in weeks or months at the most, had grown in its third year into World War I on a grand scale. A doomed generation of young men went solemnly to slaughter in the killing fields of France, Eastern Europe, the Balkans, and the Middle East. On the stalemated western front, where gas warfare had raised the level of savagery, the gain of a few thousand yards of barren, shell-pocked real estate might cost hundreds of thousands of casualties. In the two major battles of 1916, at Verdun and at the Somme River, an estimated two million troops were killed, wounded, or captured with no lasting advantage for either side. The principal belligerents, Germany on one side and France and Britain on the other, had neither the power to win under the conditions of battlefield parity and international restraint then in effect nor the compassion to stop the carnage for anything less than total victory.

The United States stood out for both its potential to change the course of the war and the confusing reality of its posture. Britain and France wanted the U.S. to fight on their side because it offered their best hope for victory. Germany wanted to keep the United States out of the war because its leaders thought that Germany could prevail if only the Americans would stop supplying its enemies. The Americans themselves were divided. Many sympathized with the Allies, but President Woodrow Wilson doggedly pursued a policy of neutrality that dovetailed nicely with the isolationist sentiments of a large body of American opinion. Standing beneficently above the fray, Wilson was ready to mediate the conflict as a nonbelligerent friend of both sides. Germany liked American neutrality but not American shipments of food and war materials to Britain and France. It was only business, the Americans said. They wanted to trade with Germany, too, except that a British blockade of Germany made it virtually impossible.

German militarists thought they had a way to deal with the problem—unrestricted submarine warfare against merchant shipping. The U-boats would attack "without warning," which meant merchant crews would have no time to lower lifeboats before the deadly torpedoes were launched. Unrestricted submarine warfare had been tried earlier with disastrous results. On May 7, 1915, the U-20 struck the *Lusitania* off the west coast of England. The Cunard liner sank in eighteen minutes with the loss of 1,198 passengers and crew, including 128 Americans, most of them women and children. Neutral sentiments in America turned to outrage against Germany. The feeling spread that the United States would soon join the war, but Wilson stood firm in his detachment and rode out the storm.

Taken aback by the American reaction, Germany suspended its submarine campaign four months later but held on to the idea. German shipyards went on a crash program to upgrade the U-boat fleet to a war-winning level. In their new calculations, German militarists, led by Gen. Erich Ludendorff, assumed that unleashing the submarines would bring the United States into the war. They believed that with enough U-boats, however, they could choke off neutral shipments and bring Britain and France to their knees before the American troops could make an impact on the ground in France. Chancellor Theobald von Bethmann-Hollweg, chastened by the *Lusitania* fiasco, fought a losing political battle against the plan as new U-boats continued to slip from their cradles.

In this setting, the explosive Zimmermann telegram unhinged the murderous stalemate in Europe.

———————

Capt. William Reginald ("Blinker") Hall served throughout most of World War I as Director, Intelligence Division (DID) of the British Naval Staff, later

Director of Naval Intelligence (DNI). The day would come when the rank would be upgraded to admiral, and the man would be awarded the honorific "sir." In his late forties and small of stature with a balding, pinkish pate rising above a semicircle of white hair, Hall was blessed with a quick mind and shrewd judgment. From childhood, he was stuck with his nickname because he had a habit of constantly blinking his eyes. He blinked more than usual in midmorning, January 17, 1917, when handed a partially decrypted telegram by one of his top decoders, Lt. Cdr. Nigel de Grey, who had emerged from his codebreakers' burrow in Room 40.

"DID, d'you want to bring America into the war?" de Grey asked excitedly.

"Yes, my boy. Why?"

"I've got something here which—well, it's a rather astonishing message which might do the trick, *if* we could use it."[1]

Hall read what there was of the intercepted telegram from German Foreign Minister Arthur Zimmermann to Count Johann von Bernstorff, the German ambassador in Washington:

> Most secret for your Excellency's personal information and to be handed on to the imperial minister in (?) Mexico with . . . by a safe route.
> We propose to begin on 1 February unrestricted submarine warfare. In doing so, however, we shall endeavor to keep America neutral . . . (?) If we should not (succeed in doing so) we propose to (? Mexico) an alliance upon the following basis:
> (joint) conduct of war
> (joint) conclusion of peace
> Your Excellency should for the present inform the president [of Mexico] secretly (that we expect) war with the U.S.A. (possibly) (. . . Japan) and at the same time to negotiate between us and Japan . . . (Indecipherable sentence [inferred to mean] please tell the president) that . . . our submarines . . . will compel England to peace within a few months.[2]

Blinker Hall could hardly contain his excitement. He mulled the salient points: unconditional submarine warfare, a German alliance with Mexico at America's doorstep, negotiations with Japan. He knew the ominous language about U-boats "compel[ling] England to peace within a few months" was no idle boast. Britain's only real hope, he thought, was to bring America into the war. Maybe the unfettered submarines would do the trick. But maybe not. Wilson was a strong-willed man, unyielding in his commitment to neutrality. If not, public disclosure of the telegram with its implications of Mexican and Japanese intrigue would be a bombshell, but Hall wasn't sure how to make it public. At all cost, he must keep the Germans from learning that London could read their codes. If they found out, they would change the codes and shut off a priceless source of intelligence. That's what de Grey had meant when he said, "*if* we could use it." It was also important to have a full and accurate text; the partial decrypt left the Germans too much room for denial. So he locked the telegram in his desk, imposed the utmost secrecy, and asked de Grey to keep working toward a completed text with his fellow codebreaker, the Reverend William Montgomery. Hall himself had some thinking to do.

He was taking on a grave responsibility. With the future of Britain on the line, he was unwilling, at least for the time being, to share this vital information with anyone outside his small circle, even with his superiors. To say the least, it was an extraordinary act of nerve and self-confidence to put his judgment implicitly above that of the nation's naval and political leaders. No common bureaucrat would have dared. How far does one take the duty of the office to preserve the secrets? Hall alone would determine that in his own time. He would decide when and to whom he would divulge the provocative Zimmermann telegram. He would decide if it was even necessary and whether it could be done without compromising Room 40. If Hall was playing God with the fate of his nation, he had full confidence in his own divinity.

Hall was used to making lonely decisions. As a career naval officer and the son of a career naval officer, he had thrived in the command of ships at sea. His superiors noticed that his ship usually outperformed the others. He also gained renown in Navy circles for strict but fair discipline and for the efficiency and high morale of his crews. In what seemed misfortune at the time for the British Navy but turned out to be a stroke of good luck for all of Britain, Hall's last command at sea, as captain of the new battle cruiser *Queen Mary,* was cut short by ill health two months after the onset of war, and he had to be relieved of command. In October 1914, he was appointed DID.

Despite his lack of experience in the intelligence field, he was not a haphazard choice. Years earlier, his father, Capt. William Henry Hall, had been the first DID. Blinker Hall himself had already demonstrated an aptitude for the intelligence game. In 1908 as captain of the cadet training cruiser *Cornwall,* the Admiralty (Navy Department) asked him while on a visit to Kiel to count the shipbuilding slips in a restricted area. How he obtained the information was left to him. At Kiel, he borrowed a fast motorboat from the Duke of Westminster, who happened to be lying over during a cruise in his royal yacht. Hall took the boat on a "pleasure run" of the Kiel Fjord and found a way for it to conveniently break down opposite the building slips. While the boat was being "repaired," two of Hall's officers below were snapping pictures so the Admiralty would have no doubt as to the number of slips.

Consequently, when the old sea dog entered the starkly different environment at naval intelligence, he fit cleanly into his new command. Hall saw naval intelligence in expansive terms, not confined to strictly naval matters, and impossible to separate from diplomacy and overseas business. He brought bright and talented civilians into the Intelligence Division as its functions grew with the demands of war. He deployed British agents to hotbeds of espionage around the globe to negate German gunrunning to the Irish Republican Army, to monitor German machinations in Spain, and to counteract German sabotage against British shipping in the Americas.

Hall had it within himself to act boldly on matters that were not strictly his business. On his own authority, he opened secret negotiations with Turkey to break off relations with Germany and allow the Allies transit of the Dardanelles so that Western aid could reach Russia. Hall's emissaries carried a letter to Turkish leader Enver Pasha that gave his personal guarantee of 3 million pounds, with discretion to raise the bribe to 4 million. Though cordial, the talks ultimately failed, primarily because Hall's own Navy superiors, including the politically powerful First Lord of the Admiralty Winston Churchill, had no idea what Hall was doing and they were working at cross-purposes with him. In the end, Churchill opted for the mailed fist over the money-laden velvet glove and undertook the disastrous Gallipoli expedition that ended in humiliating defeat for the Allies.

Consistent with his broad outlook, Hall chose assistants who moved in circles beyond his own. Lord Baron ("Dick") Herschell had connections to the royal court as former lord in waiting to Kings Edward VII and George V. Claud Serocold had been plucked from the financial world where he had been a stockbroker. Both were graduates of Eton, the preparatory school of the English elite, and both proved invaluable in their service to Hall. Hall also knew how to make friends in the right places. He was on good terms with American Ambassador Walter Hines Page and had an excellent personal and working relationship with the second secretary of the American Embassy, Edward Bell. These friendships were bound together with genuine respect and affection. Page, an unrestrained Anglophile, thought Hall to be a genius.

While Hall reached out shrewdly to others, he never surrendered his tenacious independence of thought. He tells one story of a late-night session with Churchill that reveals a lot about the character of both men. Churchill possessed such formidable forensic skills that he often won approval of projects that his crusty admirals diametrically opposed. With words as his weapon, he would beat them into humble submission by sheer force of argument. Late one night, he summoned Hall to discuss a point that years later Hall did not even remember. He remembered only that he disagreed completely with Churchill's argument, but, because of its brilliance, he feared that he would be brought around to Churchill's view. So, as Churchill carried on, Hall started muttering to himself, "My name is Hall. My name is Hall. . . ." Churchill broke off to ask what he was mumbling about. "I am saying to myself that my name is Hall because if I listen to you much longer I shall be convinced it's Brown." Churchill laughed, "Then you don't agree with what I've been saying?" "I don't agree with one word of it," said the Navy bureaucrat to the First Lord. The conversation ended, and a tired Hall went to bed. Of course, only Hall and Churchill were witness to the conversation, but author Patrick Beesly, who repeats the story, reports that friends of both men found it to ring true.[3]

In the course of building his espionage network, Hall was ever mindful of the important intelligence supplied by the codebreakers in Room 40. He had not been there at the birth of the British codebreaking unit, and, for the first two years of the war, he wielded influence on Room 40 and used its product but did not directly control it. Therefore, he could not fully coordinate it with the broad needs of his intelligence operation.

––––––––––

Room 40 did not exist when war began at midnight, August 4, 1914, but the cable ship *Telconia* took the first relevant act in its birth only a few hours later. In the half-light of dawn, August 5, in the North Sea off the German port of Emden, the *Telconia* severed five German telegraph cables that ran through the English Channel to the world beyond. This led Germany to rely heavily on Guglielmo Marconi's relatively new wireless invention for rapid communications. The airwaves were soon crackling with wireless messages heard in England. Antennas belonging to the Post Office, the Marconi Company, and individual radio hams supplemented the Admiralty's one receiving station. Before long, encrypted German radiograms were piling up in the office of Rear Admiral Henry F. Oliver, the DID at that time. In that form they did him no good, but Oliver recognized their potential. He enlisted his friend, Sir Alfred Ewing, Director of Naval Education, to organize a codebreaking unit. Ewing reached out to the naval colleges of Osborne and Dartmouth for talented young instructors willing to volunteer for temporary service during the summer recess. Several did, and some stayed permanently after college classes resumed in late September. Thus, from humble beginnings was born one of the most successful intelligence operations in history which made important, if not decisive, contributions to Allied victories in two world wars.

The initial recruits, among them Alastair Denniston, who would become head of the Government Code & Cypher School between the wars, were fluent in German but knew very little about codes and ciphers. They were getting nowhere with the German cryptograms until the fortunes of war turned in their favor. Within twelve weeks, three important German naval codes came into their possession. The first, used for major operations, was turned over in mid-October by Britain's Russian ally after it was recovered in late August from the grounded German cruiser *Magdeburg* off Estonia. The second was a German merchant marine and naval code from the German-Australian steamship *Hobart*. Although seized on August 11 in Australia, the code did not reach Room 40 until the end of October. Finally, in December, came a German code used by flag officers (admirals), the most fortuitous catch of all. This code had been among secret papers tossed overboard in a leaden box from a German destroyer going down in the North Sea during a mid-October gun battle. A month later, the box was snagged off the bottom in the net of a fishing trawler in what Room 40 always referred to as "the miraculous draught of fishes."

With these three codes in hand, Room 40 made dramatic progress. Before long the decoders could read much of the German Navy's signal traffic, which helped them to keep track of the High Seas Fleet and locate menacing submarines and dirigibles. Success brought a greater recognition of need at high policy levels, and growth naturally followed. The Admiralty authorized more receiving stations. Room 40's complement of personnel mushroomed, and the unit became an official subsection of the Intelligence Division with an official designation of ID-25, but still referred to as Room 40 by the people who worked there. Room 40 played a part in two major naval battles of World War I, Dogger Bank and Jutland. In both battles, the Admiralty set out to destroy the German fleet, which rarely ventured out of safe harbor, but both opportunities were lost. The failures resulted partly from a lack of sophistication in the distribution of the intelligence derived from codebreaking, although the codebreaking itself was judged an overall success as a tactical aid in battle. As the war dragged on, Room 40 made positive contributions to British defenses against U-boat attacks on merchant ships at sea and dirigible bombing runs in England.

The naval achievements, however, pale in comparison to the codebreaking coup scored with the Zimmermann telegram. The background to that event began in April 1915 when a diplomatic code known as 13040 turned up in Room 40. Where it came from is not entirely clear, but it appears to have been left behind by a German diplomat vacating his consulate on the Persian Gulf.[4] Up to that time, nonnaval codes were proving unbreakable. The Admiralty authorized Hall to establish a diplomatic subsection. To run it, he picked Etonian George Young, a diplomat and accomplished linguist. The tiny staff of codebreakers included de Grey and Montgomery.

The diplomatic section soon learned that Berlin was sending coded messages by way of Swedish and American diplomatic cables. Unknown to the Germans, both cables went through a relay station in Cornwall on the English southwest coast. Hall saw to it that the messages in transit were copied for referral to Room 40. The Swedish cable ran between Stockholm and Buenos Aires, which became the transfer locale to and from the German embassies in Washington and throughout the Americas. It came to be known in Room 40 as the "Swedish Roundabout." In neutral Sweden, the Germans had found a sympathetic ear for their cause, but Sweden, by allowing a belligerent nation the use of its trans-Atlantic cable for coded official messages was in callous disregard of its neutral status. German use of the American State Department cable was also a breach of international norms because the messages were sent in German code so the Americans did not know the actual contents. Col. Edward M. House, a close advisor to President Wilson, had made the arrangement over the State Department's vigorous protest. Berlin had given its word that the subject would be limited to the peace negotiations so dear to President Wilson, but the good-hearted Wilson would learn in due time that his trust was cynically betrayed.

Code 13040 helped Room 40's codebreakers to read some but not all of the diplomatic traffic. This code, in fact, had been in use for some time, and the Germans were in the process of replacing it. But that was not the problem it once was for British codebreakers. They were getting the hang of cryptanalysis and were no longer as desperate as they once were for the new codes to fall fortuitously into their hands. Early in 1916, they obtained a slim classified American textbook, *Manual for the Solution of Military Ciphers,* written by a U.S. signals intelligence officer, Capt. Parker Hitt.[5] It taught them how to break down ciphers with alphabetic frequency tables. Hitt's system was based on the theory that the letters of the alphabet of any language appear in a predictable frequency,[6] but, for the deductions to come out right, the cryptanalyst needs a large volume of traffic. Hitt also offered valuable advice about finding clues in a message's preamble, which contains such information as "place from," date, address, signature, and even the subject of the main text. The preamble was always easier to solve because for the benefit of the operator it was encrypted in a simpler cipher than the main text.

By 1917, Room 40 was probably the best organization in the world for solving codes and ciphers. The Zimmermann telegram came through in a new code, known as 0075, that Room 40 was trying to break by cryptanalysis and for which it had only partial solutions.[7] That is why the version handed to Hall on January 17 was so tantalizingly incomplete. By this time, too, Ewing had departed as day-to-day head of Room 40, so that the totality of naval intelligence, including all codebreaking functions, was in Hall's capable hands.

In Washington, late in the day on January 31, 1917, German Ambassador Bernstorff informed U.S. Secretary of State Robert Lansing of his government's decision to resume unrestricted submarine warfare. Although President Wilson reacted with shock and anger, he did not display enough of either to suit Blinker Hall. Wilson broke off diplomatic relations with Germany and declared a state of armed neutrality but not war. Hall knew then that the Zimmermann telegram would have to come into play. De Grey and Montgomery had made some progress in further decrypting it but still did not have a full text. Hall began making plans. He would first need to approach British Foreign Secretary Arthur James Balfour, whom he had come to know and admire when Balfour was First Lord of the Admiralty. Hall respected Balfour and more important, knew that the Americans trusted him as well. To gain access to Balfour, he went through Lord Hardinge of Penshurst, permanent secretary at the Foreign Office, on February 5. Thus, Hardinge was the first Briton outside the Intelligence Division to see the partially decrypted Zimmermann telegram. Hardinge promised to show it to Balfour and advised Hall to obtain a full text.

Hall intended to do just that and, at the same time, to deflect suspicion from Room 40 once the telegram was leaked. The Zimmermann message had been transmitted in two legs, Berlin to Washington and Washington to Mexico City. Hall possessed the cipher text of the first leg in code 0075, partially decrypted. He guessed that the second leg would be transmitted from Washington to Mexico City in a different code, 13042, a variant of 13040, used by smaller German embassies. Room 40 was very familiar with 13042 and would find it easier to break than 0075. Also, the message from Washington to Mexico City would have a different preamble from the one locked in his desk, including a different date of transmission. When Berlin went looking for the source of the leak, suspicion would fall on Washington or Mexico City, not London.

Hall had the assets he needed in Mexico City to carry out his plan. Sometime in 1916, Sir Thomas ("Tom") Hohler, who was then British Charge d'Affaires, had established a close friendship with two English brothers living there, one a printer and the other an employee in the telegraph service. It was the kind of friendship born of the highest obligation—for life itself. Hohler had persuaded Mexican authorities to spare the printer's execution on a false counterfeiting charge. He then accepted the brothers' grateful offer to return the favor by enlisting the telegraph employee to obtain copies of all telegrams between German Charge d'Affaires Heinrich von Eckhardt and his Swedish counterpart, Folke Cronholm, who handled von Eckhardt's diplomatic correspondence by way of the Swedish Roundabout. This practice continued after Hohler transferred out of Mexico City at the end of the year. Hall instructed Hohler's successor, Edward Thurston, to expedite copies of all cables since mid-January from Bernstorff, the German ambassador in Washington, to von Eckhardt.

By February 19, Hall was holding the plaintext of the Zimmermann telegram, which contained the preamble marking it as a cable from Washington to Mexico City. The British Foreign Office had not decided yet on a course of action, but Hall, on his own initiative, decided to prepare the way. He called his friend Edward Bell at the American Embassy. A half-hour later, Bell sat in Hall's office reading the telegram in shocked disbelief. The full text contained the following incendiary language:

Mexico is to reconquer the lost territory in Texas, New Mexico and Arizona. . . . [The President of Mexico] should on his own initiative invite Japan to immediate adherence and at the same time mediate between Japan and ourselves.[8]

It must be a fraud, was Bell's first reaction. Hall assured him that it was genuine.

"Then this means war," Bell said.

"If it becomes public," Hall replied.

Bell was now beginning to realize the significance of the telegram, for he and Ambassador Page were on the same wavelength with Hall in believing that the United States must join the war against Germany. Zimmermann's secret proposal to give Mexico a large slice of the United States, combined with the suggestion that Japan might join in the plunder while publicly professing peaceful intentions, would be enough to convince the most diehard isolationist—even the stubborn neutralist in the White House—that Germany was the unscrupulous enemy of American interests.

Bell returned to the embassy and informed Page, who became a willing partner in Hall's plot. Page joined friendly, informal conversations over the next few days on just how to make the telegram public. Balfour and his aides in the Foreign Office had been discussing the question since Hall's visit to Hardinge and remained undecided. Balfour's instinct was to leave the solution to the trusted Hall. Page believed it important to keep the disclosure on a high diplomatic plane, and, because Balfour was held in high esteem in Washington, Page thought that Balfour, as foreign minister, should officially present the telegram to him, as the American ambassador, to head off suspicions in Washington of a British trick.

Given Bell's initial skepticism, Hall realized that even the truth would be a hard sell to a doubting American public. The truth! There was only one truth that Hall wanted to sell—that the Zimmermann telegram was the real thing. The truth about Britain tapping American and Swedish cables and the truth of British codebreaking success would have to be covered up. The Germans must not know because a priceless source of intelligence would dry up, and, if the Americans found out, it would cause a public uproar on the other side of the Atlantic. Hall wanted the Americans to focus their anger on Germany, not Britain. He also recognized that he would have to give up one of Room 40's secrets to high American officials for what he considered the greater good of bringing America into the war, and he was ready to tell them Britain possessed Germany's old diplomatic code 13040 and its variant 13042.

The formula for disclosure took shape in Hall's mind. Balfour would officially present the telegram to Page, and Page would officially notify his government. The Americans could then find the coded Washington-to-Mexico City telegram in the Washington office of the private telegraph company, Western Union, which would verify its authenticity. At the same time, it would support the fiction that the Americans had discovered it, rather than the British, but the Americans would have to come to London to decrypt it. Hall was willing to let them use code 13040, but he would not let the code out of Room 40. The cryptogram found at Western Union in Washington would be sent to London, where Bell would decrypt it with de Grey guarding the codebook. In effect, de Grey would do the actual decryption. Thus, the plan was set. It remained for the players in the Zimmermann drama to carry it out.

On February 23, Page went to the Foreign Office to receive the telegram from Balfour, along with a cover story prepared by Hall to protect the source. Page worked the rest of that day and through the night until early the next afternoon in composing a letter of explanation to President Wilson and Secretary of State Lansing. In it, Page revealed for the first time that, early in the war, Britain had secured a copy of "the German cipher code used in this message" (code 13040, not 0075) and had "made it their business" to obtain copies of all coded German Embassy telegrams to Mexico for decryption in London. Repeating Hall's cover story, Page said that the copies "were not obtained in Washington, but were bought in Mexico." Britain, Page continued, requested that the American government keep the source of the information and the method of obtaining it "profoundly secret" but "put no prohibition on the publication of Zimmermann's telegram itself."[9]

Page's cable reached Washington on the evening of Saturday, February 24. The President read it that evening and was described as "indignant." Secretary of State Lansing was away for the weekend, so Wilson decided to await his return before deciding what to do. Meantime, the State Department obtained a copy of the coded Bernstorff–von Eckhardt telegram from Western Union and had its confirmation. On Tuesday, Lansing (pro-British like Page) went to see Wilson. He brought still another version of the Zimmermann telegram, this one the original in code 0075 from Zimmermann to Bernstorff, which was dug out of the State Department's own cable files. When the President learned that the Germans were using the cable line, which he had generously lent them for peace negotiations, for the purpose of plotting war, he is said to have exclaimed, "Good Lord! Good Lord!" which is allegedly as close as Wilson ever came to profanity.[10] He decided then to make the telegram public. It was leaked to E. M. Hood of the Associated Press, dean of the Washington press corps. The story broke in bold headlines across the country on March 1. It had the predictable chilling effect on isolationist sentiment, except for a small number of pacifist senators who branded the telegram a British forgery. Even they were silenced the next day when Zimmermann himself admitted to a pro-German American journalist looking for a denial that the telegram was genuine. Hall was as relieved as he was surprised. Zimmermann himself had closed the door unwittingly to any lingering argument against American entry into the war.

President Wilson realized that the Zimmermann telegram would destroy public support for his neutralist policy, and that he could do nothing to stop the U.S. from spiraling inexorably into war. Two months earlier, when Germany had announced the resumption of unconditional submarine warfare, Wilson had refused to budge from his neutralist stance. He was unwilling to take the Germans at their malicious word unless they committed an overt act. This act occurred on March 18 when U-boats sank three U.S. merchant ships with heavy loss of life. Two days later, on March 20, Wilson convened his Cabinet and the members expressed unanimous support for war. The next day the President recalled Congress for a special session to begin April 2. Citing the Zimmermann telegram as "eloquent evidence," he observed, "Germany means to stir up enemies against us at our very doors."[11]

When war was declared on April 6, the United States found itself woefully unprepared (not a unique circumstance in its history). The "Yanks" were coming over there, as the song promised, but it would take time. Raw troops had to be trained. Once they were ready for combat, the British and French had to supply much of their equipment, especially artillery. Not until the end of May 1918 did the Americans take part in their first memorable action at Château-Thierry. From then on, they were in the thick of the fighting and distinguished themselves in battle. The war ended less than six months later with the American army fully engaged in its assigned sector beside the British and French. Blinker Hall had got his wish for the United States to enter the war and the result he expected with an Allied victory. Due credit must go to Herr Zimmermann's colossal blunder and Hall's shrewd manipulation of it.

PART 2

THE CIPHER WAR

CHAPTER 2

The Enigma Demystified

The Enigma was not the only rotor cipher machine in its time, not even the first and maybe not the best, but it became the most famous because, despite its excellent design, it failed spectacularly during World War II. The failure was no fault of Arthur Scherbius, the Berlin engineer who created it, or the German technicians who improved it in later years. The machine itself was close to invincible. An enemy could own an exact copy, know its internal movements, and still not read its ciphers unless he knew exactly how the machine was set up when the German operator began his message. That information was in the message in the form of a disguised "key" that notified the receiver how to adjust his machine. To dig out the key, an enemy had to devise a system that relied, at least in the first instance, on theft or human error.

Poland was first to attack the ingenious German machine. In the fall of 1932, the Polish secret service singled out a brilliant young mathematician, Marian Rejewski, put him in a sparsely furnished room in a centuries-old building, and assigned him the task of deducing the Enigma's internal wiring. As he grappled with the problem, he received stolen coding material. By year's end he had solved the Enigma, and in January 1933, just before the Nazis came to power in

Germany, he turned his calculations over to what for the thirties was a "high tech" Polish factory for the production of Polish Enigmas that could duplicate the function of the German machines. The solution of the Enigma's internal wiring was the essential element for all that followed in the Enigma story. Poland went on from there to devise both manual and machine systems for recovering Enigma keys. In 1939, just prior to the start of war, copies of the Polish-built Enigma, along with key-recovery technology, were turned over to French and British intelligence. The British were utterly stunned to learn of the Polish success in solving the military Enigma when their own cryptanalysts, with a long and distinguished history of codebreaking, had tried and failed. The simple truth is that the British initially tried to penetrate this new genera-tion of encipherment the old-fashioned way, that is, they attacked machine-made ciphers by traditional "pencil-and-paper" methods. The Poles were years ahead of other nations, except the United States, in using mathematicians to bare the inner secrets of cipher machines.

British cryptanalysts saw the light during the late thirties, even before re-ceiving the Polish technology, and tried to interest mathematicians in their problem. Then came the war, and the search for an Enigma solution shifted into fast forward. To a new center for cryptanalysis—an old Victorian estate in the English countryside called Bletchley Park about midway between Oxford and Cambridge—came some of the best brains in the world, including a recog-nized genius, Alan Turing, and a practical-minded Cambridge professor, Gor-don Welchman. Turing looked at the Polish key-recovery system and found a way to improve it. Welchman looked at Turing's system and made it simpler, and they agreed that simpler was better. They designed a key-finding machine that proved very successful at unraveling the Enigma ciphers of the German air force and navy; German intelligence and security agencies; and, to a lim-ited extent, the German Army. The ability of the codebreakers at Bletchley Park to read these machine ciphers became what Gen. Dwight D. Eisenhower, supreme Allied commander, called "a very decisive contribution to the Allied war effort."[1] Without it, Britain might not have survived, the Allies might not have won the war, and the political map of today might look very different.

The Enigma Machine

The Enigma had its roots in a machine first offered to the German navy in 1918 by Scherbius.[2] The navy and then the Foreign Office turned it down, but Scherbius did not give up. He formed a company, the Cipher Machines Stock

Corporation, tinkered with the machine, made it better, and put it on the commercial market in 1923. A promotional pamphlet called it "The Glow-Lamp Ciphering and Deciphering Machine 'Enigma.'"

Someone looking at the Scherbius commercial model for the first time might mistake it for an unconventional typewriter.[3] It had a letters-only German keyboard, without numbers or symbols, in three rows instead of four in a pattern differing from the American keyboard as follows:

Q W E R T Z U I O

A S D F G H J K

P Y X C V B N M L

Above the keyboard was a panel of "glow-lamps" with the same arrangement of letters on round glass windows and a tiny lightbulb under each window. Above the lamp board were five disks on a single axis, which comprised the machine's scrambling unit. The two outside disks were fixed and immovable. The one on the right was the entry-exit drum (really an in-out switch) and the one on the left was the reversing drum or reflector. The three disks on the inside rotated round the axis and could be arranged in different sequences, for example I-II-III, III-I-II, II-III-I, and so forth. These were the so-called rotors, or cipher drums. Each was flanged and to each was attached an adjustable ring numbered 01 to 26 and labeled A to Z. With the lid down, the flanges protruded and three letters, one at the top of each drum, showed through small openings in the lid. A switch to the right of the drums allowed the user to choose between battery and house current.

To the uninitiated, the Enigma was a wondrous gadget. If the user pressed a key on the keyboard, a different letter lit up on the lamp board. "A" on the keyboard might illuminate "T" on the lamp board. At the same time, the right cipher drum rotated one notch (one twenty-sixth of a revolution). By pressing "A" again, still another lamp letter lit up, say "G," and the right rotor turned another notch. When pressing any letter, a different lamp letter glowed and the disk rotated.

The genius of the machine was in its internal wiring. When a key was pressed, the current flowed directly to the entry-exit drum, through each of the cipher drums to the reversing drum or reflector, back through the cipher drums to the entry-exit drum, and on to a lamp letter. The drums made of a nonconducting material, such as hard rubber or Bakelite, were the Enigma's scrambling mechanism. Each cipher drum had twenty-six electrical contacts on each side, spring-loaded contacts on one side, and flat circular terminals on the other. Each rotor was internally wired differently from the other two. The current did not flow directly through a drum (e.g., never "A" to "A" or "B" to "B") but zigzagged according to some pattern (e.g., "A" to "P" or "B" to "K"). The reflector was wired with contacts only on one side, so the current did not pass through it but merely from one letter to another and back through the cipher drums.

Each rotor could be fixed with a turnover point once every full revolution (one turnover point out of twenty-six notches) to trigger the movement of the next rotor. The turnover point was set by adjusting the inner ring and locking it into place before inserting the rotor. Once locked, ring and drum moved as one. When the operator closed the lid, he could use the protruding flanges to set the rotors to the desired key as indicated by the letters showing through the small openings. At its turnover point, the right rotor stepped the center rotor one notch (one twenty-sixth of a revolution), with both rotors moving at once. When the center rotor reached its turnover point, it stepped the left rotor one notch, with all three rotors moving at once. Not until the slow left rotor had turned a full revolution could the starting circuit be repeated. By that time, the current would have found 16,900 different paths from keyboard to lamp board.[4]

It took at least two men to send or receive a message—one to operate the keyboard and another to operate the radio. A message entered into the Enigma in plaintext would be radioed as cipher; when received in cipher at the other end, it would be fed into the Enigma at the exact setting and emerge as plaintext. In other words, the Enigma was reversible. The reflector made it so. At the same setting, if the letter "A" lit up "T," the letter "T" lit up "A."

———————

Scherbius was ahead of his time. He intended his Enigma as a way for corporations to keep their correspondence secret, but they showed only modest interest. The Enigma was a commercial failure. Along the way, several governments, including those of Germany, Japan, Poland, and the United States, bought commercial Enigmas in the open market. In the sphere of government, rather than business, the secret writing machine was destined to make history. Even before Hitler arrived on the scene, Germany chafed over the restrictions imposed on its armed forces by the post–World War I Versailles Treaty, so it was especially alert for opportunities to upgrade its military capabilities. A machine that advertised secure military communications was too tempting to ignore. The German armed forces studied it and then adopted it. The German navy began using an improved commercial version of the Enigma in 1926, and the army followed two years later. In 1930, a military version was introduced, and, in 1934, with the Nazis then in power, the military Enigma became the basic unitary cipher system of the Third Reich. The German air force and spy agencies soon adopted the Enigma in one form or another. When the war began in 1939, about forty thousand German Enigmas were in use.[5]

The military Enigma differed from the commercial model essentially by the addition of a plug board, or "commutator," similar to a telephone switchboard, with one socket for each letter of the alphabet. This further complicated the Enigma's circuitry. By plugging telephone cords into two sockets, the letters thus paired could be exchanged. The current now passed from keyboard to plug board to entry-exit drum to cipher drums to reflector and back through the cipher drums to entry-exit drum to plug board to lamp board. For example, if "A" on the commutator was plugged to "W" and "Z" to "F," and the user pressed "A" on the keyboard, the current flowed to the plug board, was switched to "W," and entered the scrambler. After undergoing its many permutations inside the rotors, it exited, say, as "Z", flowed to the plug board where it was switched to "F," and "F" lit up on the lamp board—all that in much less time than it takes to read about it. Initially, the Germans used six cords to exchange six pairs of letters. A letter unplugged remained unchanged when the current passed through it.

The Germans continued to refine the machine and improve operating procedures up to and through World War II as they tried to make the recovery of keys as difficult as possible for potential eavesdroppers. The various services and intelligence agencies made separate improvements in the Enigma; these are noted as the narrative of this book warrants. The Germans had thought through the possibility that Enigma machines would be captured in war and believed that they would be useless to the enemy because of all the potential settings. The Germans were so confident of the Enigma's invincibility that, when they studied British army Typex cipher machines captured during the French campaign in 1940 and found them to be Enigma knockoffs, they made no more than a feeble effort to attack the British cipher system. They assumed it was impenetrable— like the Enigma.[6]

The Polish Solution

It is said that truth is the first casualty of war. The truth about the Polish solution of the Enigma remained comatose for three decades after World War II as a casualty of state secrecy and false reporting. The truth was too prosaic to be imagined. A studious, unassuming, twenty-seven-year-old mathematician, Marian Rejewski, unwrapped the Enigma's mysteries by applying mathematical formulas that he devised. There was one element of intrigue that Rejewski knew nothing about at the time. In performing his calculations, he benefited from cryptographic materials stolen by a German traitor working for French intelligence, which supplied them to the Polish Cipher Bureau.

Rejewski came from the city of Budgoszcz in western Poland.[7] His family had lived under Prussian or German rule for a century and a quarter until 1919, when Poland emerged as an independent nation from the chaos of World War I. The occupiers had imposed their language in the schools, so Rejewski grew up fluent in German. One of his relatives owned an insurance company in Poznan, and, in his youth, Rejewski aspired to be an actuary. He entered Poznan University to study mathematics.

In January 1929, the Cipher Bureau of the Polish Army General Staff organized a cryptology course at the university with only two prerequisites, skill in mathematics and fluency in German. Rejewski was one of about twenty students who attended the cryptology classes in addition to their regular studies. There, he met Jerzy Rozycki from the Ukraine and Henryk Zygalski, a native of Poznan. All three excelled in cryptology. In March, without completing the course, Rejewski graduated from the university with a master's degree and moved on to the University of Goettingen in Germany for advanced studies in mathematics. After a year, he returned to Poznan and accepted an offer to be a teaching assistant. While Rejewski was away, the Cipher Bureau had singled out Rozycki and Zygalski for further extracurricular training in cryptanalysis. When Rejewski heard of it, he asked to be included. The three of them worked in their spare time on breaking down simple German cryptograms.

In the summer of 1932, they moved to Warsaw to work full time in the Cipher Bureau's German section, BS4. They occupied quarters on the third floor of the old Saxon Palace, built in the seventeenth century for the elected Saxon kings of Poland, which, in 1932, served as headquarters of the General Staff. The room overlooked a square where Poland's unknown soldier was buried. Rejewski soon found himself separated from the others. During the next several weeks, he worked alone as he focused on a cipher that he had never seen before (from the Enigma) pledged to secrecy about his new assignment.

His work boiled down to two seemingly impossible tasks: (1) to build a duplicate Enigma and (2) to match the machine settings used by the German cipher clerks. The settings were called the "key." For the system to work, both sender and receiver had to begin their enciphering and deciphering with the same settings of scrambler and plug board. It would be difficult to overstate the complexity of the challenge. The number of possible keys for a three-rotor commercial machine, in which the rotors could be positioned six different ways, came to 105,456 (the multiple of twenty-six letters on three rotors in six possible sequences—26×26×26×6). When the military machine's plug board, initially with six exchanges, was factored in, the possible key settings exceeded 100 billion—100,391,791,500,[8] but these numbers pale in comparison to those of the inner connections. "Given three drums," Rejewski said, "the possibilities [for the internal connections within the rotating drums] come to 500 million . . . million [million written fifteen times], and that after all is the most important matter, because it is synonymous with reconstruction of the machine."[9]

Before Rejewski settled into his new assignment, he had the benefit of a briefing from his boss, Capt. Maksymilian Ciezki, the head of BS4. Ciezki told him of previous unsuccessful Polish efforts to fathom the machine's wiring and handed him some examples of Enigma ciphertext. Thereafter, Ciezki remained in daily contact. At some point, he put a commercial Enigma at Rejewski's disposal.

To solve the wiring problem, Rejewski applied his Poznan and Goettingen training in mathematics. It involved the manipulation of cipher letters, the use of complex equations, and a certain amount of enlightened guesswork. At the heart of Rejewski's problem were the permutations of the current caused by the cipher drums and plug board. He would not solve it until he received the critically important information stolen by the German traitor, Hans-Thilo Schmidt, and supplied to BS4 by Capt. Gustave Bertrand of French intelligence.

In each message, the Germans used two keys, a daily key from a key list issued by general headquarters and a message key chosen at random by the sender and repeated as a hedge against a garbled transmission. This double encipherment was contained in the first six letters of the message. At the receiving end, recovery of the message required that the recipient first set his machine by the daily key to learn the sender's message key and then reset it by the message key to recover the text. Those first six cipher letters, together with the lazy keying habits of the German cipher clerks, were the chinks in the Enigma's formidable armor that started Rejewski on his way to a solution.[10]

Intent on bringing order out of the randomness of the cipher letters, Rejewski focused first on the message key. The double encipherment meant that the first and fourth cipher letters represented the first letter of the key twice permuted by the rotors and plug board. Similarly, the second and fifth cipher letters came from the second key letter and the third and sixth cipher letters from the third key letter. He asked Ciezki for sixty to a hundred enciphered messages transmitted on the same day so they would have the same daily key. For his experiment, Rejewski did not have to know what the daily key was but it had to be the same one. Because in each message the same three plaintext letters would be pressed twice, that would give him ample room—120 to 200 strikes of the same three letters—to search for patterns in the ciphertext. He describes where he went from there:

> I arbitrarily chose a key [from the stack of messages] and wrote down the first letter, and next to it the fourth. Then I sought out a key that had as its first letter the fourth letter of the previous key, and I wrote the fourth letter of the second key next to the fourth letter of the previous key. Continuing in this way, after a number of steps I arrived back at the first letter that I had written down. I did not write down this same letter a second time, but put in parentheses the letters written down so far.[11]

What emerged within the parentheses were letter connections, and when Rejewski arrived back at the first letter he had completed a "cycle" of letter connections, which might look like this: (dvpfkxgzyo). He would go on in the same way until he had exhausted every letter of the alphabet without repeating any letter. Then he would do the same for the second and fifth and the third and sixth cipher letters. He called the set of cycles thus formed a "characteristic," or a "picture" of the key. In the following example of a characteristic, AD designates the first and fourth cipher letters, BE the second and fifth, and CF the third and sixth:

AD = (dvpfkxgzyo) (eijmunqlht) (bc) (rw) (a) (s)

BE = (blfqveoum) (hjpswizrn) (axt) (cgy) (d) (k)

CF = (abviktjgfcqny) (duzrehlxwpsmo)[12]

It was not a picture to hang on the wall, perhaps, but, in Rejewski's quantitative mind, it gave shape to the amorphous Enigma product. Rejewski found that what he thought were random cipher letters had a pattern after all. Although the letters within cycles changed, he noticed that "cycles of the same lengths occurred in every line always in even numbers."[13] Andrew Hodges, biographer of British mathematician Alan Turing and himself a mathematician, described the cycle solution as "elementary group theory," and elegantly pinpointed the importance of the discovery. "[T]he *lengths* of these cycles," Hodges said, "were independent of the plug board. They would depend only on the position of the rotors, the plug board affecting *which* letters appeared in the cycles, but not *how many*. This observation showed that in a rather beautiful way the rotor positions left their fingerprints upon the cipher-text. . . ."[14] (Emphasis Hodges's.) The "fingerprints" were the cycle lengths of each three-letter characteristic. A complete catalog of cycle lengths for every possible three-letter key would permit the Poles to determine the rotor position by consulting the list.

Rejewski's next task was to trace the wiring in the cipher drums. He put together six arcane equations representing the flow of current from keyboard letters to lamp board letters.[15] In each equation, there were four unknowns: (1) wiring from keyboard to entry drum, (2) plug board exchange, (3) wiring of the right rotor, and (4) wiring for the rest of the scrambler. Rejewski assumed that he knew the wiring to the entry ring from the commercial Enigma, but he assumed wrong. That mistake would later cost him much time and grief. The plug board connections turned up in daily key lists for September and October 1932 handed him by Ciezki on 8 December 1932 (from Schmidt through Bertrand). Factoring out the less accessible of his two remaining unknowns (the middle and left rotors and the reflector) left him with a single problem to solve, the wiring in the right cipher drum, or fast rotor that turned with each depression on the keyboard.

This he proceeded to calculate. At first, the numbers did not compute. As he racked his brain, reexamined the equations, and recalculated the figures, the Cipher Bureau almost gave up on the project. This is where his false assumption about the order of the entry ring letters got in the way. In the commercial Enigma on his desk, the letters were arranged on the entry ring as on the keyboard, and he thought it was the same for the military Enigma. After weeks of frustration, he tried out a new assumption, that the letters on the entry ring were in alphabetical order. "This time, luck smiled upon me," Rejewski said. ". . . From my pencil, as by magic, began to issue numbers designating the connections in [the fast rotor]."[16] At that time, the sequence of the cipher drums was changed quarterly; because September and October belonged to different quarters, a different drum was in the right-hand position in the two months. So Rejewski applied his equations to calculate the wiring in two of the three rotors. From that vantage point, the third rotor and the reflector "presented no great difficulties."[17]

Rejewski turned over his calculations to the AVA Radio Manufacturing Company to make military Enigma analogs. AVA, a small Warsaw company under Cipher Bureau control, had carried out a number of secret projects, including construction of radio transmitter-receiver stations. One of its directors, Antoni Palluth, had served in BS4 as a civilian cryptanalyst and had been an instructor for the Poznan cryptology course. Palluth provided the link between Rejewski's theoretical calculations and the physical construction of the Polish-made military Enigma. Working from Rejewski's equations, together with the commercial Enigma and a picture of the military Enigma supplied by Bertrand, AVA produced about a dozen workable machines.

Rejewski, meanwhile, was reunited with his colleagues, Rozycki and Zygalski. From that point on, they worked together on the recovery of the message keys by cryptanalysis. Only by finding the initial settings for a message—ring positions, plug connections, rotor settings, and sequence—would they be able to break the ciphers. Of all Rejewski's initial efforts, key recovery proved the most tedious. The best he could do at the time was a series of labor-intensive pencil-and-paper methods, but they did work. By the time Hitler was taking power, his Polish neighbors could recover message keys and decipher Enigma messages on Polish-built machines that Rejewski had designed. The world at large, however, would know nothing about these activities for more than three decades.

In solving the Enigma's internal wiring, Rejewski readily acknowledged his debt to Bertrand and, by extension, to Schmidt. Not until years later did he realize the source of the daily key lists and the instructional pamphlets so important to his success. Yet, ". . . [t]he intelligence material furnished to us," Rejewski said shortly before his death in 1980, "should be regarded as having been decisive to the solution of the machine."[18] Thus, the foundation for the great British intelligence coup of World War II can be traced beyond the Poles through French intelligence to a German traitor. American code expert David Kahn calls Schmidt "the spy who most affected World War II."[19]

Schmidt was born into a family of high achievers, to whom he would ultimately bring dishonor. His mother was a baroness, his father a distinguished professor. His brother Rudolf, older by two years, was rising fast as a career officer in the German army. In World War II, Rudolf Schmidt would attain the rank of colonel general and command the 2d Panzer Army on the eastern front. Hans-Thilo grew up in Rudolf's shadow. Like his brother, he fought in France during World War I and earned the Iron Cross, but Hans-Thilo was caught in an Allied gas attack and returned to civilian life. He tried his hand at business, but his soap factory failed. With a wife and two children to support, he turned to his brother for help. Rudolf, who had been head of the army's Cipher Center in Berlin, prevailed on his successor to hire Hans-Thilo as a civilian clerk to handle cipher material. The job paid poorly, and Hans-Thilo sent his family away to live with his in-laws in Bavaria while he took up residence in a furnished room. The contrast between his own desperate finances and the success of his parents and brother could not have been more glaring.

When Rudolf headed the Cipher Center, he approved the Enigma for army use, but Hans-Thilo would betray it. It was, Kahn said, "one of the most exquisite ironies of intelligence history."[20] At age forty-three, Hans-Thilo made his first contact with the French Embassy in Berlin on June 8, 1931. He followed up with a letter dated July 1 to the French intelligence service in Paris and offered to sell important documents, including instructional pamphlets on the army's Enigma. Intrigued but cautious, French intelligence assigned to the case an experienced operative, an agent named Rodolphe Lemoine, née Rudolf Stallman of Berlin, who had taken French citizenship and the last name of his French wife. At a meeting in Verviers, Belgium, on November 1, Lemoine sized up Schmidt, examined the documents, and concluded that both were genuine. A week later, when they met again, Lemoine brought along Bertrand, who completed the deal. Schmidt went home ten thousand marks richer, and Bertrand had his valuable documents. About this time, as Schmidt was setting himself up in the business of espionage by selling out his country, he joined the Nazi Party—before Adolf Hitler took power. "Asché," as Schmidt was code-named (the French pronunciation for H-E), amounted to a personal triumph for Captain Bertrand, chief of Section D, Decryptment and Interceptions, of French intelligence. Bertrand had witnessed the failure of French codebreakers to solve the military Enigma and had come to the conclusion that France would need to launch undercover operations to tap its secrets. He had proposed forming this special unit charged with the mission of buying or stealing the necessary information. A secret business arrangement with a well-placed German traitor was made to order.

On his return to Paris from his meeting with Schmidt, Bertrand took the documents to the French cryptography unit, but the response was disappointing. Interesting, he was told, but certain essential information was missing, namely, the internal wiring of the rotors and the key lists. Bertrand met again with Schmidt in November and three more times in 1932—May, August, and October. Eventually, he obtained permission from his superiors to show his material to cooperating intelligence agencies outside France. He turned first to Britain, but the feedback was also negative. So, in the first week of December 1932, he went to Warsaw where Maj. Gwido Langer, chief of the Polish Cipher Bureau; Col. Stefan Mayer, the director of intelligence; and Ciezki enthusiastically greeted him. Bertrand and Langer were to become good friends. The Poles took two days to study the documents and then carefully explained to Bertrand that they had learned certain valuable information about the military Enigma, especially the addition of the plug board, but they needed more details along the lines expressed by the French and British codebreakers. They did not know yet just how valuable the information was. Within the month, it would lead Rejewski to his historic solution of the Enigma.

Through the thirties, Bertrand and Schmidt would get together about three times a year, and Bertrand often followed up with a trip to Warsaw. He knew of the three mathematicians by code name, but whether he actually met them before 1939 is not clear. In 1934, Schmidt left the Cipher Center to work in a Nazi codebreaking agency, thus ending his Enigma contribution (although not his relationship with French intelligence). But it made no difference. The Polish Cipher Bureau never used the stolen Enigma materials after December 1932. From that point, the Poles broke the German ciphers without the help of espionage.[21]

Schmidt eventually paid the ultimate price for his treason. After Germany occupied southern France in the wake of the Allied invasion of North Africa in November 1942, Schmidt's first French contact, Lemoine, fell into the hands of the Gestapo. Under lengthy and grueling interrogation, which probably included torture, Lemoine gave up Schmidt to save himself. Schmidt was stripped of his party membership and executed in July 1943. His brother Rudolf also suffered. While searching through Hans-Thilo's belongings, the Gestapo came upon letters from Rudolf, which Propaganda Minister Josef

Goebbels characterized as "very disparaging of the Führer."[22] Rudolf was one of Hitler's favorite generals, but that did not save his career. He was relieved of command and dismissed from the army. He managed to survive the war and died in 1957.

From January 1933 until the Wehrmacht overran Poland in September 1939, Rejewski, Rozycki, and Zygalski worked as a unit to keep pace with German improvements in both the Enigma machine and the keying procedures. Initially, they spent most of their time recovering daily keys with the unwitting help of lazy German cipher clerks who tended to choose simple message keys such as "AAA" or "ABC" or successive keyboard letters. The three Polish wizards could test the assumed keys by using the characteristics worked out by Rejewski. Once confirmed, the message key would be turned over to one of several clerks, hired in February 1933, to decrypt the message on the Polish-made Enigma.

Relations between Poland and Germany were calm through 1935, probably because Hitler was preoccupied with the buildup of the German Army. The peace was formalized by a nonaggression pact, and such high Nazi officials as the fat and pompous Hermann Goering were periodic visitors to Warsaw. During a ceremonial wreath laying at the Tomb of the Unknown Soldier, the three codebreakers looked down on the German officials from their third-floor office with the inner satisfaction of knowing their secrets without the Germans knowing that they knew.

As they labored over the daily keys, they looked for ways to improve their own procedures. Their most significant innovation—and the indispensable ingredient of the British success in World War II—was the mechanization of the key-recovery system. Logically, it was the only way to go, machine against machine, but it was neither easy nor fast. First came a cyclometer, consisting of the three-rotor sets from two Enigmas. The cyclometer worked by comparing the length of message key cycles on a given day against the predetermined cycle length of each rotor setting. Before the codebreakers could make that comparison, they had to catalog the known cycles for every rotor setting—all 17,576 (26×26×26). It took a year, as time from their regular duties permitted, but, when completed, the cyclometer could run through the catalog in twenty minutes, and, with a little extra effort, the codebreakers could discover by hand the letters swapped in the plug board (now exchanging five to eight pairs instead of six).[23] In November 1937, as the cyclometer was coming on line, however, the Germans installed a new reversing drum with different wiring. So the benumbed Poles, after first reconstructing the new connections, had to redo the catalog.

All this time, the universe of German agencies using the Enigma was growing. The German air force adopted it in August 1935; the Nazi Party security service, the Sicherheitsdienst (SD), in September 1937; and other military and paramilitary agencies along the way. They all used the same machine with different daily keys, so the task of Polish cryptanalysts was becoming ever more arduous. Despite all the problems, an internal Cipher Bureau test conducted in January 1938 found that three out of four intercepted messages were being decrypted. That sort of self-evaluation carries an inescapable bias, but there seems to be no other measure available.

The Germans were also stepping up their spying activities in Poland. Abwehr (German military intelligence) agents strolled outside the Saxon Palace and snapped pictures with miniature cameras of personnel entering and leaving the building, something the Poles learned about from an Abwehr manual stolen by one of their own spies in Germany. In 1937, fearing the compromise of their greatest secret, they detached BS4 from the rest of the Cipher Bureau and moved it to an isolated forest compound near the town of Pyry, 6 miles south of Warsaw. The work went on with minimal disruption. The second and more important mechanical invention was still to come.

In September 1938, when the German uniformed services changed their keying procedures, it was impossible for Rejewski and his colleagues to form cycles. That meant the Poles' key-recovery system was kaput, with one exception. The SD did not adopt the new keying system until July 1939; for nearly a year, the Poles were able to continue recovering SD keys.

To get back on the track of the military keys, Rejewski again sought a mechanical solution based on the message keys. As the Polish codebreakers studied this new system, they noticed that in a single day's volume of a hundred or so messages, the identical cipher letter might show up in three messages as the first and fourth cipher letter in one, the second and fifth in a second, and the third and sixth in a third. From this observation, they worked out a system to recover the message key by rigging a machine with the three-drum sets from six Enigmas. They called their new machine the "bomba," reportedly in honor of an ice cream concoction that Rozycki was eating when they came up with the idea. It would run through the 17,576 possible rotor positions in about two hours and signal when it had made a hit. (At this stage, they were still ignoring the plug board exchanges, which they would work out by hand afterward.) With six bombas running at the same time in the six possible rotor sequences, they could determine the order of the drums. Rejewski wrote out the specifications and turned them over to Palluth at AVA.[24] The bomba put Poland's key-recovery technology in a class by itself.

Alas, on December 15, 1938, only weeks after the introduction of the bomba, the Germans added two cipher drums to their Enigma. The cipher machine still took only three drums at a time, but, by interchanging the five drums, the number of possible drum sequences rose from six to sixty. Because the SD continued the old keying method for another six and a half months, Rejewski had ample time to calculate the wiring for the two new drums, but now the Poles would need sixty bombas for their mechanical key recovery. This number was theoretically possible but beyond their resources in money and manpower in the time left to them. With Nazi pressure tightening, they knew that the game was up, and they began to rethink their situation.

Bertrand remained on the friendliest of terms with Langer. On periodic visits to Warsaw up to 1934, he turned over Enigma key lists obtained from Schmidt. The material was always gratefully received but not fully reciprocated. Langer gave Bertrand intelligence summaries and, in 1938, showed him the new BS4 facility near Pyry but, in all their meetings save the last one prior to war, never offered Enigma decrypts or mentioned the Poles' spectacular success in building their own Enigma and key-recovery machines. So Bertrand naturally assumed that they had not been successful. That was no different in his mind from the failure of his own colleagues at the French intelligence service. Given the Poles' keen interest in his visits and their two countries' mutual fear of German rearmament, he had no thought but to continue the contacts.

In fact, Bertrand wanted to enlarge them. He tried to involve Czechoslovakia in a three-way exchange of intelligence, but it did not pan out because the Poles and Czechs were not on good terms. Then, he reached out to Britain, but British intelligence showed little interest in sharing information until after the German annexation of Austria in March 1938. Finally, after that eye-opening event, Bertrand accepted an invitation to London and met with British cryptanalysts. He handed them some of the same documents from Schmidt that he had given the Poles, but the British gave him nothing in return because they were prohibited by a ministerial (Cabinet) committee from sharing secrets about cryptanalysis.[25] From that point on, Bertrand set his sights on a conference of French, British, and Polish cryptologists and managed to bring it off the following January in Paris. The meetings turned out to be of little use. The Poles were not about to give away their most precious secret unless they received equal value, and the others had nothing like it to offer. They played along with the conclusion of the conference that reconstruction of the Enigma by cryptanalysis was "practically impossible."[26] The participants agreed to meet again if one intelligence agency sent the others a message that "something new" had turned up. The term, "something new" ("Il y a du nouveau"), was not to be taken literally; it was merely a code that signaled a desire for a meeting.

Events were rapidly propelling Europe toward war. The previous October, Germany had occupied the Sudetenland under terms of the notorious Munich Agreement. In March, German troops swept unopposed through the rest of Czechoslovakia. Poland now faced the German menace on three sides— Czechoslovakia on the south, East Prussia on the north, and Germany itself on the west—and had no illusions about its Soviet neighbor to the east. Intelligence revealed a gradual buildup of German troops along the three borders. Germany sought access to Danzig (Gdansk) and demanded "extraterritorial" highway and rail links through Poland. Poland responded by ordering the partial mobilization of an army ill prepared for modern warfare. As the weeks passed, the Nazis stepped up the pressure. France and Britain signed an agreement to defend Poland in the event of a German attack. In June, Langer received permission from the chief of the General Staff to reveal Poland's Enigma secrets to its allies, and the "something new" message went out.

Langer invited French and British cryptology teams to Warsaw on July 24–25. Bertrand and Henri Braquenie, a cryptanalyst, represented France. Alastair Denniston; Dillwyn ("Dilly") Knox, chief cryptanalyst; and Cdr. Humphrey Sandwith of the Royal Navy attended on behalf of Britain. The British were reluctant to make the trip because they were skeptical that any useful intelligence would come out of it. Mayer, Langer, and Ciezki represented Poland, and, for the first time, the mathematicians Rejewski, Rozycki, and Zygalski and the AVA specialists, including Palluth, were brought in to meet with foreign intelligence. The lid was off within this limited circle.

In a working session at the forest compound near Pyry, the Poles unveiled their homemade Enigmas to the astonished visitors. Questions flowing from

Knox in rapid succession indicated that he had invested considerable time in studying the German Enigma. When he learned the order of wiring in the entry drums, he was said to be furious to find out how simple it was. Rejewski had stumbled over that problem in 1932, so he could relate to the Briton's frustration and remembered him years later for his keen intellect. "Knox grasped everything very quickly," Rejewski said, "almost quick as lightning."[27]

The Poles held back nothing. In another room, they unveiled the bomba and explained in detail the Polish techniques for recovering keys. Denniston and Knox wanted to call London for technicians to fly in and take down the specifications, but that would not be necessary, Langer told them and sprang yet another pleasant surprise. Two Polish Enigmas, each with five rotors, would be sent to Paris in a few days by diplomatic pouch, one for the French and the other to be shipped to England. With a machine and the knowledge gained from their meeting, he added, they would be able to carry on. They had the resources that Poland lacked to make all the bombas needed to keep up with German improvements in the Enigma and in keying procedures. This would be a Polish contribution to the war effort against Nazi Germany.

All was done as Langer promised. When the package arrived in Paris in mid-August, Bertrand joined a British courier on the last leg across the English Channel. At Victoria Station in London, he turned the cipher machine over to Col. Stewart Menzies, soon to become the wartime chief of MI6 (the British Secret Intelligence Service). In barely six months of hesitant cooperation, the British had reaped an enormous harvest from Bertrand's seven years of cultivating the Poles.

The British Solution

On September 4, 1939, a day after Britain declared war on Germany, streams of very bright people with a high tolerance for tedium began converging on Bletchley Park about fifty miles northwest of London, site of the Government Code & Cypher School (GC&CS). The newcomers consisted of mathematicians, linguists, chess players, puzzle solvers, and assorted academics. They formed the vanguard of a cryptological army that would swell to ten thousand before the war ended. Among the vanguard from the faculty at Cambridge were Turing and Welchman, two first-class mathematicians, who would build a key-recovery machine from Polish technology to make the laggard Britain competitive in the cipher war. Before long, Bletchley Park would become the secret nerve center of a vast, bustling intelligence network engaged in the interception and decryption of German signals transmissions, the translation and evaluation of the decrypts, and the distribution of processed intelligence to Allied commanders. The activity never ended until the enemy surrendered nearly six years later.

GC&CS relocated from London to Bletchley Park in the summer of 1939 for security reasons. The new site was roughly equidistant between the intellectual wellsprings of Oxford and Cambridge, with convenient transportation links to each, as well as to London. A visitor to the large estate would be struck by the nineteenth-century Victorian mansion that flaunted a fatuous copper dome. Wartime personnel spoke of the dome with such unflattering adjectives as ugly and hideous. From a stately downstairs room, one could look out of bowed windows past an expanse of lawn to a sparkling pond with flower beds bordering both house and pond. GC&CS rescued the estate from the clutches of a developer who wanted to carve it into building lots, only to lay waste the graceful lawn and flower beds in order to erect single-story frame huts for various intelligence functions. The ravages of war! Denniston commandeered the downstairs room for his office. Soon after the war started, GC&CS became Government Communications Headquarters (GCHQ).[28]

GC&CS was a school only in the sense that if one did not know something about codebreaking or a related line of work upon arrival, it would be taught provided that the newcomer had the knack for it. GC&CS's main business was learning the enemy's secrets by codebreaking. The worthy successor to Room 40, the British codebreaking unit of World War I, its biggest challenge at the start of World War II was to break the machine ciphers spun out by the German military Enigma. Dilly Knox had been working on the problem; during the Spanish Civil War he had enjoyed limited success by reading ciphers from a commercial Enigma used by the fascist side, but the military machine with extra layers of complexity had tripped him up. Knox was an outstanding codebreaker, but his background specialty had been linguistics, not mathematics. Solving the Enigma required mathematical skills. Polish mathematicians had already done it. Now British mathematicians Turing and Welchman were at Bletchley to reshape the Polish technology for the expanded needs of global war.

The package from Warsaw, which included the Poles' military Enigma, specifications for the key-recovery machine, and other keying instructions, reached Bletchley in mid-August.[29] Armed with the Polish technology, Knox's small prewar team renewed the British attack on the Enigma. Turing, who had been an occasional collaborator, joined them full time in September at Bletchley's remodeled coachman's residence known as the Cottage.

The science of numbers and symbols was in Turing's genes. His paternal grandfather, a graduate in mathematics from Cambridge University in 1848, was ranked eleventh in his class, but then opted for the clergy. His father, an administrator in the colonial Indian Civil Service, was on leave in England at the time of Alan's birth in 1912. From the age of one, Alan, along with an older brother, was raised by a retired army couple on the English Channel coast.[30] He won a mathematics scholarship to Cambridge and, upon graduation, was made a fellow there so that he could continue his studies. In 1936, at the age of twenty-four, he published a paper in which he imagined a machine capable of computing anything. His idea caught on as the Universal Turing Machine and was eventually referred to as the conceptual forerunner of the computer. So, when Turing showed up at Bletchley Park in September 1939, he had already made a name for himself. He was also keenly interested in ciphers, and, as a quasi-insider, had kept in touch by occasional visits to GC&CS after attending a 1938 introductory course. It seemed only right that he should be handed the Polish keying technology and given the vital task of making a better cryptological bomb.

Turing found inspiration in the world of abstractions, which seemed to nourish in him equal amounts of genius and oddball behavior. When he first came to Bletchley, he buried silver ingots, his life's savings, in a nearby forest; when he came to retrieve them after the war, he couldn't remember where he had buried them. Among his many other eccentricities, he chained his coffee mug to radiator pipes to keep it from being borrowed or stolen. When bicycling in pollen seasons, he wore a gas mask against allergens. His bicycle chain was loose, but, instead of repairing it, he preferred to count the number of pedal pumps until he knew the chain was about to fall off and then adjust it.[31] This might be taken as a recognition of the superiority of his mathematical skills over the mechanical, except that his Bletchley colleague, Donald Michie, informs us that Turing "was intrigued by devices of every kind, whether abstract or concrete—his friends thought it would be better if he kept to the abstract devices but that didn't deter him."[32] Engineers who worked with him found him easy to understand when he expressed complicated ideas, but, in the words of W. W. Chandler, an engineer at the Post Office Research Station, "The least said about him as an engineer the better."[33] Turing's homosexuality was unknown to most of his colleagues at Bletchley until after the war. Although his idiosyncratic personality was a turnoff to many of them, he was held in respect and even awe for his intellectual achievements. "When he attacked a problem he liked to start from first principles," said Jack Good, who worked with Turing at Bletchley Park, "and he was hardly influenced by received opinion. This attitude gave depth and originality to his thinking."[34]

Turing's critical first step in attacking the Enigma was to remove the doubly enciphered message key as the basis for learning the settings and sequence of the cipher drums. This procedure had been the mainstay of the Polish solution. When the Germans stopped using the double encipherment in May 1940, the Polish bomba became obsolete. Turing and his colleagues must have anticipated that possibility because, immediately in the fall of 1939, they shifted the break-in burden from the message key to the "crib," or probable word(s) in the message text. The art of the crib was old but tricky. It amounted to an educated guess that certain letters in the ciphertext represented a certain word or words in plaintext. What made that possible was the stereotypical nature of the messages, especially the way they were addressed. For example, the word "general" often appeared early because the message was addressed to some general.

The Germans were sensitive to such stereotypes and often tried to hide them by padding the message with nonsensical words, so crib-seekers had to be on the alert. They used one feature of the Enigma to their advantage. No keyboard letter ever lit up the same lamp board letter. So, by running their probable word(s) beneath the ciphers, if any letter in the probable plaintext matched the cipher letter directly above, they knew they were in the wrong place and moved further into the message until they found a total mismatch. Unmistakably, codebreakers needed special powers of concentration.

As a simple example, suppose that a Bletchley cryptanalyst came upon the cipher letters DMRPLGN in a message and suspected they represented the word GENERAL. Had there not been letter-swapping in the plug board, the problem would have been theoretically easy for an accomplished mathematician. Bletchley scientists could have built a machine to search through all the possible rotor positions for the one that, in seven successive strokes, produced the cipher letters DMRPLGN from the word GENERAL. The addition of two new Enigma rotors (now five rotors for three slots in the scrambler) complicated the problem by creating a tenfold increase in the number of possible rotor sequences from six to sixty and in the total number of possible rotor positions from 105,456 to 1,054,560.

To further torment enemy codebreakers, the Germans had built the military Enigma with that irksome plug board and, by this time, had made it even more irksome than it had been for the Poles only a year earlier. In 1938, with the Polish bomba operational for a brief period, the Germans were cross-plugging only five to eight pairs of letters and leaving ten to sixteen letters of the alphabet unpaired. The Poles designed their bomba to ignore the letter-swapping, which they would figure out by hand after the machine helped find the rotor positions and sequence. Now that the Germans were cross-plugging ten pairs of letters and leaving only six letters unpaired, the results from the Polish bomba left a still virtually impenetrable ciphertext. The British version (called the "bombe") would have to deal with the plug board pairings as it located the correct scrambler positions, and not afterward. The ten cross-pluggings elevated the number of possible keys into the stratosphere. There were (and still are) 150,738,274,937,250 possible ways of connecting ten pairs of letters in the twenty-six-letter alphabet.[35] That figure is, for all practical purposes, an abstraction even before it is multiplied by the possible rotor settings times the possible rotor sequences.

Turing ignored the intimidating numbers and put his trust in what he knew—mathematical logic. His challenge was to find and verify the crib. He based his system on the principle that proof is the absence of contradiction. The idea was to assume a plug board connection and rule out contradictions until a consistency appeared. The test for letter exchanges on the plug board involved only the twenty-six letters of the alphabet, but it had to be done while searching for the right setting and sequence of the rotors. Unfortunately, Turing devised a very complicated test for confirming a crib by passing an electric current through "loops."

The loops had to be invented from the crib. To illustrate from the simple example above, the probable word is lined up with the cipher letters:

G E N E R A L

D M R P L G N

The possible loop in this example might start with the letter N in GENERAL. The N is in line with the cipher letter R and matches the R in GENERAL. From there, R goes to cipher L, to the L in GENERAL, to cipher N, and back to the N in GENERAL, thus closing the loop and confirming the key. With all the possible rotor settings and sequences and plug board exchanges, the loop was even harder to achieve than it is to understand. But, still worse for Turing's purpose, the crib had to be long enough for three loops to satisfy his conditions for consistency. Longer cribs were harder to find. Yet, under the right circumstances, the system worked and was a giant leap forward. Turing took his plan to Harold ("Doc") Keen, an engineer at the British Tabulating Machinery factory at Letchworth, who started the process of converting the Turing concept into a working machine.

When Welchman, another product of the 1938 introductory course, arrived at Bletchley Park, he was assigned by Denniston to work with Turing and the other cryptanalysts at the Cottage. He soon found himself frozen out by Dilly Knox, however, who exiled him to another building, Elmers School, to study call signs and discriminants in Enigma preambles. The call signs identified both the sending and the receiving radio stations. The discriminants distinguished among different types of Enigma traffic, such as army or air force.

Welchman never quite understood why he got the cold shoulder but concluded that Knox simply did not like him, and "apart from a few lifelong friends, by and large Dilly seems to have disliked most of the men with whom he came in contact."[36] On the other hand, Welchman, whose father was a country parson and the Archdeacon of Bristol, was described by the American author David Kahn as "austere and reserved," a man whom friends regarded as "a solemn old stick, without a great sense of humor."[37]

Also something of a busybody, Welchman seemed incapable of restraining his restless intellectual energy. When Knox exiled him to Elmers School, he spent many long days alone poring over Enigma intercepts. Although he was assigned to study call signs and discriminants in the message preamble, he could not keep his fertile mind off the doubly enciphered indicators. It was the same feature that had attracted the interest of the Poles seven years earlier, although, at the time, Welchman did not realize it. He proceeded methodically to work out a system for exploiting the double encipherment to recover the message keys.[38] It was truly brilliant work, especially for a man so new to cryptanalysis. The Poles, however, had already made this discovery and had passed the idea on to British intelligence. When Welchman showed Knox what he had done, the chief codebreaker was not very gracious about the wasted effort. "Dilly was furious," Welchman said. "What I was suggesting was precisely what he was already doing. . . . Dilly reminded me that I had been told to study discriminants and call signs, not methods of breaking the Enigma."[39]

Welchman returned to his exile, head in hand, to resume his study of call signs and discriminants. Unable to read the message texts, he soon realized that his task had nothing to do with the decryption of individual messages. He was dealing with the communications network of the German army and air force, and it told him something about their structure: "The call signs came alive as representing elements of those forces, whose commanders at various echelons would have to send messages to each other. The use of different keys for different purposes, which was known to be the reason for the discriminants, suggested different command structures for the various aspects of the military operations."[40] David Kahn noted that Welchman was "independently inventing" a branch of cryptology known as traffic analysis,[41] another extraordinary feat for a beginner. Welchman was, so to speak, reinventing the wheels of cryptanalysis; however, his efforts were not wasted. From his careful study of the German traffic, he wrote a comprehensive plan for the productive management of the expected flood of incoming messages and submitted it to GCHQ Deputy Director Edward Travis. Welchman urged a twenty-four-hour operation and close coordination of intercept control, traffic analysis, and cryptanalysis within Bletchley, plus a major expansion of intercept facilities. Again, he had gone beyond the call. His work led to the reorganization of the growing codebreaking bureaucracy and its coherent operation for the duration of the war.

Next, Welchman turned his attention to the bombe. He was still musing over call signs, discriminants, and organization charts when he reviewed the Turing plan for a key-recovery machine. He quickly grasped and appreciated what Turing had done; but he saw how cumbersome the loops were. In a flash of inspiration, he conceived an improvement that made the Turing bombe infinitely more efficient. The idea was based on the simple fact that any pairing of letters in the plug board was a two-way exchange: if A was connected to B, B was connected to A. He devised a board with 676 squares lettered A to Z on all four sides. The layout of the board allowed each letter to be wired exclusively to each other letter. The test did not need three loops or even one. Consistency required only the reversibility of the assumed plug connection. Further, the cribs could be shorter and therefore easier to find in ciphertext.

Skeptical of his own idea, Welchman sketched out a wiring diagram of what would become known as the diagonal board. When he finally convinced himself it would work, he tucked the sketch under his arm and headed for the Cottage. This time giving Dilly a wide berth, he took it to Turing, who, according to Welchman, "was incredulous at first, as I had been, but when he had studied my diagram he agreed that the idea would work, and became as excited about it as I was. He [graciously] agreed that the improvement [over his own design] was spectacular."[42] With Turing's support, Welchman approached Travis, who sent him on to Doc Keen. Keen shifted gears from the Turing design to the Turing-Welchman design. It took several months, however, to finally build the Bletchley bombe, which came on line sometime during the summer of 1940.

Until then, Bletchley codebreakers had to recover the Enigma key by hand as best they could. They did well, too, thanks to the sloppy keying habits of German air force cipher clerks. From a careful study of previously decrypted messages, the British learned of two grievous security lapses committed by the Enigma operators. In one case, John Herivel discovered that clerks tended to place the ring settings for a new key close to the letters visible through the apertures of the closed lid, which meant that the middle and left rotors would step either very quickly or only after a nearly full revolution of the adjacent rotor to the right. In the other case, Stuart Milner-Barry observed that the clerks often selected unsophisticated message keys, such as successive horizontal or diagonal letters of the keyboard. By diligently exploiting these practices, the British succeeded in recovering keys that should have been inaccessible. History was repeating itself. This was the same sort of carelessness that had benefited the Polish wizards in the early thirties.

During his study of preambles, Welchman was in the habit of underlining the discriminants of incoming messages in different pencil colors. Each grouping had its own key, with the result that the Enigma keys were color-coded for purposes of identification at Bletchley. For example, green represented the administrative network of the German army; blue, the air force; and red, the coordinated activities of the army and air force. Welchman was soon able to link call signs to the key colors, and he relayed the information to the intercept operators at Chatham so they could more easily identify the source of a message and weigh its value amid the volume of traffic. Before long, the keys had so proliferated that Bletchley ran out of colors and started coding them by other classifications.

This system, which Welchman formalized as the "traffic register," was the beginning of a busy wartime organization, to be known internally as Hut 6, that concentrated on German army and air force traffic and had its greatest success with the latter. As Hut 6 grew, Welchman settled in as its administrator.

Although he occasionally had a go at recovering keys, he became more involved in the details of management. His days of Enigma discovery were over. Eventually, after Travis succeeded Denniston as the overall chief at Bletchley Park, Welchman moved up as his assistant for the duration of the war.

Turing took over Hut 8, which handled cryptanalysis for the navy, but he ran a loose ship. Once, he engaged a newcomer, Peter Hilton, in an all-day discussion about chess before outlining the young man's duties.[43] It would not be fair to say that Turing was cavalier about his nation's wartime peril, but when a specific problem occurred to him, he became preoccupied. He had not yet reached his thirtieth birthday, but the men and women at Bletchley called him "Prof," in a respectful manner, because he was "at home" with profound ideas and "away" when it came to nitty-gritty administration. As chief of Hut 8, he proved to be more the professor and less the administrator and soon found himself eased out by Hugh Alexander.[44] Alexander ascended to Turing's job, and Turing's role became ill defined as a sort of honored intellectual-in-residence.

———

For all of the foresight applied to the Welchman organization plan, it did not deal with the intelligence utilization of the Enigma decrypts. That was left to another live wire, Grp. Capt. F. W. ("Freddy") Winterbotham, who created a unit at Bletchley Park to translate decrypts and assess their intelligence value. In virtually the same creative motion, he devised an efficient and secure distribution system so that the priceless intelligence derived from codebreaking could reach the top political and military leaders—including field commanders—without tipping off the enemy.

Winterbotham was an able intelligence officer with a flair for adventure. As a teenager, he had traveled and learned French. At the tender age of seventeen, he signed up for World War I. In 1916, he became a fighter pilot but was shot down in a dogfight over Belgium in April 1917. The hardships of eighteen months in a prisoner-of-war camp caused him lasting health problems but did wonders for his German, which he learned to speak fluently. During the twenties, he lumberjacked in the Canadian wild, jackarooed in the Australian bush, and safaried in African jungles. Global economic depression brought him back home where he found employment as the Air Staff's representative in the Secret Service, assigned to keep tabs on foreign air forces. Even in the routine of government service, he managed to find adventure. When his German sources dried up during the Nazi takeover, he traveled to Germany in the pose of an

English businessman and Nazi sympathizer. There, he rubbed shoulders with the high-muck-a-mucks of Nazi officialdom, including Hitler himself, and pumped them for information. In 1938, the Germans learned that he was a British agent and warned him never to come back. Undaunted, Winterbotham switched to aerial photography and flew reconnaissance missions over Germany at safe altitudes until the outbreak of World War II.[45]

Freddy Winterbotham was later seen poking around Bletchley Park and puzzling over the distribution problem. He anticipated a flood of intelligence from the Enigma decrypts. In normal circumstances, high-grade information went first to the intelligence chiefs of the uniformed services for forwarding as they saw fit. Winterbotham feared that the various chiefs might transmit the same information in different ciphers, a cryptologically dangerous practice, and that the sheer volume of traffic could get out of hand and arouse enemy suspicions. He proposed to Stewart Menzies, then deputy director of MI6, a plan to combine the translation and analysis of decrypts into a single unit at Bletchley and distribute the resulting intelligence through MI6. Winterbotham envisioned the joint participation of all three commands—army, air, and navy. He expected resistance from the navy based on traditional elitist thinking, however, so he planned to start by asking the army and air force to assign three or four German-speaking officers to the new unit. This was to become Bletchley Park's Hut 3. He hoped that the navy would join after the unit became operational, but the navy went its own way.

For distribution, Winterbotham wanted to expand the MI6 shortwave radio network to include overseas military and air commands. To these commands, he attached small units of trained radio and cryptological personnel. These special liaison units (SLUs), sometimes including codebreakers for decrypting local traffic, were linked directly to Bletchley Park so that they could receive intelligence from Hut 3 earmarked for their individual sectors and pass it on to area commands. Transmissions would be enciphered with the "one-time pad," a system in which sender and receiver use one set of keys for one transmission and then destroy the used keys. It is foolproof from the standpoint of denying timely cryptanalysis by a third party. The Germans, in fact, never read the SLU ciphers.

With this distribution plan, Winterbotham was offering Menzies a rational, workable plan that was good for both men—for Winterbotham, an important wartime niche; for Menzies, in line for the top MI6 job, the chance to take charge of what promised to be an important intelligence source that would lend a much needed boost to the agency's sagging prestige. Menzies gave the proposal five minutes' thought, approved it, and left it to Winterbotham to see it through. Within days, Hut 3 was up and running with six army and air force translators. In time, there would be sixty.

After consultation, Winterbotham hit on a name, "Ultra," for the Bletchley activities because they were ultra-secret. The code name Ultra applied for all the services. SLUs were set up wherever large-scale British and, later, American land and air forces operated, starting with the Battle of France. By and large, the SLUs did not fit the needs of the seagoing fleet, but where the Royal Navy had a presence at major bases, such as Malta, Cairo, Algiers, and Colombo, it shared SLU services with the air and military commands.

Polish Agonies

The great Polish achievements in reconstructing the military Enigma and recovering the message keys did Poland precious little good.[46] For that matter, Poland's generous gift did not help France either. Only in British hands did the technology developed in Poland become a major weapon of war. It became a British monopoly, shared later with the Americans, who became the senior partner in the alliance, but not with the Poles who invented it.

Rejewski, Rozycki, and Zygalski fled Poland ahead of the German army and made their way to Romania and on to France, where they and other refugees from the Cipher Bureau were warmly received by the newly promoted Major Bertrand, who would ultimately rise to general rank. Bertrand had been appointed head of wartime radio intelligence and decryptment (code-named "Bruno") located at Château de Vignolles, an old mansion about 25 miles northeast of Paris in the town of Gretz-Armainvillers. He put the Poles together in one group, Team Z, to break German codes and ciphers without their machines, which the Poles had destroyed to keep the Germans from knowing their secret. At the same time, Bertrand maintained close links with Bletchley Park. Visitors from the two cryptography centers plied the channel from one side to the other to strengthen ties and trade ideas. One visitor to the Poles at Vignolles was Alan Turing. Of course, their friendly, informal conversations were not recorded for posterity, but it seems a safe bet that Turing picked the Poles' brains about the bomba. Indeed, why wouldn't he? The harmony lasted through the period of the so-called Phony War from the fall of 1939 until the spring of 1940 when German assault forces, using Enigma ciphers to communicate by radio, blitz-krieged the powerful French army in little more time than they had taken to defeat the much weaker Poland.

Thereupon Bruno was disbanded. The Poles retreated to a place code-named "Cadix" near Marseille in Vichy France under Bertrand's protective wing to continue decryption of German military ciphers. It was a precarious situation at best. German agents operated without official interference in the unoccupied southern zone. During this period, the war began to take its toll on the Polish contingent. Rozycki, returning from a temporary mission to Algeria, was drowned in January 1942 when his ship sank for reasons unknown. In November that year, after the Allies invaded North Africa and the Germans occupied southern France, the Poles went on the run again. In the flight across the Pyrenees to Spain, Langer, Ciezki, Palluth, and others fell into German hands. Langer and Ciezki survived the war, but Palluth died in a concentration camp near Berlin, possibly from Allied bombs. Their captivity was noteworthy for the fact that the Enigma secret never escaped their lips. Rejewski and Zygalski were among the few to reach Spain safely. After several months, some of the time spent in a Spanish prison under harsh conditions, an experience common to many refugees, they made their way to England in August 1943.

Their welcome was less than royal. In reconstructing the Enigma and solving the daily keys, Rejewski had performed one of the greatest cryptanalytical feats in history. Zygalski was an able contributor to the Polish success. For Poland to have given its cryptotechnology to its allies on the eve of war was both farsighted and unselfish. It would seem to have been in Britain's own self-interest—never mind its debt of honor—to make room for Rejewski and Zygalski at Bletchley Park, but it was not to be. The pair were shunted to the Polish army in exile. They ended up with a codebreaking unit in Boxmoor outside London, where they spent the rest of the war in breaking the ciphers of the Schutzstaffel (SS), Hitler's most fanatical troops.

Bletchley insider Milner-Barry later lamented, "It was always a mystery to me that the Polish contingent was not incorporated at Bletchley during the war. . . . I can only assume there were security doubts . . . but I feel there must have been a sad waste of resources somewhere."[47] Milner-Barry's mystification reflects a commendable fair-mindedness, but he was not in charge at Bletchley and obviously knew little of the Polish codebreakers' odyssey.

He was probably not aware that, in December 1939, the British proposed that Langer put his cryptanalysts under their command, only to have the idea shot down. Langer said that he preferred to keep the Cipher Bureau close to the Polish Army, which was reorganizing in France. Left unmentioned was Langer's warm eight-year friendship with Bertrand that contrasted sharply with his formal and rather cool relationship with the other British whom he had known for less than a year. Polish author Wladyslaw Kozaczuk links this episode—and Langer's part in it—to the cold treatment Rejewski and Zygalski received in 1943.[48]

Security or pique? Who knows? The British treatment of the Polish cryptanalysts is simply difficult to understand. Whatever "security doubts" there might have been, it is obvious that the new leadership at Bletchley did not fight very hard for the Poles. Denniston and Knox, participants at the 1939 Pyry conference, were gone, and with them went any personal feeling of debt. Denniston had been pushed aside in favor of his more dynamic deputy, Edward Travis, late in 1942; Knox died of cancer in February 1943. Moreover, the Bletchley technology had grown well beyond the vision of the Poles. The British bombe, itself a more refined machine than the Polish bomba, was soon to be complemented with an even more sophisticated device, the Colossus, for key recovery of a non-Enigma German cipher, which the British called the first electronic computer. With the tide of war having changed for the better, Bletchley's leaders must have concluded in the cold calculus of realpolitik that it no longer had anything to gain from the Poles.

In his blueprint of the distribution network, Winterbotham saved a plum for himself. He personally delivered the most important Bletchley decrypts to Prime Minister Churchill, who called them "my golden eggs" laid by geese who "never cackled." That is, no geese cackled until three decades after the war, and, when the cacklers started up during the mid-seventies, some were out of tune.

Even now that the facts of the Poles' Enigma breakthrough are out in the open, they must still compete in the marketplace of knowledge with earlier fictions. After British intelligence let the secret out of the bag in the 1970s and triggered the wholesale rewriting of the history of World War II in Europe, English-language books hit the stands in rapid profusion. Winterbotham's *The Ultra Secret* in 1974 seems to have been first. In it, he wrote, "It is no longer a secret that the backroom boys of Bletchley used the new science of electronics to help them solve the puzzle of Enigma."[49]

Winterbotham instantly found himself embroiled in controversy. Ex-Polish Army officers in London got wind of his claim, and informed him that Polish mathematicians had long since solved the Enigma. Winterbotham noted their complaint but refused to correct his story, which, he lamely said, "is the one told me at the time."[50] He did not say who told him, but it is a reasonable guess that he was referring to colleagues in the secret service for whom disinformation is standard tradecraft—all that aside from the fact that electronics had nothing to do with solving the Enigma puzzle.

Another untruth (again, probably invented by the purveyors of disinformation) crept into Winterbotham's book about an unidentified Polish mechanic employed in a German factory that manufactured "some sort of secret signaling machine." In 1938, according to Winterbotham, the Gestapo discovered the mechanic's nationality and had him deported. Back in Warsaw, he was in touch with British intelligence, who smuggled him to Paris. French intelligence allegedly found him a workshop and carpenter, and the man built a wooden mock-up of the machine he had worked on in Germany. Bletchley Park, said Winterbotham, identified it as the Enigma.[51] This fiction so infuriated the former chief of French counterespionage, Col. Paul Paillole, that he spoke publicly about the role of Hans-Thilo Schmidt, whose theft of Enigma keys played such a vital part in the Polish solution of the Enigma.[52]

Anthony Cave Brown apparently read Winterbotham's book but missed Paillole's denial. Cave Brown followed Winterbotham by one year with his widely read epic, *Bodyguard of Lies,* about the undercover operations that led up to D-Day. A prolific writer with an elegant style, Cave Brown, early in his book, gives a lively account of the Enigma breakthrough, which is essentially a zestier version of the Winterbotham fabrication. As Cave Brown tells it, British intelligence learned of a Polish Jew, "Richard Lewinski (not his real name)," who had worked as a mathematician and engineer in the Berlin factory where the Enigma was built and was then kicked out of Germany because he was a Jew. Afterward, he offered to sell his expertise for 10,000 pounds sterling to MI6. After checking him out, so goes the story, MI6 set him up in a Paris apartment where "Lewinski" drew up from memory the specifications for an Enigma copy. When the Germans overran France in the spring of 1940, "Lewinski" was allegedly flown out ahead of the advancing Wehrmacht. After establishing residence in London, Cave Brown said, he simply "disappeared."[53]

Author William Stevenson put out still another bogus story. In his best seller, *A Man Called Intrepid,* Stevenson says that Poland obtained the Enigma early in 1939 when its agents hijacked a German military truck delivering Enigmas to the frontier. They allegedly replaced the Enigma with another machine and burned the truck to make it look like an accident.[54] This story was picked up by Welchman in *The Hut Six Story* in 1982,[55] much to the consternation of writers Christopher Kasparek and Richard Woytak, who lamented finding "such a cock-and-bull story repeated with approval in Welchman's otherwise sober and valuable book."[56] British scholars who published later were more accurate in giving the Poles due credit.[57] Kasparek translated the definitive book on the Polish success, *Enigma: How the German Machine Cipher Was Broken, and How It Was Read by the Allies in World War Two* by Wladyslaw Kozaczuk. Published in English in 1984, it told the story as given earlier in this chapter.[58]

For a decade before the truth emerged about the Polish achievement, however, most of the English-speaking public was fed a steady diet of fiction masquerading as fact. Winterbotham's *The Ultra Secret,* Stevenson's *A Man Called Intrepid,* and Cave Brown's *Bodyguard of Lies* all made the *New York Times* Best-Seller List during the mid-seventies. Kozaczuk's *Enigma,* in the mid-eighties, never reached such heights, although it has sold well as an academic book with a smaller readership and even went to a second printing. The idea that the British were primarily responsible for solving the Enigma remains generally lodged in the public mind.

The fact that a Polish mathematician broke the Enigma several years ahead of the British diminishes the role of Turing, who is most often given credit in the popular media for that achievement. Although he made an important contribution in attacking a more complicated German Enigma than the Poles had mastered, it is hard to imagine how the Bletchley bombe could have handled the enormous volume of Enigma traffic without Welchman's diagonal board.

Turing is justifiably celebrated as the conceptual father of the computer. Beyond that, he is a rather tragic figure who committed suicide at a relatively young age after his homosexuality became public knowledge. During the war, when his work on the Enigma was finished, Turing was asked to collaborate on an electronic key-recovery machine for the German teleprinter cipher, but he declined. Alas, the machine that evolved, the Colossus, was a step in the direction of Turing's dream, the "Universal Turing Machine," so the man justly celebrated for thinking ahead of his time missed what could have been a golden opportunity for some measure of fulfillment.

"Without the Poles," authors Kasparek and Woytak have written, "the British would not have been able to read Enigma. . . . The chief British contribution was an expansion in scale of operation to keep pace with the expanding requirements of the war."[59] The general public might have difficulty accepting that conclusion based on the way British and American authors and media have glorified Bletchley Park. But it cannot reasonably be denied. The crucial element in the Polish gift of the home-made military Enigma was Rejewski's solution of the internal rotor wirings. Without it there could have been no bomba, and no bombe. Without the bombe Bletchley Park would have been hard pressed, indeed, to recover Enigma keys. In that light, it seems the only answer to Kasparek and Woytak is an expression of faith in British mathematicians. Perhaps they could have come up with their own Enigma solution in time to save the nation from defeat—and perhaps not. The historical fact is that the British based their extraordinary codebreaking capability on Polish technology. Therefore, anyone who believes that Bletchley Park paved the road to victory in World War II must give credit to Poland for designing the road and mixing the pavement.

CHAPTER 3

The Longest Battle

F. W. Winterbotham described Bletchley Park's new Enigma key-recovery machine, the bombe, in near-mystical terms: "a bronze-coloured column surmounted by a larger circular bronze-coloured face, like some Eastern Goddess who was destined to become the oracle of Bletchley."[1] It is understandable how Freddy Winterbotham, who invested much of his life in Bletchley Park, could be so carried away with this marvelous technology. But it is also important to remember that the bombe was only a machine, wholly dependent on human input to make it effective. If the code-breakers fed it the right crib, it could do wonders to find the right key. Otherwise, it would only sparkle and sputter, then sputter some more, and come up empty.

The earliest success at Bletchley Park came against German air force keys, partly as the result of sloppy keying by the German cipher clerks. In the beginning, the bombe did little for the Royal Navy in its long, bloody struggle against the German U-boat fleet for control of the North Atlantic sea-lanes. Solving the German navy Enigma went beyond Turing's elegant mathematical formulas and Welchman's commonsense observations and even beyond the "bronze goddess" that they created. The German navy introduced fiendish improvements to its Enigma machine and took much greater care to protect its keys than did its air force counterparts, which frustrated the early efforts of the codebreakers in Hut 8 at Bletchley Park. The Royal Navy came to the rescue and searched the high seas for up-to-date key lists and the latest Enigma machines. It took courage and nimble thinking by British sailors who boarded disabled U-boats to recover the essential coding material. In one incident, two heroic young men went to the bottom of the sea in a sinking U-boat. To the extent that Bletchley Park helped the Royal Navy win the Battle of the Atlantic, Bletchley could not have done it without the Royal Navy.

The Battle of the Atlantic was a decisive struggle, perhaps *the* decisive struggle of World War II. If Britain, a resource-poor island nation, could not assure its basic food supplies and the armaments to pursue the conflict, it would have to accept defeat. The Germans and the Allies fought relentlessly from the first day to the last at great cost to both. During the five years and eight months of the war, 2,450 Allied ships (12.8 million tons) and more than 100,000 British, Canadian, and American lives were lost. Germany lost more than 900 U-boats, and of 40,900 German submariners in the war, 25,870 (63 percent) were killed.[2] It did not take the entire war to decide the issue. Not until the autumn of 1940 did the U-boat campaign become a struggle for Britain's very survival, and, by the spring of 1943, the Allies had essentially won it. During that time, it was touch and go, with first one side and then the other gaining the upper hand. Central to this deadly war at sea was the silent cipher war, which pitted the on-and-off British ability to break German U-boat ciphers against the early success of German navy intelligence in reading the ciphers of the Royal Navy and Allied merchant shipping. On both sides of the conflict, the Battle of the Atlantic demonstrated a strong connection between knowing an enemy's secrets and success at war.

When the war started, all German services used five Enigma rotors, and the Polish mathematician, Marian Rejewski, had solved all five by cryptanalysis. Soon, the German Navy added three rotors to its Enigma, making a total of eight for three slots on the machine. For Hut 8 to find the daily keys on a regular basis (i.e., for the bombe to work consistently) they had to know the wiring for the new rotors. They could have learned this by cryptanalysis whenever the wiring of two of the three rotors in the machine was known. With Turing's formula, however, it would have required very lengthy cribs. Another way was to capture the rotors and look inside. That happened, but it was not enough. Hut 8 still had to get a handle on the German Navy's careful keying procedures.

In the beginning, therefore, naval key-recovery in Hut 8 was slow at best. From the summer of 1940, when the Bletchley cryptological bombe was introduced for general use, until the spring of 1941, Turing and his charges had difficulty finding cribs to feed it. They even turned to tedious hand methods first developed by the inventive Poles. It was counted a good effort if a message could be read within a week of receipt. By that time, merchant ships affected were usually out of danger or at the bottom of the sea.

The British and German codebreaking organizations were markedly different. Britain consolidated cryptanalysis for all uniformed and intelligence services at Bletchley Park. The Germans fractionated their system into no fewer than seven intelligence authorities: army, navy, air force, military high command, foreign office, Research Bureau under Reichsmarschall Hermann Goering, and Reichsicherheitshauptamt (RSHA), the Nazi agency that controlled all German police. Of all these, the best at handling codes and ciphers, both in breaking the enemy's and in safeguarding its own, was the navy.

By the time World War II started, German naval codebreakers, the Beobachtungsdienst (B-Dienst, pronounced Bay-Deenst) had broken the two major British naval codes, the administrative and the officers' codes, by eavesdropping on the Royal Navy during the Abyssinian crisis in 1936 and the Spanish Civil War of 1936–39. Aware of this, the British made adjustments by issuing new cipher tables when they entered the war against Germany in 1939, but that was not enough. The Royal Navy did not follow the army and air commands in adopting the Typex cipher machine but stayed with the same numbered hand codes enciphered from additive tables. The B-Dienst managed to recover the new tables within a few months, partly by cryptanalysis but mostly from captured coding material.[3] The consequences were apparent in April 1940 when the Germans outmaneuvered the British fleet during the invasion of Norway. In August of that year, the embarrassed British Admiralty again upgraded its ciphers for capital ships, but the B-Dienst continued to read convoy ciphers and was able to put U-boats in the paths of Allied cargo ships.

The battle over the sea-lanes from North America to Britain went Germany's way during the first year and a half of the war, especially after the fall of France in June 1940 when U-boat bases were moved from northern Germany to the west coast of France, about 450 miles closer to the Atlantic hunting grounds. The boats now had more time on patrol, which partially offset their meager numbers. That summer and early fall were also Britain's time of greatest peril from the threat of German invasion. Destroyers had to be pulled from convoy duty to strengthen the Home Fleet, which denuded convoy escort screens. It became "happy time" for the U-boats. They sank 153 ships from July to September (51 per month on average) and another 66 in October. Including the sinkings from mines, surface ships, and air attack, Britain's losses were greater than its replacement capacity—"quite sufficient," according to German historian Juergen Rohwer, "to give some idea of what could have been done . . . with effective long-range reconnaissance and more U-boats."[4] Then, in the spring of 1941, a turnaround occurred in the secret struggle for supremacy in codes and ciphers.

The German navy utilized two major Enigma keys differentiated by geography, home waters and foreign waters. The latter covered raiders in the South Atlantic and Indian Oceans and was never broken. All North Atlantic vessels, U-boats, and surface fighting ships used the home waters key. At Bletchley Park, naval codebreakers were putting things together a piece at a time. The Royal Navy captured two of the German navy's three new Enigma rotors after sinking the U-33 in February 1940, and it found the third within a few weeks. Hut 8, however, still struggled to come up with cribs. They had a break in April 1940 with the capture of a German key list for four days, which enabled codebreakers in Hut 8 to read retrospectively a small amount of naval Enigma traffic, but it went no further. Another capture opened a window into a non-Enigma hand system known as the dockyard cipher, which was used for communications between shipyards and small coastal vessels. Oddly enough, it proved more fruitful. One subject frequently communicated was the status of minefields. Had mines been cleared? Or not cleared? Because such information was of interest to larger ships as well, the same message transmitted in the dockyard cipher would be repeated in the Enigma home waters key. A solved dockyard message thus provided cribs for the Enigma message thought to be a repeat. Such cribs Bletchley called "kisses."[5]

As sweet as they were, the kisses did not fully satisfy the British desire to read the ciphers of the marauding German U-boats. Yet something had to be done. The high rate of shipping losses was putting tremendous pressure on the Admiralty. Although not enamored with the way naval codebreaking was organized outside their control, the lords of the sea had to make do by cooperating with Bletchley Park.

The Admiralty channeled its formal contact with Bletchley through the Operational Intelligence Centre (OIC), which had been established in 1937 under Cdr. Norman Denning to coordinate the various strands of naval intelligence for use by the battle forces. In the bowels of the OIC's new quarters, a building called the Citadel that had been erected between German bombing raids during the Battle of Britain, the submarine tracking room displayed a large wall map to plot positions and courses of ships and U-boats at sea. A middle-ranking reserve officer, Capt. Rodger Winn, ran the operation. It was a demanding job for which Winn, a lawyer in civilian life, was chosen strictly on merit. His superiors in the Admiralty thought so highly of his performance in the No. 2 job that, in the autumn of 1940, they promoted his superior officer to make room for Winn at the helm in the tracking room. Winn had a knack for reading the enemy's mind. Up to this time, he had relied largely on direction finding, which told him a U-boat's location at a certain past time but not where it was headed. As he saw it, his job was to plot a U-boat's future course so that he could alert the convoys and steer them out of danger. Although he was good at guessing without actually reading the U-boat traffic, he was by no means perfect and desperately needed the exact information that only cryptanalysis could provide.[6]

Bletchley was eager to oblige but, to break the naval Enigma, it needed codebooks, key lists, and even the machine itself. To this end, a series of raids was planned and executed against soft targets in the spring of 1941, but none of them produced enough coding material. Ultimately, the Royal Navy got what the codebreakers needed from a crippled U-boat.

The British struck their first blow in early March with a raid in the Lofoten Islands off Norway, above the Arctic Circle, where the Germans occupied an airfield and maintained a small army garrison. The Lofotens had little strategic value. The people lived off the fishing industry, which produced a limited amount of fish oil that the Germans might use for the manufacture of munitions. But the operation's hidden mission, to capture Enigma ciphering material, gave it a high priority with British military, air and naval brass and the codebreakers at Bletchley Park. In effect, this was a fishing expedition of a different sort. The raiding force included commandos to stage a landing and five destroyers to sweep the surrounding waters for small German craft. The landing party captured a few Germans and blew up the oil plants, but found no Enigmas. The only resistance was encountered at sea from an armed whaler, the *Krebs,* which was quickly subdued by the destroyer *Somali.* A boarding party recovered two rotors and the Enigma key tables for February, which listed the rotor settings and the plug board exchanges.[7]

Bletchley already had the rotors from previous seizures, but the key list proved a valuable find. Almost immediately upon receiving this material, Hut 8 broke into the German home waters naval traffic for February and subsequently much of the same traffic for March, April, and part of May. Of course, the February decrypts were already old and the later ones, solved with painstaking cryptanalysis, carried time lags measured in several days or even weeks. This meant that Hut 8—still led by Turing—could not yet produce intelligence fast enough to affect directly the war against the U-boats. But careful analysis of the decrypts, which, as Turing's biographer Andrew Hodges bluntly put it, the Admiralty "would never have had the time or wit to make," turned up something of interest. Lightly armed German weather ships patrolling the Norwegian Sea north of the Faeroe Islands used the Enigma to send weather reports back home.[8]

The Admiralty certainly had the wit and the wherewithal to follow up on the discovery. Several small German ships, some of them converted fishing trawlers, took turns for weeks at a time on lonely vigils in the frigid northern waters. The Admiralty devised a plan to capture one of them and, in Kahn's phrase, "seize the Enigma." Seven warships—three cruisers and four destroyers—would sweep an area 70 miles wide east of Iceland. The sweep was carried out on May 7. Late in the day, the cruiser *Edinburgh* and the destroyer *Somali* caught sight of the trawler *Muenchen.* Armed with only a machine gun against the firepower of two floating fortresses, the crew of the *Muenchen* wisely offered no resistance. As the ships closed in, a radio noncom (noncommissioned officer) gathered up the Enigma, along with as many papers as he could find, stuffed them into a leaded canvas bag, and threw them overboard. Boarding parties turned up a short weather cipher and the home waters key list for June, which the noncom had missed. With the June key list Bletchley Park read home waters traffic for that month almost concurrently. The short weather cipher, also used by U-boats to send weather data from the North Atlantic, became a source of still more cribs for breaking into operational U-boat traffic.[9]

Two days after the *Muenchen* incident, the Admiralty got lucky. Convoy OB318, made up of thirty-eight merchant ships with a strong escort, had departed Liverpool on May 2 and headed west. The Germans sighted it on May 7 southwest of Iceland. The hungry wolves who made up the U-boat wolf pack gathered for what they thought would be a feast. But the hunters became the hunted. U-110, under command of Fritz-Julius Lemp, torpedoed two tankers before suffering damage in a depth charge attack. Lemp brought his boat to the surface, and the crew began pouring out of the conning tower. While the *Aubretia* picked up survivors, a boarding party, led by twenty-year-old Sub-Lt. David Balme, spent several hours in a systematic search of the U-110 for virtually anything that could be moved—great or small, important or trivial. Among the spoils were an Enigma machine, a complete set of rotors, a U-boat codebook of short signals for reporting Allied ship sightings, and the special settings for a doubly enciphered U-boat officers' code. Bletchley Park had hit the jackpot!

Though it was probably unnecessary, Bletchley requested one more raid to capture the home waters key list for July. It was carried out in late June with a sweep against the weather ship *Lauenburg,* which patrolled so far north it sometimes came within sight of the polar ice cap. As happened during the capture of the *Krebs* and the *Muenchen,* the Enigma itself was a thousand fathoms deep by the time the boarding party arrived, but searchers managed to retrieve the July key list amid a dozen or so mailbags full of documents and manuals.

This was the last such operation. Bletchley Park had decided not to push its luck further lest the Germans connect the raids to codebreaking. In fact, another raid would have been superfluous. June 1941 marked the beginning of a period of almost unbroken success with the naval Enigma that lasted until January 1942, and it translated into success against the U-boats. During four months, March through June 1941, the U-boats sank 282,000 tons of Allied shipping per month. For the following six months, the sinkings averaged 120,000 tons a month, less than half the earlier rate. In November, the U-boats accounted for only 62,000 tons. Ultra made all the difference in two ways. First, because of heavy losses to ships supplying Rommel's troops in North Africa that had resulted from Ultra decrypts, Germany transferred twenty-one boats to the Mediterranean theater, thereby weakening the Atlantic force. Second, now that Bletchley Park could read the U-boat bearings, Allied ships could be diverted around the danger zones.[10]

Soon after the United States entered the war in December 1941, the German U-boat fleet enjoyed its second "happy time." In Operation Drumbeat, the German U-boat commander, Adm. Karl Doenitz, deployed several long-range boats in the western Atlantic. During the first quarter of 1942, Allied shipping losses in the North Atlantic came to 216 ships (1.25 million tons), most of them in the unguarded coastal routes off the eastern seaboard of the United States. More than half the ships sunk were tankers, a priority target for the U-boats.[11] The slaughter continued for four months until, with British prodding, the Americans adopted a system of convoys with armed escorts.

The German U-boat offensive in American waters coincided with a series of British reversals in the cipher war. On February 1, the U-boat service switched to a new four-wheel Enigma (called Shark at Bletchley) that blinded the British naval codebreakers. This was an important innovation, designed exclusively for the U-boats but adaptable for wider use. The fourth wheel, positioned on the left next to the reflector, did not rotate like the other three. It could be set at any of the twenty-six letters of the alphabet or in a neutral position that put it in synch with the standard three-wheel naval Enigma to allow submariners to communicate with the rest of the German navy. The Germans also issued a new book of short weather ciphers that, for a time, deprived Bletchley of useful cribs.

While these moves stymied Bletchley Park, B-Dienst managed to penetrate Britain's naval cypher No. 3 used by the British, Canadian, and American navies for convoy communications. The first break came in February 1942, and B-Dienst stayed on top of No. 3 through most of the year. By December, the Germans were reading 80 percent of the messages intercepted in No. 3, and Doenitz estimated that half of his operational intelligence came from B-Dienst.[12] The Battle of the Atlantic went decidedly in Germany's favor during the first seven months of 1942. Allied shipping losses exceeded 4.5 million tons worldwide from all causes, about 70 percent of which were brought about by German submarines in the North Atlantic.

Throughout the second half of 1942, armed surface escorts accompanied North Atlantic convoys for the entire journey, but midway in the crossing south of Greenland, the ships went without air cover. Doenitz always exploited Allied weaknesses to minimize his own losses. When the Germans pulled back from the American coast as the U.S. Navy initiated effective convoy defenses, the "Greenland gap," the weak link in the North Atlantic convoy route, became the focal point of the next big U-boat offensive. B-Dienst continued to read the

Royal Navy cipher, which helped locate convoys, while Bletchley remained generally blinded by the introduction of the four-wheel Enigma and the dearth of useful cribs.

The campaign in the Greenland gap ("Torpedo Junction" to American seamen) raged on and off from August 1942 until the following spring. It began with furious give-and-take attacks in which the Allied side usually had the worst of it, and ended with the effective elimination of the U-boat threat once the Allies had extended their air cover over the gap, equipped their planes with the latest radar, and reestablished mastery of the Enigma. That left a year for the uninterrupted Allied buildup to D-Day and the final phase of World War II. But no such outcome could have been anticipated in the late summer of 1942.

Bletchley's big break that allowed it to master the latest Enigma technology came from a singular act of heroism by three British seamen (actually two men and a boy) in the eastern Mediterranean far from the main arena of U-boat combat. In the predawn darkness of October 17, just six days before General Montgomery launched the decisive Battle of El Alamein, a British scout plane reported radar contact with a suspected submarine about 90 miles north-northwest of the Suez Canal. Four destroyers based at Port Said, Egypt, sailed out to search the area. They included the *Petard* under the command of a tough career officer, Lt. Cdr. Mark Thornton. He and 1st Lt. Tony Fasson had discussed the need to go beyond the mere sinking of a U-boat by capturing its secret codes. In their long hours at sea, they organized and drilled a boarding team that Fasson would lead.

The destroyers quickly made asdic (sonar) contact and spent the afternoon and part of the night in trying to bring the U-boat to the surface with depth charges. Finally, at about 10:40 P.M., the battered U-599 rose up out of the pitch-black sea. The *Petard*'s searchlight illuminated a white donkey painted on the U-boat's conning tower, a drollery in appreciation of a rumor that the Greek salami eaten by the crew came from donkey meat. Instinctively, Thornton gave the command to open fire. Then, seeing men pour out of the conning tower with the boat defenseless and sinking, he ordered a cease-fire. There was not enough time for the boarding routine. While a whaleboat was lowered on the far side of the destroyer and brought around, Fasson and Able Seaman Colin Grazier stripped off their outer clothes and swam to the U-boat. Not far behind them came the canteen assistant, Tommy Brown. He was not part of the boarding team and probably did not have a clue about what the other two men were doing. Still, they made good use of him.

Waves were already lapping over the U-boat's deck, and the conning tower was riddled with shell holes, including a 4-inch gash at the base where the sea poured through it to compound their peril. Unknown to the Britons, the U-boat commander, Lt. Hans Heidtmann, had opened the seacocks to scuttle his boat. In the control room, Fasson and Grazier sloshed around in water above their ankles. With a burst from his machine gun, Fasson broke open a locked cabinet in the captain's quarters. When Brown climbed down, he instantly became a courier carrying papers back up to the whaleboat. After his third trip, with the U-boat slipping fast beneath the waves, Brown was ordered not to go back and to call down for Fasson and Grazier to get out fast, but it was too late. U-599 took the two British heroes to the bottom. Each was posthumously awarded the George Cross, Britain's second highest decoration for valor.[13] For his part, Brown also received the George Cross and was then discharged from the Navy. He was only sixteen years old and had lied about his age when he enlisted. He found his hero's death two years later while trying to rescue his sister from an air raid fire at their tenement home in the slums of North Shield.[14]

Hut 8 at Bletchley Park was back in business. The documents from U-599 included the latest editions of the short-signal book and the short weather cipher. With the latter, cribs were again possible. On December 13, Hut 8 turned up a key with the fourth rotor in the neutral position. The codebreakers soon learned that three letters of the four-letter U-boat key were the same as the three-letter weather key. Thereafter, once the weather key was recovered with cribs from the new short weather cipher, finding the fourth letter of the U-boat key was a relatively simple matter of testing up to twenty-six letters of the nonrotating left cipher wheel.

That day, a Sunday, Hut 8 telephoned the submarine tracking room with the good news. The first decrypt, forwarded by teleprinter an hour later, located fifteen U-boats in the North Atlantic. One decrypt followed another until early next morning. Reserve Lt. Patrick Beesly was on duty because it was Captain Winn's day off. Beesly immediately called his commander to share his excitement, only to learn that Winn was seriously ill with exhaustion and dangerously low blood pressure. "The gods must have decided, at this moment, to amuse themselves at the tracking room's expense," Beesly wrote later, "for on a single day in December they removed with one hand the lynch pin of our organization, and with the other restored to us our most precious source of intelligence."[15] Winn was in such bad shape that his doctors said he might never resume the arduous duties of the tracking room, but he returned four weeks later and served out the war.

The pieces in the anti–U-boat campaign came together for the Allies in dribs and drabs. Bletchley Park codebreakers broke the four-rotor Enigma on December 13, 1942, but, even with a new four-rotor cryptological bombe and collaboration with U.S. Navy codebreakers in Washington, they could not always read Shark traffic currently. In Correlli Barnett's words, they were "veering between periods of clear vision" and "temporary loss of sight."[16] The life and death of convoys hung in the balance. Often, the British codebreakers could read the orders from Doenitz that put the U-boats in the path of a convoy. That would trigger a timely warning followed by a change of course so that the convoy might steam around the danger. Often, however, Bletchley came up empty, which left the convoy on a course for ambush and sometimes disaster. In January 1943, for example, when B-Dienst learned of a nine-tanker convoy carrying fuel from Trinidad to the North African theater that gave Doenitz an opportunity to organize a pack of U-boats to intercept it, Bletchley failed to read the U-boat deployment in time to prevent the loss of seven of the nine tankers. This on-again, off-again capability continued until August 1943, after which Bletchley (and Washington) always read Shark within twenty-four hours.

Just as important as mastery of the four-rotor Enigma was the discovery that B-Dienst was reading the Allies' convoy cipher. Bletchley suspected it after breaking Shark in December 1942. The following March, a U.S. Navy cryptanalyst in Washington, Lt. Knight McMahon, proved it when he discovered that Doenitz had sent a message to redeploy U-boat pickets soon after the Allies had sent their own message rerouting a convoy around the pickets.[17] A replacement cipher was already in the works, but its distribution to the British Navy was not completed until June 1943. From then on, B-Dienst lost sight of convoy routings, and it stayed that way for the rest of the war.

During this time of uncertainty, the biggest crisis of the U-boat war occurred. The violent storms that lashed the North Atlantic that winter of 1943 created a fitting background to the ferocity of the struggle. As many as forty U-boats prowled the air gap in shifting cordons and interchanging wolf packs. In February, they engaged nine convoys totaling 242 ships and sank 34 of them; another 29 ships sailing alone went to the bottom.[18] Most of the Allied losses occurred in two convoys in which B-Dienst was operationally superior to Bletchley Park. In other words, B-Dienst had perfect vision, whereas Bletchley was groping in semidarkness.

February, however, was merely a prelude to the disasters during the first twenty days of March. For seven of the first ten days, Bletchley experienced above-average delays in reading Shark and, from March 10–19, went completely blank when the Germans issued a new short-signal book. In two running battles, March 7–14, U-boats dispatched thirteen cargo ships in Convoy SC121 and sank four merchantmen and a destroyer escort in Convoy HX228, with a total loss of two U-boats. A worse fate befell successive Convoys SC122 and HX229, which together numbered ninety fully laden eastbound cargo vessels. Although the convoys went to sea at different times from separate North American ports, the vagaries of weather and the onslaught of submarines brought them together in confusion and terror as a single concentration of floating targets. With air cover only during daylight, eighteen escort ships slugged it out with thirty-eight U-boats in the greatest convoy engagement of the war. The final toll in this battle was twenty-two merchant ships sunk against one U-boat destroyed and two severely damaged—a major German victory.

Almost overnight a dramatic turnaround occurred. Recently devised anti-submarine tactics were put into effect. Escort aircraft carriers began protecting the convoys, and the air gap suddenly ceased to exist. The next two eastbound convoys, SC123 and HX230, lost only one ship, a paltry score for the Germans considering the fact that Admiral Doenitz had massed forty U-boats. Similar encounters during early April produced only slightly better results for the Germans, far below their expectations. Bletchley managed to divert some convoys out of danger and read encouraging signals from newly trained U-boat commanders suggesting a loss of nerve from the constant threat of sudden air attack. In late April, a large U-boat force pounced on three convoys but sank only four ships against its loss of three boats.

A furious battle involving westbound Convoy ONS5 with forty-three ships raged in early May off the southern tip of Greenland, where the combatants fought each other amid roiling seas and dangerous icebergs. In a running battle beginning on April 29 and continuing until May 6, the Germans sank twelve ships at a cost of seven U-boats lost and five severely damaged. Such a standoff amounted to a German defeat, but more was to come. The U-boats moved south against eastbound Convoys SC129 and HX237; the score was three ships versus three boats. When the wolf packs took on eastbound Convoy SC130, it was zero ships to five boats, and one of the five carried Doenitz's twenty-year-old son, Peter, to his death. On May 24, Doenitz shifted most of his U-boats to an area southwest of the Azores. It was the day Germany acknowledged it had lost the crucial Battle of the Atlantic.

The Allies quickly went on the offensive. In that decisive month of May, the British stepped up radar-aided air attacks in the Bay of Biscay and sank another six boats. Now, however, the primary targets became the U-boat tankers ("milk cows") that prolonged the patrols of fighting U-boats by refueling them at sea. Altogether, Germany had ten U-boat tankers in its inventory. With the help of Bletchley decrypts, six were dispatched by midsummer. Germany pressed into service seven of its larger fighting U-boats as tanker replacements, and the Allies went after these with equal intensity. By the summer of 1944, every one of them had been sunk. Only one milk cow survived the war, U-219, which had been assigned to Japanese-controlled waters in the Pacific.

Codebreaking is only part of the story of the Allied victory in the savage U-boat war. Radar, airpower, improved weaponry and tactics, and America's capacity to build ships faster than the Germans could sink them all played a role. In assessing the contribution of codebreaking, the facts speak for themselves. Early in the war, when B-Dienst read the British naval cipher and Bletchley Park did not read the German naval Enigma, the U-boats had their first "happy time." In mid-1941, the tables were turned, and Bletchley helped guide the convoys around the U-boats. B-Dienst solved the Allies' convoy cipher in 1942 and introduced the four-wheel Enigma, which caused Bletchley to go "blind." The U-boats had their best year, thanks in no small part to their second "happy time" along the East Coast of the United States and the absence of adequate Allied air cover in the mid-Atlantic. When Bletchley broke the four-wheel Enigma, it set the stage for the climax of the U-boat war in the spring of 1943, and when the Admiralty introduced a new convoy cipher that blinded the Germans, the U-boats were fighting a losing battle. Historians agree that the Allies narrowly won the Battle of the Atlantic. Chances are they would have lost it by a wide margin had they not achieved the advantage and, ultimately, the victory in the cipher war.

CHAPTER 4

Outfoxing
the Desert Fox

When German Gen. Erwin Rommel arrived in North Africa in February 1941, he hit the ground with his motor running. He came to rescue the Italian army from the British, who threatened to push it off the African continent. The British Middle East commander, Gen. Sir Archibald Wavell, predicted the Germans would not be ready for desert warfare before May. He obviously did not know much about Rommel, who attacked at the end of March. By mid-April, Rommel had driven the British back 400 miles to the Egyptian border. For the next eighteen months, Rommel would parry and thrust, fall back and push forward, step aside and close a trap, suffer defeat and drive to victory—and ultimately lose North Africa. Prime Minister Churchill, anxious about the survival of the British Empire and his own political skin, twice dismissed unsuccessful commanders until he chose Gen. Sir Bernard Montgomery, who beat Rommel back for good in one of the decisive battles of World War II.

The most remarkable thing about Rommel's performance is that he never entered the field of battle with his Afrika Korps of elite German troops in a dominant position—not even in a position of parity. Generally outnumbered and outgunned, Rommel consistently outmaneuvered his adversary until the late summer of 1942 when, finally, the string ran out. By then, the Afrika Korps was so exhausted, its lines so extended, its supplies and reinforcements so constricted, its intelligence so compromised, and the enemy so much stronger that even Rommel's genius could not save it.

Through it all—the great German victories and the ultimate crushing defeat of the Afrika Korps—intelligence played a key role. On both sides, the most valuable intelligence came from reading the enemy's codes and ciphers. Although it cannot be said that intelligence alone determined the outcome of any particular battle, it is striking how good information, expertly used, so closely accompanied victory during the ebb and flow of the great desert campaigns. The cipher war in North Africa explains a lot about the legend of the "Desert Fox," as Rommel was called, and how the Fox was beaten at his own game.

Although never a Nazi Party member and eventually done in for his part in a plot to kill Hitler, Rommel gained favor with the Fuehrer before the outbreak of war for his authorship of a treatise on infantry tactics that Hitler read and admired. Rommel believed in mobile warfare and that battles are won with superior force at the point of attack. When the Wehrmacht punched through Belgium and northern France during the spring of 1940, Rommel was in the spearhead as commander of the 7th Panzer Division, whose many distinctions in that campaign included the capture of nearly one hundred thousand enemy troops and several French admirals and generals.[1]

Less than a year later, Hitler sent Rommel to North Africa to bail out his friend, Italian Premier Benito Mussolini, and shore up the demoralized Italian army. Wavell knew of Rommel's arrival from the German air force's Enigma messages decrypted at Bletchley Park. He knew when and where Rommel landed in Africa, the German general's assigned mission and the makeup of his striking force. Rommel would command the newly created Afrika Korps comprising two armored divisions, the 5th Light Motorized, scheduled to arrive in April, and the 15th Panzer, due in May. Also, Rommel had the nominal support of the numerically superior Italian army, but he did not fully control it and had little regard for its abilities in mobile warfare.

Both German divisions arrived ahead of schedule, but Rommel did not wait for the heavy Panzers before going on the offensive. Starting from El Agheila in

Libya, where the southeastern Gulf of Sidra laps the shore about 400 miles east of Tripoli, he struck boldly with only a brigade of the 5th Light Motorized Division. He had full confidence in the German system of "blitzkrieg" (lightning warfare), which featured a tight, efficient interdependence of forces. The surprised British, their ranks thinned by the redeployment of air and ground forces for the unsuccessful defense of Greece, fell back in disarray. They managed to hold on to the Libyan port of Tobruk with thirty-three thousand defenders, who stood out like a thorn in Rommel's back as he pressed on to the Egyptian frontier. There, he paused.

Not least of the British problems was the inadequacy of their intelligence. The Ultra decryption of German Enigma ciphers at Bletchley Park was not yet fully developed. At the time, Bletchley was able to recover only German air force keys, and they had little impact in the field in North Africa. Besides, at this early stage of the campaign, the decrypts went no further than Middle East Command headquarters in Cairo, Egypt, out of fear that the secret might fall into enemy hands. Wavell filtered the information and attributed it euphemistically to "a reliable source" or the like before sending it on to his field commander, Lt. Gen. Sir Richard O'Connor, who was not told that it came from codebreaking. The great tragedy for British fortunes at the time was that Wavell grossly underestimated the Afrika Korps, which put O'Connor off balance. Wavell had assured O'Connor that Rommel could not attack for at least a month. When Rommel did attack, Wavell reassured his subordinate that the Germans could not go far. O'Connor, who had so recently crushed the Italians, soon became Rommel's distinguished prisoner.

In this initial thrust, Rommel's best intelligence asset was his mobile radio intelligence unit, the Horch Company, which set up close to the front lines and listened in on the enemy troops by using a form of information gathering called "traffic analysis." The process was far more sophisticated than the Indian warrior of the old American West putting his ear to the ground to listen for the hoofbeats of an approaching enemy war party, but it was the same principle. The Horch Company generally could not read encrypted signals, but it became familiar with call signs that identified enemy units. Then, it used special direction-finding equipment to pinpoint a unit's location. Although the Horch Company had state-of-the-art technology for that period, the leadership made it effective. Capt. Alfred Seebohm, the company commander, possessed a special ability to discern patterns of enemy activity from seemingly meaningless scraps of information.[2] The British had their own mobile intelligence unit with comparable technology. It was called the "Y" service and would become no less effective than the Horch Company as the British gained battlefield experience.

Rommel had surprised even his own superiors in his dash across the desert. The nervous Italians asked the German high command to restrain what they considered his reckless advance. They found a receptive ear in the less than dynamic Gen. Franz Halder, chief of the German General Staff. Halder sent Gen. Friedrich von Paulus (who would later surrender at Stalingrad) to tour the North African front. In late April, with the 5th Light at full strength, Rommel tried unsuccessfully to capture Tobruk. When that failed Paulus ordered a halt to further attacks and signaled Berlin that Rommel's troops were tired and overextended and could not advance farther without doubling his force. Halder, anxious that Rommel not drain off troops earmarked for the invasion of the Soviet Union two months later, breathed a sigh of relief. So did the British who read the Paulus dispatch through cryptanalysis. Hitler, preoccupied with his eastern strategy, failed to support Rommel, who, flushed with victory and anxious to forge ahead, had to sit tight in a defensive posture and wait for the British to regroup and strike back.

As Rommel waited impatiently, a very important breakthrough at Bletchley Park deterred him from pressing the attack. Rommel was firmly convinced that the British strongholds in Cairo and the Nile delta were within reach if only the German troops could be adequately resupplied. In June, however, Bletchley Park broke an Italian machine cipher used to coordinate Mediterranean merchant shipping, and the cipher was read without interruption for the rest of the war. As Rommel bided his time and waited for his war materials, British naval and air forces based on Malta took a rising toll of the Italian merchant fleet. In December, half the ships leaving Italian ports failed to reach North Africa. The British were careful to hide their foreknowledge of Italian shipping schedules. Each time they learned of a departure through codebreaking, they sent out a surveillance plane, not to spot the ship but to make sure the ship's crew spotted the plane to allay any suspicion that Axis codes had been compromised.

Wavell tried twice to relieve Tobruk and twice failed. During his second attempt in June 1941, he was reinforced with 238 tanks released by Churchill after the threat of German invasion of the home island had passed. Wavell promptly drove them into Rommel's tank traps lined with deadly 88 cannon. Half of the newly arrived British armor was knocked out on the first day of combat, and the remainder of the attacking forces barely escaped envelopment from a German counterstroke. A shocked Churchill relieved Wavell of command.

His replacement, Gen. Sir Claude Auchinleck, spent five months training and equipping the new Eighth Army made up of units from the British Isles and Commonwealth nations. When Auchinleck attacked in November 1941 in Operation Crusader, he had a 4 to 1 manpower advantage over the Germans and a 2 to 1 advantage over German and Italian troops combined. He also had the advantage of two other important breakthroughs at Bletchley Park. In September 1941, the codebreakers temporarily recovered, first, the German army keys used within the Afrika Korps and, second, the Army keys used in Rommel's communications with Rome and Berlin. For the first time, the Eighth Army received advance information about the status and movement of Rommel's formations. Alas, not long after Auchinleck launched Operation Crusader, Bletchley lost the army keys,[3] but the damage already had been done. Auchinleck relieved Tobruk in short order and kept on rolling until he had driven Rommel all the way back to El Agheila whence the Afrika Korps had started eight months earlier and where it could regroup behind defensible positions.

The Afrika Korps spent the holiday season at El Agheila and received a priceless cryptological gift, for which it was indebted to Loris Gherardi, an obscure Italian messenger, and the Italian Military Information Service (Servizio Informazione Militare, or SIM). In August 1941, Gherardi helped SIM steal a valuable set of documents, the so-called Black Code used by American military attachés, from an American Embassy safe in Rome.

Gherardi, an embassy employee for two decades, was doubling as an agent for SIM. One of his duties was to carry enciphered telegrams from the embassy to the Italian telegraph bureau. Copies were made available to SIM, but they were no help without knowledge of the American cryptosystem. Gherardi solved that problem by gaining access to the military attaché's safe. One soft Roman night, he slipped into the embassy, opened the safe, removed the code and cipher books, photographed them, and carefully put them back as he had found them. The Americans never knew about the theft until after the war. SIM shared its bonanza with German intelligence, and the Axis powers were soon reading secret American diplomatic correspondence from embassies around the world.

Rommel was the most outstanding beneficiary. The American military attaché in Cairo, Col. Bonner Frank Fellers, used the Black Code (named for the color of its binding) to send detailed reports about the British army in North Africa to Washington. The information came directly from the British, who confided in him with the hope, perhaps, of influencing Washington's Lend-Lease policy. Little did Fellers or the British know that he was unintentionally sharing these reports with Rommel.

Exactly when Rommel started receiving the Fellers intercepts is not clear. If he had them at the time of Operation Crusader, they did nothing to stop the British advance, but there is no question that they paid high dividends beginning in January 1942. Rommel was doubly blessed without knowing it because Bletchley Park still had not recovered the German army cipher keys lost the previous November. Shorter supply lines, together with intensive German bombing of the British naval base at Malta, had allowed Rommel to build his force to its peak strength for the entire North Africa campaign.

───────────

As the confident Auchinleck was preparing to resume his offensive at El Agheila, Rommel beat him to the punch. His Afrika Korps had been upgraded to three divisions, including two panzer divisions with improved tanks. He also benefited from improved intelligence. Among the messages transmitted by Fellers in January and February 1942 were a detailed rundown on British armor, a British evaluation of Axis armor, and reports on the location and efficiency of the British 1st Armored and 4th Indian Divisions, two sizable roadblocks in his way. Author David Kahn said, "[The Fellers messages] provided Rommel with undoubtedly the broadest and clearest picture of enemy forces and intentions available to any Axis commander throughout the whole war."[4]

Rommel launched his campaign on January 21 against the newly arrived, inexperienced British 1st Armored Division and drove 100 miles in two days. During the next two weeks, the British retreated another 200 miles to the Gazala Line, only a few miles west of Tobruk, leaving to Rommel the port of Benghazi with a rich store of supplies. Rommel's advance suffered more from constant bickering with his Italian allies than from the British defenders. At Gazala, the lines stabilized and the two armies prepared for another great battle.

During the first half of 1942, while Rommel was feeding off the Fellers dispatches from Cairo, Bletchley continued to read German air force and Italian merchant marine messages. In April, the codebreakers regained one of the army keys lost in November. Cairo headquarters thus learned that Rommel would attack in late May, but did not learn the operational details. Auchinleck was left to wonder whether Rommel would hit weak spots in the British center or make a flanking move into the desert. He advised his field commander, Gen. Sir Neil Ritchie, to concentrate his armor (which outnumbered Rommel's) behind the front to be ready in either event. This was sound advice, but Ritchie did not know it was founded on codebreaking. So he weighed it against what he thought was important intelligence from the front—what turned out to be Rommel's fake signals. Rommel feinted in the center and pressed his attack on the British left flank. Once the Germans had turned the corner, they ran into fierce resistance and, at one point, appeared to be in trouble behind the British lines. Rommel regrouped in a defensive posture, dug in his antitank guns, and lured the British into a trap. In what might be called "the charge of the heavy brigades," Ritchie tore into Rommel's position piecemeal, one armored force at a time, and lost 230 of his 300 tanks. The next day, Ritchie was in full retreat. In the fallout, he was stripped of his command while Rommel became the youngest field marshal in German history.

As the British Eighth Army fell back toward Egypt, it left Tobruk exposed once again. This time, the strategic port that had become a symbol of Allied resistance was not spared. Rommel struck before the British had time to re-establish their defenses. Tobruk's capitulation on June 20 yielded to the Germans another large cache of war materials, which helped Rommel to push on halfway across Egypt until he was finally halted in July at El Alamein, the last outpost before the Nile delta. There, with victory seemingly in his grasp, Rommel was in reality at the end of his tether, his Afrika Korps exhausted and badly depleted.

———————

The battle of El Alamein was one of three decisive battles in three far-flung locations fought in 1942 that turned the tide of World War II (the others were at Midway and Stalingrad). Actually, the fighting at this outer gate to the Nile consisted of three separate battles. In the first, Auchinleck, who had taken direct command of the Eighth Army, checked Rommel's advance in July, which created a stalemate lasting through the summer. By this time, Bletchley had recovered both Afrika Korps keys, plus a new army–air force liaison key, and these messages were read within twenty-four hours on average. This favorable situation lasted through the remainder of the North African campaign. Auchinleck gave full credit to Ultra for his preliminary victory at El Alamein. Without it, he said, "Rommel would certainly have got through to Cairo."[5] If Ultra saved Cairo, it did not save Auchinleck. Churchill relieved him for not counter-attacking the battered Afrika Korps with the battered Eighth Army. He gave the Middle East command to Gen. Sir Harold Alexander and the Eighth Army command to Gen. Sir Bernard Montgomery. Under Montgomery, the Eighth Army mauled the Afrika Korps at Alam Halfa, the second El Alamein battle, as Rommel tried to resume his drive to the Nile. Finally, after a seven-week buildup, the British broke through the German lines during the famous battle that bears the name El Alamein and gives the name Montgomery an honored place in the history books.

Montgomery was better served by Ultra intelligence than any field commander who preceded him. Ultra distribution had been streamlined. For the first time, the Eighth Army was assigned its own SLU, in addition to SLUs in place at Middle East Command in Cairo, Air Command in Alexandria, and the air and sea base in Malta.[6] In a departure from normal procedure, Bletchley placed a team of codebreakers, translators, and intelligence analysts at Cairo in July to minimize delay in the flow of information to the front.[7]

Establishing an SLU with the Eighth Army extended the Ultra secret to the battlefield where it could be most useful. Now Montgomery would be privy to the same information as his theater commander, General Alexander, as well as Prime Minister Churchill. Montgomery did not like the idea of the nonsoldier politician Churchill looking over his shoulder because so much available battlefield intelligence made it easier for the boss to second-guess him. When Montgomery complained about it, he lost that minor clash of giant egos. Besides, the benefits of the Ultra intelligence far outweighed such trifling drawbacks. Getting it unfiltered by higher command and knowing the source gave it a special value. The information did not always tell Montgomery more than he already knew from local field intelligence and aerial photography, but, even as mere high-grade confirmation, it bolstered his planning resources.

Of course, any widening of Ultra distribution carried inherent security risks; however, the secret survived not only the North African campaign but the entire war and three decades beyond. Meanwhile, Montgomery played this ace up his sleeve in a way that hyped his own reputation. He appeared before his troops in godlike omniscience and told them not only that Rommel would be defeated but also what Rommel's exact moves would be. Although his information came from Ultra, the soldiers did not share in that secret, and he did not—and could not—tell them.[8]

As important as these internal British improvements was the unraveling of Rommel's entire intelligence system. The British Y service, the mobile radio intelligence unit in the field, struck the first blow. It located the Horch Company at Tel-el-Eisa, "the Hill of Jesus," west of El Alamein during the second week of July. A battalion of the Australian 9th Infantry Division attacked the company and wiped it out. Seebohm himself was critically wounded and taken prisoner. He was removed to Cairo, where he died bravely with his lips sealed. The captured documents revealed the deepest German intelligence secrets— the penetration of the American Black Code and the existence of a German spy ring in Cairo. The British co-opted both of these intelligence assets and used them to feed false information to Rommel.[9] When the Americans learned of the debacle (although they did not yet know how the code was compromised), they reassigned Fellers.

The Germans put together another mobile intelligence unit, but, without Seebohm, it was never the same. Thus, Rommel's flow of intelligence was greatly diminished at the front, and, without his knowing it, he was completely cut off from the Fellers dispatches. To make matters worse, British disinformation experts skillfully skewed the Fellers dispatches and "reports" from the defunct Cairo spy ring. It was as if the Desert Fox, bereft of his senses, could not see the red-coated huntsmen, smell the sweating horses, or hear the baying hounds as they closed in on him.

Rommel's plan of attack at Alam Halfa resembled the one that had succeeded so brilliantly at Gazala. He would secretly move his armor south into the desert, turn the British left flank, drive to the sea to cut off and annihilate the Eighth Army, and then take what he hoped would be a leisurely Sunday drive to Cairo. Rommel's secret, however, was in Montgomery's hands (through Ultra) soon after Rommel radioed the plan to his superiors in Rome and Berlin, and Montgomery devised his own plan. He sought to lure the Germans into an area of soft desert sand called the Ragil, which was unfavorable for tank maneuver. For this purpose, British intelligence sent misleading information with ciphers taken from the Cairo spy ring and planted a misleading map for the Germans to find on the corpse of a British soldier. The map falsely indicated that the Ragil sand was hard and therefore suitable for tank movement.

The attack began during the night of August 30–31. Rommel wanted to drive 30 miles east before turning north, but he was met by three armored divisions instead of one, as had been reported by his own intelligence. He then decided to turn north earlier than planned—into the Ragil. From the ridge of Alam Halfa overlooking the Ragil, the British poured down a murderous fire. Rommel broke off the attack on September 4 and withdrew behind his starting line.

Soft sand was only part of the story. Rommel's armor was also hampered by a lack of promised fuel to power his panzers. The Royal Air Force and Navy had sunk the three tankers transporting the fuel after Ultra had intercepted the Italian sailing schedules. Rommel knew that he had been tricked but not how it was accomplished. His pet theory was Italian betrayal. He also knew that he could not sustain such heavy losses—fifty tanks, seventy guns, and nearly five thousand men—and still pursue his goal of taking Cairo. Hoping against hope that reinforcements would arrive in time to avert disaster, he dug in to await Montgomery's counterattack.

Montgomery, an extremely cautious commander who would not be hurried by Churchill, spent seven weeks in preparation. He wanted overwhelming superiority before taking on Rommel. Through the American Black Code, the Cairo spy cipher, and German double agents under British control, he led the enemy to believe that his preparations would take even longer. Keeping track of German movements through Ultra, he fully realized that Bletchley Park's special intelligence was vital to the success of his operation.

Rommel's health was bad and his mood somber. He complained bitterly about the failure of his supplies to get through—always blaming the Italians, never suspecting British codebreaking. As the Bletchley Park codebreakers read the shipping schedules, the British naval and air forces were steadily erasing the Italian merchant marine. The intelligence was so good that the British knew which ships were carrying what cargo and could concentrate their attacks on vessels carrying fuel and munitions. Fully a third of the desperately needed supplies sent to Rommel in August, September, and October went to the bottom of the sea. On one occasion, Bletchley received information a day late that the *Apuania* had arrived in Benghazi with ten tanks and a large supply of ammunition. The next night, the British carried out a heavy air raid on the port and made sure to hit the *Apuania,* which blew up with such force that it caused extensive damage to port facilities and other ships.[10] Four days before Montgomery began his assault at El Alamein, Ultra revealed that Rommel had only a week's supply of fuel for his too few tanks.

Montgomery's plan called for attacking the northern flank of the 40-mile El Alamein front close to the sea. To throw Rommel off the track, the British faked a buildup in the south while disguising their true buildup in the north, a sleight of hand carried out by a special unit commanded by Brig. Dudley Clarke. Clarke, a lawyer in civilian life, had served with General Wavell in Palestine in 1938, and the two men discovered that they agreed on the importance of deception in modern warfare. Before coming to North Africa, Clarke was based in England where he planned and organized commando raids against enemy coastal bases across the English Channel. When he arrived in Cairo in 1940 to rejoin Wavell he set up shop in a building that once housed a bordello and began meticulously choosing special men for a special line of work. He hand-picked his officers for their professional talents—among them Lt. Col. Geoffrey Barkas, a designer of movie sets, and Maj. Michael Ayrton, an artist—and brought in an assortment of skilled civilians, including other artists, draftsmen, a screenwriter, an illusionist, a chemist, and a banker. This small, motley organization eventually would be called the A-Force and grow to battalion size. One of Clarke's fundamental operating principles was to understand the enemy's preconceived intelligence picture of the British forces, and he studied German intelligence appreciations of the British order of battle, for which Ultra eventually became the prime source.

The concealment in the north had to be accomplished where the flat, barren land offered no natural hiding places and under the watchful eye of enemy air reconnaissance. Working at night, the British concealed 2,000 tons of fuel in preexisting slit trenches and stacked 4,000 tons of supplies and a thousand guns under camouflage nets in such a way as to resemble trucks and bivouac tents. To bolster their feint to the south, they openly pretended to build a 20-mile water pipeline. After digging a section of trench and carefully laying empty fuel cans alongside it so that they would look like pipe to high-flying daylight reconnaissance crews, they filled in the trench after dark and moved on to the next section. All along, they followed a schedule to make it appear that the pipeline would not be finished until after the appointed day of the attack. Also, in the south, the British laid in stores of fake supplies and dummy guns. They saved the tanks, self-propelled guns, and armored cars for last and parked them in plain sight well to the rear and near the north-south junction. To the Germans, the location was consistent with the buildup in the south.[11]

At the last moment, however, Montgomery changed the plan. Ultra had revealed the movement of a German division to the north to strengthen the Italian troops covering that sector.[12] His advisors urged him to take the path of least resistance—the center between the German and Italian armies—and that is where Montgomery struck on the night of October 23–24. Rommel, persuaded by his own befuddled intelligence that the battle would not begin before November, had flown to Germany to restore his failing health and to plead with Hitler for more supplies. When he returned, he saw that his deprived forces could not stop the reinforced and amply supplied Eighth Army. Despite their desperate plight, the Axis held on at the El Alamein front until November 4. By then, Rommel knew he was beaten and cabled Hitler for permission to retreat. Hitler replied by ordering Rommel to hold out "to the last man . . . [to] victory or death." Rommel asked for a repeat. Either Hitler's message was garbled, or Rommel was pretending so. Before the "clarification" reached Rommel, the Afrika Korps was in full retreat. Bletchley Park eavesdropped on the entire conversation with unmitigated delight.[13]

A week after Montgomery began his offensive at El Alamein, Anglo-American forces landed in Morocco and Algeria and began driving east. Hitler tried to salvage his strategic position in North Africa by pouring reinforcements into his Tunisian stronghold as the Allies closed in on two sides. Temporarily renewed, Rommel fought skillfully to avoid defeat. He marched under radio silence to the western front to bloody the untested Americans at Kasserine Pass. Then, he doubled back to the east to attack an exposed advance division of the Eighth Army at Medenine. Unfortunately for Rommel, Montgomery was forewarned by Ultra and other intelligence sources in time to rush reinforcements to the Medenine front and throw back the Germans with heavy losses. The Desert Fox, who owed so much of his reputation to German radio intelligence, now wondered what made Montgomery so smart. For this final insult, he again blamed Italian treachery. He never learned the truth about Ultra.

Medenine was Rommel's last battle in North Africa. He already had been relieved of command, but the timing had been left to him. Sick and disillusioned, he returned to Germany to recover his health. On May 7, 1943, British and American troops marched into Tunis to accept the surrender of a quarter of a million Axis troops, including what was left of the once proud Afrika Korps.

CHAPTER 5

·Colossus

So much has been written about Bletchley Park's triumph over the Enigma that an achievement more far reaching tends to get lost in the rhetoric. Bletchley Park ushered in the age of the electronic computer by building Colossus, a key-recovery machine. Far from the Universal Turing Machine conceived by Alan Turing, it would not even fit the description of a general-purpose computer. It was built for a special use with limited flexibility, but it was electronic. Both computers and electronics were then in early but separate stages of development. For the first time, they were joined in the Colossus, and it proved to be a useful and long-lasting union. To put it in a bolder and truer context, the Colossus ushered in the "Information Age."

The Colossus possessed logic in the sense that it could make simple yes-or-no or true-or-false determinations and do them with blinding speed. Although both the cryptological bombe, the key-recovery machine for the Enigma, and the Colossus filled important needs in their time, only the latter served as a stepping-stone to the new dominant information technology. The Colossus was a crude device, to be sure. The electronic components were vacuum and gas-filled tubes, which made the machine very large by later standards, but they also made the Colossus a thousand times faster than the electromechanical devices then in existence. In its time, the Colossus was on the cutting edge of technology.

Contrary to some accounts, the Colossus was not invented to attack the Enigma.[1] Rather, it was a response to a new generation of German cipher machines based on the non-Morse five-unit international teleprinter code.[2] Before anyone thought of building the Colossus, a young Cambridge chemistry student turned mathematician, W. T. Tutte, deduced in 1941 the internal structure of the new German teleprinter cipher machine from intercepted messages, a feat comparable to the reconstruction of the Enigma's internal wiring by the Polish mathematician Marian Rejewski in 1932. From Tutte's calculations, replicas were made to aid laborious pencil-and-paper cryptanalysis of the teleprinter cipher. To speed recovery further, still another Cambridge mathematician, Maxwell H. A. Newman, came up the following year with the idea that led to the Colossus. Newman's work was also based on Tutte's fundamental contribution.

The Colossus had the same relationship to the teleprinter cipher as the cryptological bombe to the Enigma. They were functional cousins, so to speak, performing similar key-recovery tasks on two distinctly different ciphers. The bombe came first, was used more often, and made a greater impact earlier in the war, but the Colossus was a far more muscular and intelligent contrivance that emerged late in the war and made a large contribution to the Allies' strategic thinking. There were really two Colossi. The Mark I came on line late in 1943. A second, more powerful model, the Mark II, was first delivered to Bletchley Park in June 1944. A prototype, the Heath Robinson, preceded them both. The ENIAC, the first American computer, still larger and more powerful than the Colossi, followed them by nearly two years.

––––––––––

The teleprinter was developed in the nineteenth century as an alternative to the telegraph. It had the advantage of automatic transmission and eliminated the human error that plagued the reception of Morse code signals. An operator simply typed out a text in one location to be printed in another location without further human intervention. The teleprinter gained common usage early in the twentieth century for the rapid transmission of stock prices and news stories. Without it, there would have been no ticker tape for Wall Street parades.

The five-unit teleprinter code was devised by Emile Baudot, a Frenchman, and streamlined by Donald Murray, a Briton. It was a binary code—a unit was either occupied or unoccupied, a mark or a space. For example, the following are the first three letters of the alphabet in the Baudot-Murray code:

A   * * - - -

B   * - - * *

C   - * * * -

The asterisk represents a mark and the hyphen, a space. There are thirty-two ways to arrange the five units in the binary style, enough for the twenty-six letters of the alphabet plus six functions, such as spacing, carriage return, and line feed. As the operator typed the message, the teleprinter automatically formed these patterns on tape and sent out positive or negative pulses. These could be transmitted either by landline or through the ether.

The teleprinter code offered an opportunity for a new, more automated generation of cipher machine with savings in both manpower and time. It was known that encipherment could be achieved by introducing a random key, such as:

* - * - *

* * - - -

* - - * -

A mark in the key (1) changed a space in the Baudot-Murray unit to a mark and (2) changed a mark to a space. A space in the key left the Baudot-Murray unit unchanged. To mathematicians, this can be expressed as "non-carry binary addition."[3] Following the ABCs of Baudot-Murray, the ciphers would come out as follows:

	Letters	+/-	Keys	=	Ciphers
A	* * - - -		* - * - *		- * * - *
B	* - - * *		* * - - -		- * - * *
C	- * * * -		* - - * -		* * * - -

Bletchley Park first detected machine-ciphered teleprinter signals in 1940, but they were intermittent and presumably experimental. They became regular in the middle of 1941, and, before the year was out, Bletchley identified new cipher systems for all three services and the elite SS. C. Lorenz, AG, made one version of the new German cipher machine called the Schluesselzusatz (cipher attachment). Lorenz had two models, SZ-40 and SZ-42, the latter of which came into widespread use by the German army. A second version, made by Siemens & Halske, AG, and used by the German air force, was known as the Geheimschreiber (secret writer) and carried the designation T-52. Bletchley decided in mid-1942 to concentrate on the SZ-42 for two reasons. First, GCHQ lacked the resources to attack all of the German teleprinter systems. Second, the codebreakers were having good success in breaking the air and naval Enigma keys but finding the army Enigma keys very difficult. In other words, the need was greater for intelligence about the German army.[4]

The SZ machine, based on an encipherment system invented by American Gilbert Vernam in 1918, was very different from the Enigma. It had twelve wheels that were nothing like the Enigma's cross-wired rotors. The SZ wheels had peripheral pins, or "teeth," that could be extended to make marks on the tape or be folded up to leave spaces. There were two sets of five coding wheels (corresponding to the five units of the Baudot-Murray teleprinter code), one set called (at Bletchley) the "chi wheels" and a second set called the "psi wheels," and two motor wheels to regulate the stepping of the second set. Encipherment was accomplished by passing the plaintext message in teleprinter code through the two sets of coding wheels. The chi wheels advanced one notch for every letter, but the psi wheels advanced according to the settings of the motor wheels. Each wheel had a different number of pins that could be set each day in different patterns of mark or space that determined the key and could be rotated to any position by the cipher clerk to start a message. On the chi wheels, the pins numbered 23, 26, 29, 31, and 41; on the psi wheels, 43, 47, 51, 53, and 59; on the motor wheels, 37 and 61. Setting those 501 pins from a general key list was the work of the cipher clerk. It was usually a daily task and always required the utmost concentration. The wheel positions were the sender's decision, so they were different for each message, but the wheel positions had to be transmitted to the receiver.[5]

With sending and receiving machines matched as to pin settings and wheel positions, the message went in one end as plaintext, through the ether (or landline) as cipher, and came out the other end as plaintext. The ciphering and deciphering were as automatic as the teleprinting. Once the machines were set, the only human input was to type out the plaintext on the sender's teleprinter.

Through the magic of non-carry binary addition, any randomly selected set of keys that turned the teleprinter code into cipher at the sending end also turned the cipher into teleprinter code at the receiving end, as long as the keys were identical at both ends. This can be demonstrated on paper in nine steps with the ABCs and random keys:

Steps	A	B	C
#1 Sender input (plaintext):	* * - - -	* - - * *	- * * * -
#2 Through Chi:	* * - - *	- * * - *	- - * - *
#3 = #1 + #2:	- - - - *	* * * * -	- * - * *
#4 Through Psi:	* - * * -	- - * * -	* - - * *
#5 = #3 + #4 (cipher transmitted to receiver):	* - * * *	* * - - -	* * - - -
#6 Through Chi (= #2):	* * - - *	- * * - *	- - * - *
#7 = #5 + #6:	- * * * -	* - * - *	* * * - *
#8 Through Psi (= #4):	* - * * -	- - * * -	* - - * *
#9 = #7 + #8 (= #1) (plaintext):	* * - - -	* - - * *	- * * * - 6

In brief, the key is the sum (in non-carry binary addition) of the chi and psi wheels. The cipher is the sum of the key and the plaintext, and, reciprocally, the plaintext is the sum of the key and the cipher. The formula is the same with only one set of coding wheels, or two or three or a hundred, as long as the keys are identical at both ends. Presumably, the Germans chose two sets of coding wheels as their compromise between the need for security and the danger of overcomplexity.

———————

Theoretically, the ciphers were unbreakable if the keys were truly random, but, as with the Enigma, a sloppy German cipher clerk came unwittingly to the rescue of enemy cryptanalysts. At Bletchley Park, a section called the "Testery" under Maj. Ralph Tester employed pencil-and-paper methods to attack the teleprinter ciphers. The break into the SZ came when alert British radio interceptors noticed in August 1941 that a German clerk had repeated a long message starting from the same initial setting of the wheels with slight variations in text. For example, early in the message the German word "spruchnummer" (message number) was shortened to "spruchnr" (message no.). From that point, the ciphertext in the repeated meassage was different from that in the original.[7] The Testery team turned its attention to this breach of security like a pride of hungry lions pouncing on a wounded antelope. They started by placing one ciphertext under the other and, using non-carry binary addition, succeeded in breaking out the two streams of plaintext and one useful stream of key.[8]

These results were turned over to Tutte, who went on to calculate the structure of the machine, which took about two months. It was the breakthrough, Turing's biographer Hodges said, "equivalent to what the Poles had achieved with Enigma in 1932," the logical first step and the sine qua non of all that followed, including the machine that thrust the world into the computer age.[9] From Tutte's deductions, a team of engineers, led by Tommy Flowers at the Post Office Research Station at Dollis Hill, built the British analog of the SZ-42. Dollis Hill, more than what the words "post office research" implied, was a communications company in the broad sense. To build its teleprinter cipher machine in the shortest time possible during a war for survival, the company used the components at hand—telephone equipment. The machine that emerged was not a physical copy of the German machine, but it performed the same functions. Bletchley always referred to it and to the German original as "Tunny" and to the SZ cipher emissions as "Fish."[10]

Bletchley Park's codebreakers used Tunny to test keys deduced from the Fish ciphers. It was a small help. Key recovery—discovering which of 501 individual pins was extended or folded on the twelve wheels, plus the starting wheel positions—had to be done the old-fashioned way. Jack Good, who worked on Colossus, estimated the possible settings for Tunny to be 4 times 10 to the 131st power (i.e., 4 followed by 131 zeros). He said, "Such a work factor could never be achieved [by classical cryptanalysis] even if the moon were completely converted into an electronic computer."[11] After Turing lost his position as the leader in Hut 8, he participated as a quasi-consultant—a kind of mother hen to newcomers—in the Testery and suggested some ideas based on Tutte's findings that helped in key recovery. Others did the actual calculations and managed with commendable persistence to break into some of the Fish traffic. Extracting Fish keys by hand was a task for sharp minds. Good remembered that Peter Hilton, in particular, had "exceptional powers of visualization and could see two teleprinter characters merging [in non-carry addition] in his mind's eye."[12]

Max Newman was not particularly adept at this practice and came up with a plan for letting a machine find the starting positions of the chi wheels by doing the work of a thousand Peter Hiltons. The pin patterns would still be left to the Testery. With the kind of numbers that Tunny threw at the cryptanalysts, Newman reasoned, the machine would have to be electronic. Newman took the idea to Edward Travis, who had replaced Alastair Denniston as Bletchley's chief, and Travis gave it his full support. Newman carried it from there and drew many of Bletchley's brightest young minds into his new unit known as the "Newmanry."[13] The first two were Good, who had worked under Turing on the cryptological bombe in Hut 8, and Michie, who moved over from the Testery where he also had been associated with Turing. Good held a Ph.D. in mathematics from Cambridge, whereas Michie apparently learned his math on the job at Bletchley Park, and, no doubt, gained much from Turing's tutelage.[14]

The first machine delivered early in 1943 was not a Colossus and hardly colossal. On the other hand, it was not meant to be more than a prototype. It earned for itself the wry designation Heath Robinson, equivalent to a Rube Goldberg contraption in American idiom, because of its odd arrangement of wheels and pulleys and its loops of perforated paper tapes. Built jointly by Dollis Hill and the Telecommunications Research Establishment (better known for its radar program), the Heath Robinson featured two photoelectric scanners designed to read two synchronized tapes at a speed of 2,000 telegraphic characters a second and feed the information to electronic binary counters for comparison.[15] Apparently, it never achieved that velocity. By some accounts, it was more like 200 characters per second.[16] The Heath Robinson had many defects. It was prone to overheat. The paper tapes stretched and broke. Electrical relays caused interference with electronic counting. Most fundamentally, its creators were unable to synchronize the two high-speed tapes that passed through the electronic counters.

Little of operational value came out of the Heath Robinson, but the cryptanalysts were sufficiently encouraged to try for a better machine. Flowers, who designed the Tunny analog but had not worked on Heath Robinson, was called in for consultation at Turing's suggestion. Considered an electronics wizard, Flowers concluded that the two tapes never could be mechanically synchronized and recommended that Fish key patterns be internally stored, thus eliminating the need for one of the tapes. To achieve this, more electron valves would have to be installed, a risky proposal, because experience had shown the valves to be unreliable when used in radar. From his own studies, however, Flowers linked the valve failures to the start-up of power and believed the valves would perform reliably if the power were never turned off. Newman went along with him, but the top brass at Bletchley Park did not. Flowers had to get approval from Dollis Hill for the funds to build the new all-electronic machine, which he modestly called a "string and sealing wax sort of thing."[17]

Dollis Hill went on a crash run with day and night shifts to complete the first Colossus, Mark I, in eleven months. The machine was built in sections, with only Flowers and his top engineers, S. W. Broadhurst and W. W. Chandler, knowing its overall design and purpose, and then assembled at Bletchley Park. The codebreakers put it to work in December 1943 and soon found, to the surprise of the doubters and the delight of the engineers, that its 1,500 electron valves allowed it to function smoothly and accurately for long periods with the power continuously left on. With a redesigned photoelectric reader and electronic counters, it reached a speed of five thousand characters per second. Good and Michie discovered that they could do manual switching with the machine running at full tilt. They developed a mode of operation by which a cryptanalyst would sit at the Colossus and issue instructions to a Wren (WRNS, Women's Royal Naval Service) for revised plugging depending on the machine's output. "At this stage," Good said, "there was a close synergy between man, woman and machine." From this experience, Good worked out decision trees that assigned some basic cryptanalytic routines for Wrens to follow on their own. Michie came up with the idea for programming that enabled them to perform functions on the Colossus hitherto left to cryptanalysts in the Testery to carry out by hand.[18] This led to a call for an even more automated and flexible machine and resulted in the second-generation Mark II with 2,400 electron valves.[19]

The Colossus was built for logic, not to crunch numbers. Its initial purpose was to find the chi wheel settings for individual messages. Later, it was programmed to look for the patterns of extended or folded chi wheel pins, which had previously been done in the Testery. After the war, the Newmanry mathematicians discovered that the Colossus could have been programmed to break the motor wheels and that, with complicated plugging, it was almost possible to do multiplication. "It was further evidence," Good said, "that Colossus could be regarded as the first large-scale electronic computer, albeit for a specialized purpose."[20]

The SZ and the Enigma were complementary parts of German army communications. The more portable Enigma served mobile forces for short, tactical messages among armies, divisions, or smaller units. The bulkier SZ was the instrument of major commands—army groups, the high command, and Hitler himself. The teleprinter messages that reached Bletchley were longer than those of the Enigma. Often, a single teleprinter transmission carried more than one message. Also, the messages were strategic in nature, according to F. H. ("Harry") Hinsley, official historian of British intelligence during World War II, and of "exceptional significance for the light they threw on the intentions and the condition of the German Army and on the thinking and planning of the whole of the German High Command" and "lost nothing of their intelligence value" from the fact that they usually required several days to decrypt.[21] The first decrypt of a Fish message came by the hand method in the spring of 1942 on an experimental link between Vienna and Athens. As the German teleprinter links grew and the British developed machinery to cope, further successes yielded valuable intelligence late in the North African campaign and in communications between Berlin and Rome and between Berlin and the Soviet front. By far the biggest haul from Fish, however, was the intelligence derived before and during the Allied assault on Western Europe and from teleprinter communications between Berlin and the German commands in the West. Thanks to Colossus, Hinsley said, the availability of Fish decrypts was the "outstanding signals-intelligence achievement in this last phase of the war."[22]

When the war began in earnest with the German invasions in Scandinavia and the West in the spring of 1940, Bletchley Park was busy round the clock until the Nazi regime collapsed five years later. A day's first order of business in the hours after midnight was to grapple with the daily keys. Recovery was the norm but never a foregone conclusion. There were many hiccups and gaps along the way. Huts 6 and 8 handled the Enigma ciphers. When Fish came on stream, the Testery and the Newmanry worked on that traffic. Hut 3 took care of the translation and intelligence evaluation of army and air force decrypts and Hut 4 of the navy's decrypts.

Sections were established to deal with traffic from German military intelligence (Abwehr), which utilized both Enigma and hand ciphers. Until his death in 1943, Dillwyn Knox headed the Enigma unit, ISK (Intelligence Service Knox), and Oliver Strachey was in charge of the decryption of hand ciphers from Abwehr agents in the field at ISOS (Intelligence Service Oliver Strachey). The Abwehr's Enigma differed from the military and naval models in that it had more turnover notches to step the middle and left rotors but no plug board. ISK and ISOS decrypts were passed on to British intelligence.

Nor did Bletchley Park ignore Germany's Axis partners. ISK was responsible for Italian ciphers because many of them were sent by way of the Enigma without plug board. Bletchley also formed a unit devoted to Japanese signals with outposts at Delhi, India, for the army and air force and at Colombo, Ceylon, for the navy, and assigned personnel as far away as Australia. It used the American-made Purple machine to break high-grade transmissions from the Japanese embassy in Berlin to the Foreign Office in Tokyo. Purple was an early gift from the Americans who had reconstructed the original Japanese machine in 1940 from intercepted messages, an achievement equal to those of Rejewski and Tutte. American personnel came to Bletchley Park later in the war to share the workload with their British colleagues, and the American company National Cash Register built an American bombe to cope with the four-wheel Enigma. From 1942 on, wherever major British and American forces fought, Freddy Winterbotham set up his SLUs, the last vital links in what was arguably history's most effective intelligence organization.

Ultra, the intelligence derived from decryption, whether from Enigma or Fish, did not make an impact on the war until 1941. Regarding claims that Ultra made a difference in the Battle of Britain (the air war over England during the second half of 1940), no less an authority than Hinsley has said flatly, "[T]here is no substance to them."[23] Enigma decrypts contributed to the defeat of the Italian Army in North Africa in February 1941 and the destruction of the Italian Navy at Cape Matapan in Greece the following month. They also gave advance warning of German attacks in Greece in time for a safe British withdrawal and on Crete where German airborne forces paid dearly for their victory. This last event, Winterbotham tells us, erased any lingering doubts that Churchill might have harbored over Ultra's value.[24] Later events justified the Prime Minister's faith. In three major campaigns of the war—the U-boat war, North Africa, and the invasion of Normandy—Ultra played very important, if not decisive, roles.

CHAPTER 6

Who Broke Purple?

Bletchley Park had the right formula for success—talent and good luck. The Poles turned over their technology to demystify the Enigma in 1939, and the "backroom boys" added the necessary refinements to make it work in more demanding wartime conditions. In 1941, the Americans presented the British with another cryptological gift, the analog of a sophisticated Japanese cipher machine that needed no improvement. All they had to do at Bletchley Park was to plug it in and follow the keying instructions. The Japanese called it their "B" machine; the Americans called it Purple.

The American reconstruction of Purple from intercepted cryptograms in 1939–40 was every bit as extraordinary as the conquest of Enigma, but its historical significance seems oddly out of place. For years, people wondered, "If the Americans could read the Japanese code, why didn't they learn of the Japanese plan to attack Pearl Harbor?" The reason is simple: Purple was a diplomatic cipher. The Imperial Navy had its own cryptosystems, and, although there is controversy about whether or not the Americans read the naval ciphers prior to the Japanese attack, that issue had nothing to do with Purple. Halfway round the world two and a half years later, however, Purple intercepts made an important contribution to Allied preparations for D-Day. For that reason, it is appropriate here to outline this significant American addition to Bletchley Park's formidable array of codebreaking tools.

In early accounts of the Purple breakthrough, cryptological giant William F. Friedman received all the credit.[1] Between the world wars, Friedman was the principal cryptologist for the U.S. Army's Signal Intelligence Service (SIS) and in overall charge of the team that labored for eighteen months to solve Purple. His bona fides were without parallel—an accomplished codebreaker, highly esteemed by his peers, chief spokesman for army cryptanalysts, and the public persona of army cryptology—but whether he deserved the credit for Purple is an entirely different matter.

Shortly after the war, Friedman testified before a congressional committee investigating the Pearl Harbor disaster and left a mixed message about his role. "After work [on Purple] by my associates when we were making very slow progress the Chief Signal Officer [Maj. Gen. Joseph O. Mauborgne] asked me personally to take a hand," Friedman told the committee. "I had been engaged largely in administrative duties up to that time, so at his request I dropped everything else that I could and began to work with the group." He also testified that the conquest of Purple was a "collaborative, cooperative effort" in which "[n]o one person is responsible for the solution, nor is there any single person to whom the major share of credit should go."[2] There can be no doubt of Friedman's rank as a world-class cryptologist. His comments also proved that, after nearly three decades of government service, he had mastered the political art of unequivocal ambiguity. His reputation was such that even an expert on the subject could easily infer from the testimony that Friedman came to the rescue of a faltering team on the brink of failure and, at the end of the day, generously shared the glory.

A different story emerges from the memoir of his illustrious protégé, Frank B. Rowlett.[3] His book, edited by David Kahn, contains a foreword and epilogue written by Kahn, author of *The Codebreakers: The Story of Secret Writing,* and other important works in the field of cryptology. The Rowlett book shows that Friedman's latter statement, the one about "collaborative, cooperative effort," is far closer to the truth. No reasonable person could dispute that Friedman was indispensable to the solution of Purple. Not only did he hand-pick the cryptanalysts on the SIS team, he taught them the fundamentals of codes and ciphers. He taught them so well, in fact, that his best people, including Rowlett, could handle the most complex cryptological problems on their own. From Rowlett's account—although he does not say it in so many words—Friedman is not "*the man* who broke Purple" as Friedman's biographer would have us believe, but only one person among several who had a hand in it. The Purple Section did the nitty-gritty intellectual work while Friedman was otherwise occupied, and Rowlett led the charge at ground level.

Rowlett not only deserves more credit than he has received for the conquest of Purple, he is also the man who, under a blanket of government security and over the initial resistance of Friedman, conceived the principles that made America's own cipher machine, called Sigaba by the army and ECM by the navy, impenetrable during World War II. His work on Purple and Sigaba saved countless (and uncountable) American lives. In 1964, Congress awarded him $100,000 for his cryptological inventions, the same bonus that it had already voted Friedman. Had Rowlett worked in the private sector, he could have beaten that paltry sum by orders of magnitude. An unbreakable cipher machine was more valuable than the crown jewels. Swedish manufacturer Boris C. W. Hagelin became a millionaire after Friedman approved Hagelin's machine for use by the U.S. Army. Rowlett's machine was every bit as good, if not better.

———————

Rowlett grew up in rural southwest Virginia. He always loved science. As a boy, he built radios and did chemical experiments. He studied chemistry and physics at tiny Emory and Henry College and gravitated to mathematics. While he was still in school, his math teacher urged him to take the civil service examination for federal employment. Rowlett passed with high marks and earned a place on the mathematics register of the Civil Service Commission. After graduation, he married Edith Irene King and both landed teaching jobs, he at Franklin County High School in Rocky Mount, Virginia, and she at Stickleyville School in Lee County, 250 miles away near the Cumberland Gap.

At the time, Friedman was scanning the federal register for young men proficient in math to be junior cryptanalysts for the Signal Intelligence Service, which had taken over the cryptological functions of Herbert O. Yardley's defunct American Black Chamber. Friedman recognized sooner than the rest of the world, with the notable exception of Polish intelligence, that the cipher machine would soon dominate the little-known field of cryptology. The design of the cipher machine was based on mathematical principles in contrast to old-fashioned, handwritten code-and-cipher systems underpinned by linguistics. Friedman set out to build an SIS cryptology unit of skilled mathematicians from the ground up. Initially, the SIS allocated three positions for a rigorous training program designed by Friedman. Rowlett was first to answer the call in April 1930. His first bimonthly government check for $88.33 in that Depression year was almost double his pay as a schoolteacher and exceeded the combined teaching salaries of husband and wife.

One of the remarkable facts of this infant phase of SIS cryptology was the unerring quality of Friedman's selections based on mathematical test scores. His recruits knew nothing about the cryptology field. On his first day at work, Rowlett ventured to ask the meaning of "cryptanalysis." (A less confident man might have shied away from the question.) He had looked for the word in the dictionary and consulted friends and colleagues, he told Friedman, but could learn nothing about it. The question amused Friedman. The word and its various forms did not exist until he invented it and only recently had been officially adopted by the army. A cryptanalyst is a codebreaker—and a cipherbreaker to boot. Cryptanalysis covers the entire range of solving cryptosystems. Soon enough, Rowlett would fill in the blanks in his knowledge and get a firm grip on the subject. Within weeks, he was joined by two other junior cryptanalysts, Abraham Sinkov and Solomon Kullback, both math graduates of the City College of New York, who were equally in the dark at first and equally adept at learning the arcane mysteries of the new science. From time to time during their training, Friedman put the three of them into competition to solve cryptosystems, and Rowlett was pleased to discover that he, the country boy from "Podunk," could keep up with the graduates of one of the finer academic institutions in urban America.

Rowlett lived and breathed cryptology. He and the others worked in an area called the "vault," a large office on the third floor of the Munitions Building, half-filled with filing cabinets in which some of the secrets were kept. It was in every respect an ordinary room, except for the double steel doors secured by locks. (The Munitions Building is long gone from its setting on Constitution Avenue, not far from the Lincoln Memorial, in Washington, D.C.) Rowlett was usually the first to arrive for work and often the last to leave. When deeply involved in a project, he took his work home in his head. Often, he awoke in the middle of the night and thought through problems yet to be solved.

In Rowlett's world, separation between home and office hardly seemed to exist. He managed even the most important family events without interrupting his work. Once, after the Purple breakthrough, he and two colleagues, Robert Ferner and Albert Small, were working on a new Japanese code system and trying to coax an IBM tabulating machine into doing the tiresome and time-consuming cryptological grunt work, but the machine was too slow. It needed an attachment to further automate the tabulating. At home that night, Rowlett woke up, thought about it, and hit on a solution. Next day at the office, he sketched out a device and promised his colleagues that he would build it over the weekend.

His timing could not have been worse. Edith was showing signs that their second child was about to arrive. That Friday night, they saw the doctor, and he arranged for her to go into the hospital the next day. After dinner, Frank closed himself off in his home workshop and put together the baseboard and mounts for the new device. On Saturday, he went shopping, did some house-hold chores, and, late that afternoon, drove Edith to the hospital. After dinner, he was back in his workshop to assemble the components. As he watched the device grow into the unruly shape of a Rube Goldberg contraption, he won-dered if it would really work. Sunday morning, he took it to a screened-in porch where he could connect the wires while helping his mother-in-law keep an eye on his restless firstborn, four-year-old Frank Jr. The doctor called before noon to report the birth of another son. Frank finished his wiring job and later went to see his wife and baby. They named him Thomas. Next morning at the office, Rowlett, Ferner, and Small tested the new device on the IBM tabulator. It functioned perfectly.[4] Thus, on that one Sunday, Rowlett had become the proud father of two newborns, a little boy and a little machine.

Rowlett was still working his way through Friedman's training course when he gave America the priceless gift of an unbreakable cipher machine. In the process, he grew in stature from a promising student to a cryptological pro-fessional. The event, however, was marred by grave tension between him and Friedman that almost led to a rupture in their relations and the end of Rowlett's cryptological career before it really got started.

As part of their training routine, Rowlett, Sinkov, and Kullback studied the known cipher machines, including the commercial Enigma and Friedman's own invention, the M-134. Later, Friedman gave Rowlett the task of preparing keying procedures for the M-134. The work did not go well. The machinery kept break-ing down. Rowlett did not think it was his fault, but Friedman seemed to imply that it was. The two of them argued about it. Finally, Rowlett suggested that he give the job to someone else, but Friedman would not hear of it.

Even before this confrontation, Rowlett began thinking about better ways to key the Friedman machine. His mind leaped forward to a special keying attachment for the M-134 and from there to the design of an entirely new cipher machine with revolutionary new principles. Rowlett never specified these principles in his memoir, but in a foreword to the book, author David Kahn describes one important idea as that of "using keying rotors to irregularize the rotation of enciphering and deciphering rotors. . . ."[5] Rowlett became fully absorbed with his invention. In his free time, he drew up sketches, prepared three variations of his basic design, and even traced the imagined permutations of electrical impulses on paper to encipher and decipher small samples of text.

One day when he and Friedman were clashing again over the M-134 keying system, Rowlett broached his idea for an entirely new system that promised even more security. Friedman agreed to schedule a meeting to hear him out, but when the time came, he cut Rowlett short, dismissed the idea as unworkable, and told him to get back to keying the M-134. What most angered Rowlett was Friedman's refusal to explain why the new idea would not work. Early one morning, he confronted Friedman in his office and vowed to take the issue to the chief signal officer. That gave Friedman pause. He scheduled another meeting and gave Rowlett more time but still not enough for a full explanation of his ideas. Before Rowlett was finished, Friedman called a halt and left the office. But the next morning, Rowlett said, Friedman told him he had made a "wonderful discovery."[6]

Friedman assigned Rowlett the task of drawing up the patent specifications and promised to work with him in their preparation. Friedman cleared his schedule, and they spent the day together in Friedman's office. Rowlett finally had the chance to present his ideas in full. The more he explained, the more enthusiastic Friedman became. "During our discussion," Rowlett said, "his attitude toward me had changed, and I had never before found him so friendly and so agreeable to work with. He still retained his 'boss-employee' attitude, but I could see that as he reached a more comprehensive grasp of the principles I had discovered, he was accepting me as a professional cryptanalyst rather than as a student."[7]

Rowlett's troubles with Friedman, however, did not end there. When Rowlett finished drafting the patent application, he went back to keying the M-134 with new equipment ordered by Friedman. This time, he was able to finish the job. Friedman, meantime, received permission from higher authority to reveal Rowlett's invention to the navy cryptology unit, Op-20-G. ("Op-20" refers to the Navy's Department of Communications, "G" to the Code and Signal Section.) The navy experts wanted to build a new cipher machine and were definitely interested in such revolutionary ideas—and it appears that they assumed the ideas were Friedman's. The true inventor was never invited to periodic army-navy meetings. One meeting took place in Friedman's office. From his desk in the vault, Rowlett watched the navy men file in. After Friedman seated them around his conference table, he walked over and closed the vault door. When the door was reopened, the navy men were gone and Friedman had left for the day.[8] It took another two years for the army and navy both to accept the unbreakable Rowlett-designed cipher machine that they used during World War II.

This was not the only instance of Friedman's taking credit for the creative product of another. In his epic history of codebreaking published in 1967, three decades before Rowlett's book, Kahn mentions nine inventions attributed to Friedman that were the basis for Congress granting him $100,000 in compensation for being shut out of the private marketplace. Two of the nine, Kahn said, were built "with Rowlett's aid." Two were so secret they were not even filed in the Patent Office. Of the seven that were filed, Kahn judged at least five (and "probably" the other two) to be "derivative"—"mere improvements upon the basic creations of others."[9]

From this point in Rowlett's memoir, there seems to be a jagged edge in his relationship with Friedman. Several times in the narration, Rowlett expresses his irritation. It comes through at random like heat escaping the earth's crust, even though Rowlett tells his story without rancor or, as Kahn puts it in the foreword to Rowlett's book, with "modesty, refusal to stray beyond first-hand knowledge, and restraint in judgment, all of which anchor faith in his honesty."[10] They worked together, did Friedman and Rowlett, tutor and student, boss and employee, professional and professional, all for the good of the country, but Friedman did not single out Rowlett for praise as he did others and seemed unwilling to give him due credit for his successes. He continually cast doubt on Rowlett's proposed solutions of cryptanalytic problems until they could be demonstrated beyond question.

Rowlett and Kullback teamed up to analyze the first of Japan's machine-made diplomatic ciphers. The Japanese called their machine "Type A," but the Americans gave it the cover name of "Red." The U.S. Navy had already broken the Red machine after discovering in 1935 that the Japanese naval attaché in Washington was using rotor machine ciphers to communicate with Tokyo. Agnes Meyer Driscoll, a civilian employee and the top codebreaker at Op-20-G, manually solved the ciphers (most likely from cribs—that is, guessing probable words from the ciphertext—and other classic cryptanalytic means). From Driscoll's analysis, Lt. Jack Holtwick constructed a Red analog to facilitate decipherment, and, by 1936, the navy was reading Red naval attaché traffic on a regular basis.[11] The navy claims to have turned over all technical details of the Red machine to the SIS for its assault on the diplomatic ciphers, but Rowlett, drawing from a conversation with Friedman, leaves the impression that the navy fell well short of full disclosure.[12]

The two Friedman protégés had little to work with except enciphered diplomatic messages. They singled out one of the lengthiest messages they could find. Their first step was to separate the ciphers that corresponded to the six vowels of the alphabet from those that obscured the twenty consonants. The "subset of six," as they called it, was the easier of the two because the vowels comprised about half of all letters used. They tried to guess which ciphers stood for which vowels with the help of a gifted linguist, John Hurt. It was educated guessing that required a familiarity with the Japanese language, somewhat analogous to searching for cribs. They were not looking for assumed whole words but for patterns of cipher letters corresponding to assumed vowel arrangements of plaintext. Soon, with the help of an IBM machine, they recovered all of the vowels in the long message. With a little more work, they recovered the consonants and, ultimately, the entire plaintext message. After they learned the principles, they attacked other messages and, with adjustments for the rearrangement of keys and the shift in the machine's stepping patterns, came up with the same happy results.

Once they had the hang of it, they discovered that the Red machine was not that complicated for skilled cryptanalysts. Friedman congratulated Rowlett and Kullback on their success, a shared compliment for a shared achievement. "You have clearly demonstrated," he told them with a dig at the navy, "that the Signal Intelligence Service does not need cryptanalytic assistance from anyone."[13] From Red diplomatic decrypts, U.S. Army intelligence was able to pass valuable information to American policymakers, including details of the secret negotiations for the Tripartite Pact involving Germany, Italy, and Japan.

At this point, thanks to the Red breakthrough, the SIS cryptological unit underwent considerable expansion. Kullback was posted to Hawaii for two years, and Sinkov already had been assigned to Panama, which left Rowlett in Washington to manage the Japanese diplomatic ciphers. Rowlett turned his attention to the inner workings of the Red machine. He had never seen it, but he visualized it from the intercepts as having a keyboard, printer, and "a cryptographic mechanism." The last element, he theorized, would contain a pair of electrical commutators that could be set in either an enciphering or a deciphering mode, plus a plug board dotted with twenty-six jacks for the letters of the alphabet and wired to both keyboard and printer. The plug board would serve as the keying device. Rowlett learned from the intercepts that the plugs were rearranged every ten days, on the 1st, 11th, and 21st of each month. By further study, he detected a pattern of routine plug board sequences within the ten-day periods. He reasoned that knowing this pattern would eliminate the need for the cryptanalysis of each sequence, thus saving time and energy. Because Friedman seemed to disagree, Rowlett worked out a statistical formula to predict the ten-day sequences. To his delight, it worked every time and cleared the path for a significant shortcut because it bypassed some of the laborious pencil-and-paper decrypts.[14]

At the turn of the year, 1938 to 1939, the SIS began reading messages from Tokyo in the Red cipher that notified Japanese embassies around the world of a new "Type B" machine soon to be distributed. In late March, they detected the first messages in the new cipher, and the Japanese phased it in over the following month at the major embassies. Smaller embassies and consulates continued to use the Red machine for another three or four years. Sticking to its color theme, the SIS called the new machine and its ciphers "Purple." Enticed by the idea of facing a new challenge, the Rowlett team was eager for the chase. The team had grown substantially during the SIS expansion generated by the success with Red. Among new personnel in the unit were cryptanalysts who would figure prominently in the solution of Purple—including Ferner, Small, and Genevieve Grotjan.

They would find Purple, designed by a Japanese naval officer, Capt. Risaburo Ito, to be unlike any existing cipher machine. They began their attack the same way Rowlett and Kullback had penetrated Red—by breaking down the ciphers into subsets of six vowels and twenty consonants. They turned to the sixes first and looked for cribs. Their initial wedge was the Japanese practice of numbering the messages and placing the enciphered number, spelled out, at the beginning of each cryptogram.

From this, they were able to design what Rowlett called "a 'pencil and paper' analog" to decipher the sixes. It consisted of a chart six columns wide and twenty-five rows deep "representing a polyalphabetic substitution system of twenty-five differently mixed alphabets composed of the same six letters."[15] The term *polyalphabetic* simply means more than one cipher alphabet used alternately from message to message. In a "substitution" system, the plain letters are replaced by cipher letters and not transposed (i.e., not scrambled).[16] With the chart, the SIS team was able to decipher the sixes of any key period. After this relatively easy success, they proceeded to decipher the sixes of incoming messages while, at the same time, turning their attention to the principles underlying the other subset, the twenties. That's when the going got tough.

To begin, the pencil-and-paper deciphering of the sixes proved to be hopelessly time consuming, and the IBM tabulator did nothing to speed up the process. They decided to build a machine of their own to recognize the sixes from the intercepts and decipher them. It would have to include an entirely new cryptographic mechanism patterned after their substitution chart. Friedman approved the idea and suggested that they take on Leo Rosen to build it. Rosen was a former electronics student at the Massachusetts Institute of Technology and a member of the campus Reserve Officers Training Corps when he was snatched up for active duty and assigned to the SIS. He came to the Japanese Diplomatic Section in August 1939. He was a whiz with machines and a good match for Rowlett. It did not take him long to get up to speed with the activities of the Purple team. After observing the unit decipher the subset of sixes, he brought Rowlett a brochure from a telephone equipment manufacturer that described stepping switches of twenty-five positions. One set could handle six separate circuits—exactly the design needed. After gathering all the necessary equipment, in part by cannibalizing one of Friedman's precious M-134 machines, Rosen built the so-called Six Buster in short order. It worked so well that he built two more. Cryptanalysts engaged in the plodding pencil-and-paper work of the substitution chart were thus freed up for the attack on the subset of twenties.[17]

Ultimate success, however, would take another year of intense, tedious cryptanalysis, with allowances for a disruptive move to larger quarters. Rowlett and other creative people in the Purple Section speculated that because they had used stepping switches to decipher the sixes successfully, perhaps the Japanese had actually built the entire B Machine with the same equipment. They also considered the possibility that it was a rotor machine like the Enigma, but their analysis of the intercepts eventually told them otherwise.[18] They designed a machine with four twenty-five point, six-level stepping switches for the subset of twenties, a big brother of the Six Buster, but they did not build it right away because they still were not sure that it was the correct solution. The cryptanalysts continued with their eye-glazing task of perusing the daily ciphergrams for plaintext equivalents among the twenties. Although they realized that it could take months, they could not think of a better way.

It did take months. Finally, one day in late August 1940, Genevieve Grotjan popped into Rowlett's office where he, Ferner, and Small were in conference. With uncontrollable excitement, she invited them to look at her worksheets. At her desk, where the worksheets were laid out, she pointed out four areas, which she had circled, showing a pattern of relationships between ciphertext and plaintext. This was what they had been looking for all those months. The three men were so excited that they broke the nearly sacrosanct silence of the deciphering room with full-throated whoops of delight. The other cryptanalysts interrupted their research and gathered around. Then Friedman came in wanting to know what was going on. Rowlett explained the discovery and the significance of the circled areas. "[I]t was obvious he grasped their implications," Rowlett said.[19]

Friedman suddenly looked tired. Offered a chair, he sat down and asked, "What are you going to do now?"[20] Unlikely that the "man who broke Purple," supposedly a man deeply involved in the inner workings of the unit, would ask that question. A few weeks later, Friedman was hospitalized with a nervous breakdown. Clearly, he was overworked but not, as historians have written, because of Purple.

Everything quickly fell into place. In succeeding days, the cryptanalysts discovered more ciphertext-to-plaintext relationships like Grotjan's, and the more they discovered, the more they understood about wiring the commutators. They decided that the Japanese had indeed used telephone stepping switches for the subset of twenties, as well as the sixes, and Rosen went to work. He first had to build a mechanical analog because the stepping switches were not immediately available. (The SIS team never bought them at local equipment outlets, as some authors have written.) When the switches arrived, Rosen built the machine by expanding on the Six Buster. One night, he and Rowlett worked late to complete the wiring for the master switch. When they finally had it working, it was past 9 P.M. and they had not noticed they missed dinner. Before leaving, they fed the machine a message in ciphertext, and it came out in plaintext. At last, they had broken Purple!

They shut down for the night and demonstrated the machine for Friedman the next morning. Friedman called it "beautiful" and congratulated Rosen. They decided, on the spot, that Rosen could and should build two more with the two Six-Busters and the equipment on hand. After demonstrating the machine for Lt. Cdr. Laurance F. Safford, head of Op-20-G, and Gen. George C. Marshall, army chief of staff, the design was turned over to Cdr. D. W. Seiler at the Naval Code and Signal Laboratory in the Washington Navy Yard, who supervised the construction of additional copies. Eventually, six American Purple machines were built.

In his "Preliminary Historical Report" on the solution of Purple, written in 1940 and released, heavily censored, in 1979, Friedman gave joint credit to Rowlett and Ferner for the "direction and coordination" of the project, and called their "indefatigable labors and brilliant analytical work . . . a credit to their cryptanalytic skill, training and experience." He also mentioned Rowlett for collaborating with Rosen in the construction of the Purple machine.[21] Friedman's high praise, lavish though it was, did not overstate the magnitude of the achievement when one considers that it was done not by reverse engineering but strictly from the analysis of enciphered messages and that the Americans never laid eyes on the Japanese machine. After the war, Japanese cryptology experts could not believe that the Americans had succeeded without a machine to copy. Missing from the Friedman report is full credit to Rowlett for his conscientious, low-key, levelheaded, team-oriented, and self-effacing leadership. Without it, a successful outcome is hard to imagine.

Purple decrypts began emerging by September 1940 and before long, with the army and navy handling the intercepts on alternate days, they were flowing at a rate of fifty to seventy-five a day.[22] Noncryptanalysts privy to the work of the Friedman-Rowlett team thought the new machine to be magical, and they called the decrypts "Magic." The distribution of the intelligence from codebreaking to a small number of high-ranking officials, including the President, also came to be known as Magic. The contents of Magic were not limited to Purple decrypts but also included those from lesser diplomatic cryptosystems. With SIS and Op-20-G woefully short on funds and manpower, they naturally gave priority to Purple because it carried the most sensitive messages. Alas, certain clues to the Pearl Harbor attack were contained in the lesser systems used by the Japanese consulate in Honolulu.

The Purple machine became currency, in a sense, in an American plan to exchange cryptological assets with Britain. Early in 1941, a four-man team, Sinkov and Rosen from SIS and Lt. Prescott Currier and Lt. Robert Weeks from Op-20-G, crossed the Atlantic with the machine on the British battleship *King George V* to meet with their British counterparts at Bletchley Park. Friedman himself was supposed to have led the American team, but he had been hospitalized with his nervous breakdown. At Bletchley Park, the visitors were treated cordially and became the first Americans ushered inside the old Victorian estate since it had become the setting for the Government Code & Cypher School. Although the Americans received no hardware in return for the Purple machine, they did come away with an Enigma design, and the two sides had a full exchange of information. It was the start of what ultimately would become a close and rewarding collaboration between the two allies.[23]

The British promptly made use of Purple and were not disappointed. In early June 1941, they (and the Americans) intercepted a message from Hitler's great admirer and confidant Gen. Hiroshi Baron Oshima, Japanese ambassador to Berlin, to the Foreign Office in Tokyo, which convinced them that Germany was about to invade the Soviet Union. When it proved to be correct, British intelligence knew that in Oshima they had an unsuspecting mole in the Hitler camp. Later, he would be of further assistance as the Allies prepared for the D-Day invasion of Normandy.

CHAPTER 7

Masters of Deception

Almighty God—Our sons, pride of our nation, this day have set upon a mighty endeavor . . .

—President Franklin D. Roosevelt
D-Day, June 6, 1944

For this "mighty endeavor," the Allied nations of World War II raised deception to the level of art.

By spring 1943, the Germans had been driven out of North Africa and hurled back from the Caucasus. Wondering where the hammer would fall next, they well knew that the Anglo-Americans and their Allies were coming ashore in Europe but not where or when or in what force. The possible invasion sites abounded—Scandinavia, the Low Countries, France, Italy, the Balkans, or a Mediterranean island. That summer, the Allies landed in Sicily and later in Italy, where the Germans fought stubbornly in mountainous terrain ideal for defense. During the first half of 1944, all other options remained open, especially Norway, the Balkans, and France. Foremost in German strategic thinking was an Allied invasion of the channel coast from Belgium to Normandy. Hitler and many of his generals, especially those sycophants of his inner circle, were convinced that the main blow would be struck at the Pas de Calais north of the

Somme River but never excluded the possibility of diversionary landings else-where. When it came at Normandy, southwest of the Seine River, Hitler failed to recognize it for what it was. The powerful German Fifteenth Army, which might have demolished the tenuous Allied lodgment in Normandy, sat staring at the empty Dover Strait waiting to pounce on an invasion force that never arrived.

To gain tactical surprise in this manner was a distinct advantage and a remarkable achievement when one considers that the Allied forces came directly across the English Channel in numbers much too large to hide against an enemy anticipating their arrival. Except for the accident of weather, the German mis-takes were the product of carefully laid Allied deception plans. The Allies knew how much Hitler valued Norway for its deepwater ports accessible to the open sea. They knew that he placed a high premium on the Balkans to obtain oil and other raw materials and to protect the flank of the German Army in Russia. They also knew that he had strengthened the defenses around Calais, partly to protect his rocket-launching sites from which he intended to rain havoc on England and snatch final victory from the jaws of defeat. They knew all these things by reading German and Japanese ciphers at Bletchley Park. So they rein-forced what Hitler already believed with a stream of half-truths and plausible lies to shield their real intentions.

Unlike the campaigns in North Africa and the Atlantic, for which the Ger-mans possessed significant codebreaking assets, the invasion of France in June 1944 found the Allies with an overwhelming advantage in all phases of intelli-gence. During the critical weeks leading up to D-Day, Bletchley Park could read current Enigma ciphers of the German air force, navy, and Abwehr; non-Morse teleprinter ciphers of the German army with only tolerable delay; and current Purple ciphers of the Japanese Foreign Office. By contrast, British and American ciphers by this time were entirely secure. Even the British naval ciphers, which the German navy had so productively read until mid-1943, were now a closed book. Worse for Germany, every agent sent to spy on Britain was dead, imprisoned, or working for the British as a double agent. As a result, all information turned in by Berlin's "trusted" spies was screened or invented by the Allies.

Hitler's own intelligence apparatus was in serious disarray. High-ranking officers of his military intelligence agency, the Abwehr, had been plotting his overthrow and doing what else they could to undermine Nazi power. When Hitler learned part of the truth in February 1944, he placed the Abwehr under the control of the Nazi Party's intelligence arm, the SD, which gained him loy-alty but left intelligence in the hands of less experienced Nazi ideologues.

In effect, the Allies enjoyed an intelligence monopoly of which the Germans were totally unaware—a perfect setting for subterfuge. The Allies took full advantage by adopting a series of plans bearing such code names as "Bodyguard," "Zeppelin," and "Fortitude," to deceive the German high command about the time, place, and strength of the approaching invasion. They sought to convince the Germans that the target was any place but Normandy, the timing later than early June 1944, and the invasion force much larger than its true size. The special means used to achieve their end included double agents, mock encampments, bogus radio traffic, rumors, lies, dirty tricks, and, one should never forget, ingenuity. Without the codebreaking resources at Bletchley Park, these stratagems could not have worked. Ultra revealed what the Germans did or did not know about Allied preparations for the invasion, but there was more to it than just keeping tabs on the enemy. Reading its mail helped to generate ideas for deception. By keeping track of enemy reactions to their deceptions—in large part through Ultra—the Allies could learn whether an idea was working and make any necessary adjustments.

It was a complex web, to say the least. Major elements of the story, such as codebreaking and the double-cross system, grew out of separate experiences. Other components, including simulated wireless traffic (audio deception) and the construction of dummy armaments (visual deception), were an inspired use of the tools at hand adapted from wartime experience and fitted to the circumstances. When they all came together in the service of creative minds, they had the deceptive effect of the ancient Trojan Horse, except that this creature of World War II was far more intricate than the awkward Greek contrivance that led to the fall of Troy.

———————

The double-cross system, like British codebreaking, had prewar origins. The ancient spy game became a growth industry after the Nazis rose to power in Germany in 1933. As war approached, the Abwehr stepped up its surveillance of neighboring countries, but German spying was rather slipshod in Britain. The network there consisted of second- and third-rate agents who did not catch the British napping. When hostilities began, MI5 (British Security Service) and the Special Branch of Scotland Yard rounded up all the spies. Among them was Alfred George Owens, a Welshman who was considered the best of the lot. Owens grew up and studied engineering in Canada. Upon his return to Britain, he went to work for a navy contractor. His job took him frequently to Germany. He returned from his trips with bits of intelligence and offered them to the British Admiralty. At his request, Owens became an agent for MI6, but his new British spymasters soon learned from an intercepted letter that he was also spying for the Germans. At the onset of war, he was arrested along with the other German spies.

Owens was held at Wandsworth Prison and given cause to contemplate his mortality. His jailers offered him the chance to live in exchange for his undivided services, and he, a rational man, readily agreed. They brought him his radio transmitter and told him to reopen communications with his Abwehr control in Hamburg. MI5 dictated the message, Owens tapped it out on his transmitter, and the Germans took it as the real thing. Thus, he gained the "distinction," if that is the right word for a twice-turned turncoat, of becoming the first inductee into the British double-cross system.[1] He received the code name "Snow," but he did not last long. He had to be phased out early in the game under suspicion of pulling a double-cross on his double-cross controllers.

After Germany conquered France in the spring of 1940, the Abwehr began infiltrating more spies into Britain. They were dropped by parachute at night, smuggled in by small boat, or disguised as refugees from occupied countries. Generally ill suited for the task, they were remarkable only in the sense that most of them enjoyed remarkably short espionage careers. Of the first four spies to land in September 1940, only one spoke English. All were apprehended within twenty-four hours, and three were eventually executed. Usually, their German sponsors notified Snow or subsequent double agents in advance of their coming; they did not realize that such notice made it possible for MI5 to meet them on arrival. Eleven spies came in a second wave of infiltration and were also caught. Many other would-be spies followed, to be greeted by a British "welcoming committee" and to face one of three fates—death, imprisonment, or the double cross.[2]

Controlling double agents was obviously a delicate game. German intelligence expected them to perform certain underhanded tasks, such as the theft of secrets or sabotage. The British had to decide how to meet those expectations in a way that would make the double agents credible to the enemy without doing harm to Great Britain's interests. A blue-ribbon panel, the XX-Committee (which can be translated as either the "Twenty Committee" or the "Double-Cross Committee"), was formed to monitor the problem. It included members from military, naval, and air intelligence and various other military and civilian agencies. The idea was born in MI5 and approved by Churchill shortly after he took power in May 1940. The XX-Committee held its first meeting on January 2,

1941, with Lt. Col. Thomas Robertson in charge, and met weekly thereafter until the end of the war—226 meetings in all.[3] During those years, the committee exercised tight control over the double agents. One of the charter members was Oxford historian John C. Masterman, who stayed the course and afterward became the committee's official chronicler. From Ultra or Abwehr instructions to the double agents, the committee learned what British secrets were of interest to the Germans. It then decided what information to feed back—plausible lies or verifiable facts, which, the committee hoped, would be harmless.

In his postwar report on the double-cross system, Masterman estimated that "about 120" double agents were controlled by the XX-Committee at some time during the war and listed 39 as "more interesting" than the others.[4] A few stand out for their connection to the D-Day deception. "Garbo" was one of the more remarkable men of his time. He was the famous "Counterfeit Spy."[5] A Spaniard born of a Castilian father and a Basque mother and brought up in the small Basque town of Alsasua, Garbo hated both fascism and communism. For that reason, he tried to avoid both sides during the Spanish Civil War. Eventually, he went to prison for his antiwar stance and, under pressure, joined the government forces, only to defect to the winning fascist side. When World War II broke out, he entered it enthusiastically on the British side. In January 1941, then about thirty years old, he offered himself at the British Embassy as a double agent but was turned down. Undeterred, he hit upon the idea of cozying up to the Nazis with the intention of betraying them. He proposed exactly the kind of undertaking, espionage in Britain, that most fitted German needs. They negotiated over his assignment, and the Germans eventually supplied him with money and spying paraphernalia. Leaving Madrid in July 1941, ostensibly for London, Garbo went no further than Lisbon. He holed up there for nine months and wrote fictional espionage reports. He worked, according to Masterman, from "a Blue Guide, a map of England, and an out-of-date railway timetable," in addition to any background that he could glean from magazine racks and book shelves.[6] He explained the Lisbon postmarks by inventing a courier who, he told the Abwehr, carried the reports from London to Lisbon outside the reach of British postal censors.

Garbo fabricated reports that he sensed the Germans wanted to believe. Even though they showed a lack of familiarity with common English landmarks, his Abwehr masters accepted the reports as factual. In truth, the Abwehr desperately needed successful agents in Britain where it had racked up a dismal record, so the intelligence bureaucrats at both the Madrid office and Berlin headquarters failed to give his submissions the searching scrutiny they deserved. Garbo even created three subagents to broaden his coverage, and, from a pseudo-agent in Liverpool, he once passed along word of a large convoy preparing to set sail for Malta. British intelligence learned about it from Ultra as the Germans positioned their U-boats to intercept the phantom convoy. In the meantime, Garbo had been trying through the embassies to let the British know of his work. Finally, with the help of a neutral diplomat, his activities came to the attention of the right people. In April 1942, Garbo was brought to England as a ready-made double agent and became the star of the double-cross system. His bogus network grew larger and more spread out. His fictitious subagent in Liverpool, however, fell sick and died with a severe case of being in a position to see too much of preparations for the North African campaign. The Germans sent their condolences to the widow. Had the subagent survived, they might have wondered how he could have missed all those troops embarking on a foreign adventure, and that might have been the death of the whole Garbo network. As it turned out, Garbo became a vital part of the D-Day deception. He was destined to keep an entire German army at bay during the crucial days after the Normandy landing.

Capt. Roman Garby-Czerniawski, a native of Poland, was another outstanding double agent who, like Garbo, made a deal with German intelligence with betrayal in mind. Garby-Czerniawski, cover name "Brutus," had been an officer of the Polish general staff before the war and had spent time in the cryptanalytic service. Escaping to France in 1939, he served in Polish intelligence there until France collapsed in 1940. He then went underground and formed a network in France tied to MI6, but he was betrayed in 1941 by his cipher clerk—reportedly a jealous woman angry with her two-timing man—and marked by the Gestapo for execution. While he awaited his fate, the Germans offered him a chance to survive. If he would spy for Germany in Britain, they would spare him and a hundred members of his underground network who were being held under sentence of death. He agreed, and the Abwehr arranged for him to "escape." When he reached London, he reported everything to MI6 and offered his services as a double agent. Although hesitant at first because the Germans knew he had worked for MI6 while leading his French underground network, the XX-Committee eventually accepted his offer and used him to transmit military disinformation. When D-Day approached, he was ideally situated to take part in the great deception.

"Tricycle" was the cover name for one of the first and best of the double agents, Dusko Popov, a Yugoslav businessman with connections to Yugoslav royalist circles. He was recruited by the Abwehr at the outbreak of war and sent to spy on Britain late in 1940. On his arrival in London, he had a round of talks with British intelligence officials, who were "most favorably impressed," and he wound up as a willing agent of the XX-Committee. His name will be forever linked to the Pearl Harbor story for a missed clue to the surprise Japanese attack of December 7, 1941. Japan had asked Germany to send an agent to America, whose assignments would include spying on Pearl Harbor. The Abwehr chose Popov, who promptly reported his unusual mission to the XX-Committee. The committee sent him to Director J. Edgar Hoover of the Federal Bureau of Investigation (FBI) in the summer of 1941 along with his Abwehr assignment sheet containing suspicious questions from the Japanese about Hawaiian air bases, ammunition dumps, and the Pearl Harbor naval bases. Hoover, like most Americans in those prewar days, however, paid no heed to Pearl Harbor, and he took an intense dislike to Popov and double agents in general. He accused Popov of espionage profiteering and declared that the FBI did not need foreign spies working in the United States. The XX-Committee hastily recalled Popov and put him back to work as Tricycle in its double-cross game, where he served with distinction.

Tricycle was being groomed for the D-Day deception. At the eleventh hour, however, he had to be scratched because one of his contacts in Lisbon, Johan Jebsen, had been arrested by the Gestapo and taken back to Germany for interrogation. In fact, this man was more than a contact. Jebsen was an old Freiburg University chum of Popov's and an Abwehr agent who had originally recruited Popov to spy for Germany. Later, Popov was instrumental in luring Jebsen into spying for Britain. The two had reunited in July 1943 in Lisbon, where Jebsen was stationed. Jebsen expressed disenchantment with Hitler, which Tricycle duly reported to London. Four months later, when Popov and Jebsen talked again in Lisbon, Jebsen divulged important information about German V-weapons (rockets) and the internal anti-Hitler conspiracy known as the Schwartze Kapelle (Black Orchestra). After further investigation, MI5 enlisted Jebsen, cover name "Artist," as the only double-cross agent working on the continent. The XX-Committee was uneasy with this unusual German, coming as he did from the Abwehr and situated so far beyond its control. It made the committee even more nervous that he must have known the British connection of Tricycle and possibly of Garbo. Artist's arrest in May 1944, a month before D-Day, raised the fear that, under torture, he might blurt out Tricycle's double role to save his own skin. As it turned out, the Gestapo's questions to Jebsen centered on financial irregularities involving his Lisbon duties. Nevertheless, the XX-Committee closed the book on Tricycle and considered itself lucky that the entire D-Day deception plan did not blow up in its face.

The loss of Tricycle placed a greater burden on Brutus, but did not disrupt the deception plans for D-Day. Garbo was not affected at all; his destiny as the main player in a small cast of characters remained on track.

Ultra had not yet proved itself conclusively and the XX-Committee had not held its first meeting when General Wavell, the Middle East commander, suggested the idea of the London Controlling Section in a memorandum to Prime Minister Churchill. Deception always has been a part of war, and Wavell, like Churchill, was an ardent believer in it. Wavell proposed to fit deception to the circumstances of modern global warfare, specifically, to put it under the control and coordination of the chiefs of staff in London so that stratagems in one theater would be consistent with the pattern of deception in another. In other words, local tactics should be wedded to a global strategic concept.

Wavell then demonstrated the effective use of deception by routing a numerically superior Italian army at Sidi Barrani, a coastal town near Egypt's border with Libya. Two hundred thousand Italian troops were poised there in September 1940 for a drive to the Suez Canal against a mere thirty-six thousand British defenders, the so-called Desert Rats, who desperately hoped that reinforcements would arrive in time to save them from almost certain defeat. One advantage held by the defenders was Italian ignorance about the size of the British force. Had Marshal Rodolfo Graziani realized that he outnumbered his adversary by more than five to one, he might have been more aggressive, but Wavell literally blew dust in his eyes. He brought in Brigadier Clarke, one of the more creative officers of the war. Clarke set out to mislead the Italians into believing that the desert was crawling with the Desert Rats until reinforcements could arrive. He used a variety of fake equipment made on location out of available materials to resemble tanks, guns, trucks, and other equipment. From the air, for example, a telephone pole between two or four oil drums beneath camouflage nettings looked like a big gun. A celebrity magician, Maj. Jasper Maskelyne, made trucks look like tanks and tanks look like trucks, and he dolled up patches of desert waste so that they appeared to be airfields. Fake roads were roughed out to Graziani's southern flank, and local people, with their camels and horses dragging mats across the desert floor, created great clouds of dust, as though the animal caravan were a large column of tanks. Any Italian observation plane that tried to come too close was met with a barrage of antiaircraft fire. To Graziani, looking at high-altitude photos, the British seemed to have assembled an armored force larger than his own. Instead of attacking, he dug in. In December, after Wavell's reinforcements arrived and his troops secretly massed at the point of attack, the British struck. Graziani fell back with the loss of 130,000 men, 400 tanks, and 1,290 guns.[7]

The contribution of the A-Force to the humiliation of the Italian army reinforced Churchill's own conviction that deception and maneuver must be integral parts of a winning war strategy, a strategy that would also save lives. In particular, he wanted to avoid the mindless slaughter of static trench warfare that the belligerents had experienced during World War I. Even though, overall, the second war had more victims than the first, Churchill would be vindicated by future events in Normandy. Until the end of 1940 in the European theater, deception took the form of fake airfields and the camouflage of real facilities and equipment, purely defensive measures that helped to dilute the effect of enemy bombing raids during the Battle of Britain. At this point, the London Controlling Section (LCS) made its entry.

The LCS came into existence early in 1941 under Col. Oliver Stanley, a former Cabinet minister and a member of Churchill's Conservative Party, but Stanley proved too passive in the job and lasted only a brief time. Churchill replaced him with John Bevan, a stockbroker and scion of financiers with wide experience in the field of intelligence. Bevan seemed to have a better feel than Stanley for the nether world of subterfuge. He was amply supported by likeminded souls from his and Churchill's privileged class, whom Anthony Cave Brown vividly portrayed as "the aristocratic cream of a caste of blood, land and money, and who now dominated the British secret agencies" and "had at their disposal a wealth of experience in stratagem and special means."[8] Bevan's No. 2 man, Maj. Sir Ronald Wingate, had served in the Middle East and India. He came from a long line of imperial warriors. His father was Wingate Pasha, whose name evokes images of colonial Egypt and the Sudan. The LCS's inner circle included a novelist, civil administrator, industrialist, tea merchant, and respected scientist. From the physical and political protection of Churchill's reinforced underground bunker at Storey's Gate, London, they infused the mushrooming bureaucracies of war with a common secret agenda and reached out to important military, intelligence, and diplomatic agencies and to every major theater except the Pacific. Notable among cooperating entities were the Chiefs of Staff in London, the XX-Committee, the A-Force, MI5, MI6, and the Political Warfare Executive (PWE, engaged in propaganda). When the Americans entered the war they joined with the LCS and established an American counterpart known as the Joint Security Control (JSC) under the Joint Chiefs of Staff in Washington. The FBI, Office of Strategic Services (OSS), and the Office of War Information (OWI) also participated. Of special importance was the Committee of Special Means (CSM) at Supreme Headquarters, Allied Expeditionary Force (SHAEF). CSM planned and executed the deception for D-Day, just as the A-Force had done for Sidi Barrani and El Alamein. Although decisions about where and when and in what force to strike Europe were made at the highest levels of Allied military command and ratified by the political leaders, the coordination of planning to mask the grand strategies was the function of the LCS and its cooperating agencies.

The means of achieving deception ranged from the mundane to the macabre, from spreading poisonous rumors to planting false documents on dead bodies. A common artifice was the use of bogus radio transmissions. The Allies sent out false information by wireless, ostensibly from one friendly unit to another but, in reality, for German ears, to establish illusory units all the way up to army group and coax the enemy into overestimating Allied strength. The transmissions had to be believable because the Germans were experienced at analyzing radio traffic. They could detect nonsense even when they could not read the ciphers. Equally important were the reports of double agents to corroborate what the Germans heard by radio and to suggest a real purpose for an unreal unit. Through Ultra, the British kept a close watch on German intelligence and skewed their information according to what the Germans wanted to hear—with due caution about the risks of tipping off a genuine Allied operation. Calculated leaks of personal information, such as soldiers in nonexistent units getting married or running afoul of local law, helped to fill in the picture like the final brush strokes of a work of art—in this case, the art of deception.

From the birth of the LCS, deception played a part in every major Allied offensive. Although the El Alamein deception in October 1942 was the work of the A-Force, it was done with the knowledge and full approval of the LCS.

General Montgomery, following the example of Wavell at Sidi Barrani, used Brigadier Clarke's transplanted stagehands to feign a buildup against Rommel's southern flank while concealing preparations for an attack in the north. The effect of the fake buildup was not in the least diminished when, at the last minute, Montgomery decided to attack the center instead. All that was to Clarke's credit, even though Clarke was not there when the attack came. He had gone with Bevan to Washington to discuss deception planning with the Americans. Col. Noel Wild, Clarke's deputy, ably filled in for him at El Alamein.

Two weeks later, American and British forces landed in Morocco and Algeria and took the Germans completely by surprise. The British had concealed the purpose of troop assemblies in England with rumors delivered to German intelligence by double agents that suggested attacks were pending against Norway and France. When those rumors lost their punch, the target was changed to tropical Dakar. Support for a tropical offensive was advanced by a diplomatic request from the United States to Haiti for permission to use Haitian waters for amphibious training. The Americans emphasized the need for absolute secrecy, which was, according to historian Charles Cruickshank, "a line usually taken by the deceptive planners when they wanted to encourage leakage."[9] Despite these busy efforts to mislead the enemy, credit for achieving surprise in North Africa was probably attributable more to tight security than to deception.[10]

The invasion of Sicily in the summer of 1943 also caught the Germans napping. They were led to believe that attacks would come against Sardinia and the Peloponnesus to gain bases for later operations against southern France and the Balkans. Deception for Sicily was highlighted by one of the most famous intrigues of the war involving "the man who never was," the corpse of a man in his early thirties that was commandeered from a London mortuary and dressed in the uniform of a captain in the Royal Marines.[11] In a briefcase chained to his wrist were documents suggesting that reports of an imminent attack on Sicily were invented by the British to cover up plans to invade Sardinia and Greece. The Germans went for the bait—body, chain, and briefcase.

Other ploys advanced the Sicily deception. In London, a Spanish diplomat known to be pro-Nazi seized upon an intelligence leak to inform his friend, the German ambassador in Madrid, that the Allies were preparing to attack Greece. From Ultra, the British knew how well their stratagem was working. The codebreakers decrypted orders from Hitler that authorized the transfer of one SS brigade to Sardinia and three panzer divisions—one from France and two from the Soviet front—to Greece. Rommel went to Athens to form an army group. Just as he was setting up his headquarters, the Allies hit the beaches in Sicily.

———————

In August 1943, Allied leaders agreed at a summit meeting in Quebec that Normandy would be the invasion beachhead. Two months later, Bletchley Park reaped a huge intelligence windfall from its American-built Purple cipher machine at a time when very little Enigma or any other German radio traffic was coming out of Western Europe. Japanese Ambassador Oshima, an admiring friend and confidant of Hitler, had toured some of the coastal defenses along the Atlantic Wall (although not Normandy or the Pas de Calais) and interviewed key staff personnel of the German Army West. A competent military man and obviously unaware that his dispatches in the Purple cipher could be read in London and Washington, Oshima reported his findings in revealing detail.

He told his superiors that forces deployed in coastal positions consisted of four divisions in Holland, nine between the Rivers Rhine and Seine (including Calais), eight from the Seine to the Loire (including Normandy), four from the Loire to the Spanish frontier, and six on the French Mediterranean Coast. These were "static" units, many of them laden with East European conscripts and two-thirds of them short one full regiment. The coastal divisions were backed up by a mechanized General Reserve, consisting of fifteen first-rate divisions that could be "rushed anywhere at short notice." In all, Germany defended the West Wall with forty-six divisions—1.4 million men, not counting those in training or occupation duty—under the command of Field Marshal Gerd von Rundstedt. (Later, Rommel was given command over the reserves, except for key armored divisions controlled directly by Hitler.)

The defensive line close to the shore featured heavily fortified individual strong points armed with large and small cannon to engage ships and landing craft or mortars and machine guns for the defenders to pour down enfilading fire on the beaches. Stretches of beach not covered in this manner were heavily mined. "The German plan," Oshima said, "is evidently to smash the Allied landing operations as far as possible at the water's edge." Where coastal defenders might fail to hold back the invaders, the mobile reserves were to be called in to finish the job.[12]

These deployments in the fall of 1943 reflected the Germans' defensive priorities, that is, where they thought the main blow would fall—Calais first,

Normandy second, followed by all the rest. But they could not rule out other threats or diversionary landings anywhere from the Arctic Circle to the Black Sea. So even before Eisenhower became supreme commander, the Germans were digging in for a cross-channel invasion. When Eisenhower showed up in London in January 1944 to establish his headquarters, the Germans became convinced that the Allies would strike that year.

The LCS tapped A-Force for the man to take charge of the D-Day deception. Colonel Wild, originally with the cavalry, had been Dudley Clarke's No. 2 officer and acting commander of the A-Force at El Alamein. Clarke recommended him for the job. When Wild arrived in London in December 1943, he was told that he would head the CSM under the Chief of Staff, Supreme Allied Command (COSSAC). The deception plan, "Operation Bodyguard," was formally adopted in January 1944. It had been in preparation for several months at COSSAC, originally as "Plan Jael" with audio and visual components such as simulated wireless traffic and fake armaments. In reworking the plan, Wild incorporated double agents. It was a brilliant addition but not an original idea. He and Clarke had used double agents successfully at El Alamein.

Bodyguard aimed at three major deceptions: (1) that training and logistics for a cross-channel invasion by fifty divisions were so involved that no landing could be attempted before late summer, (2) that, in the meantime, the Allies planned campaigns in the Balkans and Norway and further landings in Italy, and (3) that the Allies gave the highest priority to a full-scale campaign of bombing Germany, in the hope that the air offensive alone would bring the Nazis to their knees without the need to invade and that this focus on the air war complicated and delayed preparations for the main amphibious assault. "Without doubt," according to historian Hinsley, these deception themes were guided by the decrypted Oshima report in the Purple cipher of his tour of the Atlantic Wall.[13] After much delay, the Soviets agreed in March to play a part in Bodyguard.

Even before Bodyguard was formally adopted, it became apparent to the Allied planners that they needed an updated deception to divert German attention from Normandy as the main landing site. In December, Bletchley Park decrypted a message from Rundstedt in the army teleprinter cipher taking note of Allied landing exercises in southern and western England, which would point to Normandy or Brittany as the invasion target. Another Oshima message to

Tokyo that month reported on an interview with German Foreign Minister Joachim von Ribbentrop, who said that the Allies might well begin their attack in Normandy or Brittany. So SHAEF, the LCS, and MI5 went back to the drawing board and came up with a new plan code-named "Fortitude." It called for coordinated threats to Norway and Calais. Prior to D-Day, the Germans were to be persuaded that an attack on Norway would come first and, after D-Day, that the landing in Normandy was only preliminary to the main attack to follow at Calais.[14]

The Norway deception conformed to a familiar pattern. A handful of over-aged officers and radio specialists under the command of Col. R. M. McLeod, a battle-scarred veteran of World War I called out of retirement, set up headquarters in Edinburgh. By simulating wireless communications among bogus military units, they pretended to assemble a fictitious army, the 4th British, in preparation for a cold-weather operation. They left it for the Germans to infer from orders for such activities as ski training and cliff-scaling instructions that the target was Norway. The XX-Committee activated a pair of Norwegian double agents, "Mutt" and "Jeff," who had been captured and turned in during April 1941. Mutt informed his German controller that a Soviet officer, Klenenti Budyenny, was in Edinburgh (which was true), apparently to coordinate a joint British-Soviet attack against Scandinavia (which was false). He also identified a nonexistent British corps headquartered at Stirling, Scotland. Jeff, who was not always cooperative with the British, was in jail at the time, but his MI5 handler knew his wireless style and reported on his behalf that another fictitious corps was located at Dundee. Garbo and Tricycle, the agents under British control most trusted by German intelligence, confirmed the news from Mutt and Jeff. Newspaper articles about "4th Army football matches," "the marriage of a 4th Army major," and other suggestive tidbits of local gossip were clipped and forwarded to the Abwehr station in Hamburg. German air reconnaissance spotted military aircraft (made of wood) on Scottish airfields and warships (destined for Normandy) at anchor off the Scottish coast. British agents in Norway asked about levels of mountain snows and whether mountain bridges were strong enough to support heavy tanks. The Soviets leaked false stories about troops training on the Kola Peninsula in the far north for an attack on Norway. British commandos conducted a series of raids along the Norwegian coast, the kind that might precede an invasion. The Germans were never sure that the threat against Norway was real, but they kept eighteen divisions in Scandinavia just in case—and most of them were still in place when the war ended in 1945.[15]

The main component of the Calais threat took the form of a fictitious command called the First United States Army Group (FUSAG). It had the usual sham ingredients—simulated radio traffic, mock encampments, fake armaments, camouflage of the real buildup to the west, false leaks, misleading espionage reports, and more—the same old stew in a bigger pot. It drew from the cumulative experience of past deceptions and benefited from the imposition of tight security that kept the truth under wraps. A continuous strip of land 10 miles deep along the entire English Channel coast from Lands End to Dover and more than 100 miles up the North Sea coast to The Wash became a restricted zone where travel was limited. Had there been a true German agent in Britain not controlled by MI5 and had he penetrated the restricted zone (not an impossible task), he would have seen the real buildup in the southwest against the flimflam in the southeast, and that would have doomed the Calais deception. But no such agent existed.

Lt. Gen. Omar N. Bradley became the first FUSAG commander, but then Supreme Commander Eisenhower changed his mind. Bradley was slated to lead the American assault on Normandy, but he could not command in Normandy and prepare for a Calais invasion at the same time. He was dropped in favor of Lt. Gen. George S. Patton, an inspired choice that made a great impression on the Germans. Patton was a general after their own hearts—a slashing, offensive-minded tank commander and a believer in the principles of blitzkrieg. He was just the man, they thought, to take on the toughest assignment of the war. The Germans would be waiting for him, and the Allied Supreme Command would let them wait. Patton was told in January that he would take over the Third Army when the Allies were ready to break out of Normandy. In the meantime, he would play the decoy as commander of FUSAG. Patton liked the Fortitude plan but not his role in it. He always saw it as his destiny to command a great army in a great battle. His day would come, but it would have to await the imperatives of the great deception.

Fortitude was first tested on the Abwehr in February 1944 when the double agent Tricycle traveled to Lisbon with a report, which, he told his Abwehr control, came from subagents, but it was actually fabricated by the XX-Committee.

Much of the report dealt with the bogus Norway operation. It also contained scraps of information that suggested a large force, ultimately revealed as FUSAG, forming in southeast England. The report did not overemphasize FUSAG but left it for the Germans to seize on the significance of various items suggesting a major buildup opposite Calais. This was London's big gamble because FUSAG was far more important in their deception plans than they dared to suggest. When the Abwehr man in Lisbon read the report, he angrily rejected the FUSAG information as "warmed-over gossip," but Tricycle argued back and demanded that the report be forwarded to Zoessen (outside Berlin) for assessment, which was done. There, at Fremde Heer West (FHW, or Foreign Armies West)—the German army intelligence unit responsible for evaluating the Anglo-American forces—the information was accepted as authentic.[16] The fictitious FUSAG thus took hold in the German mind. From this foundation, the Allied agencies of deception built FUSAG piece by piece into a formidable paper tiger that haunted the German leaders who were preparing the defense of Western Europe.

How FHW came to embrace the inflated Allied order of battle remains a treasure of wartime intrigue. Col. Alexis Baron von Roenne, the chief of FHW, had earned Hitler's favor by his meticulous attention to detail and shrewd intelligence evaluations. While occupying a lesser intelligence position in 1939, Roenne had predicted that the British and French would not attack Germany from the west while the Wehrmacht gobbled up Poland, and, in 1940, he had said that the French army would crack under the lightning thrust of German armor through the Ardennes. He was right on both counts. Later, he served with distinction in battle and suffered serious wounds on the Russian front. When he recovered, Hitler insisted that he be elevated over senior officers to the top job at FHW. Early in 1944, Roenne warned the German High Command that Anglo-American forces massing in England would launch a cross-channel invasion of France that year. He reached this conclusion from radio traffic analysis of Allied units transferred from the Mediterranean to the British Isles, but he could not predict the precise landing site or rule out the possibility of diversionary attacks. Nor could he say with any certainty how large a force the Allies were assembling.

Hitler's trust in Roenne was oddly misplaced. The latter's roots were in the Prussian military aristocracy, which Hitler despised, and the feeling was mutual. By 1944, Roenne had joined in the Schwartze Kapelle, for which he was eventually hanged. The conspirators wanted to get rid of Hitler, seize power, and negotiate an end to the war. As German patriots, they preferred to negotiate from a position of strength, and a successful Allied invasion of Western Europe did not serve their interests any more than it did Hitler's. Roenne, however, was caught up in a more personal struggle within the larger conflict. In particular, he resented the SD, which was staffed with Hitler loyalists who eyed Roenne's military establishment friends in the Abwehr with great suspicion while vying with the Abwehr for control of the Reich's intelligence system. In this cutthroat bureaucratic warfare, the fanatical SD was gaining the upper hand. By 1944, the SD was screening FHW intelligence evaluations to Hitler and the German High Command. Estimates of Allied strength submitted by Roenne were routinely and arbitrarily cut in half. Hitler, unaware that the reduced estimates were not those of the trusted Roenne, began shifting units needed for the defense of France to other theaters.

It was a dilemma for Roenne, who believed that the Atlantic Wall should be strengthened, not weakened. He felt powerless to do anything about it until one of his subordinates, Lt. Col. Roger Michel, the section chief for evaluating Allied forces in England, suggested that the FHW double the figures on the Allied order of battle so that when the SD halved them, the estimates seen by Hitler would be roughly accurate. The higher estimates could be justified by accepting agent reports from Britain at face value—reports that the experienced Roenne must have viewed with skepticism. Roenne hesitated, partly because his operations officer, Col. Lothar Metz, would not join in the scheme. What if, Metz asked, the SD stopped halving the FHW estimates? When Metz was soon transferred out of FHW, Roenne went ahead with Michel's idea. Metz's question became prophecy. In May, Roenne submitted a report estimating the Allied order of battle at eighty-five to ninety divisions when the reality was thirty-five divisions. By then, the SD officer responsible for halving the FHW estimates also had been transferred, so the SD stopped interfering. The report went through untouched.[17] From this skewed appreciation of Allied strength came a skewed German perspective for the defense of Western Europe.

Across the English Channel, the Allied command had no idea of the gamesmanship within the German intelligence system but learned from Ultra what it needed to know. The FUSAG deception was working even better than expected. At Calais, the Germans poured more concrete, built deeper defenses, concentrated more guns and tanks, and positioned their most powerful army in the west. Ultra decrypts in March and April revealed that the Germans were aware of Patton's presence in England and another decrypt in May made it clear that they associated Patton with FUSAG.[18] In this light, the deception planners put their heads together and came up with a bold refinement to Fortitude.

During the early planning for D-Day, Eisenhower had told Noel Wild that if Fortitude could hold the German Fifteenth Army north of the Seine for just two days after the invasion, it would give the Anglo-American forces enough time to secure the Normandy beachheads and gain the strength necessary to withstand inevitable German counterattacks. That was all the Calais segment of Fortitude was designed to do—give the Allied troops time to gain a solid foothold. Fortitude was now divided into "Fortitude North," with a waning focus on Norway, and "Fortitude South," directed at Calais. The new idea in Fortitude South was to extend the life of FUSAG (and the threat to Calais) for several weeks beyond D-Day. Eisenhower would get his two days plus another two months, enough time for the Allied breakthrough to the French interior. Fortitude was a major factor in the paralysis of the Fifteenth Army, but so were Allied air superiority, disruption of German army communications, and destruction of the bridges over the Seine.[19]

In May, with D-Day fast approaching, the planners set about to persuade the Germans that the coming attack in Normandy would be only preliminary to the main event, with the notionally more powerful FUSAG poised to storm ashore at Calais. Garbo and Brutus filed a series of reports to supply the Germans with an Allied order of battle that located the real Twenty-First British Army Group and the fictitious FUSAG with the main weight of Allied forces in southeast England. Toward the end of the month, Bletchley Park received confirmation of initial success in a decrypted report from Oshima of a conversation with Hitler.[20] The Fuehrer estimated eighty to ninety Allied divisions stationed in Britain and reasoned that, although the invasion might start in Normandy or Brittany, the main attack would come at Calais. The planners of Fortitude South could not have asked for more.

They were in for a shock, however, when, during the month prior to D-Day, Bletchley Park decrypted alarming news that the German army was reinforcing the Cherbourg Peninsula "in a re-disposition larger and more purposeful than any they had previously made."[21] This crucial information came primarily from a teleprinter link between Berlin and Rundstedt's headquarters in the west that had been broken in March with the aid of Colossus. Some last-minute adjustments in both the invasion and deception plans were needed, but there was no stopping the invasion itself.

D-Day had been scheduled for June 5. On June 4, with the English Channel churning in a frenzy of wind and high sea, Eisenhower postponed the attack for one day. On the 5th, after his weather forecasters predicted a twelve-hour break in the storm, he gave the go-ahead for the 6th. It was not much of a break. The seas were still rough, although not as rough as the previous day. German weathermen missed it entirely. German meteorology had been devastated by the Allied destruction of weather stations in remote North Atlantic locations and the sinking of weather ships and submarines that, earlier in the war, had reported conditions far out to sea. By now, such reports were few and far between. At this critical moment, the Germans, not fully aware of how important the moment was, received no hint of a letup and predicted that the storm would last for several more days. Because the German High Command believed that a successful invasion needed a stretch of calm weather, many senior officers, including Field Marshal Rommel, took leave at exactly the wrong time.

So the storm, together with deception and purposeful bombing, gave the Allies tactical surprise. The invasion armada of 6,500 vessels, including landing craft, slipped undetected in the dark of night to within 11 miles of the invasion beaches. German patrol boats that normally cruised the Bay of the Seine were hunkered down in port. The Allies had knocked out most of the German radar in Normandy with air strikes, and they jammed what still worked that night. They left radar in the Calais area operational so it could detect diversions that drew German sea and air defenders away from Normandy. One diversion of Calais-bound vessels towing radar-reflecting balloons anchored to rafts drew a response, but, when German warships arrived on the scene, the Allied fleet had vanished. In another diversion, bombers on the way to Germany emitted radar-reflecting foil. The German air force went for the foil and missed the British and American paratroopers who dropped on Normandy after midnight.

The test of the Fortitude deception depended on the disposition of the German armored reserves. Strong panzer counterattacks against the tenuous Allied beachheads during the earliest hours of the invasion, as the Germans had planned, could have changed the course of the war. Rundstedt had been awakened shortly after 2 A.M. on June 6 with news of the paratroop landings, but it was not yet clear to the Germans if anything unusual was happening. Parachute drops in France were common in those days. Later, Rundstedt received word that noise from ship engines could be heard off the Normandy shore, but the disabled radar could not confirm it. Rundstedt decided by 4:30 A.M., based on the strength of the airborne assault and even before the Allied landing craft had reached the shore, that a major operation was under way. He ordered two first-rate panzer divisions, the 12th SS (Hitler Youth) and the Panzer Lehr, to begin moving up from their encampments in the rear. Had the order stood, these powerful units might have engaged the invaders at the beaches before the day was out and, together with the 21st Panzer Division already deployed around Caen, driven them back into the sea. Rundstedt notified the German High Command of his order and asked for approval. Both Hitler and Gen. Alfred Jodl, chief operations officer, were asleep, and no one dared to wake them based on Rundstedt's report. Jodl awoke at 6:30 and, convinced by the Allied deception that the Normandy action was a diversion, countermanded Rundstedt's order. Hitler, who had taken prescription drugs to aid his sleep, did not rise until 10 A.M. Initially, he backed Jodl, but, late in the day, he released the two panzer divisions to Rundstedt—too late to stop the Allies at the Normandy beachheads but powerful enough to hold Montgomery in check around Caen.[22]

The Germans could still hope to turn the tide of battle by moving up the armored reserves, especially those deployed north of the Seine with the Fifteenth Army. At this point in the double-cross game, agents Garbo and Brutus made their most important contributions of the war. Early in the morning of D-Day, Garbo had gone on the wireless to give his German control in Madrid details of the Allied invasion, including the number and identity of the troops involved. This was a risk calculated by the deception planners to boost Garbo's credibility. The Germans would learn these details soon enough on the battlefield, probably during the first day or so of combat. All the better that it should come from Garbo and be confirmed on the ground. The key point of Garbo's report was that no FUSAG unit took part in the Normandy operation, and so this supposedly powerful force was waiting for the right moment to strike north of the Seine. And the right moment would come when the German reserves were transferred to Normandy.

Roenne took his cue from Garbo and concluded in his midday intelligence summary that FUSAG was still a major threat to Calais. Later that day, however, German soldiers found important papers on dead American officers that indicated far-reaching American objectives in Normandy. Although some of his officers thought that it was another Allied trick, Rundstedt became convinced Normandy was no diversion. Rommel, back at his post in France, shared this opinion. Rundstedt called Hitler and asked that the reserves be placed under his command. This time, Hitler, who also had seen the American documents, granted his request. When this news reached Allied headquarters through Ultra, it caused great anxiety. Air reconnaissance brought back photos that showed the German reserves beginning to move out. In a war that lasted nearly six years, this was a moment of extreme gravity.

The Allies held nothing back. They poured more men and arms ashore as the assault troops pressed inland to consolidate the beachheads. They brought their overwhelming air superiority into play. Hundreds of American and British warplanes converged on the French countryside like swarms of locusts and waged a vicious campaign to cut rail and road lines that could carry German forces to the front. After dropping leaflets warning French residents to get out of town, they pounded important transportation hubs into rubble. French Resistance units did their part by sabotaging rail and communications lines and ambushing German troops on the move. The deception plan went into overdrive to make the Germans think that the Calais attack was at hand. There was a marked increase in radio transmissions from FUSAG. Signals both real and fake from the Special Operations Executive (SOE, Britain's wartime sabotage and commando organization) went out to the French underground networks in the Calais area. On June 8, Brutus reported FUSAG units getting ready to embark from ports in southeastern England and told of visits to Patton from Britain's King George, Prime Minister Churchill, General Eisenhower, and on down. Even U.S. Army Chief of Staff General Marshall, Brutus said, was coming all the way from Washington to give Patton and FUSAG a proper send-off. On the 9th, Garbo radioed a long message to Madrid to review the situation and offer his "conviction" that the Normandy invasion was a trap set by the Allies to draw the reserves away from Calais. Garbo's thoughts were endorsed and transmitted by his handler to the German High Command. Roenne, as key German intelligence officer, urged that Hitler reverse his orders to the Fifteenth Army reserves and said that he had independent information of a major Allied attack at Calais on the 10th. Hitler, who had always believed that the main blow would come at Calais, canceled the order and halted the Fifteenth Army reserves in their tracks. Units already on the move were called back.[23]

The artificial threat against Calais continued to immobilize the Fifteenth Army well after D-Day. By early July, Hitler was coming around to the opinion of Rundstedt and Rommel that Normandy was indeed the main event and that any Allied attempt to land at Calais would be the diversion. He still believed that his V-1 rockets packed with 4,000-pound bombs would drive Britain from the war. He had begun raining them on England a week after D-Day. Until Churchill came to his senses and threw in the towel, Hitler thought, it remained only for German troops to contain the Allied invasion in Normandy by stubbornly defending every inch of territory. The German defenders were truly stubborn, but they paid a high price for their heroism. When Rundstedt reported the serious deterioration of German strength from the bloody war of attrition around Caen, Hitler relieved him of command and ordered Rommel to prepare a counterattack. Finally, he yielded on the Calais issue by detaching one armored division and six infantry divisions from the Fifteenth Army to reinforce Rommel in Normandy. But, it was too little, too late! Montgomery, warned in advance by Ultra, struck first but made little headway as long as the German panzers blocked the way. On that same day, July 17, Rommel was seriously wounded and knocked out of the war when Royal Air Force (RAF) fighter planes strafed his command car.

Meanwhile, Patton had moved to Normandy during the first week in July, and his place as commander of FUSAG was taken by Gen. Lesley J. McNair.[24] Despite McNair's credentials as a senior army general, the transfer of Patton was bound to reduce the threat of FUSAG in German eyes. In France, Patton would command the Third Army under Bradley's 12th Army Group but not until month's end. His arrival was supposed to be hush-hush, but the publicity-minded Patton let it be known to the press and the Germans learned of it. On July 25, the Americans began the offensive at Saint-Lô that would lead to the Third Army's breakout from Normandy. By the first week of August, Patton's armored spearheads had driven across Brittany and were racing eastward toward the French interior. Hitler then ordered a new counterattack to capture Avranches on the southern coast of Normandy and isolate Patton from his supply base. He shifted panzer divisions from the Caen front and infantry divisions from the Fifteenth Army. These moves were also revealed by Ultra.[25] Bradley called it a "reckless" attack that, more than any other decision, cost Germany the battle for France.[26] The U.S. 30th Division stalled the German advance until the First Army moved up reinforcements while Allied warplanes demolished a long column of German tanks on the road to Avranches. At last, Montgomery's British and Canadian forces broke through the weakened defenses around Caen, and Patton's Third Army swung north from Le Mans. Within days, the Allies caught the enemy in a pincer near Falaise that consumed most of the German Army in Normandy and put the rest in full retreat with the Allies in hot pursuit. Montgomery's forces entered the Belgian port of Antwerp on September 4. On the way, they passed the Pas de Calais, perhaps pausing for tea but nothing else, while across the Strait of Dover, FUSAG took its place in history beside the Trojan horse.

After the war, Jodl agonized over the fatal strategic error of fifteen well-trained, well-armed German divisions defending the empty Calais beaches as, day by day, the Allied armies strengthened their grip on Normandy.[27] Half that formidable German force deployed in a timely manner might have beaten back the Allied invasion. At the very least, it would have raised the Allied casualty toll to a horrifying level. It must have haunted Jodl to his dying day to realize that he and others in the German High Command were so thoroughly duped by Fortitude South. For that, the rest of the world need have no regrets. On the contrary, those who cherish an open society and personal integrity are forever in debt to the magnificent schemers who worked in darkest secrecy to deceive the great German war machine.

PART 3

THE ESPIONAGE WAR

CHAPTER 8

Learned Spies

The air at the upscale Kaikan Restaurant in Tokyo was heavy with smoke and booze. But no one seemed to notice as one toast followed another, drowning out the rigid formalities of the official, full-dress government reception in a roar of lively chatter. Off to the side, at the correspondents' table where inhibitions long had been abandoned, the discussion shifted to the Spanish Civil War. The year was 1937, and the war in Spain was in full stride. This conflict with ideological overtones pitted the right against the left, with each side supported and supplied by larger European powers—Nazi Germany on the right and the Communist Soviet Union on the left. The German reporter from the *Frankfurter Zeitung,* his eyes glazed from the effects of too much alcohol, emptied his glass for the umpteenth time and shouted across the table at the man from Tass, Vladimir Koudriatsev. "It's a good thing the Soviet Union is supplying the Spanish Republicans with tanks and planes," he taunted, "or else we in Germany would not have enough scrap iron."[1] Koudriatsev glared at his tormentor, but his response was lost in the renewed clamor as the other reporters picked up on this new thread of conversation. As a Tass correspondent, Koudriatsev was also a Soviet intelligence agent. He would have been astonished to know that the boorish German was a colleague in the Soviet spy business.

Richard Sorge belonged to the Nazi Party, but he hated the Nazis. Most of all, he despised Hitler. He had joined the party so he could work as a correspondent for a German newspaper, which served as cover for his real job of espionage. Sorge was a dedicated communist and an agent for the Fourth Department (intelligence) of the Soviet army, but not a spy in any ordinary sense. He was top drawer as a journalist, advisor to German diplomats, womanizer, raconteur, drinking companion, and, above all, secret agent. Public scenes displaying Nazi bravado were made to order for him because it was Sorge's style to hide his true purpose in plain sight.

Sorge ran a sophisticated ring of European and Japanese Marxists monitoring Japanese policy toward the Soviet Union, especially military policy. He and his chief lieutenant, Hotsumi Ozaki, had both achieved deep penetration into official circles—Sorge at the German Embassy, Ozaki in Japanese left-wing political circles. These two, along with Yotoku Miyagi, an energetic Japanese artist; Branko de Vukelic, a Croatian journalist of lesser stature; and Max Clausen, a radio operator posing as a German businessman, made up the core of the apparat. The Sorge spies did not openly demonstrate against the capitalist system. They did not use guns or plot subversion or carry out sabotage against the government in power. They were information specialists who fulfilled their espionage mission by delivering a stream of reliable intelligence that kept Moscow current about Japanese intentions toward the Soviet Union.

Deep penetration of a real or potential enemy is the most desired goal of intelligence agencies. Sorge ran the Tokyo ring as a foreigner in one of the world's most xenophobic societies. He had a flair for living on life's edge in defiance of social conventions. For all his élan, he was a scholarly man—Dr. Sorge, with a doctorate in political science from Hamburg University, 1920. Sorge augmented his fine intellect with an ingratiating, if bohemian, charm that made professional and social access easy for him. He turned on the charm especially for Eugen Ott, the German military attaché, later ambassador, and other unwitting officials at the German Embassy in Tokyo, where, as a trusted friend and advisor, he had virtually free run to carry on his clandestine activities.

In the early days, no one at the embassy suspected the Slavic blood in Sorge's veins. One person, the wife of a newly arrived military attaché, half-guessed the truth after Sorge had been around for five years. Col. Gerhard Matzky brought Sorge home for dinner one night in 1938. His wife surveyed the guest's dark features and high cheekbones and asked him innocently, "Aren't you really Russian? You have a certain look about you." Sorge replied glibly that he was from Thuringia, a somewhat sheltered region of central Germany, but, after that evening, he did his best to avoid Frau Matzky.[2]

She was half right. Sorge's mother was Russian, his father a German petroleum engineer. Richard was born in the grimy oil town of Adjikent near Baku in 1895. He grew up in the German culture, spoke a halting Russian, and learned English but never mastered Japanese. He attended school in Berlin and served in the German army during World War I. Life in the trenches battered and disillusioned him. While convalescing from the last of three wounds, which left him with a permanent limp, he came under the care of a father-daughter, doctor-nurse team who were radical socialists. They treated him body and soul—healed his wounds and infused his mind with Marxist doctrine. Sorge took added inspiration from the Bolshevik Revolution in October 1917. When freed of his military obligation, he picked up his studies at Berlin University, transferred to Kiel University, and joined in radical campus activities. After graduating from Kiel, already a converted Marxist, he went to Hamburg University to study for his doctorate.

Thereafter, Sorge dedicated his life to the cause of world revolution and discovered within himself a passion for intrigue. Soon, he caught the eye of Soviet intelligence and went to Moscow. He began his career with spying missions in Scandinavia, Germany, and England for the Comintern, a Soviet government agency in Moscow that coordinated communist activities worldwide. Sorge distinguished himself in these assignments, but political protocol required that he go through local communists known to local authorities, and he grew wary of exposure. In 1929, he joined the Fourth Department and received further training in espionage techniques. He went first to Shanghai to help build a new spy ring amid the wreckage of Chiang Kai-shek's savage putdown of Chinese communism. On his way, he stopped off in Germany to establish his credentials as a journalist and went on to China as the correspondent of the *Soziologische Magazin* of Berlin. He developed an analytical, somewhat turgid writing style—some might say didactic—appealing more to professionals and high officials than to the general public.

In China, as he did later in Japan, Sorge tempted fate by tearing around the narrow, crowded streets of Shanghai and Canton on a motorcycle and broke a leg already crippled by war. Perhaps his most important contact in China was an American, Agnes Smedley, a well-connected journalist and champion of communist causes. If Sorge needed an agent for a specific task, she would find him one. In 1931, the Japanese army conquered Manchuria and suddenly posed a direct threat to Russia. Sorge asked Smedley for a Japanese whom he could trust, and she introduced him to her good friend Ozaki. After three years of what his Russian employers considered highly satisfactory work, Sorge was called back to Moscow, debriefed, rested, and reassigned to Tokyo.

Sorge, ever the nonconformist, had two enduring loves—women and alcohol. As a young man, he was quite handsome and idealistic. A certain aloofness signaled an unspoken resolve to keep his sexual involvements casual, yet the opposite sex found him very attractive. A married male friend would have been well advised not to trust Sorge with his wife. Kurt Gerlach, a professor at Kiel and a communist, helped to steer the youthful Sorge deeper into party activities, in the course of which Sorge and Gerlach's wife, Christiane, fell in love or "in lust," as the case might have been. It seemed to happen without much effort on Sorge's part. "[He] was never importunate," Christiane wrote later. "He did not need to pay court to people. They flocked to him, men and women."[3] She divorced Gerlach and married Sorge, and they all remained friends. As Sorge rose in the estimation of Soviet intelligence, he was called to Moscow. Christiane went with him, only to find herself isolated and alone, feeling uneasy about the emergence of Stalin, and hearing whispers about her husband's infidelity. She packed her bags and returned to Germany; the thoughtful Sorge saw her off at the station. He soon took up conjugal living with his translator, a free-spirited Russian named Katya Maximova. Before leaving for China, he married her so that she could receive his army pay and they could exchange letters. If any woman captured his heart, it was she. They corresponded, but except for two interludes in Moscow, he saw very little of her.

In China, Sorge and Smedley lived, traveled, and worked together. By all accounts, Smedley was not much of a looker. She was a "feminist" before her time. She wrote to a friend, "I'm married . . . , so to speak . . . ; he's a he-man also, and it's 50-50 all along the line, he helping me and I him. . . ."[4] In Tokyo, Sorge indulged the embassy women, Helma Ott, his friend's wife, and the dazzling but vacuous Anita Mohr. In 1935, at the age of forty, he took a Japanese mistress, Hanako Miyake, age twenty-five. They met at the Rheingold Bar and Restaurant where she worked as a waitress. The day Sorge set up housekeeping for Hanako and her mother, he wrote a letter to Katya and told her how much he missed her. Though considerate of Hanako on one level and guiding her into reading and study, he treated her as little more than a convenience while he carried out his professional duties and carried on with other women. In his last year of freedom, 1941, he and a German harpsichordist, Eta Harich-Schneider, were a hot item of gossip at the German Embassy.

More worrisome to Eugen Ott than Sorge's love life, including the personal betrayal with his disunited wife, was the heavy drinking. Ott was anxious about his own career and feared that Sorge, in his cups, might divulge embassy secrets and create a public scandal. The concern was justified, if misguided. The greater risk for Sorge was the compromise of his spying activities. To Hanako, he once made drunken references to a secret life and "friends in Moscow" that she did not fully understand until the police brought espionage charges against him. In the spring of 1938 after a night of heavy drinking, Sorge crashed his motorcycle into a wall at high speed. Badly hurt, his face bleeding from multiple cuts, several teeth knocked out, still in an alcoholic daze, he retained an amazing presence of mind. He asked not for his friend Ott but for his co-conspirator Clausen, who found him in the hospital. After ordering the room cleared so that the two could be alone, Sorge handed Clausen his American money and secret reports written in English, which, if discovered by the police, would have put him out of the spy business in Japan. Then Sorge passed out. When he recovered, he disposed of the motorcycle but would not give up the bottle. Over time, the alcohol sapped his intellectual powers and made him more careless about security.

Sorge handpicked his ablest deputy, Ozaki, who, as an esteemed newspaper correspondent and China expert, gained access to the upper echelons of prewar Japanese politics. Thus, he became even better situated than Sorge to draw out Japan's internal secrets. Born in Tokyo in 1901, Ozaki grew up in Japanese-occupied Formosa (Taiwan), where his father edited a newspaper. The Chinese culture and Chinese problems had occupied his fertile mind from boyhood. He studied political science, economics, and sociology in Tokyo and then found work with the prestigious *Asahi Shimbun*. After an inauspicious start as a city reporter, *Asahi* transferred him to its Shanghai bureau in 1928 to take advantage of his knowledge about things Chinese.

In Shanghai, Ozaki mixed easily with left-leaning foreign journalists. One of his early acquaintances was the redoubtable Smedley. They shared Sorge's faith in the Marxist dialectic, which predicted the historical inevitability of world communism. Thus, when she arranged for Ozaki and Sorge to meet, they were all on the same wavelength, but for security reasons she introduced the latter as an American journalist named "Johnson." Ozaki assumed he was a Comintern agent. The two young men hit it off from the start, and Ozaki was only too happy to provide his new friend with information about Japanese activities on the Asian mainland. Sorge quickly recognized Ozaki as his best Japanese source.

They had more in common than their Marxist ideology. They were intellectual equals and good drinking companions with a similar casual attitude toward women. It is possible they shared Smedley, although speculation that Ozaki and Smedley were lovers has never been confirmed. Ozaki was married to his first cousin and former sister-in-law, Eiko, and, although not a faithful husband, he was a devoted father to his daughter, Yoko.

In 1932, Ozaki's newspaper brought him back to Japan and installed him as the resident expert on China. When Sorge shifted his operation to Japan, Ozaki agreed to pick up where he had left off in Shanghai.

Ozaki never joined the Communist Party. He never wanted to subject himself to organizational discipline. Through his readings of Marx and other left-wing literature, he developed a decidedly communist slant on world history and acted on his own beliefs. He envisioned China as the caldron of Marxist revolution in Asia and wanted Japan to make common cause in a communist alliance with China and the Soviet Union. Although that kind of thinking put him at odds with the right-wing militarists who dominated politics in prewar Japan, Ozaki considered himself a Japanese patriot. He simply believed that the army was leading the nation to disaster. Thus, he could rationalize his treasonous actions as consistent with his own view of Japan's best interests.[5]

Ozaki, who described himself as "gregarious," possessed the kind of social graces that made him popular in Japan's clubby, male-dominated society. As his professional star rose, his usefulness to Sorge grew. When *Asahi* set up a think tank descriptively named the East Asia Problems Investigation Association, Ozaki was asked to join the staff in Tokyo. The event that catapulted him into the stratosphere of Japanese political life was the 1936 Yosemite Conference of the Institute of Pacific Relations, an international organization for the study of Pacific Rim problems. He went to Yosemite Park, California, as a member of the Japanese delegation and delivered a lecture that appeared sympathetic to Japanese aggression on the Asian mainland. Through his participation at Yosemite, he cultivated valuable political connections, including Tomohiko Ushiba, a friend from school days, and Prince Kinkazu Saionji, the adopted son of a revered elder statesman. Ushiba and Saionji were leftists but not communists.

They probably did not suspect they were helping a Soviet spy penetrate the inner sanctum of Japanese power.

Ozaki's incisive writings on China brought him membership in still another think tank, the Showa Research Association, a policy advisory group for the future premier, Prince Konoye, a moderately left-of-center politician who emerged in prewar Japan as an alternative to the far right. At Showa, Ozaki came under the sway of a political heavyweight, Akira Kazami, who later served in Konoye's cabinet and temporarily employed Ozaki as his *shokutaku,* or unofficial advisor on China, thus unwittingly placing a Soviet agent for a period of about six months in a basement office in the premier's residence. Ozaki quit his newspaper job to join the premier's team. As a lower-level consultant, he had little, if any, influence over policy, but he was well placed for espionage. His position was further enhanced by participation in an informal breakfast group of Konoye aides who met at increasingly frequent intervals to talk politics and strategy. These meetings offered him his best opportunity for discovering state secrets, either volunteered in confidence by others or elicited by Ozaki in casual conversations. He retained his place in the breakfast group even after going to work in 1939 for the investigation department of the South Manchurian Railway, where he could monitor the Kwangtung Army, the would-be striking force of any Japanese invasion of Siberia.

Miyagi and Vukelic joined Sorge on orders from Moscow. Miyagi, born in 1903 in Okinawa and raised by his maternal grandparents, was doubly wounded in his psyche, first, by the superior attitude of mainstream Japanese against Okinawans and, second, by the then prevailing American prejudice against Asians generally, a prejudice formalized in immigration law. At sixteen, he immigrated to the United States to join his parents and hoped that the dry California air would heal his incipient tuberculosis. After graduation from art school in San Diego, he settled with his brush and easel in Los Angeles. He channeled his anger into the study of Marx and began associating with leftists. He was briefly married to a leftist woman named Chiyo. Together, they joined the Communist Party and then split up. Through leftist friends, he rented a room at the home of the Kitabayashis—a fateful connection because the woman of the house, Tomo, herself a communist at the time, would one day trigger the downfall of the Sorge spy ring. While Miyagi was at the Kitabayashis', Comintern agents recruited him for assignment in Japan. Miyagi thought his mission was to start a Comintern cell. He did not realize that he was embarking on a dangerous career in espionage.

From Miyagi, Sorge received more than he expected. Intellectually, Miyagi was not in a class with Sorge or Ozaki, nor did he have their connections. But he was friendly, bright, and industrious with a retentive mind. His art gave him a perfect cover and, besides, he did not have a record in Japan, where police kept a close watch on the communist movement. He proved to be the hardest-working member of the Sorge ring, the one who, eventually, most fit the classic mold of a spy. His chief assignment was to keep tabs on the Japanese military, including troop movements in Manchuria. In his unremitting pursuit of information, he was not above snooping around a military base or schmoozing with soldiers in some seedy bar. Also, he energetically developed a subring of agents from the Japanese left who supplied a copious stream of information that Miyagi passed along to Sorge. Before Ozaki took his position with the South Manchurian Railway, Moscow had directed Sorge to find a Japanese officer for military spying. Sorge saw it as an impossible task, given the nationalistic zeal of the Japanese army. But Miyagi came through with an eager recruit, Cpl. Yoshinobu Odai, who served in the Kwangtung Army in Manchuria and turned out to be more than satisfactory.

Although Vukelic traveled a different road to Tokyo, the pattern of his recruitment was similar to Miyagi's. He was born in 1904, the son of an army officer, and attended secondary school in Zagreb, Yugoslavia. He also entered college there but was graduated from the University of Paris. A garrulous young man, he became fluent in several languages. After graduation, he entered the corporate world for two years but then left to serve a four-month hitch in the Yugoslav army. When he returned to Paris, his job had been abolished in the global Depression. As he walked the streets looking for work, he ran into two friends whom he had known in a Marxist study group during his days in Zagreb. Vukelic had let his Marxism lapse, but his friends lured him back with the promise of interesting work—espionage. Unlike Miyagi, he knew that he was setting out to spy but little more. For cover, he landed assignments from a French picture magazine, *Vue,* based on his photographic skills, and from a Yugoslav daily, *Politika,* which made him a special correspondent. While in Paris, Vukelic fathered a child by a Danish domestic, Edith Olsen. He married her and took her with him to Japan. Never a communist, Edith did not fit in, although Sorge did use her as a courier. Both Edith and Branko ventured into extramarital affairs as their marriage disintegrated. Edith's experiences were largely promiscuous and unhappy, but Branko fell head over heels in love with his Japanese translator, Yoshiko Yamasaki, and married her after divorcing Edith.

Clausen was Sorge's second radio operator. The first, Bruno Wendt, had been assigned by Moscow. Wendt proved slow at building radio sets and fearful about sending out messages. Sorge had him recalled, and Moscow replaced him with Clausen on Sorge's recommendation. Clausen, born in 1899, was the only true proletarian in the Sorge ring. He had apprenticed with a blacksmith while a teenager growing up on Nordstrand Island off the north coast of Germany. During World War I, he studied radio in the German Signal Corps. During the postwar years he went from job to job with time to spare for reading communist literature. He joined the party in 1927, was recruited for espionage a year later and went to China where he first met Sorge. He also met the love of his life, a Finnish widow, Anna Wallenius, whom he took as his mistress and later married. Like Edith Vukelic, she was never enamored of communism, but the Clausens stayed together through thick and thin. In Tokyo, Clausen built a radio set with mostly Japanese parts. It had power enough to reach Vladivostok (code-named "Wiesbaden") in the Soviet Union, whence Sorge's messages were relayed to Moscow.

During his early years in Tokyo, Sorge kept tight control of his spy ring. He knew each of his subordinates well and worked with each as the need arose, but they did not necessarily work with each other. Ozaki never met Vukelic and saw Clausen only twice—in 1941 at Sorge's house. Miyagi had occasional contacts with Vukelic, but three years passed before he realized that they were comrade spies. Miyagi and Clausen did not meet until 1939. On the other hand, the two Japanese worked closely together. When Ozaki was too busy to meet Sorge, Miyagi acted as their go-between. He also did the English translations of Japanese documents obtained by Ozaki at the South Manchurian Railway. Miyagi had a perfectly legitimate reason for frequent visits to Ozaki's house— art lessons for Yoko. Clausen and Vukelic also knew each other well, largely because Clausen often used Vukelic's home for radio transmissions.

Of course, the discreet spy does not ask more than he needs to know. Ozaki, for example, although he had frequent meetings with Sorge, knew him only by the code name "Johnson" for a time in China and for two years in Japan. Not until 1936, at an international reception at the Imperial Hotel, was he casually introduced to the famous German newspaperman, Dr. Sorge.[6]

In the beginning, Sorge carefully screened everything that went out to Moscow. He had full trust only in Ozaki. The others he treated like underlings. He had little use for Vukelic, whom he considered a scatterbrain and an idle chatterbox offering little more than press releases and mainstream news. Sorge thought better of Miyagi but often unfairly derogated his work. Toward the proletarian Clausen, Sorge acted something like the communist caricature of the capitalist boss with little empathy or consideration. Clausen resented such treatment but kept his feelings to himself. In time, he would settle the score behind Sorge's back.

Moscow's need between the world wars for reliable intelligence from Japan was undeniable. It was still the Age of Imperialism, and Japan, which aspired to be an imperialist nation, stood as a great power on the Soviet eastern flank harboring expansionist aims. Japan had already inflicted an embarrassing defeat on Tsarist Russia in the Russo-Japanese War of 1904–05. Despite the trappings of representative government, the de facto ruling power in Japan was the army, and within the Army was a faction advocating war against the Soviet Union. At the time of Sorge's assignment to Tokyo, the restless Kwangtung Army occupied Manchuria, Korea, and most of northern China and faced the Soviet army across a long border with Siberia.

Sorge constructed a flawless cover. He brought letters of introduction from eminent Germans in the field of publishing, some with high Nazi connections. His tour de force was membership in the Nazi Party. He played that role so well while attending meetings of the small Tokyo branch that he was asked to be its leader (he turned down the offer with thanks). At the German Embassy, Eugen Ott and Amb. Herbert von Dirksen laughed when Sorge told them. They knew that his party bona fides went only as far as getting clearance to work for a German newspaper. With Ott, Sorge found a special bonding born of shared combat experience on the western front during World War I. They also played chess together and engaged in deep, informal political discussions.

The Sorge-Ott relationship was mutually beneficial. When the two had first met in 1933, Ott was an exchange officer with a Japanese artillery regiment in Nagoya. Their friendship did not fully blossom until Ott reported to the embassy as military attaché the following spring. Then, Sorge, the trained Soviet agent, cultivated a close personal and professional relationship. Ott came to rely on his judgment. Sorge, meantime, was applying his scholarly skills to the study of Japanese society. Sorge's growing expertise about Japan combined with the inside information collected by his spy ring made him invaluable to the embassy. When asked for advice, which was often, Sorge freely gave it (with Moscow's permission), and Ott freely gave Sorge access to official documents, ranging from sensitive to top secret, that came across the attaché's desk—an arrangement that had the full knowledge and approval of Ambassador Dirksen.

In 1938, Dirksen resigned as ambassador because of ill health, and, to everyone's surprise, Ott was offered the job. No doubt, Sorge's wise counsel had a lot to do with Ott's high standing in Berlin. When Ott asked Sorge's opinion about the promotion, however, Sorge warned him that he would lose his integrity and advised him to turn it down. (This was Sorge the friend talking, not Sorge the spy.) Ott ignored the advice and took the job, which, ironically, was in the best interest of Soviet intelligence. Sorge now became even more solidly entrenched as the secret "red eminence" at the embassy. Ott tried to make Sorge's role official by asking him to take a staff position, but Sorge begged off because he feared that a thorough security check would reveal his communist ties. Under Ott's persistent prodding, they struck a compromise whereby Sorge spent a few hours each morning in coordinating information flows in and out of the embassy without becoming a government employee. These quasi-official chores were often preceded by breakfast with Ott at the ambassador's residence.

Solidifying his position at the embassy and putting the apparat in place took Sorge about two years. All was ready early in 1936 when rebellious Japanese army troops, led by company-grade officers, occupied government buildings, targeted several high officials for assassination, and succeeded in killing three of them. The rebels held out for four days until the soldiers were persuaded, in the emperor's name, to return to their barracks. The rebel leaders were executed. Sorge set out to analyze this bizarre episode, the so-called February 26 Incident, so that Japan's intentions could be understood in Moscow. He asked Ozaki and Miyagi to interpret events for him and discussed matters with Ott, who showed him confidential documents from Japanese military sources. Whether the mutiny presaged a Japanese attack on the Soviet Union or elsewhere depended on the army faction in control. Perhaps the shrewdest observation came from Miyagi. Based on the twists and turns of the Army's power struggle, he predicted that Japan would take the easy road to conquest and attack China, not Russia. A year later, this prophecy would come true.

When Sorge had all the pieces together, he wrote a report for the German Embassy, submitted articles for publication in Germany, and, most important, put together a bundle of valuable embassy documents that he had photographed surreptitiously and sent it by courier to Moscow. He received high marks all around. His report for the embassy was passed on to Berlin, where it was seen and admired by top officials, including Gen. Georg Thomas, chief of the German army's economics department, who asked him to do a special study on the incident. This gave Sorge even greater access to embassy files.

The handling of the February 26 Incident set a pattern for things to come. The spy ring was superbly situated, with Sorge nestled securely in the German Embassy and Ozaki burrowed deep inside the Japanese government. Miyagi oversaw a far-flung network of subagents, and Vukelic covered other Western embassies. From his embassy sources, Sorge was able to report secret German talks with Japan, which led to the Anti-Comintern Pact of 1936 aimed at containing the Soviet Union. In 1940, he was privy to German-Japanese-Italian negotiations resulting in the Tripartite Pact, in which the parties pledged mutual assistance in the event of war. Between these events, Sorge put together comprehensive studies of the Japanese armed forces and war industries. Without Sorge's knowledge, Moscow was also keeping track of secret Japanese diplomacy by means of codebreaking. All through this period, in fact, Soviet signal intelligence, made possible by the theft of Japan's codes and ciphers, served Moscow as a check on Sorge's reporting.[7]

Sorge's Japanese comrades proved indispensable. When the Marco Polo Bridge Incident erupted in 1937, a minor clash between Japanese and Chinese troops over a missing Japanese soldier, Berlin and Moscow were equally in the dark about Tokyo's intentions. Thanks to Ozaki and Miyagi, Sorge was able to keep the two European capitals informed. Both agents believed that the Kwangtung Army staged the incident without consulting the government in Tokyo—a case of the tail wagging the dog. It served as a pretext for a full-scale Japanese invasion of China, thus fulfilling Miyagi's prophecy of a year earlier. Ozaki now predicted a long war, and Sorge accepted Ozaki's insight as his own. Japan soon found itself bogged down on the Asian mainland.

Ozaki and Miyagi distinguished themselves further with excellent intelligence work on two Japanese incursions across the Soviet border. The first incident flared in July 1938 at Chang-kufeng, a high point near Korea that overlooked the Trans-Siberian Railroad and the highway to Vladivostok. They quickly produced evidence that the aggression had no support in Tokyo. Sorge advised Moscow that the conflict would be of short duration. It lasted four days and ended with a restoration of the original borders.

The second attack was far more serious. It broke out almost a year later at a desolate site called Nomonhan where the borders of Manchuria, Siberia, and

Outer Mongolia met. The Japanese committed heavy artillery, tanks, and aircraft to the battle and enjoyed early success. The Red Army forces, commanded by Lt. Gen. Georgi Zhukov (later of World War II fame), defended as best they could to gain time and strength for a counterattack. Ozaki advised Sorge that the Japanese government did not want an all-out war and would try to localize the conflict. Miyagi submitted valuable detailed information about Japanese troop strength that he obtained largely from Odai. Even Vukelic contributed a useful report on his field trip to the Japanese side of the front as an invited member of the press corps (Sorge was not invited). Zhukov had Sorge's intelligence in hand before launching an offensive with a three-to-one manpower advantage that crushed the intruders. In September, after four months of fighting, Japan agreed to a cease-fire. It was a humbling defeat for the zealots of the Kwangtung Army.

Sorge's motorcycle accident proved to be a watershed event. He had exercised exemplary leadership of his fellow agents, who held him in the highest respect. For Clausen, however, the accident cast a different light on his leader. He was duly impressed by Sorge's willpower in retaining consciousness but aghast at his reckless alcoholic behavior. After leaving the hospital, Clausen went directly to Sorge's house and removed all espionage-related papers shortly before an official of the German News Service arrived to seal the property. "I shuddered," Clausen recalled, "when I thought of how our secret work would have been exposed had [the official] arrived before I did."[8]

Losing Clausen's respect was important because Sorge also gave up a significant measure of control over him. Having memorized the Soviet coding system, Sorge himself encrypted all messages to Moscow prior to the accident, and Clausen sent them off without knowing their contents. Because he was so badly hurt, however, Sorge decided, with Moscow's approval, to teach Clausen the system and assign him the task of encryption. After that, Clausen knew the contents of the messages, and this would have damaging consequences for Sorge.[9]

Perhaps there was always a jagged edge in their relationship, at least for Clausen, who complained that Sorge "treated me like a boy [servant]."[10] Clausen took particular offense when Sorge kept him working after the radioman suffered a heart attack in the spring of 1940. He granted Sorge's fidelity to the cause but seemed to see it as a personal shortcoming. Sorge, he said, was "a true communist . . . a man who can destroy even his best friend for the sake of communism."[11] Clausen, in fact, was developing an unmistakably capitalist mentality as he found heady success in his cover business, M. Clausen Shokai, which made blueprint copying machines.

M. Clausen Shokai, with its main business in Tokyo and a branch in Mukden, proudly boasted among its customers such Japanese companies as Hitachi and Mitsubishi, as well as government agencies, including the War and Navy Ministries, and reported a tidy profit of 14,000 yen in 1939. In Moscow, the Fourth Department was going through a budget squeeze and, having provided original seed money for M. Clausen Shokai, it decided as a payback on its investment to cap its own funding of the Sorge ring at 2,000 yen a month and let any additional expenditures come out of Clausen's profits. This did not sit well with Clausen. He had actually put up the major share of the capital, and the company's success was due entirely to his own hard work. Resisting the order to put corporate money into the spy ring, he pleaded costly new investments and other fabricated expenses.

Because of his pent-up anger against Sorge personally, his growing estrangement with communism, and an inner nationalistic pride at German success under Hitler, Clausen began holding back Sorge's reports and applying a clumsy personal censorship that made Sorge's work appear inadequate in Moscow's eyes. The fallout from this dereliction affected Sorge's warning of the imminent German invasion of the Soviet Union and his subsequent reports on Japan's "southern strategy" against Britain and the United States and away from conflict with the Soviet Union. Even though truncated, however, some of Sorge's information went through—probably enough to legitimize his place in history.

Sorge himself uncovered the German plan to invade the Soviet Union from officers accompanying couriers from Berlin. The final confirmation came on May 20 from an escort who was also Sorge's old friend, the former assistant military attaché in Tokyo, Lt. Col. Friedrich von Scholl. From him, Sorge was able to inform Moscow of the date and strength of the attack, "June 20, it may be postponed for a few days . . .," with 170 to 180 panzer and mechanized divisions.[12] Premier Joseph Stalin, however, did not believe him. Despite Sorge's faithful service in China and Japan, the dictator seems to have held it against him that Sorge was a protégé of the former Fourth Department director, Jan Berzin, whom Stalin had already executed. On hearing of Sorge's warning of a German invasion, Stalin denounced him as "a shit who has set himself up with some small factories and brothels in Japan."[13] The Fourth Department's reply to Sorge was only slightly less offensive: "We doubt the veracity of your information." On reading this message, Sorge flew into a rage and asked Clausen in pained bewilderment how Moscow could ignore his warning.[14]

The second of the Sorge intelligence coups in 1941 was a collective effort of the spy ring. On July 2, ten days after the German invasion of the Soviet Union, high Japanese military, naval, and cabinet officials met in the presence of the Emperor to chart the nation's future course. Should Japan open a second front in the Soviet Union or pursue a "southern strategy" against the Western imperialist powers? Although the world knew of the Imperial Conference, it was left in the dark about its decisions. Sorge turned to his spies. Ozaki pumped his unwitting colleagues in the breakfast group and learned that Japan would continue the struggle in China, remain neutral in the Soviet-German war but be alert for opportunities for easy territorial gain if the Soviet Union weakened, and pursue its goals in the south through diplomacy, if possible, and by force, if necessary. That still left open the possibility of a Japanese attack in Siberia if the conditions were right. While the Japanese army kept a close watch on the progress of the German advance into the Soviet Union, Sorge, Ozaki, and Miyagi spent the next several weeks trying to pin down the Japanese position. For every scrap of information he picked up about the strength and disposition of the Kwangtung Army in Manchuria and every nuanced conversation with Japanese and German officials in Tokyo, Sorge drafted reports to Moscow.

Clausen did not send them all, however, and those he did send were shortened. By Clausen's estimate, he actually transmitted only about a third of all the enciphered word groups from Sorge's reports during this period.[15] One message Clausen did not send in mid-August told of comments by the German naval attaché that the Japanese navy and civilian government had decided not to go to war with the Soviet Union, which would have been very good news in Moscow.[16] He finally did send a message on September 14 in edited form, however, that was crucial. It relayed Ott's opinion that a Japanese attack against the Soviet Union was "out of the question" for the calendar year. This was particularly meaningful because Ott had been pressing Japan on Hitler's behalf to open a second front against the Soviet Union and remained optimistic about it even as other German envoys were losing hope. Another message, sent the same day, quoted Ozaki, drawing on Japanese government sources, as being in agreement with Ott. That made it two excellent sources reporting Japanese intentions not to invade Siberia that year.[17]

These messages, together with confirmation from codebreaking, had an impact in Moscow.[18] The Soviet army transferred eleven divisions from Siberia to the Moscow region in October and November.[19] In December, reinforced with fresh troops from the east, it launched a furious counterattack that hurled back the Germans and saved Moscow from the Nazi juggernaut.

The day Hitler attacked the Soviet Union, Sorge was depressed. Those wretches in Moscow had ignored his warnings. He tried to drown his sorrow with double whiskeys at the Imperial Hotel. The more he drank, the more he brooded—Hitler was a fool to think he could defeat the Red Army; Ott was Hitler's toady; he was a fool, too; they were all fools, the whole embassy staff. Finally, overwhelmed by his own dark thoughts, he called the ambassador. When Ott came to the phone, Sorge shouted in his ear, "The war is lost." Then he repeated the performance with other embassy personnel, who considered him their friend. They all knew he was drunk, and that was not unusual. Sorge had sunk deeper and deeper into the pits of alcoholism and created scenes that embarrassed and exasperated his friends. They all agreed that, this time, he had gone too far.[20]

But, they did nothing about it. They continued to tolerate Sorge as an extremely talented advisor and a loyal, if unconventional, German patriot. The less said about his escapades, the better. If word of his latest outburst reached Berlin, there would be consequences, and if a certain Nazi in their midst found out, Berlin would soon know. Gestapo Col. Joseph Meisinger had earned a reputation as one of the most brutal and corrupt of all Nazis. On his previous assignment in Warsaw, he had committed atrocities so numerous and monstrous that his own security agency nearly court-martialed him. Instead, it sent him to Tokyo in 1940 to keep an eye on the embassy staff, especially Sorge. Headquarters personnel had turned up disturbing communist connections in Sorge's past and wondered if he, for all his useful reports, was doubling as a Soviet agent. Meisinger, however, proved to be no match for Sorge, who greeted him as a fellow Nazi, helped him drink his whiskey, told him earthy stories, and joked about his wide girth and ugly face. Meisinger was charmed. He told Berlin that Sorge enjoyed the full confidence of embassy officials in Tokyo.

Although Sorge contained Meisinger, he had other problems. He was a changed man by the summer of 1941. Cynicism and the motorcycle accident had hardened his handsome features. At forty-five, well into middle age, he found the stress of the double life increasingly unbearable. He pleaded with Moscow

A German military Enigma cipher machine. Visible are (bottom to top) the plug board, keyboard, lamp board, and three cipher wheels. NATIONAL SECURITY AGENCY

In December 1932, Marian Rejewski solved the internal wiring of the Enigma's cipher wheels, which later enabled him to design a "bomba," a machine to recover Enigma keys. WLADYSLAW KOZACZUK

Using Polish technology, mathematician Alan Turing spearheaded the British effort in 1939–40 to design a more sophisticated "bombe" to crack Enigma. PRINCETON UNIVERSITY

Shown here is a later American-built bombe to recover U-boat four-wheel Enigma keys. NATIONAL SECURITY AGENCY

Allied success in the secret cipher war was a key to victory against the U-boats. Decrypted German messages helped the Allies locate many U-boats and sink them by aerial attack. NATIONAL ARCHIVES

Aided by the intelligence gathered from reading German ciphers, British general Sir Bernard Montgomery (right) outsmarted and defeated the German "Desert Fox," Field Marshal Erwin Rommel, in Egypt. NATIONAL ARCHIVES

Rommel (left) never knew that his Afrika Korps was handicapped by compromised codes. NATIONAL ARCHIVES

In 1939–40, the U.S. Signal Intelligence Service developed an analog of Purple, the Japanese diplomatic cipher machine, after many months of analyzing enciphered messages. NATIONAL ARCHIVES

Frank B. Rowlett led the American team that broke Purple. NATIONAL SECURITY AGENCY

Genevieve Grotjan made a critical recovery of Purple cipher patterns that finally led to the breakthrough. She is shown here receiving the Exceptional Civilian Service Award from Brig. Gen. P. E. Peabody in May 1946. NATIONAL ARCHIVES

TUNNEY
1116

William T. Tutte, a science student fresh out of Trinity College, Cambridge, solved Tunny's internal mechanism by the mathematical analysis of ciphertext.
TRINITY COLLEGE, CAMBRIDGE UNIVERSITY

Left: The German army encrypted high-grade teleprinter messages with the SZ-42 machine made by C. Lorenz, AG. The British called the machine "Tunny" (or "Tunney"). NATIONAL ARCHIVES

From Tutte's calculations, Maxwell H. A. Newman led a British project to build the "Colossus," the world's first electronic programmable computer, in order to recover Tunny keys. NATIONAL PORTRAIT GALLERY, LONDON

The Colossus is pictured here in 1943 at Bletchley Park, an estate fifty miles northwest of London that became the nerve center for the British codebreaking efforts during World War II.

The ability of British and American codebreakers to read Enigma, Purple, and Tunny ciphers played a vital part in deception plans for the Allies' D-Day invasion of Normandy. As these American troops waded ashore, Hitler still believed that the real Allied invasion of France would be far to the east near Calais. FRANKLIN D. ROOSEVELT LIBRARY

Early in 1942, Lt. Comdr. Joseph Rochefort led the U.S. Navy's codebreaking unit at Pearl Harbor, which broke the Japanese navy's operations code and set up the critical American victory in the Battle of Midway. NATIONAL ARCHIVES

The "Fat Man" plutonium bomb (above), the type of bomb dropped on Nagasaki, Japan, in August 1945. Atomic spy Klaus Fuchs (right), who worked at the Los Alamos facility, provided the Soviet Union with full details about the bomb, allowing the Soviets to make an exact copy.

NATIONAL ARCHIVES, NORTHEAST REGION, NEW YORK CITY

for reassignment or, better yet, for a return home to his cherished Katya and a quieter scholarly life. At the same time, he feared that if he went back to the Soviet Union, he likely would be thrown into prison or even executed like Berzin. At the embassy, he no longer tried to conceal his Russian background and openly sympathized with the Soviet Union, but he never went so far as to admit his espionage. Sorge and Ott kept up their working relationship, but their friendship was dead. To Sorge, Ott had become "a time-server and careerist," slavishly obedient to Hitler without the slightest belief in the Nazi cause. With the two women currently in his life, the alcohol was making him megalomaniacal. One night, sloshed to the eyeballs, he told Hanako that he was "a god," and it was his mission to end the war in Europe—"all wars, in fact."[21] He promised on another drunken evening to his new love, Eta Harich-Schneider, that he would deal with the Nazi "pigs in Berlin" who had complicated her life.[22]

Richard and Eta were a fascinating pair. She, a practicing Catholic, had no use for godless communism; he, a hardened atheist, lived in the present for whatever life offered him. They shared a mutual hatred of Nazism, and she concluded that he was a moral man. She had made a name for herself in Germany as a classical harpsichordist who went on concert tours and taught at the State Academy for Music. As a state employee, she was expected to join the Nazi Party, but she refused. She stood up for non-Aryan colleagues and got into big trouble with the Nazis by including a talented Jewish student in a public concert. Friends spirited her out of the country (she left two daughters behind) and arranged for her to stay in Japan. The visit was supposed to be temporary, just another tour, but returning to Germany was impossible. She wanted to go on to South America, but she needed the ambassador's help and was reluctant to approach him. A perceptive woman, Eta could see the Nazi influence hanging over the embassy like a toxic fog. For the time being, she played the harpsichord at embassy functions and was an honored houseguest of the Otts, who knew nothing of her troubles. Sorge was the only person in whom she confided. They stole away, like schoolchildren escaping their stuffy elders, and Sorge showed her the sights of Tokyo. Eventually, he showed her to his house— and bed. Lonely and isolated in an alien land far from family, friends, and her chosen professional life, she entered into a tempestuous love affair with a charming, talented, fascinating, alcoholic journalist. It lasted only a few months until Sorge's arrest in October, when she discovered who this man really was.

Through most of the summer while Sorge carried on with Eta, Hanako stayed at Sorge's house about half of each week. It appears, however, that the two women never met. With Hanako, there were complications of a different kind. The Japanese police twice questioned her about living with a foreigner and threatened to write up an official report to higher authority. Sorge was outraged when she told him about it, but he eventually calmed down. What else could he do? He arranged a cordial meeting with police officials to ensure that no harm would come to her. Ultimately, the police burned the report in Hanako's presence. It is tempting to think Sorge bribed them, but there is no evidence of it. Soon, he sent Hanako away—ever so softly. He told her it was better that way, and she moved out. Later, on October 4, she had dinner with him on his forty-sixth birthday, exactly six years after they had first met. It was the last time she saw him alive.

Sorge was probably most concerned that summer with getting out of Tokyo. After his reassuring report to Moscow in mid-September that Japan did not intend to attack the Soviet Union that year, he felt that he had accomplished his mission. But his repeated requests for reassignment fell on deaf ears in Moscow, and he refused to slink away without the Fourth Department's permission. Sorge had been under a sporadic watch by three separate police agencies since his motorcycle accident in 1938, not because anyone suspected that he was a Soviet agent but simply because, as a foreign journalist and a prominent one at that, he was an object of official mistrust. As summer 1941 wore on, the watch intensified. He became ever more conscious that he was being followed.

Other members of his ring also felt the pressure. Vukelic was slipping totally out of orbit. Like Clausen, he was losing interest in espionage, and his efforts gradually slackened. He avoided Sorge and put off assignments. Possibly, he was reacting to Sorge's disdain for his work, but other aspects of Vukelic's life offered him greater satisfaction. His adored Japanese wife had borne him a son, and he had grown to like his legitimate occupation as a journalist. In a frank admission of an eroded commitment, he confided to Clausen that he had lost his faith in communism; he now believed communism ultimately would be defeated and "it would be useless to work for the principle any longer."[23]

Miyagi had moments of depression. He was particularly worried in the spring of 1941 when the new National Defense Security Law went into effect with penalties up to death for divulging state secrets to a foreigner—what he had been doing for years.

The same law applied to Ozaki, but his commitment never slackened. For a spy, he was careless about associating with communists known to the police. He did it out of loyalty to his friends—and got away with it because of his high status and clean record. His own informal subring included Shigeru Mizuno, and Ozaki assigned him espionage-related research even though police were keeping an eye on Mizuno. Inevitably, by association, suspicion spilled over onto Ozaki. By 1941, the authorities, anxious about leaks from the South Manchurian Railway, were screening visitors to Ozaki's office. Optimistic to the point of self-delusion, however, Ozaki continued to trust in his political connections while conducting espionage.

Japanese authorities knew that someone was sending coded radio transmissions but could never pinpoint the moving transmitter or break the code until Clausen became their prisoner and explained it to them. Clausen had had several scary moments while carrying his mobile radio between transmission sites. Once, at Vukelic's house, he was frightened half out of his wits when a roofer being lifted to his job suddenly rose up outside the second-floor window and peered inside at Clausen using the radio. Another time, at Clausen's home, a Kempeitai agent (military policeman) came into the house while Clausen was transmitting in an upstairs room. He quickly shut off the radio and closed the door on his way to greet the agent, who asked a few questions and left without conducting a search.

Sorge himself was paying less attention to details as his tight grip over the spy ring loosened. One night, to Hanako, he poured out his alcoholic thoughts in an egregious breach of security. He spoke to her about a longing for Russia and about working toward the defeat of the Japanese government.

Despite all of the police activity directed at Sorge and his fellow conspirators, it yielded no clues about espionage. The big break in the case occurred circuitously. Late in 1939, the Tokko (Japanese Special High Police Bureau, in effect, the "thought police") arrested and questioned Ritsu Ito, a known communist agitator. Although, at the time of his arrest, Ito was working for the South Manchurian Railway as Ozaki's assistant, Ozaki himself was not implicated. (Some in Japanese left-wing circles suspect, however, that the Tokko planted Ito to watch Ozaki.) During Ito's several months in prison, Tokko agents questioned him at length. Sensitive to the infiltration of communists among Japanese returning from the United States, they asked whether he knew any repatriates who had belonged to the American Communist Party. Ito named the hapless Mrs. Kitabayashi, his housekeeper's loose-tongued aunt, who had talked of her party connections in California. Ito apparently did not know Miyagi or anything about the Sorge spy ring or even if Mrs. Kitabayashi knew any real spies.

The Tokko was slow to follow up. Over time, agents questioned Mrs. Kitabayashi and staked her out but found nothing subversive about her activities. She was no longer a communist and had even changed her allegiance to Adventism. When Miyagi's name escaped her lips in the context of party members whom she had known in America, it did not much interest them. Miyagi had never been under the Tokko's scrutiny. Only when they finally got around to Miyagi almost two years after Ito's arrest and found incriminating evidence in his house did they begin to sense that they were onto something big. Then, the Sorge ring came crashing down.

The Tokko swooped on Miyagi early in the morning of October 10, 1941. Three officers rousted him from a sound sleep in his upstairs bedroom. As he dressed, they made a cursory search of the room and turned up a bounty of evidence. One document, in particular, dumbfounded them. It was a survey of Japan's petroleum stockpiles in Manchuria (obviously stolen by Ozaki). Where and how much oil Japan held in reserve was a closely guarded state secret. Yet, here on the desk of an obscure artist, who had no business knowing such things, was an inventory for Manchuria written in both Japanese and English. Under questioning the next day, Miyagi admitted owning the documents but continued to deny that he was a spy.[24] At an opportune moment just after lunch he attempted an honorable suicide by diving out a window headfirst. Unfortunately for his purpose, his two-story fall was broken by shrubbery, and he received only minor injuries. Having failed at death, Miyagi was now determined to make a clean breast of his life, as if to purge himself of a treasonous past. To police and prosecutors stunned by the scale of his disclosures, Miyagi poured forth the broad outlines of the Sorge spy ring and implicated all its inner-core members.

Miyagi confessed on October 11, and the Tokko arrested Ozaki early on the morning of October 15. After a long day and evening of intense grilling, he broke and agreed to tell the whole story. His confession jibed with Miyagi's. Next, the Tokko picked up Mizuno, who corroborated the story told by the other two men. The Tokko now had a strong enough case to go after the Europeans, a more delicate operation because of Sorge's status at the German

Embassy. Sorge, Clausen, and Vukelic were arrested on October 18, and each confessed in due course.

Sorge held out for a week, denying everything, hoping Ott would come to his rescue. On the seventh day, he was confronted with the news that all of his colleagues had confessed and the police had amassed all the evidence needed for a conviction. "Why not come clean?" the prosecutor asked. Sorge asked for paper and pencil, then carefully wrote a few words and flung the paper back at his inquisitor. "I have been an international communist since 1925," it said. Pressed further, Sorge admitted spying, then cried out, "I am defeated," and wept bitterly.[25]

From the moment that he heard of Sorge's arrest, Ott applied every pressure imaginable to see him and obtain his release. After Sorge confessed, an interview was arranged on condition that Ott's questions be submitted in advance and that there be no mention of espionage. Nor was Ott informed of the confession. Sorge, not wanting to face his former friend in the full light of his treachery, agreed only reluctantly. At the appointed meeting in a painfully stiff atmosphere, Ott asked the prearranged questions about the prisoner's health and treatment. Finally, he asked Sorge if he had anything further to say. Sorge replied somberly, "Mr. Ambassador, this is our final farewell."[26]

It was also a crushing farewell to Ott's promising career. Ott could never quite come to grips with the reality of Sorge as a spy, whether out of personal loyalty or fear for his own professional hide. He managed to survive for more than a year as a lame-duck ambassador until he was relieved of his post early in 1943. After his request for a return to active duty was denied, he sat out the rest of the war in Peiping (now Beijing).

Sorge spent the last three years of his life as a ward of the Japanese criminal justice system. After recovering from his illness and going off alcohol cold turkey, he became his old self and managed to charm those who came within his orbit. Orally, and fudging here and there in lengthy interviews with police and prosecutors over a period of months, he spelled out the particulars of his espionage career. He then offered to write out his confession. Under constant prodding for more details and spurred equally by pride in his own achievements, Sorge produced a document that facilitated his conviction.

Except for Miyagi, who died of recurrent tuberculosis during the trial, the others were also convicted. Vukelic received a life sentence; his life ended in the bitter cold of Absiri Prison in Hokkaido (the northernmost main island) on

January 13, 1945. Of the five members of the inner spy ring, only Clausen survived the war. He had wasted away to less than one hundred pounds when the Americans occupied his prison in Akita in October 1945. After he recuperated, he found Anna in Tokyo; she had received a three-year sentence. When the Americans became aware that they had rescued a communist spy, the Soviets extricated the Clausens from Japan to a hero's welcome in Moscow. Having forgotten their disillusionment with Marxism, they reaffirmed their eternal loyalty to the cause and settled down in East Germany as honored communists.

Sorge and Ozaki were sentenced to death. After exhausting all appeals, they thanked their guards for treating them well, and calmly, albeit unwillingly, submitted their necks to the hangman's noose at Sugamo Prison on November 7, 1944. Although they died with courage and grace, neither had expected execution. They both thought that Ozaki's political connections would save him. Sorge believed that he would be exchanged for a Japanese prisoner in Soviet hands, but Stalin let him die.

In the sixties, nearly two decades after his death and well after Stalin's, Sorge received a rare tribute for someone who plies his trade in the shadow world of spying. He was declared a hero of the Soviet Union. A street in Baku and a ship were named after him, and a postage stamp bearing his picture was issued. After the war, Hanako reclaimed his skeletal remains. From his dental gold, she had a ring made that she wore for the rest of her life. Sorge was all hers in death, as he had not been in life. She had him cremated and, a year or so later, buried his ashes in Tokyo's Tama Cemetery. A stone marks the site with the inscription "Here lies a hero who sacrificed his life fighting against war and for world peace."

CHAPTER 9

"Lucy,"
Man of Mystery

Lucy" is either the most important spy of World War II or his generation's Mata Hari, of whom much has been written about meager accomplishment. The myths that surround Lucy are larger by far than the humdrum life of the real man, Rudolf Roessler. Some writers glorify him for winning the war almost single-handedly; others disparage him as a mere cutout used by anti-Nazi conspirators to channel German military secrets to Hitler's enemies. He had powerful friends in high places inside Germany, say some; he obtained his information from British codebreaking, say others. Those who argue the former do not agree on whether the information reached him by radio, diplomatic pouch, or a combination of telegraph and courier. Those who believe it was codebreaking think either he or people around him were double agents. The truth is that more than half a century since Roessler breathed the neutral Swiss air in war-torn Europe nobody knows the truth. Roessler made it a condition of his cooperation with Soviet and other intelligence organizations that he not reveal his sources. Because information, like power, hates a vacuum, keeping a secret is a sure way to create a myth. The bigger the secret, the greater the myth.

This attempt to unravel the story of Lucy and the spy ring that bears his code name is not an easy task. Although a writer of some achievement, Roessler never wrote about his own wartime espionage experience or even talked about it for public consumption. Many who did were careless with the facts either because they were caught up in Cold War politics or they sought to satisfy the voracious demands of the marketplace. Others who have tried to get the story straight have ultimately failed to penetrate Roessler's wall of silence. That he was a key figure in World War II is beyond dispute. Vital German secrets passed through his hands to the Soviet spy network in Switzerland and on to Moscow to the Chief Intelligence Directorate of the Soviet General Staff—the GRU for its Russian name—where the information was put to good use, particularly at the decisive Battle of Kursk in 1943. What is missing from the picture is how this mysterious man came to possess such valuable intelligence. The whole truth might never be known.

The Lucy ring started, without Lucy, as a textbook Soviet apparat. Its leader was Sandor Rado, a Hungarian. In 1937, he took over a network in Switzerland founded by Maria Josefovna Poliakova, who returned to a Moscow desk as Rado's immediate superior.[1] Rado, born of the middle class just outside Budapest in 1899, excelled at geography and became a successful mapmaker.[2] After service as a staff officer in World War I, he studied law and politics at Budapest University and devoured the writings of Karl Marx and Friedrich Engels at a time when Austria-Hungary was in the throes of a painful separation. When the communist revolutionary, Béla Kun, declared Hungary to be a Soviet republic, Rado joined the new Hungarian Communist Army as a political commissar. Béla Kun's fling with destiny lasted less than a year, however, and Rado had to flee for his life.

Rado returned to the classroom in Vienna and concentrated on geography. To support himself, he started a news agency, Rosta-Wien, and distributed reports from inside the Soviet Union that were based on government radiograms. Later, he founded another agency, Intel, which sent reports of communist activities in Europe back to the Soviet Union. The business collapsed, however, when the pariah Soviet state established diplomatic relations with Austria in 1922, but Rado had gained a measure of recognition in the communist world. He moved to Leipzig to complete his studies in geography on a modest stipend from the Soviet government. There he met and married Helene

("Lene") Jansen, a communist activist, and published a political atlas of the Soviet Union, the first of many of his works in the field of geography. Settling in Germany, he founded the world's first press agency that offered maps and geographical diagrams. When the Nazis came to power in 1933 and began to round up communists, the Rados pulled up stakes. They fled to Austria and then to France as Rado pursued his cartographic career. In 1935, while he was in Moscow on business, a recruiter approached him from the GRU, and his life changed.

His first and only assignment in his new line of work took him to Geneva with enough funds to establish a mapmaking agency, Geopress, to cover his espionage. He adopted the cover name "Dora," an anagram of Rado, which he used in correspondence with Moscow. He had a code name, "Albert," by which he was known within the apparat. Once again, his business thrived, especially during the Spanish Civil War when he was inundated with requests to update the changing political map of Spain.

Gradually, Rado acquired the networks of other agents in Switzerland. One was that of Ursula Maria Kuczynski, aka Ruth Hamburger, born in Berlin in 1907. She and her husband, Rudolf Hamburger, had been Soviet army agents in China in the early thirties. Their marriage did not last long. He stayed behind when she was ordered to Switzerland with the cover name "Sonia" sometime in the late thirties. Her new network included two Britons who had fought with the International Brigade in the Spanish Civil War, Leon Charles Beurton (alias Len Brewer) and Alexander Foote. She taught them Soviet codes and ciphers and how to use the wireless. In February 1940, she married Beurton, which made her a British citizen, and, toward the end of the year, she turned her network over to Rado and moved to Britain to organize another network.[3]

Included in the transfer were Foote, the most productive of Rado's wireless operators, and Edmond and Olga Hamel, who operated a second two-way radio. Edmond Hamel also built radios for the apparat in a shop he owned in Geneva. Foote made the first transmission to Moscow the night of March 12–13, 1941. The Hamels began transmitting by the end of the month.[4] More than a year later, Margrit Bolli, a twenty-two-year-old Swiss Communist from Basle, agreed to operate another radio. Rado recruited her on the recommendation of the Swiss Communist Party, and Foote taught her the ropes. Bolli and the Hamels worked from different locations in Geneva, while Foote moved to Lausanne on the north shore of Lake Geneva. German Signals Security picked up signals from these three radios late in 1942. The Germans correctly perceived them as an extension of Die Rote Kapella ("The Red Orchestra"), whose apparats they had just snuffed out in Germany, France, Belgium, and Holland. They called the newly discovered network in Switzerland with its three radio operators Die Rote Drei ("The Red Three"). Although the energetic but short-lived apparats in Germany and the occupied countries had very little impact on the war, Die Rote Drei, thanks to Lucy, made a major contribution to the Soviet army's victory in the decisive Battle of Kursk.

Another Rado agent of note was Otto Puenter, a Swiss Communist who, a decade earlier, had started a press agency called the International Socialist Agency (INSA) to gather uncensored news from fascist Italy for public consumption in Switzerland. At the time, Puenter had no tie to Moscow, but he developed an extensive network of informers in Italy. When the Nazis took over Germany, he built a similar network inside the Reich. During the Spanish Civil War, he shifted his focus to Spain. While there, he met a GRU recruiter and became a Soviet spy with the cover name "Pakbo."

George Blun (cover name "Long") entered Rado's network through Puenter. Blun had been an agent of the French intelligence agency, the Duexième Bureau. Using journalism to cover his espionage, he served for several years as a correspondent in Berlin. Blun became one of Rado's most valuable agents. He also delivered his intelligence to Charles de Gaulle's provisional French government in London, as well as to the British.

Most important of all Rado's networks was that of Rachel Duebendorfer (cover name "Sissy"). She was born Rachel Gaspary in Danzig in 1901 and became a Soviet agent before she was twenty years old. She put together her spy ring in Geneva, where she worked for the International Labor Organization (ILO), which consisted largely of officials with diplomatic status who traveled freely to the belligerent countries. During the war when Die Rote Drei was in full throttle, she lived in Bern with Paul Boettcher, a German communist. What made Duebendorfer so important was her agent Christian Schneider (cover name "Taylor"), through whom the Soviet apparat discovered the legendary Lucy.

French authors Pierre Accoce and Pierre Quet have trumpeted Rudolf Roessler as "one of the master spies of all time."[5] Master spy is a loose term when applied to Roessler. British historian David J. Dallin had used the term earlier,[6] but it has not withstood the test of time and close scrutiny. Roessler's value to Die

Rote Drei sprang from his relationship with the well-placed anti-Hitler conspirators inside the Reich (or British intelligence, if one believes the codebreaking hypothesis). That made him an indispensable contact, not a master spy. Essentially for that reason, the CIA reduced him, perhaps too harshly, to the humble status of a cutout.[7]

Roessler never considered himself a spy in the classic sense of a cloak-and-dagger man. He was never tutored in the arts of espionage, nor was he a trained agent of the Soviet Union. His relationship to the Center in Moscow (GRU Headquarters) was that of a businessman dealing in an important wartime commodity, information. His anti-Nazi attitude smoothed the business relationship, but it did not stop him from exacting a high price for his goods. His pay was as high as $1,700 a month, a small fortune at that time.[8] For a vital German defensive plan, "Ostwall," the Center agreed to give him 5,000 Swiss francs. In one dispatch in 1943, Rado told Moscow, "Sissy [Duebendorfer] states that Lucy group no longer works when the salary stops." Moscow replied meekly, "The group will surely be paid according to [Lucy's] demands."[9]

Quiet, competent, unpretentious, burning with a deep hatred of the Nazis, Roessler ran a small anti-fascist publishing house in Lucerne called Vita Nova (New Life) and lived with his wife Olga in Wesemlin on Lucerne's outskirts. He rarely, if ever, traveled unless one counts the daily commute from his home to his place of work at 36 Fluhmattstrasse in Lucerne's old quarter. He was born in the Bavarian town of Kaufbeuren outside Munich in 1897 and attended school (the Realgymnasium) in Augsburg a year ahead of the great German dramatist Bertolt Brecht.[10] His experience fighting in World War I turned Roessler into a lifelong pacifist. He became a journalist after the war and developed an interest in the theater. In 1928, he moved to Berlin, where he managed and publicized an organization called the Buehnenvolksbund, a sponsor of touring theater companies that performed in "a national and Christian spirit." He also wrote articles analyzing the political role of the theater. Thus, he found a niche in the literary and business circles of Berlin society, where he knew the famous novelist Thomas Mann. He became a member of the prestigious Herren Klub patronized by the fat cats of German industry, government, and military. From his activities at the Herren Klub, including lectures on the art and business of the theater, Roessler made numerous important contacts at the highest levels of society. In 1933 after Hitler came to power, Nazi Alfred Rosenberg ousted Roessler as manager of the Buehnenvolksbund and took over the lucrative theater business for himself, which turned Roessler into an implacable Nazi foe.

The Roesslers immigrated to Lucerne where Rudolf set up the Vita Nova with the help of a Swiss friend, Xaver Schnieper. Roessler and Schnieper first met in Berlin. The latter attended school at Berlin University and initiated the contact after reading and admiring Roessler's writings. Although Roessler was thirteen years older than Schnieper, they remained close friends until Roessler died in 1958. Vita Nova, which specialized in books with a Christian slant, paid the bills but little more. Later, Roessler published a magazine, *Die Entscheidung* (The Decision), to which both men contributed. The articles were of a religious and philosophical nature until, at some point in the late thirties, Roessler, under a pseudonym, began writing distinctly political articles about current affairs inside Germany that contained sensitive information obviously leaked by highly placed government insiders opposed to the Nazi regime. (This was well before Bletchley Park had broken the German Enigma cipher.)

With the onset of war, the articles delved ever more deeply into Hitler's grand strategies and military plans. Although Roessler recognized the importance of the information flowing in, he did not quite know what to do with it, but his friend Schnieper did. Called to military duty in Switzerland, Schnieper was assigned to an unofficial intelligence agency, known as Bureau Ha, located not far from Roessler on Lake Lucerne and headed by Hans Hausamann, a freelance agent. Bureau Ha, in fact, was Hausamann's creature. The "Ha" is nothing more than the German pronunciation of the letter H—for Hausamann, who ran a successful business in photographic and optical equipment. Using his own money, Hausamann started spying even before the war because neutral Switzerland did not have an intelligence service worthy of the name and he perceived a need to keep an eye on his nation's bellicose Axis neighbors. He developed an extensive network of informers inside Germany, Austria, and Italy and forged ties with British, French, and Czech intelligence and even the communist agent Puenter. In the custom of espionage, Hausamann exchanged information with friendly foreign agents and treated it as a commodity for barter.

When the war started, Switzerland's chief intelligence officer, Roger Masson, built up the official agency, Swiss Military Intelligence, to a more respectable level. He left Bureau Ha in limbo outside the government, however, the better to preserve the appearance of Swiss neutrality while Hausamann's agents dug up secrets in the fascist countries. Bureau Ha remained Hausamann's private spy network, and Roessler became a contributor. Initially, Hausamann passed the information on to Masson. Soon, Roessler was also dealing directly with the official agency, usually through Maj. Mayr von Baldeck. Roessler's intelligence was passed on to the British through a Czech agent, Karel Sedlacek (alias Karl Selzinger, alias "Uncle Tom").[11] Sedlacek was well connected to both Swiss Military Intelligence and Bureau Ha, and he knew Roessler. His superior, Gen. Frantisek Moravec, who had sent him to Switzerland in 1937, worked from exile in London during the war under the aegis of British intelligence.

Roessler's information, however, was not as useful to the British as it would become to the Soviets. It fell into Soviet hands through the agent Taylor (Schneider), a translator at the ILO. How Roessler and Schneider came together is told by British authors Anthony Read and David Fisher.[12] Sometime early in the war, Schneider answered a help-wanted ad placed by Roessler for a part-time proofreader at the Vita Nova. They met and made a deal. Working out of his home in Geneva, Schneider traveled back and forth to Lucerne to pick up and return galley sheets. He and Roessler often talked politics during these exchanges, which continued until sometime in the spring of 1941 when each realized the other had a secret life. Roessler complained that the Swiss were not putting his intelligence to best use, and Schneider offered him a channel to Moscow.

It was a tortuous channel. Contrary to some accounts of Die Rote Drei, Roessler never dealt directly with the chief of the apparat. Rado, who ran the Lucy ring, never met the man called Lucy (Roessler) who made it famous. Lucy passed his information to the man called Taylor (Schneider), and Rado "did not even know of Taylor's existence" until the summer of 1942.[13] Taylor turned it over to the woman called Sissy (Duebendorfer), who passed it to Rado (the man called Dora). Rado condensed it, encoded it, and turned it over to his radio operators for transmission to Moscow. Foote (cover name "Jim"), a fast, tireless, competent worker held in high regard by Moscow, was soon handling all the Lucy messages and also did some of the encrypting. Rado said he never found out who Roessler's sources were, but for the sake of organizing the information, he gave them "suitably allusive" code names. Information from the German army high command was code-named "Werther," from the air force high command, "Olga," and from the Foreign Office, "Anna." Other code names— "Teddy," "Ferdinand," "Stefan," and "Fanny"—referred "not to persons but to sources of information."[14]

Rado learned of Taylor's existence before he did Lucy's. During the summer of 1942, Taylor was given as the source of information received from Sissy. When Rado relayed the information to Moscow, the Center (GRU headquarters) became quite excited about its quality. As far as it knew, the information was coming from Taylor, but Rado was skeptical. What he had learned of Taylor's rather narrow life did not square with the high-grade military intelligence submitted. Were Nazi agents planting it? When pressed, Taylor acknowledged he was getting it from a friend in Lucerne who had sworn him to secrecy. Then, in November, he informed Sissy that his friend was ready to become a regular contributor to Die Rote Drei. Without knowing his true identity, Rado codenamed him after the city where he worked, and that's how Lucy was born.[15] Lucy's service to the Soviets had the acquiescence, if not the blessing, of Swiss Intelligence, according to Dallin, "and no doubt . . . the knowledge of British Intelligence chiefs in Switzerland."[16]

Although Roessler insisted that he and his sources remain anonymous, the GRU nonetheless bent over backward to find out who he was and where he was coming from because it had found errors in one of his reports late in 1942.[17] That must have aroused fears, familiar in the spy business, that Lucy was a double agent planted by the enemy to feed disinformation. The GRU put heavy pressure on Rado, Duebendorfer, and even Duebendorfer's live-in lover, Paul Boettcher, to ferret out more details about him. If Duebendorfer had not defied her masters in Moscow, the GRU might have succeeded. At one point, the Center warned Duebendorfer that the Gestapo might be on her trail and ordered her to go into hiding for two or three months and turn over the Taylor-Lucy group to someone else. She perceived a clumsy ploy to take away her agents and refused to comply, whereupon Moscow scolded her for "frivolous and irresponsible" behavior.[18] Ultimately, the GRU had to accept Lucy's terms. His sources remain a matter of speculation to this day, a subject addressed later in this chapter.

Confusion abounds about Lucy's accomplishments. In his memoir, *Codename Dora,* Rado documents Lucy's intelligence reports pertaining to the Russo-German war by citing specific radio messages between himself and the GRU chief in Moscow. Normally, that would be the best kind of evidence; however, Rado's correspondence with Moscow cannot be taken at face value. Rado did not keep a personal file because of the obvious danger of its falling into unfriendly hands in the event of his arrest. Rather, he received the documents long after the fact from "the Moscow journalist W. G. Alexandrov."[19] In the Cold War atmosphere of 1971, when Rado published his book, Soviet journalists were government employees. "Moscow journalist" could only be a euphemism for KGB, the Soviet secret police. The documents could have been fabricated, doctored, or even genuine, but, most important, they had to serve the interests of the Soviet state. Those cited by Rado tend to strengthen the Lucy legend.

The CIA grappled with the Lucy legend in *The Rote Kapella,* its study of Soviet espionage in Europe before and during World War II. It managed to accumulate a small percentage of Die Rote Drei radio traffic from outside the Soviet orbit. Of an estimated 5,500 messages exchanged between the Center in Moscow and the Rado network in Switzerland, the CIA collected from various sources were "437 messages that appear authentic," 8 percent of the presumed total. With this 8 percent, it professes to have resolved some of the mysteries of the Lucy ring and indicates that the whole truth could be unraveled with the remaining 92 percent. Despite the huge quantity of missing traffic, the CIA carefully takes credit for "the first account of the Rote Drei that is not based chiefly on speculation, fantasy, and falsification."[20] Unfortunately, it focuses largely on the structure and operation of Die Rote Drei and pays scant attention to Lucy's real accomplishments. It is on the quality of his information, however, that the issue of Lucy's real value turns.

Rado confirms that his apparat in Switzerland, like those in France, Germany, and Japan, gave timely warning of the German invasion of the Soviet Union. (Stalin, of course, ignored them all.) But did the warning come from Lucy? On this question, most authors say that it did, based on the testimony of Lucy's first "spin doctor," Alexander Foote, in his *Handbook for Spies* published in 1947, but the CIA offers strong contradictory evidence. Rado remembers sending several messages to Moscow during the winter and spring of 1941 that indicated a German buildup in the east. His sources include a Swiss army officer, a German officer, and two agents cover-named "Gabel" and "Poisson." On June 17, five days before the invasion, Rado said he learned from Duebendorfer that a hundred German divisions were massed on the Soviet frontier. She told Rado the information was from "one of her people who had been in Germany on business." Soon afterward, Rado said, one of Duebendorfer's agents pinpointed the date of the attack, June 22, 1941.[21] More than a year later, she explained that her information had come from Taylor (Lucy was still unknown to Duebendorfer and Rado). But the CIA disputes Rado's claim based on a message from the "Director to Dora for Sissy" of October 8, 1942, which refers to "Taylor" as a "new" worker. From that, *The Rote Kapella* concludes, "Moscow received no messages from Lucy and his sub-sources until [the summer of 1942]," more than a year after the German invasion began.[22]

Next to Lucy, probably the most valuable of Rado's informers was the Frenchman George Blun, whose network reached into the German emigré community in Switzerland, the Vatican, Swedish and Austrian business circles, the German Foreign Office in Berlin, the Hungarian diplomatic corps, Swiss Intelligence, the French resistance, and the Vichy government. He was also in touch with a first-rate German journalist, Ernst Lemmer of the *Neue Zuericher Zeitung* (cover name "Agnes"), who worked in Berlin and often traveled to Switzerland.[23] Blun joined Die Rote Drei in October 1941 as the Wehrmacht was bearing down on Moscow. According to Rado, Blun reported heavy German attrition at a time when the German war machine appeared invincible.[24]

The following summer (1942), the Wehrmacht launched its southern offensive toward Stalingrad and the oil fields of the Caucusus. As the Germans raced across the vast Russian steppes, the GRU began to take notice of information attributed to Taylor. In Rado's words, the GRU director "showed quite exceptional interest" and wanted more. Taylor's source, Lucy, soon came forward, and the two became the "Taylor-Lucy group," with Lucy still in the background in Moscow's eyes. On this much, Rado and the CIA seem to agree, but Rado goes on to mention one Lucy report that seems not to fit. Lucy allegedly advised that the German right flank was unprotected near a wild semidesert region, southeast of Stalingrad, known as the Black Fields, and that it became the position from which the Red Army launched the southern jaw of the pincer that enveloped the German Sixth Army.[25] Without question, that was valuable information, but it seems more likely to have come from local intelligence, such as air reconnaissance, ground patrol, or the interrogation of captured enemy soldiers.

Greater things were yet to come in the Lucy legend. By the spring of 1943, the German Sixth Army had been swallowed whole at Stalingrad and the Wehrmacht hurled back 200 to 300 miles. The front stabilized with the Red Army holding a large salient near Kursk, which bulged 100 miles wide and 100 miles deep between two German army groups. The Soviets poured large quantities of men and armor into the salient that threatened new danger for the battered Germans. Hitler replenished his army with younger, less experienced men, so that it was larger in numbers but sharply reduced in quality by the loss of veteran soldiers. From his safe haven far behind the front lines and surrounded by compliant generals, Hitler thought he saw an opportunity to encircle the Soviet forces in the Kursk salient and regain the initiative lost at Stalingrad. In his Operational Order Number Six on April 15, 1943, he outlined the plan of attack. The northern jaw of a giant German pincer, consisting of fifteen divisions (eight armored) of the Ninth Army under Col. Gen. Walter Model, would set out toward the southeast from the vicinity of Orel. The southern jaw with eighteen divisions (eleven armored) of Col. Gen. Hermann Hoth's Fourth Panzer Army would strike northeastward from Kharkov. They were to meet near Kursk. There is no doubt that news of the plan, code-named *"Zitadelle"* (Citadel), soon reached Moscow. Many authors say the news came from Lucy, but not even Rado confirms that. He says only that the Center pressed him for details from Lucy.[26]

The attack, originally scheduled for April, was repeatedly put off until it was finally launched in July. Throughout that period, Rado supplied the Center with a succession of intelligence reports important to Soviet planning. By Rado's account, a large share of it came from Roessler's sources and included information about German intentions, the order of battle, the status of reserves, the composition of General Hoth's Fourth Panzer Army, the production and delivery of tanks and war planes, the specifications and performance ratings of the new Tiger tank and a new Messerschmidt fighter, the deployment of German long-range bombers, and the effects of Soviet and Allied bombing raids on German industrial targets.[27] That kind of information, if true, would make Lucy look very good, but it came from Rado's tainted KGB source. More recently, an American scholar, Timothy P. Mulligan, reviewed the available traffic between Rado and the GRU director in Moscow and concluded that the input of Lucy and his subsources alone "cannot have provided the decisive intelligence for a Soviet victory at Kursk."[28] The available traffic amounts to no more than 8 percent of the total, however, which allows for a less than satisfactory conclusion. That Lucy was very important to Moscow is demonstrated beyond doubt by the Center's praise of his good work and its willingness to pay well for his information.[29]

Lucy was probably not the Soviets' best source of long-range intelligence for the Battle of Kursk, and he was certainly not the only source. In the months prior to Kursk, the Soviet spy agency (NKVD People's Commissariat for Internal Affairs) received a steady stream of first-rate intelligence from a mole inside the British codebreaking agency at Bletchley Park. The mole, John Cairncross, was one of the famous Cambridge spies sucked into the Soviet secret service prior to World War II. Cairncross spent nearly a year analyzing decrypted Luftwaffe intercepts that he smuggled out of Bletchley for his Soviet controller to copy and forward to Moscow. Perhaps his most important contributions were a series of intercepts exposing a German air buildup before the battle.

The Soviets launched preemptive raids against seventeen airfields identified by Cairncross that stretched from Smolensk in the north to the Sea of Azov and destroyed more than five hundred German aircraft.[30] For all the help supplied by Roessler and Cairncross, however, the Red Army probably gained its most useful intelligence for the Battle of Kursk from its assets in place, such as Soviet signal intelligence, air photo reconnaissance, ground patrols, and the interrogation of prisoners.[31]

The German High Command expected the Red Army to launch preemptive strikes to disrupt its preparations for the offensive, but the Soviet military planners decided to absorb the initial blows and then counterattack. To blunt the German thrusts, the Soviets built formidable defensive works consisting of well-placed trenches, which would have stretched hundreds of miles if fitted end to end, bolstered with thousands of tank traps, antitank and antipersonnel mines, artillery pieces, antitank guns, and Katyusha rocket launchers. There were three defensive zones, each 3 miles deep, thus fortified. The second was 7 miles behind the first and the third, 20 miles behind the second, for a total of more than 35 miles. If the Germans managed to penetrate that far, they would meet the Soviet reserves, also dug in and heavily armed.[32] Hoth's Fourth Panzer Army moved out early in the morning of July 4 and drove 20 miles by the 9th. Model's Ninth Army attacked on July 5 and advanced only 6 miles before grinding to a halt with heavy losses. The Soviets counterattacked on July 12. The Battle of Kursk featured the largest tank engagement in the history of warfare, three thousand German tanks pitted against four thousand tanks on the Soviet side. The Germans lost nearly all of theirs. After a week, Hitler came to terms with his defeat and called off the attack. In reality, the German army was already in full retreat in the southern and central sectors. It never again regained the initiative that Hitler had risked everything to achieve.

From the pinnacle of success in the Battle of Kursk, Die Rote Drei was destined for a mighty fall.[33] The Gestapo was hot on the trail of the Soviet apparat in Switzerland, even as it was mopping up the Red spy rings in Germany, Belgium, Holland, and France. The Gestapo unit, known as the Sonderkommando, assigned to track down the Red Orchestra in the occupied countries was under new leadership. Karl Giering had been in charge until the summer of 1943. Now, dying of cancer, he was forced to retire, his place taken by Heinz Pannwitz, a former Christian seminarian who gave up his theological studies to join the Gestapo. When Pannwitz arrived in France, most of the Red Orchestra leaders were already in custody. He used imprisoned leaders to play the *Funkspiel* (radio playback game) with Moscow and, in that way, uncovered more communist cells in the French underground. At the same time, he tried his hand at penetrating Die Rote Drei. It was a difficult task, given that Switzerland was a neutral country where the Gestapo could not operate openly.

Victor Sukulov (cover name "Kent") became one of Pannwitz's more cooperative prisoners. During 1940–41, Sukulov had been the No. 2 agent of the Red Orchestra in Western Europe and leader of the Belgian apparat. Under orders from the GRU director, he went to Geneva in 1940 to give Rado his code and transmission timetable. He knew a lot about the leader of Die Rote Drei—Rado's name; cover name; address; profession; and, most important, the key to his code. What he knew, he readily betrayed to the Gestapo.

In the summer of 1943, Pannwitz sent an agent to Geneva to look up a Rote Drei cutout recommended by Sukulov. The agent pretended to be a member of the French apparat sent by Leopold Trepper ("Le Grand Chef") to make personal contact with Rado. When Rado heard this, he smelled a rat and ordered the cutout to break off the contact. Pannwitz next devised a plan to kidnap Alexander Foote, Rado's best radio operator who also handled funds supplied by Moscow for transfer to the communist resistance in France. Sukulov, still doing the *Funkspiel,* sent word to Moscow that the French Communist Party was desperately short of funds. The Center answered by ordering Sukulov to dispatch a courier to Geneva to rendezvous with Foote. Of course, the courier was a Gestapo agent. When they met, the courier handed Foote a book wrapped in bright orange paper. Inside were three enciphered messages with what the courier said was valuable information that Foote was to send off immediately to Moscow. He then arranged a future meeting with Foote at a place in Geneva near the French frontier. Foote was suspicious from the start. First, the man talked too much for a Soviet agent. Second, Foote recognized that the brightly wrapped book would serve as a beacon for anyone who might follow him. Third, the messages in a cipher he did not know could help German monitors identify his transmitter. Finally, he was wary of meeting so close to the French frontier where he might easily be snatched. On his way home he hid the book under his coat and took an evasive course. When he informed the GRU of his experience, it agreed that his contact was a Gestapo agent; ordered him not to meet with him again; and cautioned him that, having been seen by the enemy, he had been compromised to some extent.

Pannwitz was getting nowhere, so Berlin took its effort against Die Rote Drei to another level. Walter Schellenberg, head of the SD, made several trips to Lucerne in 1943 to urge Masson, his Swiss counterpart, to take action against the Soviet apparat. Masson politely refused. Word soon leaked back to Swiss intelligence, however, that Hitler had ordered preparations for the military occupation of Switzerland, the only unoccupied country left in Europe with a sizable German-speaking population. The threat loomed large in September 1943 when Italy capitulated and the Germans committed a sizable force to the Italian front.

Within days of the Italian surrender, Swiss monitors were tracking Die Rote Drei transmitters. A few weeks later, an agitated Margrit Bolli informed Rado that she had observed strangers watching her apartment. He ordered her to stop transmitting at once and go into hiding at her parents' home in Basel, but she disobeyed him and went to stay with her lover, Hans Peters, who was a Gestapo mole. The Hamels continued to beep away until the Swiss Bundespolizei (BUPO) mounted a raid in mid-October and arrested them. The BUPO then tracked Bolli to her Geneva hideaway. She broke down under questioning and identified Rado as the leader of the spy network. When Rado learned this from a BUPO informant, he and his family went underground. Five weeks later, it was Foote's turn to greet the BUPO. As the police were breaking down the entrance to his building, he calmly set fire to the enciphered messages on his desk. When they entered his apartment, he politely offered them drinks. They refused and carted him off to jail. In April 1944, the police arrested Rachel Duebendorfer. Papers found in her apartment led them to Schneider and Roessler. Die Rote Drei was history.

The experience of the Soviet spies rounded up by the Swiss was literally a world apart from that of most agents captured by the Gestapo. Two thirds of the latter were either executed or died in prison. By the summer of 1944, the Swiss felt safe from German invasion, and Duebendorfer, Bolli, the Hamels, Foote, Roessler, and Schneider were all released on bail to await trial. Foote was advised sotto voce to get lost. He slipped across the border to France and made his way to the reopened Soviet Embassy in Paris.

There he met Rado, who had successfully evaded arrest, and Trepper, who, as a prisoner, had cooperated with the Gestapo and then escaped. They returned to Moscow, where both served lengthy prison terms, Trepper for betraying members of his network, and Rado for contacting the British during his fugitive days and suggesting to the GRU that he seek British diplomatic protection as the only means of continuing his espionage activity, for which the GRU had accused him of "an unprecedented breach of discipline." Rado was also suspected of diverting GRU funds for his private use.

Foote received high marks from the GRU and, after recovering from illness, was sent on a Cold War spy mission. But while stopping over in Berlin in 1947 he defected to the British. Duebendorfer also fled—to East Germany—and later vanished. Reportedly, she had also cooperated with British intelligence, which might have had something to do with her disappearance. Both Roessler and Schneider stood trial, but only Schneider did time—thirty days. Roessler went free because the court determined that he had acted in the best interest of the Swiss state. (Later, during the Cold War, he was caught spying for communist Czechoslovakia against the West and received a one-year sentence.) Bolli and the Hamels also stood trial in 1945, were convicted of espionage, and served a year or less in prison.

Rado has rightly stated, "[O]n the subject of Lucy and his sources the record is a pretty tangled and distorted one."[34] Rado did not learn Lucy's true identity until Roessler's arrest in 1944, and Roessler refused to reveal his sources. In more than a half century since, there has been much controversy over the issue, most of it fueled by speculation and distortion. By the nature of Roessler's information, it is widely (but not universally) assumed that it came from inside the German government, especially from key anti-Hitler officers in the German High Command. But who? And how did it get from Berlin to Lucerne?

Accoce and Quet assert in their book, first published in French in 1966, that Lucy's sources were ten former army buddies, half of whom the authors identified by first name and initial and the other half simply by one initial.[35] They describe how two of these friends, "Rudolf G." and "Fritz T.," paid Roessler a visit in 1939 as the war was approaching and promised to send him Germany's greatest military secrets to give away or sell as he wished, preferably to "the staunchest enemies of Nazism." They allegedly gave him the parts for a two-way radio that they had smuggled into Switzerland. Roessler, they said, promised to have Christian Schneider assemble it and teach him how it worked so he could operate it himself.[36] The book met with a chorus of criticism for factual errors, although most observers believe the authors had one basic fact right: Lucy's information came from inside the Reich. Rado, for one, doubted the "radio hypothesis" because, if Lucy's source(s) inside Germany had used it on a regular basis, the Gestapo surely would have tracked it down as it did the other transmitters of the Red networks. Besides, Rado said, he knew "for a certainty" that Schneider "had not the vaguest notion of radio technology" and had been told that Roessler did not know how to use the radio either.[37] Stung by the fallout from their book, Accoce and Quet backed off and admitted that they had made up the whole story.[38]

Spy fiction, however, does not die easily—at least, this fiction did not. The Accoce-Quet story line was subsequently picked up by others, including British author V. E. Tarrant, whose well-organized book, *The Red Orchestra,* published in 1995, gives a polished version of the radio hypothesis and cites Accoce and Quet as his source.[39] Tarrant even identified the two friends who visited Roessler in 1939 as Col. Rudolf Gersdorff and Lt. Gen. Fritz Thiele. This is not an illogical inference if you buy the original story line. Thiele and Gersdorff were prominent figures in the anti-Hitler conspiracy. Thiele, as second in command of the Wehrmacht's signals branch, had a key role in the July 20, 1944, plot to assassinate Hitler. Gersdorff attempted to kill the Fuehrer in 1943 by suicide bombing. Tarrant adds to his narrative the name of another key conspirator, Gen. Erich Fellgiebel, the Reich's chief signals officer and Thiele's superior. Even though Fellgiebel does not fit the clues offered by Accoce and Quet, the idea that he and Thiele worked together to inform Lucy is plausible but still only conjecture. Tarrant offers no credible support for his hypothesis.

British authors Read and Fisher construct a very different scenario.[40] The sources of Lucy's information, they say in their book, *Operation Lucy,* published in 1981, were the codebreakers at Bletchley Park. Allegedly, British intelligence delivered the information to the Soviets through Alexander Foote, who, the authors claim, was really a double agent under British control. For backup, according to Read and Fisher, the British used Rachel Duebendorfer (Sissy)— who allegedly had been turned into a double agent because she needed the money—and the Czech agent Karel Sedlacek. The idea that the Lucy material came from the British Ultra was earlier advanced by Malcolm Muggeridge in 1967 in the Sunday *Observer*[41] and by Richard Deacon in *A History of the British Secret Service* published in 1969.[42]

The weight of testimony seems to tip the other way but with some loose ends. Rado called the Ultra scenario "the most fantastic hypothesis of all."[43] Nigel West interviewed former SIS operatives who flatly denied that Foote was ever a British agent.[44] Duebendorfer and Sedlacek, however, are not so easily dismissed. In the investigation leading to her trial in Switzerland in 1945, Duebendorfer allegedly confessed in writing to being a British spy. (She never showed up for the trial and later disappeared behind the Iron Curtain.)[45] Sedlacek had close ties to British intelligence and easily could have fed information either way.[46]

The spy business aside, British historian Hinsley also rejects the claim that Britain used the Lucy ring to forward intelligence to Moscow.[47] It did so without Lucy. Ultra decrypts were passed directly to Soviet intelligence (in revised form to cover the source) at the insistence of Churchill and in spite of the difficult relationship between British and Soviet intelligence agencies. On the other hand, there is an uncanny correlation between the capabilities of Ultra and the highly acclaimed performance of the Lucy ring during the Kursk phase of the war. In a recent book, *Codebreakers,* that takes a fascinating look inside Bletchley Park, Hinsley, a consummate insider, reveals that intelligence of very high quality came out of the British cryptanalytic attack on the German Army teleprinter cipher. At the end of April 1943, Bletchley achieved its first breakthrough on the Soviet front between Berlin and Army Group South. "Its earliest decrypts," Hinsley says, "gave full details of the plans for the German counteroffensive against the Kursk salient."[48] Other breaks followed that yielded "comprehensive intelligence about developments on [the eastern] fronts."[49] Common sense dictates that, in its own vital interest, Britain would have forwarded that information to the Soviet Union, one way or another. There is no direct evidence, however, that it went through the Red network in Switzerland.

The CIA made a serious attempt in 1979 to nail down Lucy's sources in its history of the Soviet intelligence networks in Europe, *The Rote Kapella,* based on the assumption that the information came from inside Germany and not from British Ultra. In the book, the CIA states, "Despite the printed assertions to the contrary, Rudolf Roessler *did* divulge the identity of his sources, or at least some of them" (emphasis by CIA). He did so to a trusted friend three and a half years before his death. That friend was the son of Xaver Schnieper. According to the younger Schnieper, Roessler listed the sources as follows: "(1) a German major . . . who had been chief of the Abwehr before Adm. Wilhelm Canaris assumed command; (2) Hans Bernd Gisevius; (3) Carl Goerdeler; and (4) 'Gen. Boelitz, deceased.'"[50] Contrary to Rado's testimony that he located the sources of information within the German government by such code names as "Werther," "Olga," "Anna," and "Teddy," the CIA insists that these code names referred to real people. This is not necessarily a conflict. Rado could perceive the nature of the information without knowing who was behind it and give it a code name strictly for convenience. Whether it came from one individual or many makes no difference, but, ever since, the world has been searching for the identity of the real people. On that question, the CIA might know something Rado admitted that he did not know.

The first mentioned of the individual sources is perhaps the most important. Canaris's predecessor as Abwehr chief was Conrad Patzig, an admiral like himself and an unlikely candidate. The CIA believes that Roessler was referring to Hans Oster, a major under Patzig, who rose in rank and favor under Canaris. Oster was the nerve center of the anti-Hitler conspiracy during its early years. His lines of communication reached to all of the important elements of the conspiracy: the Army General Staff, the Foreign Office, the crime police, and such key figures as Gen. Ludwig Beck, Gen. Erwin von Witzleben, and the prominent politician Goerdeler. From 1936 to 1943, Oster used his high position in military intelligence to plan and coordinate Hitler's overthrow. The plots all failed for one reason or another, and the frustrated Oster went beyond conspiring against the Nazi government to acts of treason against the German nation. He gave advance warning of the 1940 German offensive in the West to his close personal friend Col. J. G. Sas, the Dutch military attaché in Berlin, and urged him to pass the information on to other targeted nations. He also made sure that the British received the information by way of a link he had forged through the Vatican. So, the fact that Oster gave German military plans to Germany's enemies is well established. It is entirely possible he opened still another channel to the outside through Roessler, but nobody knows this for sure.

It is difficult to imagine in one sense. Oster was politically conservative and what is known of his outreach was all in the direction of the capitalist West and not the communist East. Given his abhorrence of the Nazis, however, a turn to the East is not beyond the pale. If Oster was a source for Lucy, his contributions stopped before the Battle of Kursk because the Gestapo ousted him from his Abwehr position on April 5, 1943, and placed him under house arrest. This means that he had to have passed the baton to someone else at the very time Roessler was allegedly feeding Die Rote Drei the critical intelligence so vital to the Soviet triumph at Kursk.

Gisevius, another very likely connection to Roessler, was working for the Gestapo as a lawyer when he met Oster early in the Nazi era, 1933 or 1934, and supplied him with documentation of Nazi crimes. He and Oster were close, and they hated the Nazis with an equal passion. Even before the war, Gisevius spent time in Switzerland where he kept Western diplomats informed about events inside Germany. He went to work for the Abwehr in 1939. After the fall of France in 1940, Canaris and Oster assigned him to the German Embassy in Zurich where he could operate under diplomatic cover. He knew Roessler, so the opportunity was there to establish a regular channel of communications. The CIA believes that the important documents that came into Roessler's possession were smuggled out of Germany in the Abwehr's diplomatic pouch rather than transmitted by radio, as many authors have claimed.

It is not as easy to imagine Goerdeler as more than an occasional informer, but the possibility of a closer tie to Lucy cannot be ruled out because Goerdeler knew Roessler, just as Gisevius did. A political conservative, former mayor of Leipzig, and a member of the early Hitler cabinet, Goerdeler was the most important civilian in the anti-Hitler conspiracy and, from the very first failed coup attempt in 1938, was slated to be chancellor in any post-Nazi government. Neither Gisevius nor Goerdeler was in a position to obtain high-grade military intelligence firsthand, so if they informed Roessler on these matters they were go-betweens (or "cutouts" in the jargon of spying) carrying the information from better-placed sources. The fourth person named by Roessler, "Gen. Boelitz, deceased," was unknown to the CIA.

If the names given by the CIA are accurate, it does not appear possible those people could have been the only ones involved. For history's sake, it is too bad that Die Rote Drei ceased to exist in the fall of 1943. If the "music" from Die Rote Drei's radio transmissions had stopped in late July 1944, there could have been no doubt about Lucy's sources. That was when the Gestapo started rounding up the anti-Hitler conspirators implicated in the assassination attempt of July 20. By that time, the Red spy ring in Switzerland had been broken up. The music had already stopped.

Although Rado had the grace to admit that he knew nothing of Roessler's sources, he seemed to accept the idea that they were among the anti-Hitler conspirators in and around the German High Command. Rado said that he wrote his book in the spirit of setting the record straight, and he did offer a few comments that helped to clarify some of the issues. Foote, in *Handbook for Spies,* claims that reports from Berlin were reaching Lucy within twenty-four hours. Accoce and Quet shrank the interval to as little as six hours. Not so, said Rado, who writes that, on March 10, 1943, the Center asked Lucy to date the origin of his reports to learn how fresh they were. From that, Rado was able to estimate that Lucy's reports took three to six days from the date of their dispatch from Berlin to the date of his transmission to Moscow.[51] This was too much time to be sent by radio and, Rado believed, too little time for the enormous volumes of information to go by diplomatic pouch.[52]

Rado quotes Roessler's close friend Xaver Schnieper from a broadcast on Swiss television in May 1966 for what he called the "unequivocal answer" to the question of how the material reached Lucy. Schnieper said the reports went by way of "the Wehrmacht's service telephone line" from Berlin to Milan and were forwarded from Milan to Lucerne by courier.[53] "Service telephone line" could mean a teleprinter hooked up by landline (teleprinter messages could go by either landline or radio). A teleprinter could accommodate large volumes of copy in a relatively short time. Also, the fact that it went by landline, rather than through the ether, would account for the failure of German Signals Security to pick up the wireless transmissions because there would have been none! Sending German army secrets to the German army in Italy would be a routine matter. A well-situated conspirator in Milan might easily lift them and turn them over to the couriers. It was then a six-hour journey by road through the porous Swiss frontier to Lucerne. But that, too, is mere speculation.

Roessler might or might not have been a master spy, but he proved to be a master at keeping secrets.

PART 4

THE PACIFIC WAR

CHAPTER 10

Infamy and
Sacred Duty

When his ears caught the first distant thud of an exploding bomb shortly before 8 A.M. on December 7, 1941, Takeo Yoshikawa thought the Americans might be conducting military maneuvers. On hearing more explosions, he entertained another possibility. He rose from the breakfast table and looked out the window of his cottage on the grounds of the Japanese Consulate in Honolulu. What he saw off to the west put a thrill into the pit of his stomach. Plumes of black smoke were rising over Pearl Harbor. His elation stemmed from both nationalistic pride and personal vindication. Yoshikawa, then only twenty-seven years old, had been the key Pearl Harbor spy. He had set up the American targets that carrier-based Japanese planes now pounded with bombs and torpedoes. He had spent five years in Japanese Naval Intelligence concentrating exclusively on the study of the U.S. Navy in the Pacific. Using the pseudonym Tadashi Morimura, he had come to Honolulu the previous March under diplomatic cover. With the skill and confidence that comes with a thorough knowledge of his subject, he had kept watch on Pearl Harbor and other naval, air, and military installations in Hawaii. Now, he was witnessing the climax of his minidrama on the stage of world history.

Born in 1914, Yoshikawa grew up on the island of Shikoku southwest of Tokyo in a culture that revered the Samurai warrior. His father was a policeman, a respected protector of Imperial Law. As a youth, Takeo absorbed bushido, the creed of the Samurai, and Zen Buddhism, which together forged in him the principles of self-discipline, absolute loyalty, and devotion beyond self. He learned the military arts, became a champion at kendo (stick fencing), and could swim up to 8 miles at a stretch in the choppy Inner Sea off Shikoku's coast. He chose a naval career, and, at the age of sixteen, entered Eta Jima, the Japanese naval academy, where, he said, "my education in bushido was completed."[1]

Upon graduation in 1933, Ensign Yoshikawa embarked on what he had every reason to believe would be a successful and fulfilling career. But fate—and hard drinking—dealt him a severe setback. He was stricken with a stomach ailment the following year and removed from active duty. Forced to retire, he returned glumly to civilian life in his native Shikoku. Within weeks, however, he was asked to resume active duty as a naval intelligence officer without hope of promotion beyond the rank of ensign. He jumped at the opportunity.

At the 3d Division (Intelligence) of the Navy General Staff in Tokyo, Yoshikawa served for a time in the British section, then switched to the American desk where he stayed without interruption from 1936 to 1941. It was not a time of high excitement for Yoshikawa. A bachelor in his twenties, he devoted himself to the study of the American fleets and bases at Pearl Harbor, Manila, and Guam and to improving his English. Early on, he perceived the business of espionage to be "a hard and thankless one, based solidly on scholarly research, meticulous observation, and the painstaking attention to detail."[2] He devoured anything in print that pertained to his subject—newspapers, books, journals, especially *Jane's Fighting Ships and Aircraft* and the *U.S. Naval Institute Proceedings.* He frequently visited the offices of foreign naval attachés in Tokyo for any unclassified information he could find. He pored over reports from Japanese agents abroad and from naval attachés in foreign capitals. By 1939, he was "the Naval General Staff's acknowledged American expert—I knew by then every U.S. man-of-war and aircraft type by name, hull number, configuration, and technical characteristics; and I knew, too, a great deal of general information about the U.S. naval bases at Manila, Guam, and Pearl Harbor."[3]

At the end of 1939, he was pronounced "ready" for foreign assignment, but he did not learn until the following August that he was going to Hawaii. Another eight months elapsed before he set sail as Vice Consul Morimura on board the *Nitta Maru* with first-class accommodations and a seat for dinner at the captain's table. When the liner docked at Honolulu on March 27, 1941, Yoshikawa remained in his cabin as instructed until Vice Consul Otojiro Okuda came for him, draped a lei around his neck, and escorted him past customs to the consulate.

The two men had no idea, as they walked down the gangplank, that an American naval undercover agent was snapping their picture with a hidden camera. Counterintelligence had an interest in "Morimura" because he was not listed in the official Japanese Diplomatic Registry. The Americans wondered who he was. If not a diplomat, they reasoned, he must be a spy. Now that they had his picture, they would get to know him better in the months to come.[4]

Although Yoshikawa said he was never told, in so many words, that he would help set the stage for the opening battle of the Pacific War, his generation of naval officers assumed that Japan would go to war with the United States, just as American officers assumed that they were destined to fight a war with Japan. In Japanese eyes, the purpose of the U.S. Navy in the Western Pacific was to protect the expansion of American trade, a policy that conflicted with Japan's own aggressive geopolitical designs. As a resource-poor island nation, Japan saw its destiny tied to its own trade expansion.

The idea for a surprise attack on Pearl Harbor had been floating around Imperial Navy circles throughout the thirties—to the point even where it was simulated in naval war games—until finally it took shape in the mind of Adm. Isoroku Yamamoto, commander of the Combined Fleet. Yamamoto had studied, served, and traveled extensively in the United States and had gained a healthy respect for American industry. He did everything within his limited political power to dissuade Japan's ruling circles from going to war with America, but after losing that argument in a government dominated by the army, he made plans as best he could for the inevitable confrontation. He believed that his country's only hope to defeat the United States was to carry out a crippling strike against the powerful Pacific Fleet at Pearl Harbor. This, he thought, would buy Japan six months to establish a hold on resource-rich Southeast Asia and the Western Pacific islands. Success depended on the willingness of the United States to negotiate once Japan had carried out its "southern strategy." Yamamoto told his superiors that he could not predict ultimate victory if the war continued for two or three years, given the potential of American industry to shift into high gear for war. His strategic vision was clear, as far as he could see. What he did not anticipate was the electrifying effect of his "sneak attack" that fortified the American will to fight a long, savage conflict. Pearl Harbor accomplished a dramatic turnaround in American attitudes. It unified a divided and isolationist nation and ignited a fire in the collective belly to avenge the Japanese "infamy" and, in the bargain, to save Europe from Nazi Germany.

Inspired by the successful British strike at Taranto in November 1940, in which carrier-based planes crippled the Italian fleet, Yamamoto made his first formal suggestion for an air attack on Pearl Harbor in a paper submitted to the Navy Minister the following January. Six weeks later, tactical planning was turned over to one of Japan's most outstanding young naval officers, Cdr. Minoru Genda. From that time, Japan actively prepared for a Pearl Harbor strike, even though it had not finally decided to wage war against the United States. Yoshikawa knew nothing of these high-level decisions. In fact, his assignment to Hawaii had been decided before any specific plan to attack Pearl Harbor had taken shape, but he did not arrive until after the plan was formally adopted.

The Imperial Navy's special interest in Pearl Harbor dated from May 1940 when the U.S. Pacific Fleet moved its operating base from California to Hawaii. The Naval General Staff in Tokyo wanted regular reports on the American fleet's size, disposition, and activities in Hawaiian waters, and turned to a normal source on matters of espionage, the Foreign Office, which relayed the request to Consul General Kiichi Gunji in Honolulu. For Gunji, the assignment was not onerous. He had merely to read the Honolulu newspapers, which diligently reported all the necessary details, including the exact times of the warships' arrivals and departures.

When Gunji was transferred to Tokyo in September 1940, his deputy, Okuda, became acting consul general and also assumed the espionage duties. Okuda took more pains than Gunji to verify the press reports and sent consulate personnel to check the ships at Pearl Harbor. Eventually, newspaper coverage diminished under pressure from U.S. Navy officers worried about security implications, and Okuda came gradually to rely on his staff. He tapped the consulate's treasurer, Kohichi Seki, to be the principal scout, or "outside man." Seki had attended Eta Jima but had been discharged from the navy because of ill health. He spent a few weeks studying *Jane's Fighting Ships* before venturing upon his new duties. At first, working alone, Seki took cabs to Pearl Harbor and back. Soon he had a driver/guide, Richard Kotoshirodo, a

Nisei with dual citizenship, who knew the islands like a born Hawaiian, which he was.

The permanent consul general and coordinator of espionage, Nagao Kita, arrived two weeks ahead of Yoshikawa on March 14, 1941. Kita was carefully chosen for the job in light of Yamamoto's designs on Pearl Harbor. A portly, affable bachelor with a gregarious nature and a high tolerance for liquor, he seemed to follow intrigue as his specialty. The Imperial Navy saw to it that he was posted where it had need for good intelligence. Most recently, it was Canton, near the British colony of Hong Kong, and before that, Shanghai, once an open city where espionage had flourished until the city was captured by Japanese troops.

When Kita and Yoshikawa first met on the latter's arrival in Honolulu, neither knew much about the other. Yoshikawa wanted to make sure that Kita would not interfere with his mission, and Kita wondered if this kid had what it took to make a good spy. They soon developed a healthy respect for one another and a good working relationship. In Yoshikawa, the General Staff had put its most knowledgeable agent in a position to fill a critical need for the success of its Pearl Harbor plan—a steady flow of accurate, firsthand information. In his own words, Yoshikawa set out to give Tokyo a running account of "the number of ships present at Pearl Harbor at any given time; the number of aircraft present at the airports . . . and their dispersal patterns; naval sortie and movement patterns from Pearl; air defense readiness; and reconnaissance activities and security measures mounted against attack."[5]

After the war, Yoshikawa said that he worked "strictly alone." This is essentially true if one discounts Kotoshirodo and another driver, John Mikami, a resident alien who owned his own taxi. Very often, on field trips, one or the other was at the wheel. Kotoshirodo became sufficiently involved in the operation that he carried out assignments on his own at Kita's or Yoshikawa's direction. Sometimes during the earliest days, as Yoshikawa was getting familiar with the terrain, Seki also went along and remained available if needed. Kita, of course, made the decisions, but when he concluded that Yoshikawa measured up, he gave the eager young spy wide latitude.

There can be no doubt that Yoshikawa preferred his own company when it came to his mission. He was particularly leery of involving anyone from Hawaii's Japanese community. At the time, about 160,000 people of Japanese ancestry were living on the islands; about 35,000 had dual nationality. Yoshikawa, who handled the repatriation of Japanese nationals as his cover job, discovered to his horror that many of them were coming to the consulate to renounce their Japanese citizenship. He also attended Buddhist meetings and mingled with community leaders but found that "those men of influence and character who might have assisted me in my secret mission were unanimously uncooperative."[6]

Japan had possessed another intelligence asset in Hawaii since the late thirties, a German family consisting of Otto Kuehn, his wife Elfriede, a step-daughter Ruth, and a teenage son Eberhard. The Kuehns owned two houses on the windward side of Oahu, both of which had views of Kaneohe Naval Air Station and a Marine Corps training camp at Mokapu Point. Accounts vary as to the role of the Kuehns. Either they were paid to remain in deep cover or they engaged in active spying before and during Yoshikawa's arrival. Ruth, said to be a good-looker, allegedly gleaned intelligence, Mata Hari–style, by dating American sailors and later by operating a beauty parlor in Honolulu where navy wives came to be pampered. Yoshikawa knew of the Kuehns and was in contact with them, but he could hardly have trusted pillow talk and gossip for his reports to Tokyo.

———————

Kita assigned Yoshikawa separate quarters on the consulate grounds so that he could come and go as he pleased and paid no attention to staff complaints that "Morimura" was a goldbrick who spent very little time doing consular business. During Yoshikawa's first week, the chief took him to the Shunchu-ro teahouse at Alewa where he could mix business with pleasure. To Yoshikawa, it was a taste of home. The proprietress came from Shikoku (as did Kita), and the geishas were friendly. More important, a second-floor room overlooked Pearl Harbor.

Yoshikawa wasted little time getting down to the main business of staking out the American base. He discovered different vantage points. Aiea Heights offered a commanding view of the ships. He could identify them and take notes of where they were berthed and how they moved in and out of port. That is, he took notes in his head and retained the information until he could jot it down in the privacy of the consulate. For security reasons, he never used pencil and paper in public nor binoculars or cameras where they might look out of place. A few times, dressed in work clothes, he walked through Aiea's sugarcane fields to find better views of the harbor. Maybe he liked Aiea so much because the Shunchu-ro was nearby. He sometimes spent the night there, happily diverted. At dawn, he could watch ships maneuvering and planes taking off on patrol from the airstrip on Ford Island. For a close-up look at Ford Island and Battleship Row, he donned tourist clothes and went to the tip of the peninsula below Pearl City, but he was careful not to wear the same clothes on successive visits. He made friends with the Japanese proprietor of a soft drink stand in Pearl City, who did a steady business with sailors on shore leave. The best view of the submarine base, he found, was from the Kamehameha Highway between Aiea and Makalapa. He also made good use of his boyhood swimming prowess to observe the underwater obstructions, tides, and beach gradients, and, when the occasion called for it, he took boat rides to steal as close as he dared to naval shore installations. Several times, disguised as a Filipino laborer—unshaven, barefoot, and wearing aloha shirts—he tried to walk to the Pearl Harbor entrance to find out if there were antisubmarine nets, but never got close enough to make sure.

Other air bases were not easy to observe. Sometimes, Yoshikawa went from John Rodgers Airport in Honolulu on tourist flights over Oahu with its network of airfields and bases. One fall day, he treated a geisha friend to a plane ride and snapped aerial pictures of Hickam and Wheeler fields. Another time, the military command invited the public to "gala day" at Wheeler. "Chancellor Morimura," as Kita had dubbed him, cheerfully accepted the open invitation. He counted the hangars to estimate the number of airplanes inside, measured the runways in his head, and watched P-40s in flight. He was impressed by their speed and the skill of the fighter pilots. On two other occasions, Mikami drove him to Wahiawa near Wheeler and Schofield barracks in midisland. On one of these trips, they tried to enter Schofield, which had a large training preserve, but were turned back because Mikami's taxi did not have the proper license plates. Several times during the summer, they drove along the island's east shore on the Kokokahi Road past the Kaneohe Naval Air Station. Yoshikawa even took Mikami and two consular maids for an excursion across the bay in a glass-bottom boat. Peering through the bottom, he gauged the water's depth and concluded that Kaneohe Bay was too shallow to serve as an alternate anchorage for big navy ships.

Nor did Yoshikawa ignore the outer islands. In May, he and Kotoshirodo went as tourists to Maui to observe the deepwater port at Lahaina. The planners in Tokyo hoped the Pacific Fleet would prepare Lahaina as an alternate moorage because ships sent to the bottom there, in contrast to the shallow waters at Pearl Harbor, would sink so deep they could not be recovered. But Yoshikawa saw no sign of development. Later, the two of them covered the Island of Hawaii, and Kotoshirodo went on his own to Kawai. None of the outer islands turned up much more than a few good bars to soak up Yoshikawa's generous expense account.

To avoid suspicion and frustrate American counterintelligence, Yoshikawa was under strict orders to operate within the law. The Americans had a lively interest in the consulate. The U.S. Navy's District Intelligence Office (DIO) put taps on six consular phones, plus Okuda's private line, Kita's residence phone, and Yoshikawa's cottage phone, and recorded fifty or more conversations daily. Although the Americans did not follow Yoshikawa's every move, they knew enough to decide after three months that he was indeed a spy, the consulate's new "outside man." Neither did they try to arrest him, because he stayed within the law. Besides, they knew from codebreaking that Japan had spies watching other American bases on the West Coast and the Panama Canal. In that context, Yoshikawa's spying was nothing special at that time.

Theoretically, the consular spy was most vulnerable in his communications with Tokyo, which were coded and sent in diplomatic cipher through commercial channels. The interception and thoughtful analysis of these coded messages might have alerted the American naval and military leaders in Hawaii to expect the worst. American law, however, was on Japan's side. Section 605 of the Federal Communications Act of 1934 prohibited the interception of messages to or from a foreign country.[7] Private cable companies handled Japanese consular business in Honolulu on a rotating basis. For them to show Japanese diplomatic messages to American counterintelligence would put them outside the law that the Japanese spy strictly observed.

In Washington, the uniformed services finessed the law with the argument that messages sent by radio (as opposed to underwater cable) were not covered and continued to intercept and decrypt Japanese diplomatic and naval traffic. They had penetrated all Japanese diplomatic codes, including the most secret one, transmitted in a machine cipher known to the Americans as Purple, which the Japanese had thought to be unbreakable. Tokyo used Purple for the most sensitive diplomatic communications between the Foreign Office and major embassies around the world. They relied on lesser nonmachine ciphers for consular traffic, including messages to and from the Honolulu consulate. Understandably, American intelligence assigned a lower priority to consular communications. All this traffic in whatever cipher was being picked up by far-flung radio listening stations and forwarded in raw form to Washington, where it was sorted out, decrypted, translated, and analyzed by undermanned army and navy staffs. The distribution in Washington of Japanese diplomatic decrypts went by the name Magic, and reached a very restricted list of high officials. The great irony of this special Magic was that high-priority messages in Purple contained no clues of Japanese plans to attack Pearl Harbor, whereas the lower-priority traffic between Tokyo and Honolulu had clues in abundance.

On September 24, a message from Tokyo directed Yoshikawa to divide Pearl Harbor into five "subareas" and, when reporting on ships, to locate each ship according to its subarea. Such an instruction would have been a red flag to Gen. Walter Short and Adm. Husband E. Kimmel, the commanding army and naval officers in Hawaii, but they never saw it until after the war. It took two weeks from interception of the message to final processing in Washington. When Col. Rufus S. Bratton, chief of the Far Eastern Section of Army G-2 (intelligence) and former military attaché in Tokyo, read the translated decrypt on October 9, he instantly recognized it as a bombing grid. He passed it up the army chain of command without its stirring so much as a raised eyebrow. The navy staff, showing even less interest, thought it merely demonstrated espionage in Hawaii consistent with Japanese activity at other ports. The "bomb plot" message was committed to the files and never forwarded to the Hawaii commands where it might have been taken seriously.

Yoshikawa devised a code for the subareas, stepped up his watch on the base, and dutifully plotted the ships in their sections, where one day they would become sitting ducks for Japanese dive-bombers and torpedo planes. As he watched, he also noticed patterns that, as a navy professional, he deplored. Invariably, most of the fleet would be out training on weekdays but back in port on weekends. On Sundays, air patrols were few and activity was light along Battleship Row.

In early November, the Japanese liner *Taiyo Maru* docked in Honolulu. It had been chartered, as the war clouds gathered, to carry Americans to Hawaii and Japanese citizens back home. On board were three men from Japanese Naval Intelligence disguised as crew members. They had a more sinister mission. On the way over, the ship had traveled the empty northern route that the six-carrier Pearl Harbor striking force would take a month later, and the intelligence officers recorded daily weather information. At Honolulu, one of them, Lt. Cdr. Suguru Suzuki, slipped past U.S. agents at the pier and made his way to the consulate. He gave Kita a list of ninety-seven questions about the defenses of Hawaii for Yoshikawa to answer. Yoshikawa worked a full day and managed to answer most of them. The first was the most important and easiest: "On what day of the week would the most ships be in Pearl Harbor on normal occasions?" "Sunday," he replied. To the completed questionnaire, he added sketches, maps, and the aerial photographs he had taken on pleasure flights over Oahu.[8] "We knew then," Yoshikawa said later, "that things were building to a climax and that my work was almost done."[9]

As things "built to a climax," they also intensified. Tokyo showed more urgency in the coded dispatches for Yoshikawa, which were always addressed to Kita (and Yoshikawa's messages were always sent in Kita's name). On November 15, Tokyo asked Yoshikawa to report on the movement of U.S. Navy ships twice a week. On the 18th, it wanted information about Mamala Bay off southern Oahu and other strategic points. On the 20th, it ordered special scrutiny of fleet air bases on Oahu. Yoshikawa struggled to keep up with the new requests while carrying out his normal routine of sightseeing, swimming, boating, and hiking around key locations. On November 24, he sent a report on fleet exercises. Four days later, Tokyo asked him to report on the movement of capital ships, and Yoshikawa dispatched a long report of the fleet's schedule on December 1.

The attack was now less than a week away. Japan had passed an Imperial resolution to make war on the United States, and the striking force had put to sea. It was still possible that the attack could be called off, but, for all practical purposes, the die was cast. On December 2, Tokyo requested daily reports on "the presence in port of battleships, aircraft carriers and cruisers," and asked about barrage balloons and antitorpedo nets. Another message directed Kita to begin destroying the codes. When Yoshikawa saw them burning, he was as certain as he could be, without being told in so many words, that the attack was imminent. On the 3rd, Yoshikawa met secretly with Otto Kuehn, who gave him a lengthy, convoluted system for signaling offshore Japanese ships and submarines. Yoshikawa sent it to Tokyo in its entirety. On Friday, December 5, there was another urgent request from Tokyo to "report comprehensively" on the Pacific Fleet. Yoshikawa's information was now being relayed to the striking force bearing down on Hawaii. He took one last sightseeing flight over Oahu and walked through Pearl City to the tip of the peninsula where he could see beyond Ford Island that the fleet was in. On Saturday, he told Tokyo that he saw no barrage balloons or antitorpedo nets and, letting down his guard, ventured the uncharacteristically gratuitous and wholly unprofessional opinion that there was "considerable opportunity" for an attack. A second cable enumerated the ships in port (none were carriers) and advised Tokyo about the absence of naval air reconnaissance.

Since midsummer of 1941, the Combat Intelligence Unit at Pearl Harbor, known familiarly as Station Hypo, had been tracking the movements of the Japanese fleet by traffic analysis and direction finding, measures that identify and locate a ship from its radio signals. What Hypo learned went into a daily intelligence summary written by the officer in charge, Lt. Cdr. Joseph J. Rochefort, and routed to Admiral Kimmel and the nation's naval and political leaders in Washington. In July, Rochefort had reported the reorganization of the Japanese navy to a war footing and the recall of the entire merchant fleet for strategic military purposes. In October, Rochefort outlined a two-pronged Japanese strategy, an invasion force heading south and a screening maneuver involving air units in the North and Central Pacific. Rochefort did not realize it then and never guessed it in time, but the northern maneuver turned out to be the Pearl Harbor striking force. So it was clear that the Japanese were preparing for war. The only questions were where and when. Rochefort could not say.

Two weeks before the Pearl Harbor attack, Kimmel had ordered an exercise north of Hawaii to test the Pacific Fleet's defenses against a possible Japanese raid. It covered the same area from which the attack itself was launched— actually, the only logical approach. Kimmel called it an exercise, but, deep down, he was looking for a Japanese carrier force. He had the right idea but at the wrong time.[10]

The December messages between Tokyo and Honolulu were a smoking gun. Even those in November, which were read in Washington, should have rung alarm bells. None of them reached Hawaii before the raid, but they might have arrived in time except for an amazing series of missed connections.

On October 14, President Roosevelt had invited David Sarnoff, chief executive of the Radio Corporation of America (RCA), to the White House for lunch.[11] RCA was one of the telegraph companies handling Japanese consular business in Honolulu. Roosevelt asked that RCA's Honolulu office pass the Japanese messages directly to naval intelligence at Pearl Harbor. Sarnoff, happy to oblige his commander in chief (he held a commission as general in the U.S. Army Reserve), left a few days later for Hawaii. It took several days by train and ocean liner to reach Honolulu, where he met publicly with military and civilian leaders and behind the scenes with Kimmel; Short; Rochefort; Capt. Irving Mayfield, chief intelligence officer for the Fourteenth Naval District; and RCA personnel to make the necessary arrangements. Unfortunately, RCA's turn in the rotation did not begin until December 1.

When the time came, the transfer was anything but smooth. Mayfield had been assigned to sit on a court-martial board and was away from his post. Intelligence officer Yale Maxon picked up the first batch of Tokyo-Honolulu messages on December 1 and notified Rochefort, but no couriers were available. Those messages did not arrive at Hypo until December 5.[12] Rochefort, obviously unaware of their explosive substance, assigned PO Farnsley C. Woodward to decrypt them. Woodward was not one of Hypo's best codebreakers, but he was familiar with diplomatic codes. As the preattack Japanese cryptograms piled up, ever more ominous in content, Woodward put in several long days before completing the decoding task on December 10, three days after the Japanese attack. By that time, whatever the content, the messages no long rated as intelligence. They were history.[13]

In Washington, all of the important Tokyo-Honolulu correspondence had been intercepted, but only the three earliest messages in November had been decrypted and translated by December 7. One of the others almost made it in time. The cable explaining Kuehn's signals was among a pile of "deferred" messages, still in Japanese, in Dorothy Edgers's in-basket when she came to work on Saturday, December 6, at Op-20-G. A translator in her mid-thirties, Edgers was new on the job but so fluent in Japanese, after living in Japan for thirty years, that she was certified to teach the Japanese language to Japanese students up to the high school level. Her main drawback as a translator at Op-20-G was her unfamiliarity with navy terminology. With no urgent business at hand, she quickly scanned the stack of "deferreds." Several struck her as important, including the one from Tokyo on December 2 that asked for daily reports on ship movements and inquired about torpedo nets and barrage balloons. The Kuehn message about communicating information on American fleet movements to Japanese submarines and ships offshore might not have been the most significant in the stack, but it caught her untrained eye. She stayed late to translate it on her own time so that she could show it to the chief of the Translation Section, Lt. Cdr. Alwin D. Kramer, but Kramer was not impressed. Treating her like the novice she was, he nitpicked her translation, told her it could wait until Monday, and sent her home. Kramer was a busy man in a high-pressure job and not easily deterred by a greenhorn civilian—a woman at that. After the war, when Colonel Bratton read about this incident, he said simply, "If we had gotten that [Kuehn] message on [December 6] . . . the whole picture would have been different."[14]

The toll at Pearl Harbor on December 7, 1941, was 2,403 Americans killed and 1,178 wounded. Most of them were U.S. Navy personnel, but the U.S. Army, Marine Corps, and even the civilian population also suffered. Japanese planes did not target civilians, but errant American antiaircraft shells fell into residential neighborhoods. Eighteen ships, including eight battleships, and nearly three hundred U.S. Navy and Army Air Corps planes were destroyed or damaged. Five Oahu air bases suffered extensive damage. With a loss of twenty-nine planes, one full-sized submarine, and five midget submarines, Japan hailed the Pearl Harbor attack as "a great success unprecedented in history." Its success, however, was marred by the absence of two American aircraft carriers (away on missions to Wake and Midway islands) and the failure to attack port facilities and oil storage tanks, which left Pearl Harbor still a viable base for the Pacific Fleet.

As the smoke cleared, the FBI questioned Mikami and Kotoshirodo, who told them of "Morimura's" great interest in military installations. When Yoshikawa had left Japan the previous March, he feared that he would never see it again, but his diplomatic immunity spared him from American justice. He returned to Japan in February in the repatriation of the consular staff and served out the war at a Third Bureau desk in Tokyo. He proudly considered his Pearl Harbor mission the culmination of his Navy career. Years later, he reflected on the experience. "Some things certainly are ordained," he said. "And so it was that I . . . never came to serve in action but look back on my single top-secret assignment as the *raison d'être* of the long years of training in my youth and early manhood. In truth, if only for a moment in time, I held history in the palm of my hand."[15]

CHAPTER 11

"Our Man in Tokyo"

The crew of the aircraft carrier *Enterprise* knew something big was brewing. They belonged to Adm. William F. ("Bull") Halsey's carrier task force called back on short notice from the South Pacific only to find they would have no time for the languid pleasures of their home base in Hawaii. Among the first to learn the new mission was the navigator, Cdr. Richard Ruble. Word came straight from the top in the form of a ten-page order, CinCPAC Operation Plan No. 29-42, issued by Pacific Fleet Commander Adm. Chester W. Nimitz for what history would record as the Battle of Midway.

At his station on the bridge, Ruble studied the order. He became fascinated by the rich details about the enemy's battle plan and the size of its fleet, the largest ever to set sail up to that point in history. The Japanese would send a diversionary task force against the Aleutian Islands on June 3, 1942, but their main objective would be far to the south, Midway Island, 1,200 miles westnorthwest of Oahu. Planes from four aircraft carriers of the Kido Butai (Striking Force)—four of the six involved in the Pearl Harbor attack—would raid Midway on June 4 and support the invasion two days later. They hoped to take the Americans by surprise and finish a job left undone at Pearl Harbor by drawing out the American carriers and destroying them, thus snuffing out the American presence in the Western Pacific. With advance knowledge of Japanese intentions, however, Nimitz planned to spring his own surprise. Three American carriers would lie in ambush northeast of Midway to await the Kido Butai's arrival. One of the greatest naval battles in history was shaping up.

When he finished reading the order and knew what he would be doing for the next several days, the duly impressed Commander Ruble looked up at his fellow officers on the bridge and said, "That man of ours in Tokyo is worth every cent we pay him."[1]

Appearances to the contrary, there was no "man of ours" in Tokyo, and considering the magnitude of the achievement and the niggardly pay of U.S. Navy personnel in those days, this was one of the best bargains in American history. The key to success was the astute application of codebreaking by the Hawaiian-based Combat Intelligence Unit (Station Hypo), and its officer in charge, Lt. Cdr. Joseph J. Rochefort.

Rochefort had started his naval career as an enlisted man and never really lost his blue-collar perspective. Yet, he was more than an administrator, as suggested by the term *officer in charge*. He was also more than a codebreaker, although codebreaking was the critical function of Station Hypo. In more than two decades of peacetime duty, Rochefort had gained experience as a codebreaker, radio intelligence expert, Japanese linguist, naval planner, and operations officer, all of it neatly packaged with an agile, retentive mind and a strong sense of duty. In other words, he had all the qualifications of a first-rate intelligence officer, and, in that capacity, he excelled in the preparation for the Battle of Midway.

Rochefort lacked status, however; he was not part of the U.S. Navy's Intelligence Bureau; he had no formal orders to do the things he did. It is little short of amazing that this low-ranking officer, lacking Naval Academy credentials, should turn up at the right time and place to play so pivotal a role at a major turning point of history. As one naval historian put it, "to . . . Rochefort must forever go the acclaim for having made more difference, at a more important time, than any other naval officer in history."[2]

Enduring his ordeal was no small achievement either. Of course, he was under intense and personally demanding pressure as chief of Station Hypo. He had signed on for that; he was a career navy man in time of war. Still, he got more than he bargained for. He found himself fighting the war on two fronts— against a powerful Japanese fleet and against his superiors in Washington. In the face of Washington's potentially disastrous intelligence advice, he guided his own unit to a spectacular break of the enemy code that paved the way for victory at Midway. His success put the nation forever in his debt and eventually cost him his career. Although Rochefort has correctly indicated that Hypo's Midway intelligence coup was a group effort, neither should it be forgotten that he led the group. Symbolically, he, more than any other individual, deserves to be known as "our man in Tokyo."

Rochefort was born in Dayton, Ohio, in 1898 and grew up in Southern California. He enlisted in the Naval Reserve in 1918 during World War I in what he called the patriotic "spirit of the times," and was assigned soon afterward to Officers Training School. Fourteen months later, he was commissioned an ensign and transferred to the Regular Navy. His failure to attend the Naval Academy made him an outsider in the fraternity of naval Brahmin, but it did not negatively affect the performance of his duties. He did admit later in life that, had he gained the Naval Academy experience, he might have learned better how to navigate the stormy seas of navy politics.

As much as he had a knack for it, Rochefort was a reluctant codebreaker. Before taking over Hypo, he had served only one stretch of duty involving cryptanalysis, from 1925 to 1927, first as trainee, then as officer in charge of Op-20-G, the navy's fledgling radio communications desk in Washington. ("Op-20" referred to the U.S. Navy Bureau of Communications and "G" to the code and cipher unit, located in Room 1621 of the old Navy Building on Constitution Avenue.) He had arrived at Op-20-G on the recommendation of one of his executive officers, Cdr. Chester C. Jersey, who knew Rochefort as a good bridge player and solver of crossword puzzles. What Rochefort commanded at Op-20-G borders on the farcical. His subordinates consisted of a civilian cryptanalyst and a clerk. The civilian was Agnes Meyer Driscoll, an unsung genius who was his mentor. She taught him and a succession of other promising naval officers the basics of codebreaking. Her admiring students became the top naval codebreakers of World War II.

Between the world wars, the American and Japanese navies warily regarded each other as future enemies. Consequently, Rochefort's introduction to codebreaking at Op-20-G was a Japanese code to solve, using a basic reference text, *The Elements of Cryptanalysis,* by William F. Friedman. As much as he loved the challenge, Rochefort admitted that the intense mental effort "gave me ulcers." When he went home at night, he recalled in later years, he needed three or four hours to wind down because he could not get the problems of the day out of his head. "I wanted to get in the fleet," he said, ". . . so I made every effort to keep away from cryptanalysis."[3]

He tried but never really succeeded. Through the years, Rochefort kept in touch with his friend Lt. Cdr. Laurance F. Safford, the first and most frequent officer in charge of Op-20-G, who nurtured that orphan of two Navy bureaus—communications and intelligence—as his own baby from its birth in 1924 until America's entry into war. The cryptography desk's peculiar hybrid status derived from the fact that the Communications Bureau supplied the necessary radio equipment and the Intelligence Bureau was the primary consumer of its product.

Even when Rochefort found himself happily removed from cryptanalysis, fate seemed to hand him assignments that would serve him in good stead for his coming date with destiny. He was singled out for Japanese language training from 1929 to 1932 in a farsighted program for selected army, navy, and Marine Corps officers. He spent three years in Japan to learn the written and spoken word and the culture and mind of the future enemy. Afterward, he joined the fleet staff and, although only a junior officer, found himself working at high levels of planning and operations. Along the way, he impressed peers and superiors alike. His fleet commander, Adm. Joseph M. Reeves, called Rochefort "one of the most outstanding officers of his rank" whose "judgment and ability are truly remarkable," and predicted—only half right, as it turned out—that despite his lack of academy training Rochefort would "advance to positions of high rank and great responsibility."[4]

Rochefort's assignment to Pearl Harbor was a little like Dorothy's trip to Oz. He was caught up in a political storm at Navy Headquarters that swept him along. Early in 1941, the Pacific Fleet commander, Adm. James O. Richardson, demanded tactical intelligence from Station Hypo because he refused to be put in the position of relying on Washington. Before Richardson could take advantage of it, however, President Roosevelt relieved him of command and installed Admiral Kimmel, who was destined to become the U.S. Navy's Pearl Harbor fall guy. Safford carried through with the order for Hypo to provide close tactical support of the fleet in May 1941 when he asked Rochefort to take command.

Rochefort accepted on condition that he be allowed to pick his top people. The second in command was Lt. Cdr. Thomas H. Dyer, a future mathematics professor. Dyer and Lt. Wesley A. ("Ham") Wright were two of the Navy's best codebreakers; Dyer and Lt. Jack S. Holtwick were the acknowledged experts on the IBM tabulating machines, which served as Hypo's memory bank and performed the mathematical drudgery in codebreaking. Others in the hierarchy at Hypo included linguist/cryptanalyst Lt. Joseph Finnegan and traffic analysts Lt. Cdr. Thomas A. Huckins and Lt. John A. Williams. These officers became Rochefort's unofficial brain trust, with whom he would consult informally, individually, or as a group, before issuing daily intelligence summaries or making major intelligence evaluations.

Lt. W. J. ("Jasper") Holmes became a Hypo insider even though he was none of the above. A Naval Academy graduate and submarine officer, Holmes's career had been cut short in 1936 by spinal arthritis. In retirement he taught engineering at the University of Hawaii and wrote magazine articles under the pen name Alec Hudson. In June 1941 he agreed to return to desk-bound active service in Fourteenth Naval District intelligence. His initial job was to plot the location of ships at sea and, for security reasons, he moved in with Hypo. A friendly, outgoing man, Holmes came to know his new roommates well and eventually served Hypo and its successor, Fleet Radio Unit, Pacific (FRUPac), in various administrative capacities. He stood out later in the war for his contribution to the submarine campaign in the Pacific. Holmes had a keen analytical mind and a flair for writing. In a book about his wartime experience, *Double-Edged Secrets,* he spoke of the Hypo group in admiration and "cold appraisal" as "competent, resourceful, clever, hard-working, but not geniuses." The organization as a whole he described as "efficient and smooth-working," and Rochefort as the "ablest of the group" and a leader who inspired "an ironclad morale that knit us forever into a unit."[5]

If the organization was efficient and smooth working, it was far from traditional. In a chilly, poorly ventilated basement room in the Administration Building of the Fourteenth Naval District, to which Hypo was technically attached, Rochefort ran his unit as a meritocracy. The mood was workmanlike and informal. Dyer's desk featured a menagerie of pinup girls. A sign above it read: "You don't have to be crazy to work here, but it helps." Finnegan, who was given to flashes of brilliant insight, kept his desk, as Holmes put it, like a "rat's nest," littered with "IBM printouts, newspapers, messages, crumpled cigarett packs, coffee cups, apple cores, and sundry material."[6] Rochefort trusted their abilities, however, and gave them the slack to do their work but ultimately took personal responsibility for their results.

Rochefort blamed himself for failing to discover the striking force that bombed Pearl Harbor on December 7, 1941. He lived by the credo that an intelligence officer's duty is to tell his commander today what the enemy is going to do tomorrow, but, with a war in progress, he was too busy to dwell on it. A few days after the Pearl Harbor attack, Safford put Hypo to work on the Imperial Navy's high volume operations code known as JN25. Safford's codebreakers in Washington, called Station Negat, and Station Cast in the Philippines had been reading it for several months. JN25 consisted of two separate books, one a "dictionary" with about 33,000 five-digit code groups, each meaning a word or phrase, and a second book of random numbers which when added to the code groups created ciphers. JN25 used pencil-and-paper ciphers unrelated to the famous Purple machine for high-level diplomatic messages. The only machines involved in decrypting JN25 were IBM tabulators.

Three American codebreaking units were now focused on the main operations code of the Japanese fleet. It helped that an enemy aircraft downed in the Pearl Harbor attack yielded vital intelligence, including the Imperial Navy's latest operational call signs that identified ships and shore stations. Unfortunately, on December 3, before the attack, the Japanese had abruptly changed the additive book (but not the codebook), which meant the Americans had to laboriously reconstruct the new system from intercepted messages. In this task, the codebreakers in the three units cooperated by exchanging newly recovered code values and additives. Within weeks they were beginning to read the system again.

A certain amount of disruption occurred when Station Cast retreated to Australia. There, it was renamed Belconnen, and Australian codebreakers joined the Americans. A more serious and lingering conflict developed in relations between Hypo and Op-20-G. Radio intelligence became one of the scapegoats of the Pearl Harbor attack for failure to detect the approaching Japanese fleet. Heads that rolled included those of Rear Adm. Leigh Noyes, director of communications in Washington, and Rochefort's friend Safford at Op-20-G. In their places, Capt. Joseph R. ("Joe") Redman became director of communications; his brother, Cdr. John R. ("Jack") Redman became head of Op-20-G; and Cdr. Joseph N. Wenger took charge of cryptanalysis. Rochefort never liked his new boss, Jack Redman, an academy man and strictly a communications officer with little or no experience in cryptology. He was convinced that Joe Redman had greased the skids for Safford to create an opening for his brother.

A sweeping reorganization of radio intelligence also rankled Rochefort. In Washington, the newly arrived Chief of Naval Operations Adm. Ernest J. King wanted it centralized in the mold of the British system. From the time Rochefort had arrived at Pearl Harbor, however, he had "arrogated to myself" the responsibility of analyzing the incoming information—including radio direction-finding (RDF) and traffic analysis in addition to the more vital codebreaking—and passing it on as intelligence to the Pacific Fleet.[7] With Redman at the helm, decrypted and translated messages in raw form were to be forwarded to Washington for analysis and the finished product relayed as intelligence back to the fleets. Rochefort ignored Redman by continuing to feed his own intelligence directly to the Pacific Fleet commander. Naturally, they conflicted, and the issue festered like an open sore.

Gone, too, was Rochefort's comfortable link to Washington in the person of Safford. It had always helped to have a powerful friend at headquarters. Now the worst had happened: he had a powerful enemy there. At Pearl Harbor, fortunately, his stock was on the rise, thanks in part to an equally strong relationship with the Pacific Fleet intelligence officer, Lt. Cdr. Edwin T. Layton. They had first met in 1929 on the way to Japan for language training. Now at Pearl Harbor, they were in daily contact, and, through Layton, Rochefort had access to the fleet's highest levels of decision making.

Layton enjoyed Nimitz's full confidence. He briefed the admiral each morning and was authorized to enter his office without appointment on urgent matters. Nimitz directed Layton—who had met and played bridge with Japanese Admiral Yamamoto—to adopt the mindset of the Imperial Navy and to interpret enemy intentions in advance. For this special prescience, Layton turned to Hypo, and he takes credit for giving Nimitz confidence in the codebreakers. Shortly after Nimitz arrived in Hawaii on Christmas Day, 1941, he conducted a pro forma inspection of Hypo, with Layton in tow, as part of a self-prescribed orientation in his new command. Rochefort treated them somewhat distractedly, he admitted later, and probably made a negative first impression. Outside, Nimitz turned to Layton and asked him, if codebreaking really worked, why Hypo had not given advance warning of the Pearl Harbor attack. Layton assured him that the failure was not Rochefort's and begged him to withhold judgment.

Rochefort was less forgiving of himself. He set goals he knew he could not achieve. He gloried in the rigors of navy life and seemed to have found nirvana in his earlier days of service under a demanding superior who was "very rough on his officers." That was Lt. Cdr. (later Adm.) Arthur S. ("Chips") Carpender, under whom Rochefort served on the destroyer *MacDonough* in the late twenties. "As far as I was concerned," Rochefort said, "[Carpender] set a marvelous example, which his officers just couldn't meet naturally. But that training was very valuable. . . . It wasn't very happy, but you can't expect a young naval officer to be happy."[8]

Rochefort's own high standards dovetailed nicely with Nimitz's demand for timely intelligence, and his own perceived failures spurred him to greater efforts. In general, he stayed away from the ulcerous task of solving codes and ciphers. Neither did he work on original translations, although he was a capable linguist. He picked up where the cryptanalysts and translators left off. The messages were seldom models of clarity that spelled out enemy intentions in so many words. These were operational orders transmitted by the hundreds each day. Rochefort personally handled about 140 a day after others had a go at them. Inevitably, there were blanks in what he saw. On average, no more than 15 percent of a message would be recovered. His self-assigned task was to fill in the blanks as best he could and, with the help of his colleagues, extract meaning from Hypo's imperfect labors. He had a knack for relating scattered bits of information, like fitting together the pieces of a jigsaw puzzle, and his keen memory enabled him to reach back through the volumes of traffic, along with reports from direction-finding and traffic analysis, for relevant scraps of information.

It was not long before Rochefort earned the new commander's respect. He made a number of intelligence calls at variance with Washington, and, more often than not, he was proved to be right. In late January, Rochefort predicted from a decrypted fragment the Japanese occupation of the excellent deepwater port of Rabaul on New Britain.[9] That was good news for Nimitz because it meant that the Japanese carrier striking force would be far to the south when he dispatched Halsey's carriers on a morale-boosting raid of the Marshall Islands. Admiral Halsey achieved complete surprise without interference from carrier-based planes.

After the Japanese army overran the Dutch East Indies and captured Singapore, the Japanese Kido Butai ventured into the Indian Ocean and chased what was left of the British fleet back to the Indian subcontinent. By mid-April, signs were pointing to a new enemy offensive in the Southwest Pacific toward New Guinea and the Solomon Islands. Station Belconnen detected a Japanese plan to capture Port Moresby on the southern coast of New Guinea within air-striking distance of Australia, and predicted that the large battle carriers *Shokaku* and *Zuikaku* and a light carrier, which turned out to be the *Shoho,* would support the operation. Nimitz was determined to block them, but his four carriers were widely strung out in the vast Pacific. Two of them, the *Hornet* and the *Enterprise,* were on a mission to ferry Lt. Col. James H. Doolittle and his brave flyers to their historic bombing raid over Tokyo. Only the *Yorktown* was in position near the Coral Sea, with the *Lexington* en route a day or two out of Pearl Harbor. In Washington, Admiral King was so concerned that for the only time in the war he asked Rochefort directly for a situation report. Rochefort replied within hours that the Japanese were planning two actions—in eastern New Guinea and in the Coral Sea—but no invasion of Australia, and still another Pacific operation, which turned out to be Midway, whose details were not yet clear.[10]

The *Lexington* arrived in time to take part in the Battle of the Coral Sea, May 4–8, and, alas, find her final resting place on the sea bottom. The *Yorktown* suffered major damage but managed to limp back to Pearl Harbor. In return, the Americans sank the *Shoho,* and forced the enemy to call off its attack on Port Moresby. They also inflicted heavy damage on the *Shokaku,* and the *Zuikaku* lost many of her planes. Both carriers had to be scratched from the coming Battle of Midway, a serious and possibly decisive reduction in force.

Hypo grew turbulently with the demands of war. By May 1942, about 120 officers and men were putting in twelve-hour shifts under extreme pressure. Included in that number was the band from the battleship *California,* whose instruments had gone down with the ship on December 7. Their acquisition proved serendipitous, as they adapted readily to their new duties. Their main function was to operate the IBM machines. In May, messages were pouring in at a rate of five hundred to a thousand a day. Each message contained a few to many five-digit code groups, and each code group had to be punched up. The punch cards were assembled in "books" and distributed to the decrypters and translators who were too busy to notice the unruly clutter around their desks. The disorder would be marginalized time and again, however, when Rochefort, filling in the blanks of a new message, spotted an undecrypted code group he had seen somewhere before and triggered a frantic search into the stacks. "I could remember back maybe three or four months," he recalled three decades later. "This [officer] sends a similar message to some other command. . . . In other words, everything was in my head. Eventually, of course, you've got to get away from this. You've got to get organized. But we didn't have time to get organized."[11]

Rochefort and Dyer arranged to work twenty-four hours on and twenty-four off so that one of them could be there at all times and avoid commuting at night during blackouts. Somehow, the twenty-four on always turned out longer, and when it came to crunch time, as the day of battle approached, they took to spending days on end in Hypo's stuffy basement room. Rochefort, whose wife and children had been evacuated to the States, brought in a cot to catch up on his sleep when the body rebelled against the will. He gained a certain unintended cachet by wearing a faded red smoking jacket over his uniform to ward off the chill and slippers to soften the impact of the concrete floor.

Dyer prolonged his waking hours by popping uppers. Other members of the Hypo team joined him as Benzedrine tablets were "passed around like jellybeans." But chemistry had its limits, too. The intense concentration would eventually wear Dyer down to the point where his appearance would betray him. Rochefort would hand his ragged-looking friend his empty lunch pail and push him out the door so he could go home and rest. Holmes tells of bumping into an old friend from the *Yorktown* outside Hypo's basement quarters. The damaged carrier, back from the Coral Sea, was undergoing rush repairs to make her battle-worthy for Midway (although the officer had no idea of his next mission). As they chatted, Dyer, unshaven, unkempt, almost unconscious from sleep deprivation, stumbled out. Holmes's friend eyed Dyer disapprovingly and said, "Now there goes a bird who should be sent to sea and get straightened out."[12]

———————————

The Doolittle raid on Tokyo caused insignificant physical damage, but the emotional fallout was huge. It did wonders for American morale and induced Japanese leaders to push the panic button, with far-reaching consequences. For three days the Combined Fleet combed the ocean east of Japan in a futile effort to catch the retreating American carriers that had launched the attack planes. The frenzied Japanese radio traffic yielded a substantial windfall for American codebreakers. American listening posts relayed the large volume of messages to codebreakers in Washington, Australia, and Hawaii, who built up their knowledge of the five-digit JN25 code and additive tables. More broadly, the Japanese High Command resolved, once and for all, to eliminate the threat posed by the U.S. Pacific Fleet and began to plan the decisive Battle of Midway.

Even before the enemy's southward offensive was halted with the failure of the Port Moresby invasion force, Rochefort was picking up pregnant tidbits about the larger upcoming offensive in the north. On April 27, he learned of Tokyo's interest in maps of the Aleutians. On May 4, a battleship under repair signaled that it would be ready for "the campaign." On May 5, Yamamoto's flagship ordered large quantities of refueling hose for "scheduled operations."[13] Traffic analysis revealed heavier radio communications with Saipan, which suggested it would be an important jumping-off place, and to Rochefort that meant a mid-Pacific operation.

At this point Rochefort had nothing to go on but intuition. He had a hunch that the Japanese target might be Midway, but he could not prove it, and Washington did not share his hunch. From the same decrypts read by Hypo, Naval intelligence in Washington decided that the next Japanese push would come even farther south than the Port Moresby offensive. Had Nimitz acceded to this line of thinking, which flowed down to him in a message from his commander, Admiral King, Midway would have been easy pickings for the Japanese, and enemy control of Midway would have put Pearl Harbor within range of land-based bombers. Planning for battle with erroneous intelligence is a formula for disaster. The truth had to be nailed down.

On May 14, Rochefort became convinced from partial decrypts that Midway was the Japanese objective. His reasons centered on the designator "AF," which emerged clearly as the Japanese target, and he convinced himself that "AF" was Midway. He showed the decrypts to Layton and methodically interpreted each tiny piece of evidence. He then went through the same exercise for Nimitz's war plans chief, Capt. Lynde V. McCormick. Both men came away persuaded, and that sealed it for Nimitz. Op-20-G, however, was not persuaded, arguing that the target could be Johnston Island, an American base south of Midway and closer to Pearl Harbor, and warned of a possible strike against the U.S. West Coast or the Panama Canal. Rochefort, known for his caustic tongue, scoffed at the notion of a West Coast attack because it was "simply beyond the capability of the Japanese transport and supply" to carry out a major operation that far from home.[14]

A ruse cooked up at Hypo removed all doubt. Holmes recalls a conversation at Rochefort's desk that also involved Dyer and Finnegan. In his teaching days at the University of Hawaii, Holmes had studied Midway's infrastructure, and he mentioned that a breakdown of that desolate atoll's new water distilling plant would trigger a water emergency. Finnegan casually ventured the opinion that if Japanese radio intelligence discovered Midway short of water, it would promptly inform Tokyo. Rochefort pounced on the idea. "That's all right, Joe," he said cryptically.[15] No one understood at the time what he meant because he never told them of his bitter personal feud with Op-20-G.

With an okay from Nimitz, Rochefort sent instructions by secure underwater cable directing Midway to make an emergency request for water in plain language and then use a cipher they knew the Japanese had captured at Wake Island to give details of an explosion at the distilling plant. When Midway dutifully complied, Wake Island took the bait and advised Tokyo in a coded message of the water shortage at "AF." The incident has been widely misinterpreted as a way of persuading Nimitz that "AF" was Midway, but Nimitz was already on board. The real purpose, Layton said, was to convince Washington. It did—so much so that Layton discovered after his retirement that someone at Navy Headquarters had engaged in a cover-up. ". . . [It] is significant to note," he said, "that the daily records of Cominch's [Commander in Chief King's] decryption intelligence are missing from 8 May 1942 onward. . . . Furthermore there are extensive deletions in the summaries that survive from the White House map room."[16]

Now that Nimitz knew the target and something about the force being brought to bear on it, he pressed Layton and Rochefort to find out the date of the attack. As Rochefort read through the partial decrypts about Japanese preparations, he found the indicators pointing to early June, but Nimitz needed him to be more precise. Washington's estimate of mid-June once again presented pressure from that source, but of more urgent concern were his own battle preparations. To spring the ambush successfully, timing was all important. Nimitz realized, in any case, that there was no time to lose. He had already recalled Halsey and his two carriers, the *Hornet* and the *Enterprise,* from the South Pacific and addressed a delicate memorandum to King that explained why he found it necessary to reject Washington's intelligence estimates and go against the chief's advice to keep Halsey in the south. King accepted the move partly because Belconnen, the Australian and American team near Melbourne, also detected Japanese preparations for a mid-Pacific operation.[17] Meanwhile, the damaged *Yorktown* was limping back to Pearl Harbor, where repair crews were waiting to patch her up and send her out to fight again. These three carriers—*Hornet, Enterprise,* and *Yorktown*—were Nimitz's answer to the world's most powerful armada. He desperately needed precise intelligence from Hypo.

The big break came on May 20 when Hypo received a lengthy message issued to all Japanese fleet commanders. Sensing its importance, the codebreakers began immediately to break it down. They soon realized that it was the Imperial Navy's final operations order for the Midway campaign. They kept at it day and night, this time filling in all the blanks. When they had done all they could with text encrypted in JN25, however, they found the dates and times still buried in a special cipher. Finnegan, with Ham Wright's help, went to work on it. They searched back through the IBM cards and found that the cipher had been used only twice before, and one of those times it came out garbled. Such rarity made their task more daunting. Finnegan, in a burst of inspiration, came up with the answer. The full solution yielded not only the date of the carrier-based attack on Midway, June 4, but also the number of carriers, the hour and location of the planes' takeoff, and the direction of their approach to Midway. By May 25, Rochefort had the text of the Japanese battle plan and sent it off to Nimitz and King. (Missing, however, was information about a trailing battle force consisting of several battleships and heavy cruisers commanded by Yamamoto himself.) With full confidence in the Hypo intelligence, Nimitz would be able to ignore the invasion fleet, sighted first on June 3, and wait to pounce on the four carriers of the striking force discovered the next day at almost the exact time, place, and bearing predicted.

———————

Nimitz fixed a cold stare on Rochefort as he walked into the commander's conference room on the morning of May 27 a half-hour late for the briefing. Hypo's man looked haggard from lack of sleep, and his rumpled working khakis stood out in contrast to the starched uniforms and shiny brass of admirals, generals, and high-ranking staff officers. As he started his presentation, he nervously apologized for the delay. He had taken the time for a final verification of the facts in Hypo's possession, and now he relayed them to the assembled officers. Nimitz, a fair-minded man who admired dedication and competence, allowed his blue eyes to soften. He already had made his decision and felt steadily more comfortable about going out on a limb with Hypo against the intelligence estimates from Washington.

Midway ranks as one of the greatest naval battles in history. Fortunately for the Americans, it was fought entirely with aircraft, because the Japanese had a better than four-to-one advantage in fighting ships—145 to 35. In aircraft carriers, the real focus of battle, the sides were closer—4 to 3. Counting Midway itself as a fourth aircraft carrier (it was bristling with air reinforcements), they were dead even. Superior intelligence and the benefit of surprise gave an edge to the Americans. Even so, luck smiled on the victors when the battle was joined on the morning of June 4. Midway-based high-level bombers were first to attack the Kido Butai and scored not a single hit. Next came equally unsuccessful low-level, land- and carrier-based torpedo planes, tragically slaughtered by anti-aircraft fire and the defending fighters. Finally, with the enemy Zeros distracted below and fortunate to find the target at all, let alone the right moment to attack, dive-bombers from the *Enterprise* and *Yorktown* knocked out three carriers, the *Akagi, Kaga,* and *Soryu,* in a span of five minutes. The fourth, the *Hiryu,* was fatally damaged in the afternoon after its planes had put the *Yorktown* out of action. Later, the *Yorktown* was torpedoed and sunk by a Japanese submarine. Yamamoto called off the invasion, scheduled for two days later.

Midway marked a turning point. With the sinking of the four carriers, Japan lost hundreds of skilled pilots and maintenance crewmen whom it could ill afford to lose. Although the Pacific War would last another three years with more fierce battles to come, the Imperial Navy would switch permanently from offense to defense. It cannot be said that Hypo won the Battle of Midway. That credit goes to the men who fought it. But, it is equally true they could not have won it—could not even have fought it—without Hypo and especially Rochefort, who transformed those decrypted messages into accurate intelligence.

The spin in Washington turned the Hypo achievement on its head. Op-20-G covered up its own failure and called the Midway intelligence coup an example of cooperative signal intelligence under its leadership. The Redmans elevated the level of their conflict with Rochefort. Two weeks after Midway, the elder brother Joe, the director of Naval Communications, argued in a self-serving memorandum directed to King's deputy, Vice Adm. Frederick J. Horne, that radio intelligence should be removed from its limbo status between the intelligence and communications agencies and put directly under communications.

In derogation of Rochefort, Redman charged that "an ex–Japanese language student . . . not technically trained in naval communications" ran Hypo and that the war effort was suffering because the importance of radio intelligence "was not fully realized."[18] Redman urged that Rochefort be replaced by a "senior officer trained in radio intelligence rather than one whose background is in Japanese language" (a program administered by the rival Intelligence Bureau).

Layton called these charges "outrageous."[19] Rochefort, who died in 1976, never saw them. They were buried in secret files until declassified in 1984, but he was feeling the Redmans' heat during the summer and early fall of 1942. The "opportunists" in Washington, as he later described them, were trying to control Hypo with "bullying tactics . . . to bring us in line with their thinking."[20] The atmosphere was further poisoned by a recommendation, which originated at Pearl Harbor and was endorsed by Nimitz, that Rochefort be awarded the Distinguished Service Medal. Rochefort himself advised against it because he knew it would only stir up the pot in Washington. By honoring Rochefort, the Navy would have to admit that Hypo, not Op-20-G, deserved the credit for Midway. The Redmans and others argued that no one person should be singled out, and King followed their advice.

Hypo received its reward in a more bureaucratic way—by growing bigger. In the wake of the codebreaking coup at Midway, Nimitz gained King's approval to establish a larger intelligence unit at Pearl Harbor. It would supplement, not replace, Hypo, and like Hypo it would serve the fleet under the aegis of the Fourteenth Naval District. Rochefort became the first commanding officer of the Intelligence Center, Pacific Ocean Area (ICPOA), a job about which he was not very keen because the added administrative duties diverted him from his hands-on work at Hypo, now called FRUPac. In Washington, the Redmans correctly smelled a maneuver to pry out Rochefort and FRUPac from Navy Communications, and they moved deftly to protect their turf. In mid-September, Jack Redman was reassigned to Pearl Harbor as fleet communications officer for Admiral Nimitz. Before leaving Washington, he plotted with (Joe) Wenger to hasten Rochefort's downfall. They worked out a private cipher to exchange messages on a U.S. Navy radio circuit between Washington and Hawaii. The private cipher was against navy regulations, but that did not stop Redman from signaling Wenger to see to Rochefort's transfer shortly after he settled in at Pearl Harbor.

As tenacious as the Redmans were to keep control of Hypo, Rochefort was equally determined to retain a measure of independence. He complained to

Nimitz that the persistent bickering was interfering with Hypo's intelligence gathering at a time when the Navy was taking heavy losses in savage battles off Guadalcanal. But he was shocked at the arrival in early October of Capt. William G. Goggins, a trained communications officer, assigned as executive of ICPOA. Rochefort and Goggins quickly fell into disagreement over suggestions by the latter about collaboration between ICPOA and Hypo. Rochefort sought and received reassurance about his status from Nimitz's chief of staff, Adm. Raymond A. Spruance, who had been in tactical command at Midway. Then, with Nimitz's approval, Rochefort wrote a fateful memo to Washington that said he was concentrating on future fleet operations and would no longer discuss issues from the past. In other words, he would ignore the demands of Op-20-G to fall in line. It was his personal declaration of independence but very poor political judgment. When Redman heard about it, he signaled Wenger in the private cipher: "Get rid of Rochefort at all cost." Rochefort's orders arrived on October 22. He was reassigned for "temporary" duty in Washington, but he knew that "temporary" would be a long time, and it turned out to be forever. Rochefort had been outmaneuvered. He told the people around him, "I'm not coming back." Nimitz protested to King, but the transfer stuck.[21]

Goggins took over Hypo two weeks later. Holmes recorded the loss of Rochefort as "another blow to our morale."[22] But Hypo carried on as FRUPac and gained further distinctions in the course of the war, notably a decryption that led to the shooting down and death of Admiral Yamamoto and a key role in the devastating submarine campaign against the Japanese merchant fleet. Rochefort wrote Holmes that his departure was no fault of Goggins and asked that the staff treat their new leader with the same loyalty that they had shown him. Goggins gave the codebreakers room to do their work and got along very well with them.

Jack Redman proved himself a competent communications officer. Although he had angered Nimitz with his Rochefort vendetta, Redman eventually charmed his way into the admiral's good graces. Nimitz was not one to carry a grudge or allow a personal matter to interfere with the war effort. Because he liked to break the tension of Hawaii's dreary work-oriented bachelor existence, he and Redman often played horseshoes or went bowling, and, on trips to the war zone, they sometimes passed the long hours by playing cribbage. Redman remained on Nimitz's staff for two and one half years.[23]

The Redmans had succeeded with the powers in Washington in painting a picture of Rochefort as insubordinate, obstructive, and uncooperative. Fatigued, angry, and resentful on his arrival there, Rochefort conclusively proved their case. "I made several mistakes in a great big hurry," he admitted later, "one of which just compounded the other."[24] He petulantly refused assignment at Op-20-G, which he conceded on reflection he should not have done. He asked for sea duty, but regulations prohibited anyone with his special knowledge from serving in a war zone lest he fall into enemy hands. The closest he came to achieving his career goal of commanding a ship of the fleet was command of a floating dry dock under construction in San Pablo Bay east of San Francisco. As one historian succinctly put it, "A greater waste of a first-rate intelligence expert can hardly be imagined."[25] His valuable talents went unused until late 1944, when he was assigned to a special group on intelligence planning for Admiral King.

Rochefort's Midway contribution went officially unrecognized during his lifetime. After the war, Nimitz again recommended him for the Distinguished Service Medal, and it was again denied. This prompted Jasper Holmes to comment sadly, with allowance for the navy's culture of disciplined service, "It was not for the individual for whom the bell tolled but the Navy died a little."[26] Recognition finally came ten years after Rochefort's death and after many of the principals in the Midway episode had also died. The Distinguished Service Medal was presented to Rochefort's children in 1986, not by the navy, but by President Ronald Reagan, at a modest, dignified White House ceremony. The nation had finally acknowledged its debt to a dedicated officer who had done his job and earned a place in history.

PART 5

THE COLD WAR

CHAPTER 12

The Spy Who
Knew Everything

As much as Donald Maclean hated America, his life in espionage might appear to have been an endless joy because of the grievous damage he did to American interests. But despite his great talent for collecting and analyzing information, he also hated espionage. He once compared it to cleaning toilets. A child of privilege, he was consumed by his hatreds. He led a tortured double existence chasing a secular god that drew him outside his own culture even as he worked from within it. As his brilliant career propelled him to the higher echelons of the British Foreign Service and made his espionage that much more effective, he plunged into private debaucheries that took him in a downward spiral. He drank too much, and, when he drank, he might rail against American policy, or insult someone he did not like, or abuse his American wife, or go on a binge to a seedy homosexual hangout. Ultimately, in his fury against this imperfect world to which he was nobly born, he squandered his diplomatic career in the cause of communism.

Maclean was one of the famous Cambridge-educated communists recruited during his university days for deep penetration of the British government. He went directly from the campus to the Foreign Service, and in the course of his short, highly successful professional life, he found himself in position to steal some of America's most important secrets at a critical moment in world history. From 1944 to 1948, while serving at the British Embassy in Washington, he passed confidential political documents to his Soviet control that helped Stalin bring the nations of Eastern Europe under Soviet domination. He also contributed information about America's atomic arsenal that helped the Soviets achieve parity in the nuclear arms race. As the opposing sides began to take shape during the Cold War, he gave the Soviets advance warning of the formation of the North Atlantic Treaty Organization (NATO). Later, as the officer in charge of the American desk at the Foreign Office in London 1950–51, he revealed vital American and British secrets of the Korean War.

Five of the most famous Cambridge spies are known in Moscow as the "Magnificent Five." All are worthy of the adjective—from the Soviet perspective. Maclean stood out because he happened to be in the right place at the right time and possessed the skill to exploit his opportunities. Had he been a capitalist at the turn of the twenty-first century, he surely would have become a multimillionaire. As it happened, he was a communist during the mid-twentieth century who did his utmost to bring down the capitalist system.

Cambridge University owns the dubious distinction of nurturing the best British agents ever to work for the Soviet Union. Not that this great institution of higher learning was ever a school for spies, but in the early thirties it experienced something akin to an "invasion of the body snatchers." The minds of young English gentlemen in training for leadership in the capitalist world were being infiltrated by the alien philosophy of Marxism. The times were rife with instability. Britain was still reeling from World War I, which had so cruelly sapped its manpower. The British Empire was fraying. Capitalism quivered as the world quaked in deep economic depression. When fascism reared its ugly head, the propagators of Marxism offered lofty promises of a better life for the growing masses who were seeking a way out of their dire circumstances.

The ivory tower at Cambridge was not immune to these powerful sociopolitical currents. Maurice Dobb, a lecturer in economics and a card-carrying member of the Communist Party, started a communist cell. David Haden Guest, an activist who walked the campus with his heart on his lapel in the form of a hammer and sickle pin, provided the energetic student leadership that caused the cell to grow into a robust extracurricular force. A student swept up in the communist ferment of 1933, the year that Hitler came to power in Germany, put it succinctly: "[I]n the Cambridge that I first knew, in 1929 and 1930, the central subject of ordinary intelligent conversation was poetry. . . . [By 1933] almost the only subject of discussion [was] contemporary politics . . . [and] a very large majority of the more intelligent undergraduates [were] Communists, or almost Communists. . . ."[1] This was the Cambridge of Donald Maclean and four fellow students—Kim Philby, Guy Burgess, Anthony Blunt, and John Cairncross—who live in history as the "Cambridge Five."

Maclean's father was a prominent politician. Sir Donald was the former minister of education in the Liberal government of Stanley Baldwin, and, while young Donald was attending Cambridge, held a similar post in Ramsey Mac-Donald's coalition Cabinet until he died suddenly of a heart attack in 1932. Young Donald was tall (6 feet, 4 inches) and lean, with delicate good looks that made him attractive to both sexes. Aloof and intellectually gifted, he did not relate easily to other students. His one fast friend in preparatory school was James Klugman, a Jewish boy who shared Maclean's rebellious spirit and, by his own account, declared himself a communist to annoy school officials. The two moved on together to Cambridge, where both delved more deeply into Marxism and became infected with the communist fever. Klugman morphed into a visible and outspoken party member. Maclean followed him into the party and had a dilettante's taste of proletarian advocacy by marching through the town of Cambridge shoulder to shoulder with workers on a hunger strike. Inevitably, Maclean met and, some say, lost his innocence to a fellow communist (and homosexual predator), Guy Burgess. Somewhere in the swirl of academics, advocacy, and experimentation, Maclean's communist ardor suddenly and mysteriously subsided. Nobody realized at the time that he had been recruited into the service of Soviet intelligence and directed by his handler to infiltrate the British Foreign Service.

Maclean joined the diplomatic corps in 1935 as a third secretary and spent his first three years at the Foreign Office in London. He applied himself diligently to learning the skills of diplomacy and left no doubt that he was in the fast lane to advanced diplomatic rank. His high level of performance was rewarded in 1938 with what was considered a plum in the Foreign Service—assignment to the Paris embassy. While in Paris, he courted an adventurous young American woman from a wealthy family, Melinda Marling, who, despite her ambivalence toward this dashing and rather supercilious British diplomat, married him just as France was collapsing in June 1940. The couple spent most of the war in London, where Donald continued to impress his superiors with his competence and work ethic.

Maclean's historic assignment to the Washington embassy came in the spring of 1944. For Donald, duty came first—his espionage duty. Next came his outside profession, diplomacy. His marriage was a distant third. On arrival in the United States, he informed Melinda that she would live in New York with her stepfather, whom she did not like, while he was setting up in Washington. She was pregnant at the time and wanted to stay with Donald, but her feelings were subverted to the needs of Soviet intelligence. She had to be in New York to justify Donald's weekly commute from Washington to meet with his KGB control. The arrangement lasted nine months until another Soviet agent, Anatoly Gorsky, was transferred to Washington from London, where he had previously handled Maclean and the other Cambridge spies.

That Maclean was an irresponsible husband and father is the very best that can be said for him as a family man. During his first nine months in Washington, he traveled on weekends to New York but rarely saw his wife, who was the official excuse for his visit. He did not even send her money but left her wealthy mother to take care of her financial needs. When Melinda eventually did move to Washington, she complained to embassy wives that Donald drank too much, was moody and uncommunicative, and spent too little time with the family. Theirs was an unhappy marriage, and she found her time in Washington the unhappiest of all.

Maclean, however, was a superior being in his other pursuits. He started at the embassy as a second secretary, but, within a year, he rose to first secretary and spent most of 1946 as acting head of chancery. During that time, he was the embassy's chief administrator, and in all its history, the embassy "was probably never so exquisitely efficient, so impeccably organized" as when Maclean ran it, according to a senior British diplomat.[2]

More important than his organizational skills were his damaging espionage activities. During the latter part of World War II, he was probably the most productive Soviet spy in Washington, more so than certain high-ranking Soviet informants in the Roosevelt Administration, such as Harry Dexter White, the No. 2 man in the Treasury Department, and Lauchlin Currie, a senior economist on the White House staff. Because Maclean controlled cable traffic into and out of the embassy, he saw to it that Soviet intelligence received secret documents exchanged between his ambassador, Lord Halifax, and the Foreign Office in London, as well as correspondence between Roosevelt and Churchill. Looking back on those years, former CIA Director Richard Helms considered Maclean to be Stalin's most valuable spy. Or, as the elegant Secretary of State Dean Acheson pithily observed after the Englishman defected, "[T]hat son-ofabitch knew everything."[3]

Maclean subtly left his mark on the summit conferences of Allied leaders late in the war against Germany. Churchill was to admit later in life that he attended the meetings of the so-called Big Three with a great sense of insecurity. He once pictured himself as "the poor little English donkey" with Stalin, the great Russian bear, on one side and Roosevelt, the great American buffalo, on the other.[4] Maclean reinforced that image for Stalin's benefit when he told his Soviet control in the summer of 1944 that Britain "depends almost entirely on America" for its economic survival.[5]

The fate of Poland was the Allies' great tar baby at the Yalta Conference in February 1945. Churchill and Roosevelt supported the ambition of its government-in-exile in London to take power in Warsaw after the war, a commitment so strong that to back away from it would mean political trouble at home. Roosevelt, in fact, had postponed the Yalta Conference until after the 1944 presidential election to give himself more flexibility on the Polish issue. Stalin, however, had already installed a communist government at Lublin as the Red Army advanced through Poland. He rejected all efforts to install the London Poles, and he knew from his spies that the West would not go to war over Poland.[6]

After much maneuvering on both sides, the Western leaders thought they had a deal. It called for the formation of a transition government by adding "democratic leaders" from inside and outside of Poland to the existing Lublin regime. The transition government would then prepare for "free and unfettered elections" to establish a permanent government. The question of which interim leaders to include would be worked out later in Moscow by a commission consisting of Soviet Foreign Minister Vyacheslav Molotov and Moscow Ambassadors Averell Harriman of the United States and Sir A. Clark Kerr of Britain, but the ministerial talks went nowhere. Molotov rejected almost all of the Polish leaders proposed by Harriman and Kerr.

Maclean played a mischievous hidden role by divulging internal British cables to Soviet intelligence. One telegram from "Nook" (KGB code for the British Foreign Office) to "Pool" (the British Embassy in Washington) directed the ambassador, Lord Halifax, to see Secretary of State Edward R. Stettinius, Jr., and, if possible, Roosevelt to patch up differences between the two Allies. "We believe," said the Foreign Office message, "that if we and the Americans together take a firm position, the Russians very likely will give way on some of the points [at issue]."[7] Another cable included the text of Ambassador Kerr's telegram from Moscow to London. Sir Clark wrote in part, "I do not think that Molotov, despite his stubbornness, has said his last word."[8] Presumably, Molotov read these lines, and, in any case, he did not give way. The British and Americans did. Poland lapsed into four and a half decades of imposed communist rule and became a metaphor for the Western abandonment of Eastern Europe.

Maclean was even more helpful to the Soviets in their effort to catch up with the United States in the nuclear arms race. Thanks to him, the leaders in the Kremlin knew more about the American atomic bomb program in 1947–48 than did the elected senators and representatives on Capitol Hill and most of President Harry S. Truman's Cabinet.[9] During the war, Roosevelt and Churchill had hammered out secret agreements at Quebec, Canada, and Hyde Park, New York, to share in the development of atomic arms. The agreements amounted to foreign treaties, which, under the Constitution, were supposed to have been submitted to the Senate for ratification. Congress was never told about them until the spring of 1947 nor, for that matter, was the British Parliament.

The agreements resulted in the creation of a secret American-British-Canadian Combined Policy Committee (CPC) to share technical information, allocate uranium, and resolve disputes among the partners. The CPC was run by a three-man secretariat representing each of the member nations. Maclean served as the British secretary during a nineteen-month period from February 1947 to September 1948. At the same time, Maclean represented British (and Soviet) interests in still another secret body unknown to Congress, the Combined Development Trust (CDT), formed by the CPC in 1944 to corner the world market in uranium for the Anglo-Saxon nations.

Unaware of the wartime agreements, Congress passed the McMahon Act in 1946, which made it illegal to share atomic secrets with a foreign power. So when the CPC met at the State Department on February 3, 1947, with its British, Canadian, and American representatives, its business under the three-nation accords was in violation of the new U.S. law. It was Maclean's first CPC meeting. The most important secret that he took from it was America's total dependence on foreign sources of uranium. He continued to keep track of the Congo's uranium output through monthly reports of the CDT, which detailed the amount of ore mined, its purity, its destination, and the price. Acheson characterized these data as "prime military secrets."[10] They told the Soviets how limited was the American supply.

Maclean also had access to the Atomic Energy Commission (AEC). During a ten-month period from August 1947 to June 1948, he made twenty visits to the AEC in search of classified information. In November 1947, the AEC issued him a pass, which allowed him to enter its premises unescorted, a privilege not extended to members of Congress or the President's Cabinet. It was particularly galling to FBI Director Hoover to learn in 1951, after Maclean had slipped behind the Iron Curtain, that a Soviet spy had enjoyed such special treatment. Whenever Hoover went inside the AEC in his capacity as chief of counterintelligence, an armed guard escorted him.

Maclean, through his connections at the AEC, arranged for British scientists to visit the atomic plant at Oak Ridge, Tennessee, which turned out enriched bomb-grade uranium. In a report Maclean helped to draft, one of the visiting scientists said the tour of Oak Ridge saved the British many months of work. No doubt, it was helpful to the Soviets as well. British scientists also visited the Berkeley Radiation Laboratory in California, where a 92-inch cyclotron, a powerful tool used in the production of plutonium, was under construction. The helpful hosts at Berkeley sent the cyclotron blueprints to the British (and unwittingly to the Soviets) by way of Maclean. In August 1955, after Stalin died, Western and Soviet scientists mingled for the first time since the thirties at a Geneva conference on the peaceful uses of atomic energy. One of the papers presented by Soviet scientists described "the world's most powerful" cyclotron nearing completion at Dubna. Lewis Strauss, chairman of the AEC, came away from the conference "astonished" by Soviet achievements, "notably . . . the photographs they exhibited of their new cyclotron."[11]

In November 1947, Maclean was one of two Soviet spies from Britain to participate in a three-nation conference to decide which wartime atomic secrets to declassify. The other, by pure coincidence, was the atomic spy Klaus Fuchs. At this point, Soviet and British interests coincided. Each nation was building a bomb and wanted to learn all they could about American atomic secrets. It put Maclean in the driver's seat. He could openly solicit atomic secrets for Moscow in London's name. Neither Maclean nor Fuchs overplayed his hand by arguing too strongly for declassification. Fuchs, in fact, made himself conspicuously conservative and sometimes advocated that a secret be retained in the face of unanimous opposition. Simply by being there and listening to the Americans explain why they wanted to keep certain things secret, the spies obtained useful clues about what more they needed to know.

Maclean's contribution to his Soviet masters was exceptionally wide in scope. One of his duties as acting head of chancery in 1946 was to interface between the British Joint Supply Mission (JSM) in Washington and the Foreign Office in London. For this purpose, he had a special pass to the Pentagon where the JSM was quartered. The JSM handed Maclean many sensitive documents to be forwarded to the Foreign Office. One top secret report laid out U.S. Army and Air Force strength at every base in the United States and abroad. It included the detailed composition and firepower of a U.S. infantry division and the range of its weapons. This was a bonanza for the Red Army and probably found practical use during Moscow's proxy war in Korea.[12]

By 1948, the Soviet Leviathan had swallowed most of Eastern Europe and was fixing its glare on the West where the communist tide was rising. The Soviet Union had two and a half million to four million troops under arms, compared with fewer than a million in the U.S. armed forces. Few informed observers doubted that, in a conventional war, the outnumbered Americans would be swept off the European continent. American policymakers, the Congress, and the American public, however, believed that Stalin would never start a war with the United States for fear of nuclear retaliation. But at that time America's nuclear deterrent was largely fiction, as AEC Chairman David Lilienthal learned to his shock and dismay on an inspection trip to Los Alamos in January 1947. He found the U.S. atomic arsenal in disarray. During a grim meeting at the White House on his return, he told President Truman that there were no assembled bombs, no assembly teams to assemble them, and no assurance without further testing that, once assembled, the bombs from available parts would work.[13]

That was less than the half of it. The United States was also running low on uranium. Without uranium, no new bombs could be built. The Belgian government was experiencing political pressure from the communist left, and, in the Belgian Congo province of Katanga, the mines faced the prospect of being shut down, either from the need to drill new shafts or from labor unrest, or both. Nor was the American delivery system up to snuff. Gen. Carl Spaatz, Air Force Chief of Staff, 1946–48, recalled later that no more than twenty-seven B-29 bombers were available during that time. Even those few bombers were more than necessary to carry the twelve A-bombs on hand in 1948.[14] The only bases from which they could operate were in Britain and Egypt, the latter still a British colony.

In other words, Stalin had little to fear, and he knew it because Maclean kept him informed. Fortunately for the West, Stalin blundered. A Soviet campaign of heavy-handed intimidation against Finland and Norway, together with a brutal communist takeover in Czechoslovakia, sent a chill through non-communist Europe. Instead of caving in, the West stiffened its resolve. France, Belgium, and the Netherlands began to discuss their collective security. U.S. Secretary of State George C. Marshall had already broached his farsighted plan for European economic recovery, and in the nation where foreign policy, since the time of George Washington, had steered clear of "entangling alliances," the mood began to shift in favor of an entangling alliance against communism. Exploratory low-level talks about a trans-Atlantic pact (what would become NATO) were held at the end of March in a basement vault at the Pentagon. At first, the talks involved only the CPC and CDT nations, the United States, Great Britain, and Canada. They were so secret that neither Congress nor the French government was informed for fear that word would leak out, but Stalin, the last man they wanted to learn their secret, had his agent, Donald Maclean, at the table. No one was allowed to take notes at the meetings, so Maclean later summed up the proceedings from memory in the privacy of his home and sent the notes to Moscow.

The big question for the conferees was where to draw the line. Should the American umbrella be extended to Scandinavia? Austria? Italy? Greece? Turkey? Iran? Any nation excluded was potentially a sitting duck for the Soviets. In fact, Korea was later excluded, which emboldened the communist North to attack the South.

Stalin responded to the talks by stepping up pressure on the West. The Soviets walked out of meetings to resolve the status of Austria and began a harassing campaign to dislodge American, British, and French occupation forces from Berlin, which was surrounded by Soviet troops in East Germany. This strategy backfired with the American-led airlift of food and supplies for West Berlin. Expanded high-level talks on Western security were held the following summer, and included France. Within a year, NATO became a reality. With no more pandering to Stalin, the Cold War became an open confrontation. Maclean's superior espionage notwithstanding, Soviet expansion in Europe came to a screeching stop. That upset Maclean, who had hoped for a quick communist takeover of all Europe so that he could escape from his despised double life.

The stress of undercover work took its toll on Maclean. Although a smashing success in diplomacy and espionage alike, he was temperamentally ill suited for both. He said later that, given a choice, he never would have gone into the Foreign Service and that the more he experienced the diplomatic life, the more he hated it. His anti-Americanism grew as the Truman Administration increasingly stood in the way of Soviet expansion in Europe and the Middle East. It erupted one summer night in 1945 at a dinner given by the gifted journalist Joseph Alsop, a cousin of President Roosevelt's and one of the most socially prominent men in Washington. The evening started pleasantly enough, but Maclean went heavy on the "sauce" as the night wore on. He began to ridicule American foreign policy in Iran, where Soviet troops occupied oil fields in the northern part of the country, and he condemned the CIA's role in the enthronement of the young pro-American Shah. Then he spat his venom at the stewardship of President Truman's secretary of state James Byrnes. That did it for Alsop, a close friend of Byrnes's. He ordered Maclean out of the house.[15]

Maclean had attended the Alsop dinner alone because Melinda and the children had retreated to a family farm in western Massachusetts to escape Washington's oppressive heat. When she returned to the capital, family life was no better. Donald's drinking became worse, and he began to go out late at night. Where he went, Melinda never knew. One rumor had it that he was dating a couple of CIA secretaries as part of an undercover assignment. Whatever he did during his late-night carousing, he avoided trouble with the police.

In the late summer of 1948, Maclean left Washington. His normal tour of three years had been extended an extra sixteen months, and his next posting was Cairo as the head of chancery. At age thirty-five, he was the youngest counselor at a major embassy in the British Foreign Service. His future as a diplomat never seemed brighter, but the fear of discovery began to eat at his insides. British physicist and Soviet spy Alan Nunn May, Maclean's contemporary at

Cambridge, had been caught in the fallout from the 1945 defection of Igor Gouzenko, a young cipher clerk at the Soviet Embassy in Ottawa. Just prior to Maclean's departure from the United States, Whittaker Chambers had publicly denounced another suspected Soviet spy, Alger Hiss, during hearings before the House Un-American Activities Committee. Records show that Maclean had met with Hiss, presumably about espionage because, based on their separate areas of responsibility, they had no official business to discuss. The next year in Cairo, Maclean received news of Fuchs's arrest and word from Philby by way of Moscow that he was in danger from the same American codebreaking effort that had netted Fuchs.

Maclean self-destructed in Cairo. He started drinking heavily, and the more he drank, the more his latent homosexuality surfaced. He resented it when Melinda began enjoying the diplomatic swirl by hosting dinners and arranging social events. Their marriage, never very solid, was coming apart. Once he struck her, and more than once he insulted her. An old friend of Maclean's, Philip Toynbee, son of a famous historian, stayed with the family while on a reporting assignment in the Middle East. The two spent entire weekends in an alcoholic haze. The final indignity came one night after a day of heavy drinking. They invaded the apartment of two young women who worked at the American Embassy. Although the women were not home, the door was unlocked. The intruders turned the place upside down—grown men, in an alcoholic stupor, acting like a pair of schoolboy cutups. They scattered furniture, smashed dishes, emptied drawers, and tore up underwear. The climax, perhaps apocryphal, was described by Toynbee years later: "Donald raises a large mirror above his head and crashes it into the bath, when to my amazement, and delight, alas, the bath breaks in two while the mirror remains intact."[16]

When Maclean sobered up, he was contrite. He called the women to apologize and offered to pay damages. His brilliant diplomatic career and his unhappy marriage were equally in shambles. The Foreign Office recalled him to London and put him on sick leave. After a period of rehabilitation (during which he continued to drink) he reunited with Melinda and the children and appeared, outwardly at least, to have pulled himself together. But, in fact, the demons still haunted him. At one party, high on booze and provocative conversation, he blurted out to an old friend that he was "working for Uncle Joe."[17] Fortunately for him, the remark was not taken seriously. In the summer of 1950, the Foreign Office, eager to reclaim its wayward star, put him back to work in London as head of the American Department.

By this time, the Korean War had broken out and Maclean once again had access to important information useful to the Kremlin. Despite the British government's attempt after Maclean's defection to cover up the magnitude of Korean War secrets available to him, author Verne W. Newton was able to demonstrate that cables routed to the American Department (where Maclean could read them) pertained to "highly secret operational military information originating from the British mission in Peking, the British Cabinet, the American Joint Chiefs of Staff, and from [United Nations Army Commander] Gen. Douglas MacArthur himself."[18] Detailed information about planned air and military operations coming directly out of the Pentagon war room was routinely cabled to Maclean's American Department in London.

Even more significant were the secret transcripts of a summit meeting between President Truman and British Prime Minister Clement Attlee after China had entered the war in force. From Maclean by way of Stalin, China's Mao Tse-tung and North Korea's Kim Il Sung learned that Truman did not intend to use the atomic bomb except to avoid a military disaster. Neither did he intend to bomb Chinese military and industrial targets north of the Yalu River.[19] Knowing an enemy's intentions in time of war is a gift of unsurpassing value. Maclean had scored again, but his time in the hated shadows was growing short.

———————

Maclean's exposure came out of an extraordinary feat of American codebreaking in 1951, long after he had left Washington. There to watch the codebreakers track him down was his fellow Cambridge spy, Kim Philby, assigned by the British MI6 as its representative to American intelligence. Their co-conspirator, Guy Burgess, on assignment at the British Embassy in 1951, was staying at the Philby home. At about the time Philby realized Maclean would be unmasked, the embassy sent Burgess back to England in disgrace for a gross violation of the speed limit in Virginia, a climactic event in a reckless, depraved life. Philby entrusted Burgess to carry a warning to Maclean but implored Burgess not to take flight with him. When Burgess and Maclean left together, Philby was compromised and his career went into decline until he himself defected a decade later.

A few months after Philby's arrival in Moscow in 1961, Burgess died from the long-term effects of alcohol. Philby did not bother to go to his old friend's funeral. Maclean and Philby found jobs in the Soviet bureaucracy, Maclean for the Foreign Service, and Philby for the KGB. Outside of work, they lived painfully intertwined lives in Moscow's tiny exile community. The two were a study in contrasts. Maclean, who had found espionage distasteful, was more than happy to have it behind him. Philby had thrived on it and missed the thrill of the double life. Had Burgess not compromised him, he might have enjoyed a very long and even more spectacular career as a mole.

Beyond that, personal animosities arose between Philby and Maclean. Their wives followed them to Moscow. Melinda Maclean had been there with her children since 1953. Eleanor Philby came with Kim. The couples spent a great deal of time together. Soon, Kim and Melinda were having an affair. Eleanor moved out and left Moscow. Melinda moved in and exacted her revenge for injuries past and present by inflicting a deep emotional wound on Donald. That affair lasted perhaps a year, after which Melinda, too, moved out and returned to the United States. The Macleans' grown children, married to Russians, remained in the Soviet Union for a time but eventually followed their mother to the States. Donald spent his last days alone in Moscow without family. When he died in 1983, high-ranking Soviet officials attended his funeral. His picture was hung in the Memory Room of the KGB (later the SVR, the Russian [post-Soviet] intelligence service), where he is honored as a hero of foreign intelligence. His ashes were carried back to his native Britain, where he was condemned as a traitor.

CHAPTER 13

The Spy
of the Century

Since 1950, when the German-born physicist Klaus Fuchs confessed to spying for the Soviet Union, he had been considered the No. 1 thief of U.S. atomic secrets. With the release of American decoding secrets in 1995, however, the identity of another important atomic spy became known. Theodore Alvin Hall, an American teenager out of Harvard University, reached Los Alamos some six or seven months ahead of Fuchs. While Fuchs was totally out of contact with Soviet intelligence, Hall was the first Soviet agent to send Moscow details about a crash American program to build a plutonium bomb, the kind tested at Alamogordo, New Mexico, in July 1945 and dropped on Nagasaki, Japan, on August 9. Hall's report included a description of the top secret "implosion" trigger for detonating the plutonium bomb by compression.

Although Fuchs was more advanced academically and far more experienced than Hall in atomic research, he knew nothing of the plutonium bomb until he arrived at Los Alamos in the summer of 1944 as part of the British team assigned to the Manhattan Project, the name given to the U.S. atomic bomb program. By February 1945, when he renewed contact with his KGB courier, Fuchs thoroughly understood it and wrote out a report from memory. It reached Moscow about a month after Hall's material, but Fuchs's information had greater impact. The reaction of Igor Kurchatov, scientific director of the Soviet program, tells the story. What originated with Hall, Kurchatov found "interesting" and worthy of further research; that from Fuchs, he called "exceptionally important."

Neither should it be forgotten that, for three years in Birmingham, England, and in New York City, Fuchs was feeding Soviet intelligence a steady diet of information about his research on the uranium bomb, the kind dropped on Hiroshima, Japan. His reports included work on plans for the U-235 enrichment plant at Oak Ridge, Tennessee, and calculations about gaseous diffusion, the separation of the bomb-grade isotope U-235 from the abundant U-238 found in uranium ore.

The Soviets entered the nuclear age in September 1949 by exploding an exact copy of the American plutonium bomb. Both Hall and Fuchs contributed to that event, but Fuchs's input, based on Kurchatov's reaction, was the more valuable to Soviet scientific research. Two years later, the Soviets followed up by testing a uranium bomb. Fuchs also had a hand in that test. All things considered, Fuchs remains the No. 1 thief of America's (and Britain's) atomic secrets. Judging from the impact of the atomic bomb on the conduct of nations, the nerdy-looking, bespectacled Fuchs—the antithesis of the dashing James Bond of fiction—is probably the most important spy of the twentieth century.

The impetus in the West for building the atomic bomb came largely from European scientists who had fled the Nazi terror to Britain and the United States. After the uranium atom was first split in 1938 by two German chemists, Otto Hahn and Fritz Strassmann of the Kaiser Wilhelm Institute in Berlin, the emigré scientists feared that if Germany were the first country to develop the bomb, Hitler and his Nazi henchmen would rule the world.

The tremendous energy generated from breaking the atom apart has two applications depending on the rate of fission. By slow fission, the energy can be harnessed for peaceful purposes. By rapid, virtually instantaneous fission, the energy is lost in a gigantic explosion. During the late thirties, that distinction was still only hypothetical, and scientists wondered if the bomb was practicable. In the spring of 1940, Rudolf Peierls and Otto Frisch, transplanted Europeans at Birmingham University in England, performed basic mathematical calculations that answered in the affirmative. They put their findings in a memorandum to the British government, which established an exploratory group called the Maud Committee. After studying the bomb problem for more than a year, the committee concluded optimistically that a bomb could be built within two and a half years. During the summer of 1941, the Maud Committee turned its findings over to the Cabinet Scientific Advisory Committee chaired by Lord Hankey.

Little did anyone know that a Soviet spy was lurking in Lord Hankey's chambers. In September, Anatoly Gorsky, the KGB resident at the Soviet Embassy in London, dispatched a coded telegram informing Moscow of certain conclusions of the Maud Committee report about the feasibility of the bomb. A few days later, he notified Moscow that Lord Hankey had submitted a favorable report to the War Cabinet and that Britain had decided to go ahead with an atomic bomb that would take two to five years to build. Gorsky's source was undoubtedly the mole John Cairncross, one of the Cambridge-educated communists recruited in the thirties by Soviet intelligence for deep penetration into the British government. Cairncross was secretary to Lord Hankey during the fall of 1941.[1]

In Moscow, where the war was coming ever closer at that time, there was no immediate reaction to the intelligence from Cairncross and Gorsky. The Soviets argued for a year and a half over whether to start their own program until, finally in February 1943, the State Defense Committee adopted a resolution to begin research on a Soviet bomb. A month later, Kurchatov was named scientific director. No one believed there was any chance the bomb could be developed in time to help in the war against Hitler. In the first place, the Soviet Union lacked enough uranium even to create a chain reaction, and had no access to significant deposits of uranium ore. Still, it had taken the first baby steps of its journey into the atomic age.

Fuchs began his espionage career in the fall of 1941 at about the time the Maud Committee report was being passed up the line to Moscow. Although at the age of thirty he was entering his climactic years, he had already lived an eventful life. Fuchs grew up during unstable times in a family that knew tragedy.[2] He was born in 1911, the third and brightest of four children. When he was seven years old, the German monarchy collapsed with the end of World War I. On the heels of this national trauma, Germany endured the chaotic years of the Weimar Republic. Fuchs spent his youth in eastern Germany and excelled in school. His father Emil, a Lutheran clergyman with a left-wing predilection, encouraged the children to form their own political views, but, in fact, they all accepted his socialist philosophy and eventually became communists. Some people in the community painted them as "the red foxes," a well-turned play on words in that *Fuchs* is German for fox and many members of the Fuchs family had reddish hair. When Klaus was nineteen, his mother committed suicide, and he learned that his mother's mother also had taken her own life. Later, one of his two sisters would make it three generations of female suicides in the family.

Klaus studied mathematics and physics at Leipzig University. He took an active part in student politics by joining the student branch of the Social Democratic Party and sometimes engaging with fellow leftists in street fighting against Nazi Brownshirts. He soon transferred to Kiel University in the north, where his father had been hired as a professor of theology. At Kiel, the fox's fur turned a deeper red, and he signed on with the communists. His father, disillusioned by Lutheran support of Hitler and nagged by growing doubts about Christian doctrine, joined the Quakers who preach nonviolence.

Open opposition to the Nazis was becoming dangerous. One day, Klaus confronted Nazi demonstrators on the Kiel campus, only to be beaten up and thrown in the river. On the night the Reichstag (parliament building) burned to the ground, February 27, 1933, the Nazis, who probably set the fire themselves, blamed the communists and arrested four thousand of them within twenty-four hours. Fuchs went into hiding for five months. The Nazi experience solidified his values on national loyalty. In 1950, as a naturalized (and, in his fashion, loyal) British citizen, he told an interrogator from Scotland Yard that he reserved the right to act according to his own conscience should there arise in Britain a situation comparable to that in Germany in 1932–33.[3]

Fuchs fled Germany in the summer of 1933. In England, with the help of his father's Quaker connections, he became a research assistant for the study of quantum theory under Professor Nevill Mott at Bristol University. As an outsider in a new country where he barely spoke the language, Fuchs turned inward. He socialized very little and kept his politics to himself. The socialist-turned-communist dynamo of Kiel devolved into a closet communist at Bristol. Fuchs earned his Ph.D. in four years. By then, he spoke good English with a heavy German accent that he never lost. He moved on to Edinburgh University under one of the great German scientists of the day, Max Born, where he earned another degree and enhanced his reputation by coauthoring learned scientific articles with Professor Born.

In August 1939, Fuchs applied for British citizenship. When war broke out the following month, however, his application was set aside because war with Germany made him an enemy alien. After the fall of France, he was interned on the Isle of Man in the Irish Sea and later in Canada, where he regularly attended a discussion group for communists. After six months, Fuchs returned to Britain and, in the fall of 1941, replaced Frisch as Peierls's partner at Birmingham to research the British bomb-building project called Tube Alloys. Again, Fuchs applied for citizenship, this time successfully.

Operation Barbarossa, the German invasion of Russia, had already swallowed large chunks of Soviet territory, and Fuchs wanted to help the communist state survive. Realizing the military importance of his work, he initiated contact with a Soviet agent and turned over his personal research on atomic fission. For the next year and a half, he regularly submitted his scientific reports to the GRU, initially to an agent called "Alexander" attached to the Soviet Embassy in London and later to a woman whom he knew as "Sonia," who ran a spy ring in Oxford. Fuchs and Sonia (Ursula Maria Kuczynski, aka Ruth Hamburger, who had previously spied in China and Switzerland) met several times in Banbury, about halfway between Birmingham and Oxford. His reports arrived in Moscow during the protracted internal debate over whether to institute a bomb program and must have impacted the final decision to go ahead.

Leo Szilard, a brilliant if eccentric Hungarian expatriate, pushed the nuclear agenda in the United States. Szilard was a theoretical, as opposed to an experimental, physicist. He did his best thinking while he soaked in a warm bath. In September 1933, at London's Strand Hotel, he soaked for hours and thought of creating a controlled chain reaction by bombarding the nucleus of the atom with neutrons, but he did not know which atom would split until the German breakthrough in 1938.

By the summer of 1939, Szilard had migrated to America. Fearful of a Nazi Germany armed with nuclear power, he enlisted two fellow Hungarian refugees, Edward Teller and Eugene Wigner, both eminent physicists, to join him in a crusade. They persuaded Albert Einstein to write President Roosevelt a letter urging an American nuclear program. Szilard hoped for government funding of his pet idea for research on a nuclear chain reaction, but there was only enough money for a low-budget experiment that Nobel physicist Enrico Fermi directed in cooperation with Szilard at Columbia University in the fall of 1941. It failed to reach critical mass, the smallest mass that will sustain a chain reaction. A year later, Fermi made history at the University of Chicago when he headed a team of scientists who generated the first self-sustaining chain reaction from a large atomic pile consisting of uranium, uranium oxide, and pure graphite to moderate neutron emissions.[4]

The Americans in the Manhattan Project did not know they had beaten Germany to the punch. They assumed that the nation first to split the atom was ahead in the nuclear arms race. In fact, six months earlier, German scientists had succeeded in creating an atomic pile with uranium and heavy water (which, like graphite, acted as a moderator of neutron emissions). They could see how a self-sustaining chain reaction would be possible with certain modifications to the pile. Three weeks later, however, an experiment went bad and the German laboratory burned to the ground. German nuclear research immediately fizzled and came to a virtual standstill.

Unaware of the German failure, the Americans moved rapidly to build the infrastructure for a nuclear industry. The Manhattan Project had three main components. At Los Alamos, they built the main laboratory to make both a uranium bomb and a plutonium bomb. The Oak Ridge plant produced bomb-grade U-235 by separating it from U-238. Another plant at Hanford, Washington, made plutonium from U-238. Both the Oak Ridge and Hanford plants worked around the fact that U-238, the abundant isotope found in uranium ore, was not fissionable. In 1941, American chemist Glenn T. Seaborg had discovered plutonium, a new man-made element whose active isotope had an atomic weight of 239, by neutron bombardment of U-238 in a cyclotron (particle accelerator) at the University of California, Berkeley. The laboratory at Berkeley was a satellite facility of the Manhattan Project. There were other satellite programs, notably at the University of Chicago and Columbia University and in Montreal, Quebec, and Chalk River, Ontario.

Late in 1943, Fuchs and Peierls arrived in New York as part of a British contingent to assist American scientists in the Manhattan Project. For the next eight months, they performed calculations on uranium diffusion for the Oak Ridge plant, part of a project administered by Columbia University and the Kellex Corporation, a construction subcontractor at Oak Ridge. Before leaving Britain,

Fuchs had received instructions from Sonia for contacting another Soviet agent in New York. He did not realize that he was being passed from one Soviet intelligence agency to another, from the military GRU to the civilian KGB.

He met his new contact, "Raymond," for the first time in February 1944 on Manhattan's Lower East Side. In a scene that, a few decades later, might have passed for a *Monty Python* spoof but actually conformed to the instructions given him by Sonia, Fuchs was carrying a tennis ball in his left hand while he looked for a man wearing gloves and holding another pair of gloves and a book with a green cover. He found Raymond to be a short, pudgy man with heavy eyelids magnified by thick glasses. They made the appropriate verbal signals and fell into conversation. Fuchs never knew (and never asked) Raymond's real name, Harry Gold of Philadelphia, who was born Heinrich Golodnitzky in Switzerland in 1910, the son of Russian Jews. A chemist, Gold passed industrial secrets to the Soviets before being assigned as Fuchs's contact.[5]

At the first get-acquainted meeting, Fuchs delivered no secrets, but, at future meetings, he turned over copies of his written reports prepared for the Kellex Corporation. During this period, he wrote thirteen very technical papers, such as "Fluctuations and the Efficiency of a Diffusion Plant," in four parts, all of which he gave to Gold. After each meeting, Gold reported to his Soviet control, Anatoly Yatskov (cover name "John"), who worked out of the Soviet consulate in New York. The Soviet nuclear program was well served. The uranium diffusion plant built at Podolsk outside Moscow was an exact copy of the Oak Ridge plant.[6] Fuchs and Gold had seven meetings over a period of six months in various parts of New York. Fuchs did not show up for the eighth meeting scheduled for late July in Brooklyn. He had been transferred to a new secret facility in the American southwest.

Los Alamos sits on a scenic New Mexico mesa thirty miles north-northwest of Santa Fe and nearly a mile and a half above sea level. Maj. Gen. Leslie Groves, director of the Manhattan Project, and J. Robert Oppenheimer, scientific director at Los Alamos, chose the site for both its isolation and accessibility to transportation. The Oppenheimer family owned a ranch nearby. There were railroad lines to Santa Fe and one passable highway connecting Santa Fe to Los Alamos. The first time Rudolf Peierls's wife Genia was driven up the winding road, which offered spectacular vistas at almost every turn, she thought it was like "climbing up to heaven"—until she reached the compound.

At the height of its activity in 1944–45, Los Alamos was a community of about forty-five thousand inhabitants whose functional prefabricated buildings marred the natural beauty of the countryside. It had the strict rules of a military base. Its existence was a military secret. Everyone who lived there, including a dozen Nobel laureates, had only one address, P.O. Box 1663, Santa Fe. Their mail was censored, telephones were generally not available, and the inhabitants needed army permission to be away overnight.

The highest priority at Los Alamos was the development of a trigger mechanism for the plutonium bomb. Peierls and Frisch had already invented the uranium trigger, which consisted of two separate chambers filled with U-235 suddenly brought together, as if shot from a gun, to create a critical mass and cause the explosion. This concept did not work for plutonium, however, because the heavier man-made element had a high rate of spontaneous fission and to bring it together, as in the "gun" trigger would cause it to explode prematurely. The new idea was to create critical mass for plutonium by compression, to be achieved by surrounding a plutonium core with a layer of explosives and directing the blast inward. On this theory, the scientists at Los Alamos bent to the task of developing an "implosion" trigger.

By the time Fuchs arrived at Los Alamos in the summer of 1944, Ted Hall had been in residence more than six months. Hall was only eighteen years old in January 1944, an age when most young people are in their final year of high school. He was exceptional. He had already finished his undergraduate courses at Harvard. Before he could collect his bachelor's degree, he was shipped off to Los Alamos. He knew only that this sudden turn of events had something to do with his passion for physics. The following spring, he was graduated cum laude in absentia.

He was born Theodore Alvin Holtzberg in New York in 1925, one of four children of Jewish immigrants.[7] He and his older brother, Edward ("Ed"), changed their name to Hall to enhance their career prospects in a society where Jews suffered discrimination. Their father, Barney Holtzberg, a furrier, suffered serious business reverses in the Depression, after which the family scaled down its lifestyle and shifted politically to the left. The New Deal president, Franklin D. Roosevelt, was a family hero. During the mid-thirties, Ed attended City College of New York and brought home radical literature, which included Marx's *Communist Manifesto* and the writings of Lincoln Steffens, the muckraking journalist. Ted gobbled them up and gained an elementary political awareness through a Marxist prism even before he reached his teens.

Ted Hall was two months short of fifteen when he entered Queens College in the fall of 1940. Two years later, at his brother's insistence, he transferred to Harvard University. After his initial shock over Harvard's academic rigor, which brought him to the edge of quitting, he immersed himself in such abstruse subjects as advanced math, relativity, and quantum mechanics. One of his roommates in the fall of 1943 was another Marxist from New York, Saville Sax, destined to become a partner in espionage. Hall wrapped up his course work that semester shortly after becoming eligible for the draft and rode a train to his rendezvous with history.

At Los Alamos, Hall spent most of his time working under an Italian emigré physicist, Bruno Rossi, internationally respected for his research in cosmic rays. He led a group under Rossi that contributed to the growing body of knowledge on the implosion trigger. In mid-October, Hall went home on a two-week leave and looked up his old roommate Sax, the ardent Marxist who had flunked out of Harvard. Together, they went in search of a Soviet control. Youthful idealism keyed Hall's decision to give away the greatest secret of the United States. He feared that postwar America might fall into economic depression and be consumed by fascism. A fascist America holding a monopoly on the atomic bomb, he reasoned, might use it against the Soviet Union. He admitted later in life that he did not fully understand the true antidemocratic nature of Stalin's dictatorship. Sax, a communist from his roots up, was a willing partner. His Russian-Jewish parents had supported the Bolshevik Revolution, and his mother, Bluma, worked for Russian War Relief during the war.

The two young men set out on separate paths with the same objective. Through Bluma, Hall gained an audience with a Soviet journalist, Sergei Kurnakov, who doubled as a KGB agent. Kurnakov listened to Hall's story and accepted a written report on the plutonium bomb, but he did not commit himself. Sax, meanwhile, strode boldly up to the entrance of the Soviet consulate on Manhattan's East Side, and was ushered into the presence of Anatoly Yatskov (aka Yakovlev), the same agent who handled Fuchs's courier, Harry Gold. He heard Sax out, accepted a duplicate of Hall's report, and thanked him for his interest, but he was also noncommittal. He compared notes with Kurnakov and weighed the risk of taking on a couple of wide-eyed kids coming in off the street against the pressure from his KGB superiors in Moscow to penetrate the veil of secrecy surrounding the U.S. atomic program, which they called "Enormoz." Ultimately, Hall, with his report on the plutonium bomb together with his impressive Harvard credentials and fortuitous placement at Los Alamos, represented an opportunity too good to ignore.[8]

After Hall's return to Los Alamos, Sax made a trip west between Thanksgiving and early December 1944 and met Hall in Albuquerque on the campus of the University of New Mexico to receive more classified documents. In February, Sax returned to Harvard. His place as Hall's courier was taken by Lona Cohen, the female half of a legendary husband-and-wife Soviet spy team. She made at least two trips to New Mexico, once in the spring of 1945 and again in the late summer after the A-bombs had fallen on Japan, at which time Hall turned over the results of the Alamogordo test.

While the two teenagers, Hall and Sax, were giving away America's vital secrets, Fuchs was completely out of touch with the KGB. There is no evidence that Fuchs and Hall ever met at Los Alamos or, if they did, that either one had the faintest idea that the other was also spying for Stalin.

On arrival at Los Alamos, Fuchs and Peierls joined a team headed by Hans Bethe, a fellow German refugee on loan to the Manhattan Project from Cornell University. They began work on calculating plutonium fission, something entirely new to them. A group under George Kistiakowsky of Harvard experimented on the explosive charges for the implosion trigger, and Fuchs became the liaison between the two teams. About twice a week, he witnessed explosives testing. He quickly learned how the implosion trigger functioned and devised a mathematical formula for calculating the reaction of plutonium to the inward pressure.

At Los Alamos, Fuchs talked very little about his personal or family history, as he had in his other life as a spy. Fuchs's younger sister, Kristel, was married to an American, Robert Heineman, and lived in Cambridge, Massachusetts. Fuchs had designated her to Soviet intelligence as a backup contact. When he failed to appear for his appointed rendezvous in July 1944, Gold posed as an old friend of Klaus's and visited Kristel in Cambridge. Through her, Soviet intelligence reconnected to Fuchs, who traveled to Cambridge on leave in February 1945. Gold came up from New York, and Fuchs wrote an eight-page report from memory that explained what he had learned at Los Alamos about the plutonium bomb. They arranged a June rendezvous in Santa Fe, New Mexico.

Gold and Fuchs met twice in Santa Fe. For the June meeting, Fuchs prepared his report in his room in Los Alamos and used classified papers so that he could give precise figures; he no longer limited himself to reporting only his own work. He wrote down the intricate details of the bomb and drew a diagram. This was the whole design of the plutonium bomb in all its top secret detail, as Fuchs understood it. On the appointed day, he drove to Santa Fe in his battered old Buick and arrived at the Castillo Street Bridge at precisely 4 P.M. to meet Gold, who had traveled to Albuquerque by rail and to Santa Fe by bus. Fuchs drove a short distance and parked. He told Gold that the plutonium bomb with an explosive power equivalent to 10,000 tons of TNT soon would be tested in the New Mexico desert, then drove him to the bus station, and handed him the written report. When they met again in September, the bombs had fallen on Japan and the war was over. At this last meeting, Fuchs handed over another report whose most important revelations were the production rates of U-235 and plutonium (P-239), which enabled the Soviets to measure the potential size of the American inventory.

By the fall of 1944, Soviet intelligence was aware that the Manhattan Project had brought together "a concentration of scientific and engineering-technical power on a scale never before seen in the history of world science. . . ."[9] The following February, KGB leader Lavrenti Beria received the first Soviet intelligence report from inside Los Alamos. Its contents consisted of information about the plutonium bomb, whose source must have been Ted Hall. After studying the report, Kurchatov (Oppenheimer's counterpart) told Beria in mid-March that the implosion technique "is of great interest, correct in principle, and ought to be subjected to serious theoretical and experimental analysis."[10] From that statement, it appears that the concept was entirely new to him. Three weeks later, Kurchatov went way beyond "interesting" in describing information that had been provided by Fuchs during a February meeting with Gold in Boston as having "great value" and being "exceptionally important." Stanford historian David Holloway concludes from the available evidence that Fuchs "was by far the most important informant in the Manhattan Project."[11]

There were other informants. David Greenglass worked as a technician under Kistiakowsky in the machine shop where the implosion "lens" was molded into shape. Greenglass provided information about the plutonium bomb, including crude sketches of the lens, to his sister and brother-in-law, Ethel and Julius Rosenberg, who later became the only atomic spies to be put to death. Years later, Kistiakowsky saw Greenglass's sketches and described them as "uselessly crude" and their importance to the Soviets "almost nil." Thus Greenglass can be ruled out as a useful source for Soviet science.[12]

Alan Nunn May, the first atomic spy to be caught and sent to prison, worked in Canada at the Montreal laboratory. He provided information about the design and construction of a heavy water pile at Chalk River, Ontario, and results of metallurgical testing at Chicago. He also contributed samples of two uranium isotopes, U-235 and U-233, a bounty considered so important by the KGB that the samples were hand carried to Moscow. To the scientists in Russia who needed uranium in bulk, however, the samples fell far short of sufficient.[13] May was exposed by documents carried out of the Soviet Embassy in Ottawa in September 1945 when Igor Gouzenko defected. Another spy, Bruno Pontecorvo, worked at Chalk River for six years. He initiated contact with the Ottawa resident at the Soviet Embassy and provided a steady flow of documents that the KGB considered almost the equal of those from Fuchs.[14] When things got hot for Pontecorvo in the West he defected to the Soviet Union.

Two other atomic spies, known from codebreaking by their cover names, have never been identified.[15] Also, because Kurchatov was so well informed about experiments at the Berkeley Radiation Laboratory, Holloway suspects there must have been a spy there keeping an eye on Glenn Seaborg and Emilio Segré.[16]

When the war ended, Fuchs continued his undercover career. After he returned to Britain in 1946, he became chief of theoretical physics at the Harwell atomic research facility. He did not immediately reestablish his Soviet connection, luckily for him, because British security, in accordance with its routine, put him under surveillance for six months but turned up nothing. Fuchs went back to spying the following winter. By then, he was cut off from information about the American atomic program, so his usefulness to the Soviets was diminished. Before he left Los Alamos, he sat in on a discussion of the hydrogen bomb. When asked by his new Soviet handler to describe the principles of its construction, he managed to brief him on the thinking of American scientists. American calculations in 1946 about what was needed to put the H-bomb together turned out to be inaccurate, however, so Fuchs could not have been much help to the Soviets, as he himself admits. In fact, the Soviets built the hydrogen bomb their own way with little, if any, help from their spies.[17]

Earlier, Fuchs had passed along a secret, not revealed publicly until May 1948, that Britain intended to build its own atomic bomb.[18] Because of his experience, Fuchs was a key figure in the British A-bomb program. True to his dual loyalties, he did his best for Britain and told the Soviets what he did. He revealed that the British intended to build a plutonium bomb (his recommendation), gave figures about British plutonium production to the Soviets (from which they could calculate how many bombs the British might produce), and relayed details of a British plutonium reactor under construction. His information dovetailed nicely with the Soviets' needs because they also decided to build a plutonium bomb.

Like Donald Maclean, Fuchs was unmasked by American codebreaking. Ultimately, he confessed without knowing that the authorities were already onto him. Throughout his career, he had managed to compartmentalize his espionage by pretending to wall off his covert activities from his immediate social environment. He referred to this in his confession as "controlled schizophrenia." The wall began to crumble at Harwell. As his professional status rose and his personal friendships grew, his loyalties subtly changed. The noble fight against the Nazi horror no longer justified his covert acts against the interests of a free society. Outside political influences caused him to rethink his Marxist ideals, as, for example, the realpolitik of expansionist Soviet policy. He said later that he was disillusioned by communism as practiced in Russia. Months before his confession in 1950, he had stopped giving secrets to his Soviet control. His exit from espionage, like his entry into it, was a matter of conscience. Yet, he did not seem to fully grasp the reality that, whatever his conscience told him, society would exact a price for what he had done.

The task of obtaining Fuchs's confession was assigned to William Skardon, an MI5 counterespionage officer on loan to Scotland Yard. A skillful interrogator, Skardon knew only that Fuchs had passed information to the Soviets on one occasion while he was in the United States. He met four or five times with Fuchs over several weeks and, each time, asked a variant of the same question: "Did you betray a secret to the Soviet Union?" When Fuchs finally admitted it, Skardon asked him to identify the most important secret he had revealed. "Perhaps the most important thing," Fuchs answered almost casually, "was the full design of the atom bomb." Skardon was stunned. No one in British security had the least idea it was as serious as all that.[19]

After Fuchs acknowledged his espionage, he poured out the details and signed a written confession a few days later. When he was arrested and held for trial, his colleagues were utterly astonished. An old friend from his Edinburgh days, Edward Corson, cabled him, ". . . do not believe accusations." Fuchs cabled back, "The evidence will change your mind."[20] Rudolf and Genia Peierls felt betrayed. Peierls visited Fuchs in prison and asked him to name his Soviet handlers to remove any possible suspicion of his colleagues, especially foreign-born scientists like himself. Russian-born Genia could not believe his naiveté toward the Soviet dictatorship.[21] Fuchs thought he faced death. But his offense, giving away secrets to a foreign power (not the enemy), carried a maximum penalty of fourteen years, and that is what he received. With time off for good behavior, he served twelve years, after which he was stripped of his British citizenship and banished. By that time, he was fifty years old. He spent the rest of his life in East Germany.

The fact that Soviet scientists received so much help from Fuchs and other Western spies should not be misconstrued to mean the Soviets were not capable of building the A-bomb on their own. Careful historians say only that the atomic spies saved them a year or two and that the Soviets would have built an atomic bomb with or without their help. The fact remains, however, that their 1949 plutonium bomb was a copy of the American original based on information supplied by spies, the most important one being Fuchs, and their uranium bomb, tested in 1951, also benefited from Fuchs's treachery. Whatever the speculation over how long it would have taken the Soviets to catch up, the theft of U.S. atomic secrets stands out as one of the most spectacular intelligence coups of all time.

CHAPTER 14

Speak, Ciphers!

With the hindsight of more than half a century and the release of many classified secrets, it is clear that 1945, the year of Allied victory in World War II, was the year of Soviet defeat for its espionage network in America. When Igor Gouzenko walked out the door of the Soviet Embassy in Ottawa, and asked Canada for political asylum, the alarm bells went off in Moscow. Stolen documents stuffed in Gouzenko's pockets and inside his coat contained solid evidence of widespread Soviet spying in Canada and the United States. Two months later, word reached Moscow that Elizabeth Bentley was cooperating with the FBI. Once Moscow's dedicated agent and courier for Stalin's spies in the U.S. government, Bentley knew the Soviet network from the inside. Before Gouzenko and Bentley broke away, Whittaker Chambers had already talked to U.S. authorities.

Moscow ordered contact with its American sources broken off. Soviet operatives whom Bentley might identify hastily booked passage back to the Soviet Union out of harm's way. The American spies left behind looked for shelter. The Soviets kept their American assets in limbo for two years as they waited for the storm to subside. By 1947, when they tried to breathe new life into the old network, the environment for espionage had changed. The once productive crowd of communist ideologues had faded into history. Because most of the Soviets' best sources were out of government in the cutbacks from war to peace and the transition from Roosevelt to Truman, efforts to revive the network were largely unsuccessful. In fact, it never fully recovered. Four decades later, one of America's best-informed intelligence experts, Sen. Daniel Patrick Moynihan, laid claim to an American victory. In the era of the Cold War, he boasted, Soviet intelligence enjoyed "episodic successes," but, by the end of the forties, ". . . Communism was a defeated ideology in the United States, with its influence in steep and steady decline, and the KGB reduced to recruiting thieves as spies."[1]

First came the defectors with their startling revelations, then the codebreakers who toiled quietly behind the scenes. The latter's unspectacular work gave rise to spectacular results, and the world knew nothing about it for fifty years. Not until the mid-nineties did the American government release decrypted wartime messages between Moscow and Soviet agents in the United States, finally letting one of the century's biggest secrets out of the bag—secret to the public at large, not to Soviet intelligence. The codebreakers confirmed the testimony of the defectors and discovered spy operations, most significantly, the theft of the atomic bomb, about which Bentley, Chambers, Gouzenko, and others knew nothing. Although the Gouzenko papers led to the arrest and confession of the British physicist Alan Nunn May, who did A-bomb research and spied for the Soviets in Montreal, Gouzenko could not name other atomic spies. For that matter, neither could May. The FBI knew that May was not the only one, but no good leads on the others turned up until, unexpectedly, a project to be known later as "Venona" came to the rescue. Bit by bit, a cipher here and a code group there, a word at a time, now and then a sentence, sometimes a whole paragraph, with the hours stretching into days and the days into years, the Venona codebreakers peeled away layers of conspiracy and subterfuge hidden in what should have been an unbreakable Soviet cipher and gave the FBI the break it was seeking.

Unlike other great conquests in the arcane field of cryptanalysis—the German Enigma by the Poles and British, the Japanese Purple by the Americans, and the German teleprinter cipher by the British, all of which involved the reconstruction of cipher machines—the Venona breakthrough was achieved with old-fashioned pencil-and-paper codebreaking and early model IBM tabulating machines. Venona ferreted out, among others, Klaus Fuchs, Theodore Alvin Hall, Donald Maclean, David Greenglass, Harry Gold, and Julius and Ethel Rosenberg and detected other damaging atomic spies by cover name but never found out their true identities. It also corroborated the main lines of public testimony provided by the defectors.

Altogether, in all categories of espionage activities, Venona learned that 349 Americans or others living and working in the United States—not including Soviet agents protected by diplomatic immunity—spied for Soviet Russia during World War II.[2] Not all of them worked in government. Atomic spies Klaus Fuchs, Ted Hall, and others were scientists and technicians caught in unusual wartime circumstances. Some spies, such as Bentley and Chambers, were couriers. Others, including Julius Rosenberg, carried out industrial espionage relating especially to weapons technology. Still others functioned as talent spotters and recruiters. Many spies, however, did hold government jobs, in some cases key positions at very high levels. Among them were Harry Dexter White, an assistant secretary of the treasury; presidential aide Lauchlin Currie, and most probably Alger Hiss, a political advisor to the secretary of state.

The Venona Project sprang from humble beginnings in 1943 with a small number of people sifting through tall stacks of encrypted Soviet messages between Moscow and the United States. At the time, in the midst of war, no one thought of espionage. The codebreakers were trying to track down rumors that Stalin sought a separate peace with Hitler. (Not surprisingly, Stalin harbored the same suspicion of his Western allies.) The outcome of the war proved the rumors false even before the codebreakers could read a single message. The spy scandal in the immediate aftermath gave the project new life; after years of looking up a blind alley, the codebreakers had their first pungent whiff of espionage. From then on, in collaboration with the FBI, they followed the trail leading to the atomic spies and beyond. They learned a lot about Soviet intelligence in the West, not just who many of the spies were but how they operated and the structure of the network. The revelations were never used openly in court, and the Venona Project itself, which was terminated in 1980, remained secret until 1995. Consequently, the heroes of Venona have not yet taken their rightful place in American lore. They are best known to a tiny number of scholars, intelligence buffs, high officials in the West, and, of course, the master spies of the erstwhile Soviet Union.

Most of the wartime communications between Moscow and Soviet missions in America went by slow diplomatic pouch. More urgent messages buried in codes and ciphers were sent by commercial cable or, less often, by radiogram. When the rumors popped up in 1943 about a separate Soviet-German peace deal the U.S. Office of Censorship ordered the Soviet cables intercepted. The U.S. Army's Signal Intelligence Service formed a small Russian Section to work on the encrypted messages piling up by the thousands at Arlington Hall, a former girls' academy, a few miles west of Washington. At first, the project had no name. Then, it was called "Jade"; later, "Bride"; even later, "Drug"; and finally in 1961, "Venona."[3] The last name stuck. Eventually, the Venona codebreakers decrypted and translated about 2,900 messages in whole or in part.[4] That represents a mere fraction of the total sent, but it is, nonetheless, a stunning achievement when one considers that, when they started, the codebreakers had no good reason to believe they could unravel a single message.

In theory, the Soviet cryptosystem was unbreakable because it used the so-called one-time pad. It was actually a combined code and cipher system that consisted of, first, a codebook or "dictionary," in which four-digit groups represented Russian phrases, words, proper names, and letters, and, second, the one-time pad of random additives for creating ciphers. To take a purely imaginary example, say a Soviet clerk wanted to transmit the following message: "Charles sending atomic bomb report." ("Charles" was a cover name for Klaus Fuchs.) Each word had its own four-digit group from the codebook. First, the clerk transposed the words into code:

Charles sending atomic bomb report.

4385   6113   3194   2289   8617

Second, the clerk compressed the four-digit groups into five-digit groups by shifting numbers to the left:

43856   11331   94228   98617

Third, the clerk inserted the five-digit random additives, also known as the "key." Somewhere in the message, the sender indicated to the receiver which set of additives to use. The five-digit additives added to the five-digit code groups by "non-carry" addition produced ciphers—"non-carry" meaning that if the sum of two numbers in a column was 10 to 18, the 1 was discarded:

Five-digit codes:	43856	11331	94228	98617
+				
Random additives:	36829	96589	21493	25397
=				
Ciphers:	79675	07810	15611	13904

Fourth, the cipher numbers were turned into cipher letters for commercial cable or radio transmission in Morse code. This was accomplished with a simple conversion table with ten Latin letters representing the numbers 0 to 9. If 0 = O, 1 = I, 2 = U, 3 = Z, 4 = T, 5 = R, 6 = E, 7 = W, 8 = A, and 9 = P, the message would go out as intentionally incomprehensible garble:

WPEWR   OWAIO   IREII   IZPOT.

The additives from the one-time pad were the strength of the system. Cryptanalysis requires the repetition of additives. With repetition, no system is safe. The more often the additives are repeated, the more vulnerable the system. With the Soviet one-time pad, each sheet containing a different set of sixty five-digit additive groups was used only once, after which the page of additives would be destroyed at both the sending and receiving ends.

Other countries, notably the British, also successfully used the one-time pad. The Japanese Imperial Navy chose to make ciphers with an additive book instead of the one-time pad. Early in the Pacific War, the Japanese kept the same book in operation for several months. By reusing the same additives, they made the system more vulnerable. This was at the root of the American breakthrough prior to the Battle of Midway. Using the additive book as opposed to the one-time pad was a conscious choice. Maintaining the uniqueness of thousands upon thousands of one-time pads was cryptographically difficult. The Japanese chose the greater simplicity and what they considered the slight vulnerability of their system over the complexity of the alternative, thereby fatally underestimating the abilities of American codebreakers.

The Soviets made a similar mistake to a far lesser degree. What led to the limited American success in the Venona Project was a Soviet compromise of its additives. Under the pressure of war early in 1942, when the German army still threatened Moscow, the demand for one-time pads apparently exceeded the ability of Russian cryptographers to turn them out in a timely manner so they duplicated at least thirty-five thousand additive pages. They realized that they had opened a crack in their airtight system but thought the crack to be so small that no enemy codebreakers could ever take advantage of it. To make that even less likely, the Soviets widely scattered the duplications. There was no single full pad of duplications, but thousands of one-time pads contained one or more two-time additive pages.

The breakthrough at Arlington Hall came in three stages: first, the discovery of duplicate additive pages; second, a technique for stripping away the additives to reveal the code numbers; and third, the reduction of code numbers to plain language. A fourth task, the identification of spies from their cover names, was reserved for the FBI.

At first, the Soviet diplomatic cables rated a low priority. With a war against the fascist powers still to be won, most of the experienced codebreakers and language specialists were absorbed with German and Japanese systems. Nevertheless, the first breakthrough in Soviet codes was not long in coming. During the fall of 1943, Lt. Richard Hallock noticed a number of duplicate additive pages in Soviet trade messages. Before the war, Hallock had been an archaeologist and scholar of the ancient Babylonian language at the University of Chicago. When he first began staring at the Soviet ciphers, he must have been reminded of his adventures in Babylonian. He attacked them in the classic mode of looking for cribs. On the assumption that many of the messages would have repetitive openings, he fed the first five cipher groups of ten thousand messages into IBM tabulating machines and unexpectedly found two sets of duplicate keys. More number crunching produced more duplicates.[5]

The next major break would have to wait for war's end. The discovery of duplicates meant only that the Arlington Hall codebreakers knew there was a crack in the system, but they still did not know how to exploit it. During the intervening two years, the codebreakers knocked heads with the unyielding puzzle, made worse by the fact that the duplicates were scattered not only in time but also among Soviet users of the one-time pads.[6] There were five such users. The first consisted of the Soviet trading companies (Amtorg and the Soviet Government Purchasing Agency) taken as one. These agencies sent more than half of all Soviet messages intercepted during the war, largely routine and repetitive messages about American Lend-Lease to the Soviet Union. The other four users included three intelligence agencies—the NKGB (People's Commissariat for State Security), GRU (military), and naval GRU—and the Soviet Foreign Ministry. They all had their own codebooks (the trading companies shared one) and did their enciphering with supposedly unique keys from one-time pads.

During the war, the NKGB had more than one codebook. Messages intercepted in 1942 and 1943 (when the spy agency was called the NKVD, standing for People's Commissariat for Internal Affairs) used one codebook and those picked up in 1944 and 1945 used another one. Until November 1944, the Arlington Hall codebreakers had found all duplications in the trade messages. That month, the duplications started turning up in the second wartime NKGB system.[7] It was in the later NKGB code that the Venona cryptanalysts would make history with startling discoveries of Soviet espionage.

About this time, a young prodigy, still wet behind the ears, made a useful discovery. Cecil Phillips from the Blue Ridge Mountains of North Carolina, then only nineteen years old, found that, starting in May 1944, the messages in the second NKGB system began with an unenciphered numbers group to serve as a marker for the receiving Soviet clerk.[8] It meant that the first five-number group in a message was copied straight from the additive page. The groups that followed were ciphers.

The second major breakthrough came late in 1945. After the victory over Japan, Arlington Hall reassigned many of its wartime staff to the Venona Project. Among them was Samuel Chew, an outstanding cryptanalyst who noticed predictable patterns in the repetitive trade messages that allowed the Arlington Hall teams to strip stretches of duplicate additives from trade and NKGB ciphers to reveal the code numbers. This major step paved the way for another transferee from wartime duty, this one a brilliant linguist, to turn the code numbers into words and phrases.

Meredith Gardner was thirty-four years old when he went to work in the Russian Section early in 1946. Prior to the war, he had been a university language teacher in Wisconsin and Texas. He was fluent in German and Spanish and had studied Old High German, Middle High German, Lithuanian, Sanskrit, and Old Church Slavonic. After Pearl Harbor, he joined the army and began studying the Japanese language, which—so goes the amazing story—he mastered in three months. During the rest of the war, he worked on German and Japanese codes.[9] In his new assignment, he had to teach himself Russian.[10]

Gardner led a team that reconstructed the 1944–45 NKGB codebook, that is, they found the words to match the code numbers that had been pried loose from the ciphers by other cryptanalysts. He did it, according to Phillips, "by using classic codebreaking techniques."[11]

Phillips is emphatic about this point because some who knew him said Gardner had at his disposal a partially burned Soviet codebook recovered from a Finnish battlefield during the war.[12] FBI agent Robert J. Lamphere claims to have actually seen it in Gardner's office, which he often visited because the FBI was Venona's primary client. It is possible that Lamphere saw a charred codebook there, but it was not helpful to Gardner until 1953 nor was it the codebook used by the NKGB in 1944–45.

The disputed codebook came not from the battlefield but from the Soviet consulate in Petsamo, Finland. On June 22, 1941, the day Germany invaded the Soviet Union, the codebook was confiscated by Finnish troops who overran the consulate and snatched it from its pyre before flames consumed it. The Finns turned it over to German intelligence, and it fell into American hands at the end of the war when a military intelligence unit, headed by Lt. Col. Paul Neff, on assignment from Arlington Hall retrieved photocopies from a German Foreign Office archive at a castle in Saxony. This was in the Soviet zone of occupation, and Neff made off with his booty the day before Soviet troops occupied the area. It was a Soviet intelligence codebook for sure, but not the one reconstructed by Gardner. Rather, it was the earlier version that applied to messages sent in 1942–43, which reportedly was the more difficult of the two. The Petsamo codebook did not become useful to American codebreakers until 1953 after Chew made another major breakthrough in decipherment.[13]

The important point is that, soon after his arrival on the Venona Project, Gardner began penetrating the NKGB code used in 1944–45. Late in 1946, he broke the "spell table" for encoding English letters and, before long, unraveled a 1944 NKGB message listing scientists connected with the Manhattan Project, possibly based on information passed to Soviet intelligence by Ted Hall.[14]

As Gardner and his colleagues labored quietly inside Arlington Hall, tension grew in the postwar world outside. When Gouzenko walked out of the Soviet Embassy in Ottawa, he carried his ticket to freedom under his coat—documents exposing Soviet spy networks in North America. In March 1946, Canadian

Prime Minister Mackenzie King made the Gouzenko affair public in a speech to Parliament and saw it magnified by bold newspaper headlines. The following July, the Canadian government issued a White Paper with the shocking details.

President Truman's first instinct was to ignore the outcry, but he faced harsh criticism from congressional opponents in the 1946 election year. He responded by signing an executive order that established loyalty boards in federal agencies and defined disloyalty to include membership in a subversive organization, such as the Communist Party. That failed to head off Republican control of Congress, however, and the new majority, smelling blood, used its power to hammer the Truman Administration over the espionage issue. In 1948, another election year, the House Un-American Activities Committee held hearings aimed at weeding out the spies in the U.S. government. The committee called Whittaker Chambers, Elizabeth Bentley, and other witnesses to testify. The hearings were played out in a rancorous atmosphere that put the Truman Administration on the defensive. When Chambers named Hiss as a source of documents that he had passed on to Soviet intelligence, Hiss initially denied everything—denied being a communist, denied spying for the Soviet Union, even denied that he knew Chambers. The contradictory testimony led ultimately to Hiss's conviction for perjury and launched the career of Richard Nixon as a big-time political player for his part in putting Hiss on the spot. All of it was grist for the American media.

At Arlington Hall, Gardner plugged away in secrecy. In the spring of 1947, he read two 1944 NKGB messages that indicated a Soviet mole inside the War Department General Staff.[15] He didn't know who it might have been. In July, he wrote an internal memo in which he referred to some puzzling decodes. They singled out a man with the cover name "LIB?? (Lieb?) or possibly LIBERAL: was ANTENKO until Sept. 1944" who "speaks of his wife ETHEL."[16] The world would eventually get to know the man and his wife as Julius and Ethel Rosenberg. Not until late summer 1948 did Col. Carter Clarke, assistant Army G-2 (intelligence), call FBI liaison officer S. Wesley Reynolds to tell him of Arlington Hall's progress in breaking the Soviet codes. Interestingly, no one at Arlington Hall had notified the CIA because of a mistaken fear that it had been penetrated by Soviet intelligence or even told President Truman, perhaps for fear that he would say something to the CIA director.[17]

In October, Gardner met his new collaborator from the FBI, Agent Lamphere, who described Gardner as "tall, gangling, reserved, obviously intelligent and extremely reluctant to discuss much about his work. . . ."[18] Lamphere dropped by Gardner's desk every week or so to offer encouraging words, as well as advice from his own knowledge of NKGB operations. Before long, the two men forged a working friendship that lasted until Lamphere left the FBI in 1955. Their first two years together were the most productive, as real people rose up out of the gray coded texts of Venona.

The first to emerge in late 1948 was Judith Coplon (cover name "Sima"), an employee of the Department of Justice.[19] The FBI identified her by the date of her transfer from New York to Washington, and Lamphere discovered that she worked under the same roof that he did—in the DOJ building as a political analyst for the Foreign Agents Registration Section. That meant, wrote a chagrined Lamphere, "the agency most compromised by her was the FBI."[20] Assigned to take charge of her investigation, Lamphere let her discover a partially true incriminating document and ordered her followed to New York, where she was arrested in the company of a Soviet agent, Valentin A. Gubitchev. The document was found in Coplon's purse. She endured two trials, one for espionage and the other, along with Gubitchev, for conspiracy. Although Venona was never mentioned in the government's case, the decision having been made to keep it secret, Coplon was convicted of both crimes. The decisions were overturned on appeal, however, because of the FBI's use of wiretaps.

In February 1949, Gardner broke NKGB messages quoting British Foreign Office telegrams sent to the British Embassy in Washington during 1944 and 1945. From that time on, it was clear that a Soviet mole (cover name "Homer") had been in the British Embassy. Not until 1951, however, did Donald Maclean come under suspicion. By then, Maclean held a new post as head of the American desk at the Foreign Office in London, where he was stealing important new secrets about U.S. and British operations in the Korean War.

As Gardner worked to identify Homer, Kim Philby entered the picture. He was in Washington as Britain's MI6 liaison to American intelligence. With full security clearance, he often stopped in at Arlington Hall to look over Gardner's shoulder and congratulate him on his excellent work. All the while, he kept Moscow up to date on Gardner's progress. When the FBI and MI5 had narrowed the list of possible Homers to two, with Maclean still on it, Philby sent word to him in London by way of fellow spy Guy Burgess. Just as MI5 was gearing up to question Maclean, he and Burgess skipped out to Moscow. Burgess's flight compromised Philby because the two were good friends, going back to their Cambridge days, and because Burgess had been living with the Philby family in Washington. The famous Cambridge spy ring was greatly diminished by the Venona decrypts. A decade later, Philby followed Burgess and Maclean to Moscow.

At about the time that the Soviet Union exploded its first atomic bomb, Gardner picked up the trail of Klaus Fuchs. In September 1949, the cover names "Rest" and "Charles" turned up in Venona messages. One message quoted verbatim from a paper written in 1944 on how to separate bomb-grade uranium-235 from the infinitely more abundant U-238 by "gaseous diffusion." Lamphere learned from the Atomic Energy Commission that Fuchs wrote the message while working in New York as part of the British scientific team assigned to the Manhattan Project. Another message left no doubt that Fuchs was the traitor. It mentioned that the agent had a sister who lived and had attended college in the United States. Fuchs's sister, Kristel Heineman, fit the description. Fuchs was tried and convicted in Britain without giving away the Venona secret. When Fuchs's trial was over, British authorities allowed Lamphere to interview him to identify his contact in New York, cover name Raymond, whom the FBI already suspected to be Harry Gold of Philadelphia. After considerable effort, which included new undercover pictures of Gold, Fuchs finally made positive identification.

The cover name "Calibre" appeared in Venona decodes in February 1950. Lamphere perceived this agent to be an enlisted man who had served at Los Alamos during the war. In a classic domino effect, the trail led to David Greenglass and beyond. After Fuchs identified Gold, Gold informed on Greenglass, who then betrayed his brother-in-law, Julius Rosenberg. Gold's role was pivotal because he had served as courier to both Fuchs and Greenglass during a trip to New Mexico in June 1945. That one encounter between Gold and Greenglass doomed the Rosenbergs. Later in 1950, Julius Rosenberg was linked to the Venona cover names "Liberal" and "Antenna" (previously thought to be "Antenko"). Two Venona messages implicated Ethel Rosenberg.

The Rosenbergs will be forever identified with atomic espionage, but that derives largely from their relationship with Greenglass, who was the least important of the known Los Alamos spies. Julius Rosenberg ran a spy ring engaged primarily in stealing technological secrets about advanced weapons of warfare, including radar, jet aircraft, and rocket engines. With Gold and Greenglass testifying for the prosecution, Julius and Ethel were convicted. Perversely, their death sentences and gruesome executions in a dark period of American history characterized by red-baiting and witch-hunting made them world celebrities. The evidence from Venona confirms Julius Rosenberg's guilt. His wife was sympathetic and supportive and did odd jobs for him. She also typed her brother's notes from Los Alamos. Their execution, especially Ethel's, is hard to justify four and a half decades after the event. The government threatened the death penalty as leverage to get the Rosenbergs to inform on other spies and apparently did not expect to go through with the threat, but the Rosenbergs died with their lips sealed.[21]

Sometime during the two-year period 1949–50, Gardner decoded a message about Soviet recruitment of Ted Hall. The message even mentioned Hall by name (Teodor Kholl), along with his former Harvard roommate, Saville Sax (Savil Saks).[22] Later, Hall was connected in Venona cables to the cover name "Mlad" (meaning youngster) and Sax to the cover name "Star" (meaning oldster); Sax was older than Hall by more than a year. By the time the FBI caught on to Hall and Sax in 1950, they were attending school at the University of Chicago. Hall, by then married to a left-wing activist, née Joan Krakover, was studying for his doctorate. He no longer had access to atomic secrets and wanted to put espionage behind him, as did his wife. The FBI placed Hall and Sax under surveillance but never caught them in an illegal or even suspicious act. In their frustration, the FBI brought them in for questioning in the hope of intimidating them into confessing but was unsuccessful.[23] As in the other spy cases, the Venona decrypts were not to be used for evidence. The Halls subsequently moved to England, where Ted died in 1999.

At least, Hall and Sax were singled out and eventually exposed when the first Venona decrypts were declassified in 1995. Other atomic spies have never been identified. For example, Quantum was mentioned in at least two partially decrypted Venona messages but never connected to a real person. In June 1943 at the Soviet Embassy in Washington, Quantum met with a high-ranking diplomat, possibly Deputy Ambassador Andrey Gromyko, and was turned over to the NKGB. He submitted documents detailing a variant of gaseous diffusion, the process used to separate the U-235 isotope from U-238. Also, he asked for money. After the material was evaluated, he received three hundred dollars. Whoever Quantum was, he must have been a scientist of some stature to gain an audience with a senior Soviet diplomat.[24] The atomic spy who went by the cover names of Vogel and Pers is mentioned in a partially decrypted message of February 1944 as the source of a technical report about the Oak Ridge plant.[25]

American counterintelligence tracked down the true names of about half of the 349 American citizens or residents who came out of the Venona decrypts; the other half are known only by their cover names. The list does not include Soviet agents under diplomatic cover, but it does name four Soviet illegal aliens operating in the United States outside of diplomatic protection.[26]

By 1950, Venona caught up with spies already unmasked by Chambers and Bentley. The cover name "Jurist" applied to former Assistant Secretary of the Treasury Harry Dexter White, who had died of a heart attack shortly after testifying before the House Un-American Activities Committee in 1948. The cover name "Ales" probably referred to Alger Hiss, a former State Department aide who was convicted of perjury in 1950. White House aide Lauchlin Currie had the cover name "Page." He testified at the hearings of the House Un-American Committee in 1948 and left the country in 1950. Later, he renounced his citizenship.[27] Another key spy, ringleader Nathan Gregory Silvermaster, appeared in Venona as "Robert." After he and his friend Ludwig William Ullman ("Pilot," "Donald") were forced out of government work in 1947, they formed a profitable home building business in New Jersey.[28] The FBI also pressured Victor Perlo ("Raider") and other members of his group to leave the government. Years later, Perlo surfaced as a member of the National Board of the American Communist Party and, in 1991, took a hard line against Soviet President Mikhail Gorbachev's efforts to democratize Soviet communism.[29]

One of Gardner's recoveries in 1949 led to the realization that the Soviets knew the Venona secret. From the cover name "Nick" in a decrypted Venona message, the FBI tracked down a real person, Amadeo Sabatini, who informed on Jones Orin York ("Needle"), an inventor who, during the thirties, had relayed aviation secrets stolen from Northrup Aircraft, Inc. In 1950, York identified his latest NKGB handler as William Weisband, a colleague of Gardner's at Arlington Hall. Weisband was born in Egypt of Russian parents and grew up fluent in Russian. Soviet intelligence probably recruited him before he left Egypt. He came to the United States in 1938 at the age of thirty and, starting in 1943, served at Arlington Hall as a linguist advisor. It is believed that Weisband was the first person to inform Moscow of the Venona Project, probably in 1948 when he smuggled out a horde of valuable documents as the House spy hearings rattled the Capitol dome. After his exposure, Weisband lost his job at Arlington Hall but was never prosecuted for espionage—again, to keep Venona secret, even though it was now clear that Venona was no secret to the NKGB. He did serve a year in jail on a contempt conviction for ignoring a summons to appear before a federal grand jury looking into Communist Party activities.[30]

Venona reached its peak of success in the United States during the years 1948–50 with the close collaboration of Gardner and Lamphere. It remained in operation until 1980. In 1948, the Americans shared the Venona secret with British intelligence, after which GCHQ at Bletchley Park tried its hand at breaking down the trade and NKGB ciphergrams transmitted between London and Moscow late in the war. Unfortunately, there were few ciphergrams because Prime Minister Churchill had put a hold on the interception of Soviet messages until very near the end of the war. Little, if anything, came out of that effort. American and British codebreakers eventually broke into the GRU and naval GRU codes, which yielded more inside information about the far-flung Soviet intelligence networks. The GRU ciphers dated back to early in the war and dealt to a large extent with Russian emigrés whom Stalin wanted tracked down and either shot or hauled off to a gulag.

It is hard for the noncryptanalyst to imagine the sheer enormity of the Venona effort and harder still to understand how real information could be extracted from those stupefying volumes of random ciphers. Only their fellow cipher brains can fully appreciate the striving and accomplishment of the Venona teams. Peter Wright, a British counterintelligence officer, spoke of the awe in which Meredith Gardner was held by other cryptanalysts and paraphrases him as viewing his own work as "almost an art form."[31] Gardner should know, but he apparently took some of the blame on himself for the execution of the Rosenbergs and the excesses of McCarthyism and perhaps did not fully appreciate his own contribution to the Western side during the Cold War. Venona helped to expose a vast Soviet intelligence network when the fate of the world was hanging in the balance. Gardner's art made a huge impact on the history of his time.

CHAPTER 15

Exposing
Comrade Bluster

When the Soviet Union exploded its first atomic bomb in 1949, four years behind the Americans, the East-West nuclear arms race was under way. Within a few years, each side had tested a hydrogen bomb with unimaginable explosive power that carried an explicit threat of Armageddon. Never did this peril capture the world's attention so forcefully as in the high-stakes game of chicken played during the early sixties between the youthful American president, John F. Kennedy, and the mercurial leader in the Kremlin, Nikita S. Khrushchev. The Soviet chairman had missiles and hydrogen bombs and talked as though he would not hesitate to use them, even in the face of certain nuclear retaliation. As a doctrinaire Marxist, he believed he was on the rising tide of history and, like a schoolboy playing "King of the Hill," he predicted that communism would bury capitalism in his lifetime. Kennedy came to office in January 1961 well schooled in domestic political infighting but ill prepared for an international crisis that might touch off a war to destroy civilization. Khrushchev's bombast struck full blast against Kennedy's cool, and the world wondered if the new president had the poise and willpower to withstand the onslaught.

Kennedy came through with flying colors in the two major Cold War face-offs of his presidency, the Berlin and Cuban missile crises, but a secret of his success is not so well known. His outwardly boyish charm was no help nor was his hypnotic Boston-accented oratory or any of his political assets that had made him popular with the American public. He did it with the aid of precise and voluminous intelligence provided behind the scenes in significant part by a disaffected Soviet officer, Col. Oleg Vladimirovich Penkovsky.

Penkovsky was a smart, hard-nosed, well-connected officer in the GRU with access to some of the Soviet Union's most important military secrets. He revealed information so momentous that two trained intelligence experts, an American and a Soviet defector, published a worthy book about him and found it within the bounds of hyperbole to give it the sweeping title *The Spy Who Saved the World.*[1] The words need not be taken at face value to appreciate the contribution of this unusual man at a significant crossroads of the twentieth century. In terms of his impact, Penkovsky was probably the most important spy of the Cold War.

Khrushchev had already gained momentum when Kennedy arrived on the scene. The Soviets had built a nuclear arsenal, developed rockets to deliver the bombs, and proved their rocket technology good enough to carry large pay-loads and put satellites in space—although never as good as Khrushchev would have had the world believe (they were not accurate at the time). In Cuba, on January 1, 1959, Fidel Castro and his ragtag army rode into Havana to consum-mate an indigenous Marxist revolution 90 miles south of the Florida Keys. The Soviets hastened to woo the Cubans into their Cold War camp to spearhead a campaign to spread the revolution into Latin America. Khrushchev took to boasting of his strategic gains and reached out globally for other new avenues of expansion through Egypt in the Middle East and India in South Asia.

What stuck in Khrushchev's throat, however, was the growing strength of NATO, and he schemed to exploit the enemy's weakest outpost, militarily speaking. A decade and a half after the end of World War II, the American, British, and French sectors of occupied Berlin, 90 miles inside the Soviet sphere, had become a Western showcase. East Germans disillusioned by com-munist rule found it easy to defect by way of West Berlin and did so in droves. Foremost among them were the technicians and managers needed for industrial recovery. Under pressure from the embarrassed communist leadership of East Germany, Khrushchev was determined to bring about an end to Berlin's occupation status and make the West recognize East Germany as a sovereign power. Kennedy well understood his weak position. He called Berlin the testicles of the West that Khrushchev could squeeze at will.[2]

Kennedy put himself at a disadvantage even before he took office by making an issue of an alleged "missile gap" while campaigning for president in 1960. The charge of American missile inferiority was untrue, as the Kennedy Administration would later discover, but it played into Khrushchev's hands by reinforcing the world image of growing Soviet might. When Kennedy became president, he had been weakened, to a degree, by a false perception created by his own rhetoric.

As president, Kennedy's first foreign adventure was to launch an ill-fated invasion of Cuba by anti-Castro exiles in April 1961. The Bay of Pigs plan, Operation Zapata, had been drawn up by the CIA. Although the Eisenhower Administration had passed it down to the new president, Kennedy approved it and had to suffer the consequences. It ended in disaster, at least partly because Kennedy feared Soviet retaliation against Berlin and withheld American air cover for the invaders. Consequently, the invasion utterly failed in a matter of days and left Kennedy looking foolish and inept. To his credit, he took full responsibility. "There's an old saying," he told a news conference, "that victory has a hundred fathers and defeat is an orphan." But, he admitted, "I am the responsible officer of government."[3]

In June, Kennedy and Khrushchev met in Vienna for a stormy summit conference. Khrushchev confronted the president over Berlin and demanded a German peace treaty by the end of the year. "I want peace," the Soviet leader thundered, "but if you want war, that's your problem." His position, he said, was "firm and irrevocable." Kennedy did not know if the chairman was bluffing, but he did not flinch. "If that is true" he snapped back, "it will be a cold winter."[4] Despite Kennedy's firm show of resolve, Khrushchev came down from the summit convinced that his young adversary was a weak leader who would break under pressure. Kennedy privately admitted that he was shaken by the experience. He confided to columnist James Reston of the *New York Times* that Khrushchev had probably concluded from his failure to follow through at the Bay of Pigs that he (Kennedy) "had no guts. So he [Khrushchev] just beat the hell out of me."[5]

———————

Colonel Penkovsky was a stroke of good luck for the West. He made possible a most timely penetration of the Soviet military hierarchy. The initiative for their coming together belonged entirely to Penkovsky, a career soldier and a trained intelligence officer. So eager was he to avenge a personal grievance that he risked approaching two young American students on a Moscow street late in the evening of August 12, 1960, after a performance of the Bolshoi Ballet. He walked up to Eldon Ray Cox and Henry Lee Cobb to ask for a light. The colonel was dressed in civilian clothes and spoke passable English. He struck up a casual conversation and strolled along with them but did not identify himself. His eyes darted in all directions to make sure they were not being observed. One can imagine the mixture of bewilderment, apprehension, and fascination that must have seized the two Americans.

When Penkovsky saw that the three of them were alone, he dropped the small talk. He wanted to convey important information to the American Embassy, he said, but dared not go there himself. He told them things that the Soviet government did not want the world, especially Americans, to hear. For example, he mentioned false Soviet reporting about the downing of the U-2 spy plane piloted by Francis Gary Powers on May 1, 1960. It had not been hit with a single surface-to-air (SAM) missile at 65,000 feet, as the Soviets claimed. To the contrary, Penkovsky said, fourteen missiles had been fired, and an explosion at a lower altitude had disabled the frail spy plane. A Soviet MiG-19 fighter trailing the U-2 from below had been blown out of the sky. This shattered the Soviet-created notion that their SAMs were good enough to reach the higher altitude. Penkovsky also revealed another Soviet lie that an American RB-47 reconnaissance bomber shot down by a MiG-19 on July 1, 1960, had violated Soviet air space. The RB-47 had been flying over international waters, close to but not inside Soviet air space, as the U.S. government had claimed.

It was all a bit overwhelming for the young tourists on their first visit to Moscow, but Penkovsky did not stop there. He gave them a sealed envelope to take straight to the American Embassy before they retired for the night. This act, in particular, had the odor of a provocation. The Americans had been warned of possible entrapment, to be followed by blackmail and recruitment for espionage. Suddenly two policemen appeared nearby, and the Americans hurried off with Cox clutching the sealed envelope. While Cobb returned to the hotel, Cox, impressed by the Russian's intensity and believing his spy plane stories, found a cab near the hotel and took the dangerous package to the American Embassy. It was already past midnight, but an embassy official working late accepted the envelope and carefully questioned the bearer about his experience. Then, he delivered a chilling lecture about the peril of taking such a risk in a hostile city teeming with secret police.

The envelope was opened next day in a secure room at the embassy. In it were two other envelopes. One contained a letter for the CIA from an unnamed person describing himself as "your good friend . . . who has already become your soldier-warrior for the cause of Truth. . . ." He spoke of "very important materials on many subjects of exceptionally great interest and importance to your government," which he offered to pass on "for study, analysis and subsequent utilization."[6] The second envelope had instructions for using a Moscow dead drop (hiding place) for depositing or picking up messages and materials. The letters and a report on the letter writer's encounter with Cox and Cobb, including the spy plane stories, were dispatched to Washington.

The CIA was impressed, perceiving it as high-grade information from a trained intelligence officer. From clues in the letter and interviews with Cox and Cobb, they identified the author as Penkovsky. The CIA badly needed a strategically placed mole in Moscow. Only a few years earlier, its best insider, Lt. Col. Pyotr Popov, had been caught by Soviet security and executed. Unfortunately, the CIA did not have anyone in Moscow who could handle Penkovsky, so it sent an agent (code-named "Compass") from Washington who lacked the requisite language skills and field experience and found himself unable to cope with KGB surveillance of American Embassy personnel. "Compass" never made contact with his asset and never used the dead drop for fear of exposing him.

Meanwhile, Penkovsky was tired of waiting. The GRU had assigned him to the State Committee for the Coordination of Scientific Research Work, a cover organization for espionage in science and technology. In December 1960, he was senior liaison on the Soviet delegation playing host to a British trade mission. One night in Leningrad, he approached one of the delegates, Dr. A. D. Merriman. In the privacy of Merriman's hotel room with the spigots turned on full to muffle their conversation, Penkovsky pulled some papers from his inside coat pocket and asked Merriman to deliver them to the American Embassy. Merriman, fearful of a provocation, flatly refused, but on his return to Moscow, he reported the incident to the British ambassador. When he returned to London, he informed MI6. The following month, Penkovsky tried a similar approach to a Canadian embassy official and was similarly rebuffed.

MI6 allowed the CIA to debrief Merriman. The two agencies regularly exchanged information, although, at that time, the CIA had not told the British about Penkovsky's encounter with Cox and Cobb five months earlier. Unsuccessful in their own efforts to contact Penkovsky, the Americans now enlisted British help. The British had sized up Penkovsky as an agent provocateur crudely trying to entrap one of their diplomats. Indeed, that was the view of the American ambassador in Moscow, Llewellyn Thompson, who, after the failure of Compass, refused to allow the CIA use of the embassy to run Penkovsky. In Washington, Joseph J. Bulik, chief of the CIA's Soviet Branch, had a different view. To him, Penkovsky presented a golden opportunity for deep penetration at a high level. In late January 1961 in Washington, Bulik met with one of MI6's best agents, Harold T. Shergold, and told him about Penkovsky's approach to Cox and Cobb and the spy plane revelations. Shergold agreed that the two agencies should try to reel him in. From then on, events began to move more rapidly.

Britain's December trade delegation to Moscow, when Penkovsky had approached Merriman, was headed by Greville Wynne, an industrial salesman who made frequent trips to Eastern Europe to drum up trade for a group of British manufacturers. Wynne was first and foremost a businessman but also something of an adventurer, and he cooperated closely with MI6. He allowed MI6 to debrief him after his visits behind the Iron Curtain and had received, at the very least, an orientation from MI6 in what to look for. Now, MI6 directed him to "develop relations" with the State Committee,[7] and he went to Moscow at the bidding of British intelligence to promote Anglo-Soviet trade. At State Committee headquarters on Gorky Street, he proposed to bring technicians from his British companies to tour Soviet factories and discuss trade. It was at this meeting that Wynne first met Penkovsky. In a book written (possibly ghostwritten) years later, Wynne heaped flatulent praise on Penkovsky: "Sunlight filtering through the uncleaned windows showed up his glossy reddish hair and deep-set eyes. His nose was broad-based and his mouth full-lipped and strong. A powerful imaginative face." Wynne eyed the others at the meeting through a Cold War prism. The group leader was "short and gross," wore clothes "that appeared to have been slept in," had "crumpled hair, dirty fingernails, nicotine fingers, hands like a coal-miner, rough red face covered with blackheads, needed a shave." Two other Soviet officials were "of the same ilk with variations."[8] Fortunately, Wynne kept his observations to himself. Within two days, the Soviets approved his proposal—for their own reasons, related more to espionage than to trade. When Wynne returned in December with the British technicians, he found that Penkovsky was handling their itinerary. A friendship blossomed, and they were soon on a first-name basis. Penkovsky asked Wynne to call him Alex because, he said, Oleg did not sound good coming from Wynne, but, during the December tour, Penkovsky never approached Wynne, as he had Merriman, to carry any messages to Western intelligence.

Wynne was back in Moscow in April to arrange a reciprocal visit to Britain by Soviet technicians. By now, the British and American agencies were working together and focusing on Penkovsky. Although Wynne knew there was something special about this particular Soviet officer, he kept to his main purpose of trade. When Penkovsky showed him a list of the Soviet trade delegates scheduled to make the trip to London, Wynne resisted. He recognized most of them as Soviet bureaucrats, not legitimate engineers and managers, who could do nothing to foster trade. The one scientist on the list specialized in radar and wanted to visit Jodrell Bank, but none of Wynne's clients had anything to do with radar. Wynne told his friend they were not acceptable and he would so inform the State Committee. Penkovsky, suddenly in a state of high agitation, asked Wynne not to do that because it would mean the cancellation of the trip. "It is not the delegation that matters," Penkovsky cried. "It is I who must come to London, and it is not for pleasure."[9] Then, he explained his personal mission to give away Soviet secrets. Without another thought for his industrial firms, Wynne accepted the list of delegates. Before he left Moscow, Penkovsky gave him a letter for British and American intelligence that pleaded with them to speed up at their end.

The six-man Soviet delegation arrived in London on the morning of April 20, 1961, a day when Castro's troops were mopping up the remnants of the CIA-backed invaders at the Bay of Pigs. On the way in from Heathrow Airport, Penkovsky slipped Wynne a package of documents. Wynne had no way of knowing what an extremely important bundle of classified material it was— seventy-eight pages of handwritten notes, diagrams, and photographs about Soviet rockets and missile-launching installations that would become crucial reference material during the Cuban missile crisis.[10] Wynne booked the visitors into the Mount Royal Hotel on Oxford Street near Marble Arch.

As head of the delegation, Penkovsky was entitled to a large room to himself, but he took care to see to every need of his delegates so they would speak well of him back in Moscow. Penkovsky stood apart from them. They knew him not only as their leader but also as a fairly high-ranking officer of the GRU; when he excused himself after dinner to retire for the evening, they thought nothing of it.

At 9:40, Penkovsky arrived at his room on the fifth floor. From there, he walked to the stairwell at the opposite side of the hotel, descended two floors, and knocked on the door of room 360 where MI6 and the CIA were waiting for him. Four men greeted him amiably and identified themselves with false names. One said to him in fluent Russian, "You know now that you are in good hands."[11]

Penkovsky's principal motive for walking into that room seems to have been revenge against the Communist state, which had blocked his career path. He was born to the wrong class—the upper class. His grandfather, Florian A. Penkovsky, had been a Tsarist judge in Stavropol. His father, Vladimir F. Penkovsky, a mining engineer, had fought in the White Army against the Bolsheviks in the Russian Civil War and was killed in the siege of Rostov in 1919. When Oleg launched his career two decades later, he omitted his father's oppositionism from his biographical file. If the authorities ever found out that he came from a family of Whites, his career would be ruined. Eventually, they did find out and proved his worst fears to be true.

Oleg, only four months old when his father died, had no direct memory of him and grew up a staunch communist. After graduation from high school, he enrolled in the Second Kiev Artillery School, joined the Young Communist League (Komsomol), and became a candidate for the Communist Party. He vowed with youthful enthusiasm to "fight for the principles of Lenin," and his ideological fervor made him a committed and conscientious soldier. After graduation from the artillery school in 1939, he participated in the Soviet occupation of eastern Poland and the inglorious Red Army campaign against Finland during the winter of 1939–40. In March 1940, he was accepted into the Communist Party. He carried out various assignments in the Moscow Military District, became a political officer, and met his general's daughter, Vera Gapanovich—fourteen years old at the time and nine years younger than Oleg. They would marry after the war.

Penkovsky had a certain knack for being helpful to people who could further his career. He was not a compulsive toady, but he reserved his special favors for people whom he liked and respected. This is conspicuously illustrated by his relationship with Gen. Sergei S. Varentsov. During much of World War II, what the Soviets called "The Great Patriotic War," Penkovsky stayed out of combat in Moscow throughout the pivotal battles of the eastern front—Moscow, Stalingrad, and Kursk—and the recapture of Kiev in 1943. By then, he worried that he had won no distinctions in a war that had already made a thousand Soviet heroes. Up to that point, his record would be no help to his career, so he put in a request for frontline duty and was assigned to artillery headquarters on the Ukrainian front under General Varentsov. Penkovsky soon became the Soviet Army's youngest regimental commander on the front lines. In June 1944, he was wounded and hospitalized in Moscow.

Toward the end of Penkovsky's two-month recuperation, General Varentsov suffered a serious hip injury and was removed to Moscow. Penkovsky took him gifts, and Varentsov asked him to act as his liaison with headquarters at the front. Penkovsky made several trips on Varentsov's behalf. He also took care of the general's family in Lvov in the western Ukraine because "not only was [Varentsov] a very nice person, but I knew that he would reward me tenfold for anything I did for him."[12] What Penkovsky then did for Varentsov was decent well beyond the call of duty—something he would not have done for just anybody. The general's daughter Nina was married to a man accused of black marketeering by Soviet military authorities in Lvov. He and two other men were shot. Nina was so distraught that she committed suicide. When Penkovsky heard of it, he sold his watch, went to Lvov, bought her a black dress and a coffin, and gave her a proper burial. On hearing the story, Varentsov told Penkovsky, "You are like a son to me."[13] Thus, they were bonded in a special friendship that would give Penkovsky access to secrets that he could not otherwise have learned.

After the war, Penkovsky married Vera and gained an influential father-in-law, Lt. Gen. Dmitri A. Gapanovich, who became his patron and advisor. With Gapanovich's support and Varentsov's endorsement, Penkovsky entered the Frunze Military Academy in Moscow. He graduated in 1948 and, a year later, enrolled at the Military-Diplomatic Academy in Moscow for a four-year course in strategic intelligence. Afterward, in 1953, he joined the GRU. By this time, Penkovsky was a full colonel and on the high road to success at the age of thirty-four.

For his first overseas assignment in 1955, he reported to the Soviet Embassy in Ankara, Turkey, as the GRU's acting *rezident* (chief of station) under the diplomatic cover of assistant military attaché. In Turkey, he opened his mind to the West and developed a warm, if cautious, friendship with the U.S. military attaché, Col. Charles Maclean Peeke. Penkovsky ran the station for seven months until a permanent *rezident*, Maj. Gen. Nikolai P. Rubenko, arrived. (Rubenko was a pseudonym; by his real name, Savchenko, he was known to the CIA as a GRU agent.) Penkovsky stayed on as Rubenko's assistant, but they were soon at odds. The subordinate thought poorly of the general's administrative abilities, and Rubenko accused him of not being aggressive enough in recruiting Turks to spy for the Soviet Union. An incident brought their differences to a head. Another agent working aggressively out of the embassy was twice caught spying by Turkish authorities, and, the second time, he was expelled. This occurred during a visit to Turkey by the Shah of Iran when Moscow had ordered a suspension of espionage. Penkovsky argued with Rubenko over the incident and accused him of disobeying orders by allowing the compromised agent to remain active during the Shah's visit. Rubenko threw him out of his office, and they filed separate reports to Moscow. The dispute landed on the desk of Gen. Ivan A. Serov, who was then head of the KGB. Serov passed it on to his patron, Khrushchev, who ordered an investigation. Penkovsky was upheld, but it was a Pyrrhic victory. By going over the general's head, the upstart colonel had made enemies of Rubenko's many old friends in the military bureaucracy. He had also called attention to himself at a high level on a messy issue.

Penkovsky went home on a leave that was supposedly temporary, but he never returned to Ankara. He was already angry with the regime. Had he returned to Turkey, he admitted later, he might have asked his friend Colonel Peeke for an introduction to the CIA. Unlike Rubenko, who was reprimanded and discharged from the service, Penkovsky was still in good standing with the GRU. Nevertheless, he seemed anchored in Moscow. In September 1958, with Varentsov's help, he was allowed to attend the Dzerzhinsky Military Academy for advanced courses in rocket technology. This was an old artillery school where the curriculum had been adapted, in a manner of speaking, to the higher form of artillery. Penkovsky graduated with distinction in May 1959. During those eight months, he took very detailed notes about Soviet missile technology—information that would fill the package he handed to Wynne two years later in London.

After Penkovsky's graduation from rocket school, General Serov, who now headed the GRU, thought it made sense to post Penkovsky to Delhi as the military attaché and the GRU's chief of station. Khrushchev wanted to send rockets to India, and Serov reasoned that, by his latest rocket training, Penkovsky qualified for the assignment. Penkovsky was elated. Making the necessary preparations, he eagerly anticipated the opportunity and savored his renewed career prospects. At the last moment, however, the assignment was canceled and he was transferred to the State Committee, a much softer duty. The KGB had belatedly discovered his father's service with the enemies of Bolshevism, and the information was forwarded to the GRU personnel chief who spoke to Penkovsky about it. Penkovsky knew then that he would have no further opportunity for advancement. The best he could hope for was early retirement on an inadequate pension. From that point on, his own government was his enemy, and he began plotting in earnest to work for the enemies of his enemy.

The four case officers who greeted Penkovsky in room 360 of the Mount Royal Hotel were Bulik and George Kisevalter of the CIA and Shergold and Michael Stokes of MI6. Kisevalter, who spoke fluent Russian, took the lead. He was well regarded at the CIA for his handling of the deceased mole Popov, but, with Penkovsky, the personal chemistry was not the same. Popov had been a down-to-earth guy like himself, and they could relate to each other during an evening spent at a bar swilling whiskey or vodka. Penkovsky was more driven, standoffish, and harder to control. Nevertheless, Kisevalter knew his job and did not fail. He was born in the Caucasus in 1910 and spent the first seven years of his life there. His father was a German engineer, his mother French. When the Bolshevik Revolution brought chaos to Russia, the family fled and settled in the United States. Kisevalter attended Dartmouth College, where he became a close and lifelong friend with multimillionaire Nelson Rockefeller, later governor of New York and vice president of the United States.

The volume of secrets that Penkovsky divulged in a series of meetings in England astonished his interlocutors. High-grade intelligence poured out like water cascading through an open floodgate. He revealed, in the words of Jerrold Schecter and Pyotr Deriabin, "the most fundamentally significant information about the Soviet military capacity to destroy the West."[14] Everything in the Soviet Union, Penkovsky told them, was subordinated to the arms race. While people who lived outside large cities, such as Moscow and Leningrad, were going hungry and military personnel (including the embittered Penkovsky) had taken pay cuts, the national treasury was being spent on nuclear missiles and other weapons of war and to prop up Soviet allies. Penkovsky hinted, more than a year before the fact, that Cuba might receive strategic missiles. Particulars about Soviet missile technology—type, range, payload, fuel storage capacity, and other details—were contained in the written material that Penkovsky had passed to Wynne, which Kisevalter translated between sessions.

For all of that, Penkovsky said, the missiles were not perfect, contrary to Krushchev's boasts. Short-range missiles performed well, but newer long-range versions had a high rate of failure during tests and straying from their impact area in Kazakhstan. Some had crashed into villages and caused hundreds of casualties. At fault was the missile guidance system, and it exposed a persistent weakness in Soviet electronics technology. The Soviets had also experimented with nuclear-powered rockets. These efforts were unsuccessful and had cost the life of the commander of the Strategic Rocket Forces, Marshal Mitrofan Nedelin, who was killed in the explosion of a nuclear-powered missile on the launching pad at Tyura Tam south of the Aral Sea. Beyond missiles, Penkovsky gave his debriefers chapter and verse on his own intelligence agency, the GRU, and the important role of intelligence (including the KGB's) in the Soviet hierarchy—information that later evoked the words "unique" and "unprecedented" from a CIA evaluation. He also identified more than three hundred GRU officers and a dozen or so agents active in the West.[15]

Penkovsky made one proposal that shocked the American and British agents. He said that Hitler had lost the war in the Soviet Union because the German air force had failed to knock out Soviet military command and control centers. He urged, in all seriousness, that Moscow buildings containing the General Staff of the Soviet Ministry of Defense, KGB headquarters, and the Central Committee of the Communist Party, as well as similar military and political targets in major Soviet cities, be blown up with small, pre-positioned atomic bombs. He volunteered to emplace the Moscow bombs. Of course, none of that happened. It was a crazy idea, even if he could have managed it without getting caught, and it reflected a quixotic Cold War belief that a nuclear holocaust could occur without devastating consequences for winner and loser alike. The strategy of "decapitating" the enemy by destroying leadership and communications centers was a part of Pentagon planning, however, and the spread of American missiles targeted against the Soviet Union was revised to include the vital nerve centers highlighted by their knowledgeable informant.

Penkovsky seemed tireless, at least during this initial tour. He spent half of each night talking to the Anglo-American team and, by day, joined his Soviet delegation on the itinerary arranged by Wynne. Of course, his superiors in Moscow had sent the lot of them to England for espionage and expected them to bring back a planeload of industrial secrets, so Penkovsky asked his "comrades-in-arms," as he called the British and American agents, to provide him with information worth the trip. In particular, the GRU wanted data on high-grade, lightweight steel for rockets. MI6 obliged him with enough glossy brochures to whet Moscow's appetite without giving away the store. Penkovsky also asked for money and drove a hard bargain. He needed money to pay current expenses and buy gifts for his family, friends, and favorite generals, but, more than that, he wanted money to build a nest egg for the day that he and his family would defect to the West two or three years hence. When the Anglo-Americans agreed to pay him $1,000 a month from the first meeting day forward, he reminded them that he had already put in countless hours to gather information and prepare the lengthy report he had given Wynne. He asked them to place a fair value on previous labor, and he also wanted status, a meaningful position when the time came for his defection.

The Anglo-Americans agreed to all these demands and more. They did their best to accommodate Penkovsky's every wish, including a sample of English women, which MI6 satisfied by carefully procuring a safe, high-class prostitute. They were careful, too, to stroke his enormous ego when he sought reassurance that his work be appreciated. When he asked for an audience with Queen Elizabeth II, however, it was more than the British agents could deliver. Penkovsky insisted. The Queen had received Soviet cosmonaut Yuri Gagarin, the first man in space, he reminded them. "Has he done more for you [than I have]?" Alas, he had to make do with a stand-in, Sir Dick White, then head of MI6. Sir Dick showed up at the hotel debriefing room one night with a message from Vice Adm. Lord Louis Mountbatten, a first cousin of the Queen and the highest military official in the country. Sir Dick had a certain elegant bearing that was bound to impress Penkovsky, and he had been shrewdly advised to smooth on the puffery. He told Penkovsky that Lord Mountbatten was "filled with admiration" for his contribution and placed the "highest value and importance" on the information provided. It had the desired effect. Penkovsky, himself no slouch at pouring on the syrup, promised "to fight under your banners until the end of my life" and pledged his "fealty to my queen, Elizabeth II, and to the President of the United States, Mr. Kennedy, whom I am serving as their soldier."[16] In his mind, the American president was as good as royalty. He had asked also to see President Kennedy should he go to the United States some day, and he was promised an audience with the President's brother, Attorney General Robert F. Kennedy, but he was never to see the "promised land."

Altogether, on this trip, Penkovksy spent two and a half weeks in England. When the Soviet delegation visited the industrial cities of Leeds and Birmingham, the debriefing team followed it for nighttime meetings with Penkovsky.

Most of these meetings, seventeen in all, were lengthy and substantive. Military and diplomatic strategists in Washington and London were more than satisfied, and no one thought any longer of Penkovsky as an agent provocateur. When he returned to Moscow on May 6, 1961, a month before Kennedy and Khrushchev met in Vienna, he brought with him a tiny Minox camera and enough film to copy top secret Soviet documents requested by Washington and London. Within days of his return, he visited the library of the artillery command in the Ministry of Defense, a place that would have been blown up by one of the small atomic bombs he wanted to plant. A special pass arranged by his mentor Varentsov gave him access to the library so he could research an article on nuclear strategy that he proposed to write for a Soviet journal. He pulled out top secret documents as requested by Western intelligence, took them to a private room, placed a chair under the doorknob so that no one could catch him red-handed, took out his camera, and began the next phase of his astonishing espionage career. His spirits soared at the ease of photographing the pages in contrast to the laborious handwritten notes he had taken before.

Things went smoothly for Penkovsky during this time. In late May, Wynne came to Moscow to attend a French trade show and to arrange for another British delegation to the Soviet Union. The State Committee assigned Penkovsky to look after him, so time spent with Wynne was officially on the up-and-up. On the way into town from the airport, Penkovsky turned over a briefcase full of papers and three rolls of undeveloped film, which Wynne took to the British Embassy for the resident MI6 agent, Roderick Chisholm. Wynne and Chisholm carried out their business without speaking in order to cheat the Soviet bugs concealed in the embassy walls. Chisholm had a package from London that contained 3,000 rubles and a letter for Penkovsky. Wynne carried it out of the embassy and met Penkovsky at the Karl Marx statue near his hotel, the Metropol. As they walked together, Penkovsky accepted Wynne's package and, in turn, gave him a letter for London, which Wynne took back to Chisholm. And on it went, all carried out with the time-honored subtleties of the ancient art of espionage.

Because Wynne would not have many opportunities to visit Moscow, another contact for Penkovsky already had been arranged. Janet Chisholm, wife of Roderick Chisholm, thirty-two years old in 1961, formerly a secretary at MI6, dark brown hair, attractive, intelligent, and levelheaded, had nerves of steel and ice in her veins. The first Sunday of July, she was in a park near the British Embassy with her three young children and a baby carriage. A large weekend crowd milled about. Penkovsky spotted her sitting on a bench opposite a circus and cinema, but he did not approach right away. Rain was threatening, and he waited for the crowd to thin out. Then, he started to walk by, smiled at the children, and stopped to chat. He took out a box of candy and handed it to Mrs. Chisholm, who put it under a blanket in the carriage and pulled out another box of candy for the children. In Penkovsky's box were more exposed film and two sheets of typewritten paper.

The written material was very timely. Only a month earlier, Khrushchev had met with President Kennedy in Vienna and threatened nuclear war over Berlin. After the summit, Penkovsky attended a social gathering at Varentsov's dacha in celebration of the older man's promotion to the rank of chief marshal. Varentsov updated his protégé on Khrushchev's plan for a separate peace treaty with East Germany. East German armored units, backed up by Soviet troops in full battle readiness, would block the roads to Berlin. Khrushchev believed that the NATO forces would not fight. The substance of Penkovsky's conversation with Varentsov was contained in the two pages that Janet Chisholm had tucked into the baby carriage. Penkovsky urged Western leaders to stand firm and put on an exaggerated show of military strength but not fire the first shot. Khrushchev, he said, "is not prepared for a big war, and is waging a war of nerves."[17] Penkovsky was very much in tune with American strategic thinking. In Washington, his information was distilled by the CIA and made available to President Kennedy and other high officials. In an address to the nation on July 25, Kennedy called West Berlin "the great testing place of American courage and will" and a focal point of confrontation with the Soviet Union. So that the Soviets would not mistake his meaning, he asked Congress to increase the military budget by $3.2 billion (big money at that time) and requested standby authority to call up the reserves. By his own authority, without appealing to Congress, he tripled the draft. U.S. strategy was to send a small military convoy up the autobahn to Berlin and, if it was blocked, to deliver a nuclear response. Potentially, the autobahn to Berlin was the road to Armageddon.

A few weeks later, Penkovsky came into possession of an official Soviet transcript of the Vienna summit conference, which highlighted Khrushchev's tough talk to Kennedy and played down Kennedy's firm response. The report was distributed to other communist countries and selected Third World nations in an effort to gain support for Soviet policy on Berlin. CIA Director Allen Dulles showed the report to Kennedy, who learned for the first time about the un-named Soviet colonel feeding valuable information to the Anglo-Americans. Kennedy was fascinated by the differences between the Soviet and American versions of the summit and gained important insights about his adversary's lack of integrity.

Penkovsky was getting high marks all around—in Washington, London, and Moscow. Based on his excellent performance with the trade delegation in England, he was promoted to deputy chief of the GRU Foreign Department and ordered to put together another London tour in late July. The trip was can-celed, however, partly because of a defection from a Soviet ballet company in France, so Penkovsky was told to go alone. General Serov sent his wife and twenty-one-year-old daughter along on the same Aeroflot flight and asked Penkovsky to look after them. He did so with gusto by taking them shopping and showing them the sights of London. It was a vote of high confidence and an opportunity not to be missed for Penkovsky to curry favor with his GRU chief.

Penkovsky, of course, renewed ties with his American and British case offi-cers, whom he greeted as dear old friends. This time, the meetings were held at a safe house in Kensington. For Penkovsky's gratification, they showed him the Kennedy speech incorporating his ideas about standing up to Khrushchev on the Berlin issue. He, in turn, gave them an update on Soviet war preparations, which seemed to have escalated in response to the Kennedy speech. At the last meeting in London, the case officers brought out British and American army uniforms with colonels' insignias for him to try on. The American uniform even had ribbons denoting campaigns and honors. It was meant as further compensation for denying him an audience with the queen. Before departing, the case officers gave him presents for Marshal Varentsov on his sixtieth birth-day. One was a bottle of vintage cognac with a forged label showing it to be the same age as Varentsov. At the party back home, Penkovsky poured the cognac for the guests, who included Defense Minister Rodion Y. Malinovsky, to toast the birthday man.

Shortly after Penkovsky's return to Moscow, he learned of plans to isolate West Berlin. That was four days before the scheduled event, which would begin stealthily during early morning on August 13 when East German construction crews began laying barbed wire around the perimeter, but he had no way of feeding the information to Western intelligence on short notice. He passed it to Wynne during a French trade exhibit in Moscow later that month. By then, a permanent concrete wall was under construction. In any case, the Kennedy

Administration sat on its hands as the wall was going up. The President himself, according to historian Michael Beschloss, was privately relieved that the destabilizing flow of refugees from East Germany now could be managed.[18]

When Penkovsky went to Paris the following month for a Soviet trade fair, he carried news from Moscow that was even more ominous. He revealed details about the intensive training of Soviet ground forces to prepare them for battle and the testing of medium-range and intermediate-range missiles (SS-4s and SS-5s), which would be used in the delivery of nuclear warheads. The West had detected nuclear explosions, which meant that Khrushchev had broken his word to Kennedy that the Soviet Union would not be the first to resume testing. Penkovsky added the useful tidbit that the test bombs exploded were delivered by test missiles. But he assured the case officers that, even though the SS-4 was in serial production and considered reliable, the Soviets did not have enough nuclear warheads to sustain an attack on the West. They could start a nuclear war but not finish it. Moreover, their missiles still lacked a reliable electronic guidance system and were therefore less than perfectly accurate.

The meetings took place at a safe house in a stylish residential area of Paris's Sixteenth Arrondisement without the knowledge of French officials. British and American intelligence had no intention of sharing their prize agent with the French; besides, French intelligence leaked like a sieve. They knew that the KGB had penetrated it. Wynne, in Paris only part of the time, saw his friend off at the airport for the trip back to Moscow. It was Penkovsky's final farewell to the West.

Penkovsky continued to spy in Moscow for the better part of a year. Translators at the CIA, hard-pressed to keep up with the volumes of Soviet documents generated by his Minox camera, began to wonder out loud if his work had not reached a point of diminishing return where the risks outweighed the rewards. Indeed, it had. Since January 1962, he had been under suspicion by the KGB. Methodically, the security police were closing in as he imperceptibly let down his guard. They prevented the GRU from sending him abroad, watched his movements, and built an airtight case against him.

At the CIA, Penkovsky was known by the code name "Hero." His reports gleaned from his own write-ups and the debriefings of the CIA-MI6 control team were code-named "Chickadee." The translated documents captured on film had still another code name, "Ironbark." One Chickadee report about

Soviet long-range missiles was particularly far-reaching, even though only about twenty CIA officials had access to it and the distribution list outside the agency was confined to perhaps a dozen key officials. In those Cold War years, the several U.S. intelligence agencies concerned with national security put their collective heads together at least once a year to estimate Soviet missile strength. Their product even had a stately name with stylish initials, the National Intelligence Estimate (NIE). In the spring of 1961, the official NIE was fifty to one hundred Soviet intercontinental ballistic missiles (ICBMs), operational and ready for launch. This was a consensus figure based on sources that were not particularly reliable. To some extent, it reflected unsubstantiated claims by the U.S. Air Force, which had a political stake in a higher count. The more Soviet ICBMs, which were the Air Force's responsibility to counteract, the more it could justify a higher budget. Penkovsky's Chickadee report that spring conveyed much lower figures, based on his conversations with Varentsov. But the intelligence agencies did not accept them for several months, until corroborated by a new intelligence weapon, satellite photo reconnaissance. Then, in November 1961, the NIE was lowered to thirty-five or fewer Soviet ICBMs.[19] The missile gap was a Soviet problem, not an American one. It remained for the Kennedy Administration to call Khrushchev's bluff, lest he miscalculate and push the nuclear button.

As Penkovsky was returning from Paris to Moscow, the rhetoric of the Cold War was heating up. In a speech to the Twenty-Second Congress of the Communist Party of the Soviet Union on October 17, Khrushchev declared that the Soviet Union was "stronger and more powerful than ever" and insisted that a German peace treaty "must and will be signed with or without the Western powers."[20] Four days later, the United States responded via a speech by Deputy Secretary of Defense Roswell Gilpatric at White Sulphur Springs, West Virginia. For the enemy to initiate a nuclear war against the United States, Gilpatric said, would be an act of self-destruction because ". . . we have a second-strike capability which is at least as extensive as what the Soviets can deliver by striking first." He cited hundreds of manned intercontinental bombers, ninety-six Polaris missiles in six nuclear submarines, dozens of land-based intercontinental ballistic missiles, plus carrier strike forces and land-based theater forces—"in all, tens of thousands" of nuclear delivery vehicles "and more than one warhead for each vehicle."[21] That chilled even the bombastic Khrushchev. Berlin faded into the background, but it was not entirely out of the picture.

Khrushchev had another card to play. Unable to cow the Americans by bluffing weapons superiority from long distance, he decided to bring the gun muzzle up to point-blank range. The increase in Soviet arms shipments to Cuba during the summer of 1962 made Washington nervous. From what the Americans could see, the hardware included SAMs, IL-28 bombers, and MiG-21 fighter planes. At the same time, Moscow had insisted repeatedly that its buildup in Cuba was strictly for defense. Senior Kennedy advisors, with one exception, took these assurances at face value. That exception was CIA Director John McCone, a Republican in the Democratic administration. He deduced that the SAMs, clearly visible in aerial photographs, were there for a hidden purpose, the defense of strategic missiles still to come. U-2 reconnaissance missions, sporadic during the weeks that followed, were hampered by bad weather and organizational problems that were overcome only after operational control of the Cuban overflights was transferred from the CIA to SAC on October 12. By this time, Washington was buzzing with rumors from Cuban emigré sources of large Soviet missiles arriving in Cuba. Two days later, Maj. Richard S. Heyser carried out a U-2 photo reconnaissance mission over an area of suspicious activity in western Cuba that touched off the most tense two weeks of the Cold War.

In Washington, Heyser's film was analyzed by photo interpretation teams at the National Photographic Interpretation Center (NPIC) that drew its technicians from the CIA and the military services. At a remote location near San Cristóbal, about fifty miles west-southwest of Havana, they spotted equipment and new excavation of a kind associated with the installation of missiles but different from the familiar SAM sites. What caught the eye, in particular, as they peered through their magnifying machinery, were six canvas-covered objects that measured more than 60 feet in length. After consulting their reference material, which prominently included text and diagrams, supplied by Penkovsky, of missile sites in various stages of preparation plus photographs of missiles parading through Red Square in Moscow, they concluded that they were looking at an SS-4 launching site at an early stage of construction. It was the first solid evidence of offensive Soviet missiles in Cuba. They passed the word to Arthur C. Lundahl, NPIC director, who asked the teams to work through the night and called in support personnel. That evening, two more SS-4 missile sites were discovered in the same general area.[22]

Three days later, after another overflight, the photo interpreters had another shock. Just west of Havana near Guanajay, they discovered a second missile complex under construction. This one was larger than any of those near San Cristóbal and had different distinguishing characteristics. From the reference material, they identified it as an SS-5 launching site.[23] The stunned Americans no longer doubted that the Soviets were building a significant strike capability that blanketed the most populous and strategically sensitive parts of the United States. From Cuba, the SS-4, classified as a medium-range missile, could hit any U.S. city as far north as Cincinnati and Washington and as far west as San Antonio and Dallas. The larger SS-5 (intermediate range) could reach all the way to southern California and a large part of eastern Canada. The missiles also threatened much of Latin America. Even if the bombs were still not as numerous or the missiles as accurate as Khrushchev would like, they could wreak indescribable carnage. Further overflights indicated other missile sites well east of Havana at Sagua la Grande and Remedios. By October 18, the NPIC teams had found sixteen SS-4 missile launch pads and eight SS-5 launch pads in two other locations.[24] The Soviets intended to place a total of eighty medium-range and intermediate-range missiles in Cuba, but only about half that number ever reached the island and none were SS-5s.[25]

President Kennedy was informed of the San Cristóbal discovery on October 16 and immediately called his top security advisors to a meeting. They discussed how to respond—air strikes? invasion? blockade? diplomacy? nothing? Kennedy felt that a few Soviet missiles in Cuba did not change the balance of power because the American lead in strategic weapons was so overwhelming. Yet, the missiles had to go. Otherwise, the United States would be perceived as weak, with disastrous consequences for its leadership of the noncommunist world. Over the following days, the advisors met daily in secrecy. They came to be known as Excom, short for the Executive Committee of the National Security Council. The precise, voluminous intelligence that had been supplied by Penkovsky gave greater substance to their deliberations. President Kennedy went about his normal activities in order not to stir up speculation. He campaigned to help Democrats win in the off-presidential-year elections. He met with Soviet Foreign Minister Gromyko and heard him repeat the familiar line that Soviet aid to Cuba was "solely" for defense. The news media and some members of Congress were getting wind of the missiles in Cuba from refugee sources, and the Kennedy Administration had to work hard to keep the lid on. If Khrushchev should find out what the Americans knew, Kennedy would lose the initiative.

After much soul-searching about whether to launch a military strike without warning, Excom formed a consensus around the option favored by the President—a blockade on further Soviet military shipments to Cuba. Excom sugarcoated the blockade by calling it a "quarantine," because a blockade was technically an act of war, and held off on more violent acts, such as air strikes and invasion, to give diplomacy a chance to work. Kennedy briefed his Cabinet and congressional leaders and sent special emissaries to inform Britain, France, Germany, and Canada, the most important allies of the United States. An hour before delivering a grim seventeen-minute address to the nation on Monday evening, October 22, he sent Khrushchev a copy. Kennedy called the missile buildup "a deliberately provocative and unjustified change in the status quo which cannot be accepted by this country, if our courage and our commitments are ever to be trusted again either by friend or foe."[26] Days of tension followed until Soviet ships carrying missiles and nuclear warheads turned back rather than challenge the American blockade. Afterward, Secretary of State Dean Rusk uttered the quintessential summation of the Cuban missile crisis, "We're eyeball to eyeball, and I think the other fellow just blinked."[27] The crisis was not over. Tough and sometimes rancorous negotiations remained. Another two months passed before the Soviets finally took back all their offensive missiles and bombers. In return, Kennedy pledged not to invade Cuba and to remove obsolescent American missiles from Turkey.

The same day, October 22, 1962, that President Kennedy addressed the nation from Washington, Oleg Penkovsky was arrested in Moscow. The KGB had been on his trail at least since the previous January. When he returned to Moscow from Paris in October 1961, he had immediately resumed his espionage activity. Janet Chisholm became his regular courier, and they met weekly when possible. They usually made eye contact in a park or busy store, as prearranged, and he would lead her to a residential building on a quiet street. She would follow him inside to the vestibule where, in a few seconds, they would make their exchange. Then, she would go home to wait for her husband and quietly—assuming their home to be bugged—give him the materials from Penkovsky. MI6 also arranged for Janet and Penkovsky to meet formally at a diplomatic party, and they once made an exchange at an embassy social event when he was on official duty.

Things were going so well for Penkovsky that he must have become over-confident. Certainly, he was careless. He continued to lead Janet to the same building on the same quiet street. Before long, the KGB set up a camera in an apartment on the opposite side. In January, the two were caught on film as they entered and left the building separately. The KGB surveillance had begun routinely. In response to the surprising discovery six years earlier that the spy Pyotr Popov was passing intelligence to the West in the streets of Moscow, Gen. Oleg M. Gribanov, head of the Second Chief Directorate, tightened the KGB watch on the British and American embassies. For periods lasting weeks, they shadowed anybody and everybody, including Mrs. Chisholm, who had a connection to the embassies.[28] Late in January, Penkovsky spotted two men in a car following her and broke off contact. By then, she was pregnant with her fourth child and soon returned to England.

Penkovsky was already too late to save himself. KGB suspicion of him was first aroused after he had attended a British Embassy reception without clearing his visit beforehand, as security regulations required. Since then, they had kept an eye on him at home and in his office. A remote-control camera was placed in the window box of an apartment opposite his. It caught him tuning and listening to his radio and taking notes—suspicious activity. In July 1942, when Wynne paid a visit to Moscow, the KGB kept a close watch on him, too, and caught sight of Penkovsky in Wynne's room at the Hotel Ukraine turning on the radio and the bathroom water taps to mask their conversation. One evening when they were to meet at the Pekin Hotel restaurant, they discovered that Wynne was being followed and Penkovsky urged him to get out of town first thing in the morning. On August 27, at a diplomatic reception Penkovsky made his final pass of Minox film, along with a letter warning that "the 'neighbors' [KGB] continue to study me. For some reason they have latched on to me." It was even worse than Penkovsky knew. The KGB commandeered the apartment above Penkovsky's home, drilled a small hole in his ceiling, and inserted a tiny camera. It caught him using his Minox and encryption gear. When the family was away, they searched his apartment and found all the evidence necessary to charge him with espionage.[29]

On November 2, twelve days after Penkovsky's arrest, Wynne was hosting a cocktail party in Budapest for Hungarian trade officials when he was seized by four burly Soviet security agents and carted off to Moscow. He and Penkovsky were held incommunicado until December 12, when Pravda announced that Wynne had confessed. At their perfunctory trial on May 7, 1963, Penkovsky was accused of treason and Wynne of aiding and abetting him. Conviction of both men was a foregone conclusion. Penkovsky was sentenced to death, and, on May 17, Pravda announced his execution. Wynne received an eight-year sentence, but eleven months later, Britain and the Soviet Union agreed to a swap of prisoners, Wynne for the Soviet spy Konon Molody (aka Gordon Lonsdale).

To the very end, Penkovsky remained "Hero" in more than his code name to his handlers in Western intelligence. During the months leading up to his trial, he never told his Soviet interrogators the full extent of his betrayal. Two years after his death, the CIA was still churning out reports based on his materials, some of which were so sensitive that they remained secret even after the demise of the Soviet Union nearly three decades later. In addition to what has already been mentioned, his voluminous output included information on Soviet air defense, armored vehicles, ground-to-ground missiles, nuclear combat operations, and the use of chemical weapons. His report on the technical characteristics of the SA-2 SAM missile revealed that this antiaircraft weapon, effective at high altitudes, did not become operational until it reached 4,000 feet, so SAC instructed its bomber pilots to fly below that altitude. Among the documents that Penkovsky photographed was a top secret article on the Soviet T-62 tank, which greatly influenced the design of the American M-60 battle tank.[30] Measured in both volume and importance, Penkovsky's information was so inimical to Soviet interests that it belies a theory floated after his death that he was a double agent planted by the KGB.

But what sort of hero was he who betrayed his country and his patrons? Marshal Varentsov and General Serov were both demoted and forced to retire in disgrace. Penkovsky's father-in-law, General Gapanovich, had the good fortune to die in the fifties. To see Penkovsky through the eyes of a Russian patriot, communist or noncommunist, is to put him in a class with Benedict Arnold looked at from the American perspective. Excessive pride and a modicum of greed were common to both men. It does not seem credible to argue that Penkovsky turned to spying for his nation's enemies out of a love for freedom and democracy. It probably would not have happened had he not had his run-in with Rubenko in Turkey, or had he been allowed to assume his assigned post in India, or had he been promoted to general with continued prospects for advancement. It is fortunate for the West that events took the course they did because Penkovsky was truly a key figure for the West at a critical point of the Cold War. He was a traitor, all right, but he was our traitor.

CHAPTER 16

Workers against the Workers' State

November 9, 1989, is a date for freedom's children to remember. The world watched in disbelief at the late-night news picturing Berliners as they poured through the gates of the Berlin Wall—east to west and west to east—without interference from East German guards. People held animated reunions with relatives and friends or chipped away gritty concrete shards of wall for souvenirs of the historic moment. The next day, workers methodically began to tear down the wall, thus signaling the acquiescence of the East German government in a new policy of openness to the West. For twenty-seven years, the Berlin Wall had blocked easy escape for the discontents of East Germany as they tried to flee the communist dictatorship. Now, its dismantling symbolized the collapse of the entire Soviet empire in Eastern Europe, which was already in the throes of revolutionary change.

That year, Poland held free elections that eased the way to power for supporters of the Solidarity trade union movement. In Hungary, the ruling Socialist Workers (communist) Party reconstituted itself as the Socialist (democratic) Party, a move from the one-party state to pluralism. On the day that the Berlin Wall came down, hard-line communists in Bulgaria relinquished the reins of government to party reformers. Soon afterward, Czechoslovakia experienced its "Velvet Revolution" as demonstrators took to the streets for several days in nonviolent protests until the communists bowed to the will of the people. Only in Romania did revolutionary blood spill. The Romanian army, in defense of demonstrators calling for reform, fought pitched battles against government security forces in the streets of Timisoara. When the smoke cleared, hundreds lay dead. In the capital, Bucharest, the communist leader Nicolae Ceausescu and his wife were summarily executed by a military firing squad. Three years later, the Soviet Union itself came apart as its constituent republics declared their independence.

Geopolitically, the collapse of the Soviet empire must rank as the most significant event of the last half of the twentieth century. Maybe it was foreordained. The independent peoples of Eastern Europe were never an easy fit in a one-size-fits-all system directed from Moscow. In 1956, they fought for freedom in the streets of Budapest and again, in 1968, in Prague. Each time, the Soviet army was called in to put down the uprising. The East Germans were equally resentful of their fate under Soviet dominance. In East Berlin in 1953, construction workers protesting a rise in production quotas sparked demonstrations that spread to other cities. Hundreds died while Soviet troops restored order. For nearly a decade afterward, the East German people "voted with their feet," to use a term then in vogue, by defecting to the West in a steady stream. It was easy enough to do—simply ride or walk from East Berlin to West Berlin and ask for asylum—until the East German government put up the Berlin Wall in 1962.

The end of the Soviet empire had its beginning in Poland in 1980. Polish workers had carried out major strikes in 1956, 1970, and 1976 to protest government-imposed increases in the price of food and to demand higher pay. In 1980, they took a quantum leap. Workers at the Lenin Shipyard in Gdansk struck not just for better pay but also for the right to exist as an independent trade union, which thrust at the heart of the one-party state. They called their movement "Solidarity." It gained the support of the Polish people and captured the imagination of the free world. In that case, the Soviet army did not intervene. Instead, Soviet leaders pressured the Polish communist government to impose martial law, which it did after a delay of sixteen months. That was time enough for Solidarity to grow from an organized labor movement into a worldwide symbol of freedom too powerful to contain, even after the military regime had crushed it as an organization.

During this sixteen-month period, one of Poland's brightest and most respected young army officers played a hidden role as an agent of the CIA. Col. Ryszard Kuklinski joined the Polish army's general staff in 1964 as a military planner. By the time of the Solidarity crisis in 1980–81, he was head of the General Planning Department and deputy head of the Operations Directorate of the Polish General Staff. In these high-level positions, he served as the trusted military aide and speechwriter for Gen. Wojciech Jaruzelski, the army commander and defense minister. Kuklinski was also liaison to Marshal Viktor Kulikov, the Soviet commander of the Warsaw Pact, the military alliance of Soviet bloc nations organized to counter NATO. Thus, Kuklinski became the CIA's best human source of information inside the Soviet orbit.

At times, when the Soviet Union seemed to be threatening a military solution to the Solidarity crisis, Kuklinski kept the CIA abreast of Warsaw Pact maneuvers at the Polish borders. Based on Kuklinski's intelligence, the Carter Administration issued a timely warning against Soviet invasion. Later, the Reagan Administration drew up economic sanctions to be applied should the Polish government implement martial law, which it eventually did. Kuklinski actually helped to write Poland's plan for martial law and sent a copy to the CIA. From what is known so far—and much of his work remains secret—it is safe to say that Kuklinski is one of the most underappreciated spies of the twentieth century.

Kuklinski lived in a free Poland for only the first nine years of his life until the German blitzkrieg of September 1939.[1] Six years of German occupation were followed by forty-four years of Soviet domination. By the time Poland emerged as a free nation again, Kuklinski was an American citizen.

During World War II, Kuklinski's father, Stanislaw, an apartment house caretaker, became active in the resistance. Ryszard took his toy accordion to meetings where he and the other children played their instruments to muffle the voices of the adults plotting against the hated Nazi occupiers. The Kuklinskis lived within sight of the Jewish ghetto, and, before he had even reached his teens, Ryszard frequently witnessed the depraved slaughter of his neighbors. In 1943, the Nazis caught up with Stanislaw's underground activities. He was arrested, beaten, and carted off to a concentration camp, never again to see or be seen by his family. Ryszard, then thirteen years old, ran away to join other teenagers roaming the forests in poorly organized resistance gangs. In their youthful naiveté, Ryszard and some of his friends hit upon the idea of volunteering to work for the Germans in France with the intention of escaping across the English Channel to enlist in the Polish army in exile. To their great disappointment, the Germans took them no further than Silesia, where Ryszard served eighteen months of his childhood in a Nazi slave labor camp. Ryszard escaped during the winter of 1945 and spent the last few months of the war on the run. When he returned to Warsaw after its liberation by the Soviet army, he found it in ruins. He located his mother, Anna, outside the city at the home of a close friend. At the age of fifteen, he went in a vain search for his father, who was last reported at the Oranienburg-Sachsenhausen concentration camp near Berlin, but Stanislaw was one of six million Poles, both Jewish and gentile, who had died at the hands of the Nazis.

In 1947, Ryszard joined the Polish army. He soon found out who was in charge. At officers' training school, Soviet officers replaced his commanding officer and school commandant. Nevertheless, Kuklinski excelled in his military education and ranked first in his class. He did what was expected of him by joining the Communist Party only to learn, unexpectedly, that his communist masters could not take a joke. In his last year at officers' school, just months before graduation, he was expelled from the party, stripped of his military rank, and transferred out of the school for repeating the latest witticism about Soviet efforts to collectivize Poland. On appeal, the party reinstated him and gave him his commission. For several years, Kuklinski routinely climbed the career ladder until, in 1964, he was offered a position on the General Staff in Warsaw. Initially, he devised war exercises in cooperation with Soviet military planners, traveled throughout the Soviet bloc, and gained wide respect for his skills. He worried, however, that Soviet strategic plans called not simply for the defense of the homeland but for offensive warfare against the NATO alliance in which Poland might well be the key battleground of a nuclear war.

Events in Czechoslovakia in 1968 stirred Kuklinski's conscience. Assigned to assist Warsaw Pact military exercises in southern Poland, he quickly perceived that the maneuvers were a cover for an invasion of Czechoslovakia to quell an anti-Soviet uprising by the communist government in Prague. He tried to dissociate himself by faking a family illness in Warsaw, but the ruse bought him only a week's time before he had to return to the invasion force. He became an unwilling participant in the Soviet suppression of the Czech rebellion. The invasion took the West by surprise, and it occurred to Kuklinski that he should find a way to open secret communication with NATO.

When Polish workers struck in December 1970, communist leader Wladyslaw Gomulka called up three armored divisions. One morning at the Gdansk shipyard, troops opened fire on a crowd of workers. In five days of unrest, forty-five workers were killed and more than a thousand injured. The incident reinforced Kuklinski's resolve to act against Poland's communist rulers. Soon afterward, he proposed to his superiors that he lead a military team on a "pleasure cruise" to Western ports to spy on NATO installations. His plan called for the team to travel as vacationers in an old German sailboat that he, as an avid part-time sailor, had recovered from the sea and restored. The mission was approved and Kuklinski and crew set sail a year or so later. At the port of Wilhelmshaven in West Germany, Kuklinski secretly initiated contact with a U.S. Army officer, who turned him over to the CIA.

Kuklinski made similar voyages during the next few years. On each occasion, he met with American intelligence. The Americans made sure that he was not followed. During debriefings, agents shopped for him in Western stores for automobile parts and other consumer items to justify his long absences from his Polish companions. In 1976, for unknown reasons, the voyages came to a halt by order of the chief of staff of the Polish army. From that point on, Kuklinski fell back on the connections established for him in Warsaw, primarily dead drops and brief secret encounters with American agents.

In the Polish capital, the danger of detection was ever present. Once, on the street at night while carrying a briefcase filled with classified documents, he thought that he had been spotted by counterintelligence. He immediately took evasive action by ducking in and out of subways and then walking 3 miles to his home, taking care that he did not have an unwanted shadow. To be on the safe side, he tried to remove any trace of his outward appearance that might give him away. He burned the clothes he was wearing, had a haircut, and, after removing the contents, threw his briefcase into the Vistula River. For a while, he broke off contact with the CIA.

———————————

The Cold War was carried on, to a large extent, by intelligence agencies. Hot wars, limited in scope, were being fought on the fringes in such places as Korea, Vietnam, and Afghanistan. On the prospective main battlefield in Europe, the

Warsaw Pact and NATO armies each waited for the other to fire the first shot, while the Soviet KGB and the American CIA, along with their respective allied intelligence agencies, engaged in undercover competition on a global scale. Dirty tricks, propaganda, lies, entrapment, seduction, blackmail, and even assassination were in the mix. At its core, however, the undercover war was about gathering information.

As intelligence became ever more institutionalized, it sprouted ever-growing bureaucracies for codebreaking, foreign espionage, and domestic counter-espionage. By the sixties, the halcyon days of the Marxist ideologue-cum-spy were over for the Soviet Union. Gone from active service were the likes of Richard Sorge, Kim Philby, Donald Maclean, Klaus Fuchs, and Ted Hall. A new breed of mercenaries trod the stage—John Walker, Ronald Pelton, Edward Lee Howard, and Aldrich Ames. Ironically, the most talented ideological spies were turning in the opposite direction, from east to west. The Russian, Oleg Penkovsky, and the Pole, Ryszard Kuklinski, are the two best examples.

Fortunately, there was no cataclysmic Cold War event—everyone would have lost—but both sides possessed stolen information that might have been decisive in the event of war. The Soviets received vital American coding material from John Walker. The Americans benefited from Warsaw Pact war plans for Europe made available by Kuklinski. Throughout the seventies, Kuklinski passed more than thirty thousand pages of Soviet documents to the CIA. He turned over details of Soviet weapons systems, including the T-72 main battle tank, and plans for electronic warfare. Kuklinski was able to supplement American satellite photo intelligence by identifying which Soviet missile sites were real and which were decoys and by pinpointing three top secret strategic command posts to be used only in the event of war. When he wrote Poland's strategic military plans, he saved a copy for the CIA.[2]

Because the feared clash of nuclear titans never happened, Kuklinski's potentially damaging information about Soviet war plans was never used in battle and, like Walker's betrayal of American cryptosystems to the Soviets, was ultimately reduced to a footnote. What mattered more, as it turned out, was that Kuklinski furnished the CIA with Poland's martial law plans and, from his inside position, kept the Americans fully informed about preparations for military action, whether by Polish or Soviet troops, against the Polish people struggling for their human and civil rights. "We waited eagerly for each of [Kuklinski's] reports . . . ," the CIA's Robert M. Gates said. "His information had been important to us in prompting [President] Carter's tough warning [against Soviet intervention] in December 1980 and it would be critical to us all through 1981 [after President Reagan took office]."[3]

―――――――――

The historic strike of 1980, which launched the Solidarity movement, started in July when railroad workers in Lublin walked off the job. The usual bread-and-butter issues were at play. The strike did not reach the Lenin Shipyard in Gdansk until August 14 after a popular forklift operator, Anna Walentynowicz, was fired for allegedly stealing spent candles from a cemetery. She was gathering the used wax to make new candles to honor the dead of the 1970 strike. Although the Gdansk workers were not anxious for another confrontation—the 1970 bloodbath having been etched in their memories—they shut down the entire shipyard by day's end. They demanded Walentynowicz's reinstatement and a thousand-zloty pay raise across the board. Within three days, the strike had spread to factories throughout the Gdansk area and was held together by an Inter-Factory Strike Committee led by future Nobel laureate Lech Walesa. He published a list of demands that included government recognition of free trade unions, the release of political prisoners, and limited freedom from government censorship. Walesa's position, influenced by Polish intellectuals organized as the Workers Defense Committee (KOR), won instant support from the Catholic Church. It was no longer just a strike but a political insurrection, the birth of Solidarity, and a spontaneous uprising of the working class unforeseen in Marx's dialectic—directed not at the capitalist class but at Lenin's version of the workers' state. It spread far beyond Gdansk and seized the nation's repressed yearning for freedom.

The Polish government, then headed by Edward Gierek, offered reforms and better pay but dug in against demands "aimed at destroying the [communist] social order." Yet, on August 31, Gierek signed the Gdansk accords, which promised better food supplies and granted wage increases, the right of unions to organize, limited freedom to publish, and the return of Anna Walentynowicz. With total victory in their pockets, the workers went back to work and Solidarity lived on as a national union and political movement with a membership of ten million workers, more than one fourth of the population of Poland. The movement was so strong that a million Communist Party members also joined Solidarity.[4] Despite his reputation as a defiant labor leader, Walesa had led his one and only strike. He thought Solidarity had gone as far as it could in challenging the communist regime. He became a moderating voice within the movement, counseled against radical action demanded by local unions, and maintained a dialogue with communist leaders. Walesa, operating in the non-violent tradition of Mahatma Gandhi and Martin Luther King, did his best not to give Poland's government or the Soviet leviathan next door an excuse for military intervention. It was an uncertain, nervous time in Poland's history.

In the immediate fallout from the Gdansk accords, Gierek was deposed as party first secretary and replaced by Stanislaw Kania, a politically savvy centrist born of peasant stock. While taking a conciliatory stance toward Solidarity, the new regime prepared for the worst. Defense Minister Jaruzelski ordered an update of the contingency plans for martial law, which had been in the files since 1970. Kuklinski served as one of the drafters of the new version, a mark of the high regard and trust in which he was held at Army General Staff head-quarters. He made sure the CIA received a copy of the new draft when it was submitted to the Polish government and party leaders in December 1980.

The Polish Communist Party was in a terrible bind. Solidarity, with broad public support, continued to press its pro-democracy political agenda, while the Kremlin, ever more alarmed by the threat that Solidarity posed to the communist state, increased its pressure for the Polish leadership to crack down. The Soviets postured, bullied, cajoled, and seemed to threaten invasion, but they never invaded. They had other problems. The Soviet army was bogged down in a losing war in Afghanistan. The last thing the Soviets needed was another conflict sure to generate negative world opinion and invite economic sanctions from the West. In the United States, the Carter Administration kept abreast of the Polish situation through Kuklinski and other sources, including satellite photo reconnaissance.

In late November, while Solidarity threatened large-scale strikes, the Warsaw Pact prepared for military exercises, Soyuz-80 (Alliance, 1980), in and around Poland. The maneuvers involved Soviet, Czech, and East German troops, with Polish troops confined to their bases. They had all the earmarks of the preparations that Kuklinski had witnessed twelve years earlier before the invasion of Czechoslovakia. On December 1, Soviet and Polish generals met to work out details of the plan. Kuklinski was not at the meeting, but he soon learned of it. As he understood it, eighteen Warsaw Pact divisions—fifteen Soviet, two Czech, and one East German—were poised to intervene in Poland, and Defense Minister Jaruzelski had endorsed the plan. Kuklinski fired off a "Very Urgent" message notifying the CIA.

To American policymakers, a crisis similar to past Soviet interventions in Hungary and Czechoslovakia was looming. The Carter Administration, with Polish-born chief security advisor Zbigniew Brzezinski in a key role, reacted with a public warning of "very grave consequences to U.S.-Soviet relations" if Soviet troops invaded Poland. The Americans were talking about political estrangement, economic sanctions, and cultural isolation, however, not military action. They also urged major heads of state in the West to issue similar admonitions.[5] Brzezinski, a Catholic but only a presidential aide, threw protocol to the winds and called Pope John Paul II, a de facto head of state, to inform him of the imminent Soviet threat and ask him to turn Catholic pressure on Western nations with large Catholic populations. The Pope, surprised by the quality and depth of Brzezinski's inside information, agreed to do so.[6] When the crisis had passed by late December, the Carter Administration claimed credit for getting the Soviets to back off.

Kuklinski, on the other hand, gives credit to Kania for the Soviet restraint. The new Polish leader spoke forcefully at a Warsaw Pact meeting in Moscow on December 5. He told his "fraternal comrades" that intervention would meet with stiff resistance from the Polish people and very likely the Polish army. He pleaded for more time to implement martial law. Kania's speech sounded so tough on Solidarity that Soviet leaders were convinced that he intended to crack down immediately, but they were wrong. While vigorously condemning Solidarity in the same brutish language coming from Moscow, Kania stood like a rock against the imposition of martial law and consistently blocked it during the year he held or shared power. Eventually, the Soviets backed off, and the crisis took a holiday. It helped that Solidarity cooled its agitation for a few weeks.

The Soviets have always claimed that they never intended to invade Poland but only to pressure Kania and Jaruzelski. Logic supports their argument if history does not. Why should the Soviet army, already bogged down in Afghanistan, shed more of its blood in Poland where the cost likely would be very high? Harvard scholar Mark Kramer recently uncovered documents from East German archives that show the situation to have been more complex than either Kuklinski or the Carter Administration knew. They suggest, in Kramer's words, that Soyuz-80 was "intended mainly as a cover for Polish authorities to impose martial law." Soyuz-80 was to be carried out in two stages. The first would involve only four Soviet divisions, plus the other three from Czechoslovakia and East Germany. If needed, that is, if the Polish army was not up to the task of crushing Solidarity, a second stage would activate up to eleven more Soviet divisions. Thus, said Kramer, Kuklinski, in his understandable haste, did not have all his facts straight, and the Carter Administration, deprived of up-to-date photo intelligence because of cloud cover over the region, issued its stern warning without corroborating Kuklinski's information.[7] One has to wonder, however, how Warsaw Pact troops intervening in Poland, whether seven or eighteen divisions, could have avoided conflict if the Polish army, or parts of it, sided with Solidarity—a real possibility.

During the lull that lasted into the next year, Walesa and a contingent from Solidarity went like conquering heroes to Rome, where Walesa received the Pope's blessing and the adulation of the Western press. That rankled the Soviet leaders, but something far more ominous set off alarm bells in the Kremlin. Mikhail V. Zimianian, a member of the Soviet Party Central Committee, went to Poland on a fact-finding mission and returned to Moscow with the dire warning that Solidarity, backed by the Catholic Church, was becoming the dominant power in Poland.[8]

In February 1981, the Central Committee of the Polish Communist Party, under pressure from Moscow, elevated Jaruzelski to prime minister, at the same time allowing him to keep his position as defense minister. That left Jaruzelski and Kania to share power. After a secret test of the martial law plan, Jaruzelski gave it his final approval. An important element was the timing. Martial law was to be initiated on a Saturday night to avoid resistance and bloodshed to the extent possible. Strict secrecy was indispensable; the Sejm, Poland's legislative body, could not be informed. Indeed, the Sejm was not told, but the CIA was, thanks to Kuklinski. In March, Jaruzelski and Kania went to Moscow to submit the plan, with talking points written by Kuklinski, for Soviet Premier Leonid Brezhnev's approval. As happy as Brezhnev was to see it, he was more interested in getting the Poles to set a firm date, but Kania and Jaruzelski continued to stall. Back in Warsaw, the army drew up a list of eleven thousand Solidarity members and supporters to be arrested during the crackdown.

By this time, the Reagan Administration had taken office in Washington. With Poland's tough new martial law plan in hand, administration officials began thinking through the likelihood that Solidarity would be suppressed by its own government without Soviet intervention and developed a menu of economic sanctions as their response to any implementation of martial law. The sanctions were never threatened in advance, an inaction that became controversial after the event. For all the tough talk, said the CIA's Robert Gates, Reagan's approach to the Polish problem was "nearly identical" to Carter's.[9]

Near the end of March, another serious crisis flared up when security force toughs beat up Solidarity activists in the city of Bydgoszcz while they were agitating for government recognition of a Solidarity-sponsored farmers' union known as Rural Solidarity. Aroused by the government's resort to violence, Solidarity demanded punishment for the perpetrators, assurances of future restraint, release of political prisoners, and recognition of Rural Solidarity. It then flexed its muscle by calling a four-hour general strike for March 31. The government met the Solidarity demands on police brutality but put off a decision on the other issues. Walesa responded by postponing the strike.

Moscow was aghast at even this concession to Solidarity. Once again, Warsaw Pact armies on the Polish border bestirred themselves on the pretext of field maneuvers. Polish air space was closed "for technical reasons" the night of March 28–29; the East Germans held railroad flatcars in reserve for possible military use; and the Soviet General Staff expanded its command, control, and communications networks and dispatched units to Poland for coordinating military operations. The Kremlin hierarchy was so uptight that senior Soviet officials flew to Warsaw to demand that the state transfer all its power to the Polish army and that the army accept Soviet advisors at all levels. Jaruzelski and Kania rejected the demand.[10]

The tension reached a climax on April 4. Kania and Jaruzelski were summoned to the Warsaw military airport at 7 P.M., where an unmarked Soviet plane flew in to pick them up. On board was Gen. Anatoli Gribkov, second in command of the Warsaw Pact, who said later that the two Polish leaders appeared as though they thought they were never coming back. The plane flew them to Brest on the Soviet-Polish border. There, they were driven past a huge building that looked like a prison and on to an abandoned railway car. They were greeted by KGB boss Yuri Andropov and Defense Minister Dmitri Ustinov, who, in light of Brezhnev's senility, were probably the two most powerful men in the Soviet Union. The Poles found the car well furnished with plenty to eat and drink. The four men sat alone for six hours and conversed in Russian, the Soviets urging the Poles to crack down on Solidarity, and the Poles pleading that the time was not right. The conversation finally ended with the Poles agreeing to study a Soviet document announcing martial law. Later, the two sides argued about whether the Poles had agreed to sign it.[11] From that point, Moscow put unrelenting pressure on the two Polish leaders to impose martial law. Ultimately, Jaruzelski bent to the Soviet will but not before Kania was removed from power.

The military exercises ended on April 7, with Solidarity's strike still pending, to be rescheduled for late April. Word was going around that radical elements within Solidarity were preparing to launch a campaign of violence, stockpiling Molotov cocktails and planning to occupy and destroy party and government offices. Polish leaders feared the worst. Church leaders all the way up to the Pope were appalled. Jaruzelski and Kania asked the church to intercede with Solidarity. The Polish vicar, Stefan Cardinal Wyszynski, went to Walesa and asked him to call off the strike. When Walesa refused, Wyszynski, who was dying of cancer, fell to his knees, grabbed Walesa's coat, and threatened to remain kneeling in prayer until he died. Yielding to what he called "emotional blackmail," Walesa canceled the strike. Wyszynski got up off his knees and died a few weeks later.

In September 1981, the National Defense Council of the Polish Politburo met amid Soviet hectoring to fix a December date for martial law. Everyone in the room from Jaruzelski down supported it, except Kania. In Moscow, Kremlin leaders were livid but hardly surprised. They had been getting detailed intelligence reports on Kania—about his bitter disenchantment with the Soviet style of "bureaucratized" socialism and his unhappy state of mind over the pressure to call out the troops—reports so intimate that either his house was bugged by Polish security or someone in his family was informing on him.[12] They now turned to Jaruzelski to replace the man they had elevated only a year earlier. Jaruzelski, backed by party and government leaders, confronted Kania with the warning that they were prepared to implement martial law with or without his approval. At a meeting of the Central Committee in October, Kania was removed from office. Jaruzelski became party first secretary and, from that time until 1989, held executive power alone. His first task was to carry out martial law.

Kuklinski did not attend the September meeting but something happened there of vital interest to him. One of the generals announced that Solidarity knew the army's plans for martial law and knew them in such detail that the source must have been at a high level of military planning. When Kuklinski heard of this, he realized that he would be a suspect. Soon afterward, he received a chilling visit from a high-level counterintelligence officer whose understated purpose was to advise him about how leaks could be avoided. Kuklinski thought the leak must have come at the CIA's end. In a message to his handlers, he broke off daily contact and urged them to be more careful with his information. "I am prepared to make the ultimate sacrifice," he told them, "but the best way to achieve something is with our actions and not with our sacrifices."[13]

The security service launched an investigation in September and put a watch on Kuklinski's house. In early November, Kuklinski and three other officers were summoned to a meeting at the office of Gen. Jerzy Skalski, chief of martial law planning. Skalski told them that the Americans possessed the final version of the plans, which meant one of the four must have given it to them. Each of the other three men, in turn, professed his innocence and pledged full cooperation with the investigation. Kuklinski said later that he was ready to confess when it came his turn to speak, but Skalski interrupted. "I am not a security officer," he said and closed the meeting. Kuklinski knew, in any case, that it was time for him to leave Poland. Five days after giving a prearranged signal to the CIA, he, his wife, and their two children were smuggled out to freedom. Kuklinski has not revealed how it was done.[14]

Tensions mounted as the autumn gloom descended on Poland. Solidarity was growing more radical—bolder to the point of reckless. Walesa had to adopt the hard line of his followers or he would lose out as their leader. On December 2, Polish troops raided the Army Firefighter's Academy in Warsaw and rounded up three hundred striking cadets. Solidarity, in its man-the-barricades state of mind, called for a general strike. It scheduled a huge rally in downtown Warsaw for December 17. On December 11 and 12, Solidarity's national commission met in Gdansk. Walesa, who still favored negotiations with the communist regime, listened to speaker after speaker call for free elections, worker control of factories, and a plebiscite on communist rule. When one of the speakers asked him to admit there was no longer any use talking to the government, Walesa replied, "I'm just sitting here trying to figure out what it is you guys ate today that makes you talk like you do."[15]

December 12 was a Saturday. The meeting broke up about midnight, just when troops were fanning out across Poland. Within the first two hours of December 13, most of Solidarity's national commission were under arrest. Without a lot of bloodshed, more than ten thousand Solidarity members on the government's list of troublemakers were rounded up. What was left of the organization went underground. Authorities declared a "state of war" and established a Military Council of National Salvation. The army, now in charge, took over the railroads, highways, mail delivery, broadcasting, gas delivery, fire-fighting, trade, and the manufacture of strategic goods. The borders were sealed and Polish air space closed. Television broadcasters wore army uniforms.

Without Kuklinski on the scene, the Americans did not know the precise date of the crackdown. Solidarity was caught completely off guard. Rumors of martial law had been circulating for so long that many Solidarity leaders no longer took them seriously, nor did the United States issue any advance warning of dire economic and political consequences as it had a year earlier in the face of the perceived Soviet threat of military intervention. Some Solidarity leaders felt betrayed. Jaruzelski took it as a green light, a signal that the Americans would accept martial law as the lesser of two evils. He assumed wrong. The United States, joined by other Western nations, did, in fact, impose sanctions. They were devastating and, as usual when sanctions are imposed, innocent people suffered the most.

During the next seven and a half years, Poland gradually emerged from its nightmare. The outlawed Solidarity survived as a shadow of its former self, reduced by martial law from a national power to a nagging thorn in the side of the military authorities. It continued to deliver its message of resistance through underground newspapers, magazines, factory bulletins, and radio broadcasts. On rare occasions, it broke into state-run television with pirate transmissions. These activities would not have been possible without outside help from the Catholic Church, Western organized labor, and especially the CIA. The agency managed a covert operation for all of Eastern Europe that consisted essentially of smuggling in printing materials, communications equipment, and other supplies for waging underground propaganda warfare. The CIA was most active in Poland, said Gates, by then its deputy director, and so secretive about its operation that it did not inform Solidarity that the CIA was the source.[16]

More than the undercover assistance of the CIA, the public crusade of the Polish Pope kept the freedom movement alive. When John Paul II paid his second papal visit to his homeland in 1983, he spoke of solidarity as a concept—"the fundamental solidarity between human beings." He embraced the principles of the Gdansk accords—the right of workers to organize as independent unions and to demand a just salary, job security, decent hours, and a day of rest—rights, he said pointedly, "given by the Creator," not the state.[17]

Soon thereafter, on July 22, 1983, Jaruzelski called an end to martial law and, in 1986, freed the last 225 political prisoners.

Poland was then on the path to reform, boosted by the arrival in 1985 of a reform-minded leader in the Soviet Union. Soviet Chairman Mikhail Gorbachev spoke of *perestroika* (restructuring), *glasnost* (openness), and "absolute independence" for socialist countries. Jaruzelski pursued reform with half-measures, such as a consultative council to advise on national policy, and tried, at the same time, to retain the primacy of the Communist Party. He refused to give Solidarity a role in reform or any legal status as a union. He kept censorship in place and treated Walesa as a has-been. Thanks to the Pope's intercession, President Reagan lifted the economic sanctions, but Jaruzelski's meek efforts at reform ultimately failed. A third papal visit in 1987 generated more stirring speeches in support of Solidarity. Jaruzelski then went a step further. He eased censorship and travel restrictions and appointed a noncommunist prosecutor to investigate government abuses. With the economy still in the tank despite the lifting of sanctions, he scheduled a referendum on a program of economic austerity and limited political plurality. The proposal lost because Solidarity urged voters to boycott the vote.

In 1988, wildcat strikes erupted throughout Poland. The workers refused to go back to work until the government promised negotiations for reform that included Solidarity. Jaruzelski finally gave in. Talks known as the Round Table negotiations took place early in 1989, with the church playing the role of mediator. Solidarity emerged with its legal status restored. Even more significant, the negotiators created a new legislative body called the Senate. Free elections were scheduled, and, in June, Solidarity won all but 1 of 262 Senate seats contested. Jaruzelski retained the presidency, but, in August, he called on Tadeusz Mazowiecki, a Catholic intellectual allied to Solidarity, to form a government. At last, Solidarity took power in Poland, and the communist regimes of the Soviet empire started to fall like dominoes.

Ryszard Kuklinski followed Poland's struggle for freedom from his distant exile in the United States. American officials at the highest level treated him like a hero. Brzezinski, the Carter aide who had relied on his reports, paid him a visit during his early debriefing by Pentagon and CIA officials. "You have served Poland well," Brzezinski told him, a tribute traditionally spoken to Poland's decorated soldiers. In a private ceremony, CIA Director William Casey presented him with the Distinguished Intelligence Medal, the agency's highest award, and praised him in a personal letter as "a man of high character and courage, as a Polish patriot. . . ." Kuklinski, his wife Joanna, and their two adult sons, Waldemar and Boguslaw, were given U.S. citizenship and new identities and relocated to an undisclosed place in the United States. Boguslaw's fiancée, Izabela, escaped from Warsaw with the help of the CIA and soon joined him. In spite of the secrecy surrounding the Kuklinski family, there have been two apparent attempts on Ryszard's life. Tragically and mysteriously, both Boguslaw and Waldemar have since died in separate accidents.[18]

In Warsaw, a military tribunal secretly court-martialed Kuklinski in absentia in 1986 and, finding him guilty, stripped him of his Polish citizenship and military rank and condemned him to death. In 1990, after the communist government fell from power, the sentence was commuted to twenty-five years in prison. Polls showed that most of the Polish people viewed him as a traitor. In 1995, the Polish Supreme Court annulled the conviction and returned the case to the military court for review. Two years later, the Procurator of the Warsaw Military District decided that Kuklinski had spied "out of higher necessity" to "benefit the nation." He revoked the sentence and restored Kuklinski's rights and rank. In the spring of 1998, for the first time in nearly seventeen years, Kuklinski openly visited Poland and, for the most part, received a hero's welcome. He then returned to his home in Someplace, U.S.A., where the neighbors on the block know him by another name and are unaware of his contribution to the collapse of the Soviet empire.

Introduction

1. Tuchman, *Guns of August,* 297–346.
2. Andrew and Mitrokhin, *Sword and Shield,* 130. In the history of the Soviet Union, the nonmilitary intelligence agency endured numerous name changes, starting with Cheka in 1917 and ending with KGB from 1954 until the collapse of the communist state in 1991. During World War II, it was twice NKVD and twice NKGB (see ibid., frontispiece). For simplicity, I refer to this agency as the KGB throughout, except in Chapter 15, where its name is relevant to cipher breakthroughs.
3. Ibid., 132.
4. Kahn, *Kahn on Codes,* 76–88.
5. Andrew and Gordievsky, *KGB,* 530–31.
6. *Nightline,* ABC News, Feb. 11, 1997.

Chapter 1: Herr Zimmermann's Fatal Blunder

1. Accounts vary as to how Hall first received the Zimmermann telegram. This version is taken from Hall's own description in Beesly, *Room 40,* 204.
2. Ibid.
3. Ibid., 135.
4. Ibid., 129–33; West, *Sigint Secrets,* 83–86; Tuchman, *Zimmermann Telegram,* ix–xii.

5. West, *Sigint Secrets,* 92–93.
6. Hitt was not the first to notice. Among those before him who perceived cipher correlatives relating to ordinary language were Edgar Allan Poe and Sir Arthur Conan Doyle, creator of Sherlock Holmes.
7. Details about code 0075 in Kahn, *Codebreakers,* 286–87.
8. Beesly, *Room 40,* 216.
9. Ibid., 219–20.
10. Ibid., 221.
11. Tuchman, *Zimmermann Telegram,* 197.

Chapter 2: The Enigma Demystified

1. Winterbotham, *Ultra Secret,* 2.
2. Kahn, *Seizing the Enigma,* 31. Earlier accounts say that the Enigma was first patented in Holland and bought by Scherbius.
3. This brief description of the Enigma is compiled from several sources: Welchman, *Hut Six Story,* 38–47; Alan Stripp, "The Enigma Machine," in Hinsley and Stripp, *Codebreakers,* 83–88; Hodges, *Alan Turing,* 166–70; Marian Rejewski, "How the Polish Mathematicians Broke Enigma," in Kozaczuk, *Enigma,* 247–51.
4. Stripp, "Enigma Machine," 86.
5. Kozaczuk, *Enigma,* 61.
6. West, *Sigint Secrets,* 23.
7. Rejewski's background is from Kozaczuk, *Enigma,* 1–6.
8. Rejewski, "How Polish Mathematicians Broke Enigma," 250.
9. In the commercial Enigma without plug board, this number came to $26 \times 26 \times 26 \times 6$, or 105,456, the multiple of the twenty-six contacts on each of the three rotors times the six possible rotor sequences. In the early military model attacked by the Poles, the plug board, with six pairs of letter exchanges, created a further 100,391,791,500 possibilities. The numbers grew ever more intimidating during the war but never so much that they could save the Enigma from its own sloppy operators or, in the case of the Naval Enigma, from the capture of key lists. Kozaczuk, *Enigma,* 24.
10. The goal here is merely to convey the difficulty of Rejewski's task. For interested readers, Rejewski explains his mathematical solutions in Kozaczuk, *Enigma,* Apps. D and E, 246–90. Separate accounts are in Kahn, *Seizing the Enigma,* 62–66, and Hodges, *Alan Turing,* 170–76.
11. Rejewski, "How Polish Mathematicians Broke Enigma," 251–52.
12. Ibid., 252.
13. Ibid.
14. Hodges, *Alan Turing,* 172.
15. Rejewski, "How Polish Mathematicians Broke Enigma," 253.
16. Ibid., 258.
17. Ibid.
18. Ibid.

19. Kahn, *Kahn on Codes,* 76–88. For more details on the roles of Bertrand and Schmidt, code-named "Asché," see also Kahn, *Seizing the Enigma,* 56–67, and Kozaczuk, *Enigma,* 17–19. Bertrand himself first told the story in Gustave Bertrand, *Enigma: The Greatest Enigma of the War of 1939–1945* (Paris: Librairie Plon, 1973).

20. Kahn, *Seizing the Enigma,* 58.

21. Ibid., 76–77.

22. Kahn, *Kahn on Codes,* 87.

23. Rejewski, "How Polish Mathematicians Broke Enigma," 263–64.

24. Ibid., 265–67. Zygalski devised another key-recovery technique by using perforated sheets, a very laborious system. It worked but did not have any lasting impact.

25. Hinsley, Thomas, Ransom et. al., *British Intelligence,* vol. I, 488.

26. Kahn, *Seizing the Enigma,* 78.

27. Richard Woytak, "A Conversation with Marian Rejewski," in Kozaczuk, *Enigma,* 236.

28. Bob Watson, "How the Bletchley Park Buildings Took Shape," in Hinsley and Stripp, *Codebreakers,* 306–07; Welchman, *Hut Six Story,* 31.

29. Included were the perforated sheets based on the double encipherment of the message keys invented by Henryk Zygalski. John Jeffries had them mass-produced and immediately put them to use. At Pyry, they had been known as the "Zygalski sheets"; at Bletchley, they became the "Jeffries sheets." In any case, this technology did not survive beyond May 1940 when the Germans stopped using the double encipherment.

30. Turing biography in Hodges, *Alan Turing,* 1–6.

31. I. J. Good, "Pioneering Work on Computers at Bletchley," in Metropolis, Howlett, and Rota, *History of Computing,* 34.

32. Quoted in B. Randell, "The Colossus," in Metropolis, Howlett, and Rota, 78.

33. Quoted in ibid.

34. Good, "Pioneering Work," 34.

35. Hodges, *Alan Turing,* 178.

36. Welchman, *Hut Six Story,* 34.

37. Kahn, *Seizing the Enigma,* 97.

38. Welchman, *Hut Six Story,* 59–71.

39. Ibid., 71.

40. Ibid., 38.

41. Kahn, *Seizing the Enigma,* 98.

42. Welchman, *Hut Six Story,* 81; see also Hodges, *Alan Turing,* 182–83.

43. Hodges, *Alan Turing,* 227.

44. Ibid., 228.

45. Winterbotham, *Ultra Secret,* 3–6.

46. Hinsley doubts whether the Poles gained any significant intelligence from Enigma decrypts. He notes that Polish reports of their success were short on detail and never mentioned the contents of their decrypts. Hinsley et al., *British Intelligence,*

vol. I, 490. Rejewski points out that success in reading messages depends on the number of messages intercepted. In other words, it depends, in the first instance, on the volume of traffic. The volume must have been low during the thirties when the world was not at war. Rejewski, "Remarks on Appendix I to British Intelligence in the Second World War by F. H. Hinsley," 78.

47. Stuart Milner-Barry, "Hut 6: Early Days," in Hinsley and Stripp, *Codebreakers,* 92–93.
48. Kozaczuk, *Enigma,* 98–99.
49. Winterbotham, *Ultra Secret,* 15.
50. Ibid., 16.
51. Ibid., 10.
52. Hinsley et al., *British Intelligence,* vol. I, 487–88.
53. Cave Brown, *Bodyguard of Lies,* 17–20, 34–35.
54. Stevenson, *Man Called Intrepid,* 49.
55. Welchman, *Hut Six Story,* 13.
56. Christopher Kasparek and Richard Woytak, "Polish and British Methods of Solving Enigma," in Kozaczuk, *Enigma,* 292.
57. See, for example, Hinsley et al., *British Intelligence,* vol. I, 487–95; Hodges, *Alan Turing,* 170–76; Lewin, *Ultra Goes to War,* 1978.
58. A Polish version of Kozaczuk's *Enigma* was first published in 1979. The author had initially disclosed the Polish breakthrough in another Polish-language book in 1967. A French-language book, *Enigma: The Greatest Enigma of the War of 1939–45,* by Gen. Gustave Bertrand of French intelligence, was published in 1973 and corroborated the Polish claim. The story can be read in Rejewski's own words in Appendices D and E of Kozaczuk, *Enigma,* 246–91.
59. Kasparek and Woytak, "Polish and British Methods," 317.

Chapter 3: The Longest Battle

1. Winterbotham, *Ultra Secret,* 15.
2. Van der Vat, *Atlantic Campaign,* 381–82.
3. West, *Sigint Secrets,* 189–91.
4. Quoted in Miller, *War at Sea,* 101.
5. Kahn, *Seizing the Enigma,* 118–19.
6. Beesly, *Very Special Intelligence,* 58–60. Beesly was Winn's assistant in the tracking room. After the war, Beesly wrote books on British naval history. Winn returned to the field of law and was Lord Justice of Appeal at the time of his death in 1972.
7. West, *Sigint Secrets,* 188–89; Kahn, *Seizing the Enigma,* 127–36.
8. Kahn, *Seizing the Enigma,* 129–37; Hodges, *Alan Turing,* 200.
9. West, *Sigint Secrets,* 191–92; Kahn, *Seizing the Enigma,* 189–90.
10. F. H. Hinsley, "Introduction: The Influence of Ultra in the Second World War," in Hinsley and Stripp, *Codebreakers,* 6.
11. Van der Vat, *Atlantic Campaign,* 237–39.

12. Kahn, *Seizing the Enigma,* 212–13.
13. Ibid., 218–25. Why Fasson and Grazier did not receive the highest award is anybody's guess. It is hard to imagine a more valorous act.
14. West, *Sigint Secrets,* 228–29.
15. Beesly, *Very Special Intelligence,* 157.
16. Barnett, *Engage the Enemy,* 578.
17. Kahn, *Seizing the Enigma,* 263.
18. Combat statistics for winter and spring, 1943, in Van der Vat, *Atlantic Campaign,* 320–37.

Chapter 4: Outfoxing the Desert Fox

1. Cave Brown, *Bodyguard of Lies,* 94.
2. Ibid., 102–03.
3. Hinsley and Stripp, 2–5.
4. Kahn, *Codebreakers,* 473–74.
5. Quoted in Hinsley and Stripp, *Codebreakers,* 5.
6. Winterbotham, *Ultra Secret,* 75. The SLU system, established by intelligence agent Winterbotham, ultimately served all major sectors (except the Pacific theater) where Allied troops fought. It was, in effect, the communications pipeline from Bletchley Park where German messages were decrypted to the theaters where the war was prosecuted.
7. Hinsley and Stripp, *Codebreakers,* 4.
8. Hinsley et al., *British Intelligence,* vol. II, 409.
9. Cave Brown, *Bodyguard of Lies,* 103–04.
10. Hinsley et al., *British Intelligence,* vol. II, 422–24.
11. Cave Brown, *Bodyguard of Lies,* 116–21.
12. Winterbotham, *Ultra Secret,* 78.
13. Ibid., 77.

Chapter 5: Colossus

1. See, for example, Winterbotham, *Ultra Secret,* 15: "[T]he backroom boys of Bletchley used the new science of electronics to help them solve the puzzle of Enigma."
2. Because of official British secrecy, this fact was buried until recently. Some information about the Colossus was released in 1975 by the British Public Record Office, which enabled Brian Randell of the University of Newcastle-upon-Tyne to interview key figures in the Colossus story for an in-depth article. Vital information not available to Randell and notably missing in his paper included the need for which Colossus was created. Therefore, he mentioned nothing of the teleprinter code or the new German cipher machines. See Randell, "Colossus," 47–92. Bletchley Park insiders Harry Hinsley, Jack Good, Ken Halton, and Gil Hayward now give a fuller account in Hinsley and Stripp, *Codebreakers,* 141–92.
3. Jack Good, "Enigma and Fish," in Hinsley and Stripp, *Codebreakers,* 152.

4. F. H. Hinsley, "Introduction to Fish," in Hinsley and Stripp, *Codebreakers,* 141–42.
5. Jack Good, "Enigma and Fish," 152–53.
6. Gil Hayward, "Operation Tunny," in Hinsley and Stripp, *Codebreakers,* 178.
7. Tony Sale, "The Lorenz Cipher and How Bletchley Park Broke It," http://www.codesandciphers.org.uk.
8. Jack Good, "Enigma and Fish," 161.
9. Hodges, *Alan Turing,* 230.
10. Not until the end of the war did British technicians have a chance to examine the SZ, even though Montgomery's forces captured two Geheimschreibers as they pursued Rommel after the breakthrough at El Alamein. Jack Good, "Enigma and Fish," 161; West, *Sigint Secrets,* 226.
11. Jack Good, "Enigma and Fish," 153–54. Good arrives at his estimate with this equation: 2 to the 501st power, divided by the multiple of the pins on each wheel (about 1.6 times 10 to the 19th power), equals 4 times 10 to the 131st power. (One has to wonder if he worked that out before breakfast.)
12. Ibid., 161–62.
13. Turing, conceptualizer of the "Universal Turing Machine," which foreshadowed the computer, was invited to join the Newmanry, but declined, according to Hodges, *Alan Turing,* 268. Brian Randell of the University of Newcastle-upon-Tyne said that Turing probably consulted on the prototype machine, the "Heath Robinson," but had little direct involvement with the Colossus itself. Newman recalled that his group knew the planned Colossus was theoretically related to a Turing machine, but they were not conscious of their work having any dependence on Turing's ideas. After the war, Turing received the Order of the British Empire (OBE), which Newman considered "quite ludicrous in relation to his achievements." This does not appear to be a mean-spirited comment because Newman, who, in October 1945, took the Chair of Pure Mathematics at Manchester University, persuaded Turing to join him there in 1948 because he believed that Turing would make an important contribution to a computer project then under way. Turing himself, said Randell, accepted the OBE award "somewhat as a joke." See Randell, "Colossus," 78, 82.
14. Randell, "Colossus," 60.
15. West, *Sigint Secrets,* 227.
16. Randell, "Colossus," 62.
17. Hodges, *Alan Turing,* 267; Randell, "Colossus," 64–66.
18. Jack Good, "Enigma and Fish," 164.
19. Hodges, *Alan Turing,* 277.
20. Jack Good, "Enigma and Fish," 165.
21. Hinsley, "Introduction to Fish," 144.
22. Ibid., 147.

23. Hinsley, "Introduction: Influence of Ultra," 3.
24. Winterbotham, *Ultra Secret,* 68–69.

Chapter 6: Who Broke Purple?

1. See Farago, *Broken Seal,* 95–100; Kahn, *Codebreakers,* 18–22; Clark, *Man Who Broke Purple,* 138–46.
2. Quoted in Kahn, *Codebreakers,* 21, 22.
3. Rowlett, *Story of Magic.*
4. Ibid., 224–28.
5. Kahn, Foreword, in ibid., ix.
6. Rowlett, *Story of Magic,* 97.
7. Ibid., 98.
8. Ibid., 100–01.
9. Kahn, *Codebreakers,* 391–92.
10. Kahn, Foreword, in Rowlett, *Story of Magic,* x.
11. Layton, Pineau, and Costello, *"And I Was There,"* 79.
12. Safford, "Brief History of Communications Intelligence," 8; Rowlett, *Story of Magic,* 112.
13. Rowlett, *Story of Magic,* 122.
14. Ibid., 133–36.
15. Ibid., 146.
16. Kahn, *Codebreakers,* xiii–xiv.
17. Rowlett, *Story of Magic,* 148–50. This account by the insider Rowlett is drastically different from reports of the Purple solution published two and three decades earlier. In 1967, Farago, *Broken Seal,* 98, wrote that the Purple Section spun its wheels for eighteen months until "[o]ne morning in August 1940, in the nineteenth month of the effort, a young cryptologist named Harry Lawrence Clark . . . stumbled upon what he confidently believed was the key to [Purple's] solution": stepping switches. British biographer Ronald Clark, *Man Who Broke Purple,* 144, reprinted Farago's mistake in 1977. It is now clear that Leo Rosen, not Larry Clark, thought of the stepping switches soon after he joined the Purple Section and nearly a full year before the final breakthrough.
18. Early reports on Purple that used unofficial sources, while its secret actually remained classified, described it as a rotor machine based on the Enigma; see Kahn, *Codebreakers,* 18–19. Now that the secret is out, researchers just doing their job can still be misled by the original error. See Stinnett, *Day of Deceit,* 69–70.
19. Rowlett, *Story of Magic,* 152.
20. Ibid.
21. Friedman, "Preliminary Historical Report," 8–9.
22. Prados, *Combined Fleet Decoded,* 164–65.
23. Smith, *Ultra-Magic Deals,* 54–55; Kahn, *Seizing the Enigma,* 235–37.

Chapter 7: Masters of Deception

1. Masterman, *Double-Cross System,* 36–45. The scholarly Masterman called Owens, or "Snow," the *fons et origo* of the double-cross system.
2. Cave Brown, *Bodyguard of Lies,* 209.
3. Masterman, *Double-Cross System,* 62–63.
4. Ibid., 190–95.
5. Delmer, *Counterfeit Spy.* Delmer, who ran the Psychological Warfare section in Churchill's underground bunker at Storey's Gate, London, was first to publish an account of the great D-Day deception. His version differs in some details from those of other authors. For starters, his fictitious name for the Spaniard was "Cato," his German code name, not "Garbo."
6. Masterman, *Double-Cross System,* 115.
7. Cave Brown, *Bodyguard of Lies,* 48–50.
8. Ibid., 268.
9. Cruickshank, *Deception in World War II,* 46.
10. Ibid., 48.
11. Montagu, *Man Who Never Was.*
12. Oshima, two messages to Tokyo, Nov. 10, 1943, intercepted and decrypted by Allied codebreakers and reprinted in Boyd, *Hitler's Japanese Confidant,* 186–91.
13. Hinsley et al., *British Intelligence,* vol. III, pt. II, 45.
14. Ibid., vol. 3, pt. II, 47–49.
15. Cave Brown, *Bodyguard of Lies,* 462–68.
16. Delmer, *Counterfeit Spy,* 155–56.
17. Cave Brown, *Bodyguard of Lies,* 197–99.
18. Hinsley et al., *British Intelligence,* vol. III, pt. II, 49.
19. Ibid. 177–78.
20. Masterman, *Double-Cross System,* 156; Boyd, *Hitler's Japanese Confidant,* 128.
21. Hinsley, "Introduction to Fish," 146.
22. Cave Brown, *Bodyguard of Lies,* 658–60.
23. Masterman, *Double-Cross System,* 156–57.
24. McNair died later that month when Allied bombs fell short of the German lines at Saint-Lô.
25. Lewin, *Ultra Goes to War,* 337.
26. Bradley, *Soldier's Story,* 371.
27. Masterman, *Double-Cross System,* 158.

Chapter 8: Learned Spies

1. Quoted in Prange, Goldstein, and Dillon, *Target Tokyo,* 168.
2. Ibid., 196.
3. Quoted in Deakin and Storry, *Case of Richard Sorge,* 30.
4. Quoted in Whymant, *Stalin's Spy,* 32.
5. Johnson, *Instance of Treason,* 84–91, 97–99.

6. Prange, Goldstein, and Dillon, *Target Tokyo,* 152.

7. Andrew and Gordievsky, *KGB,* 178–81.

8. Quoted in Deakin and Storry, *Case of Richard Sorge,* 98.

9. Whymant, *Stalin's Spy,* 2–3.

10. Quoted in Prange, Goldstein, and Dillon, *Target Tokyo,* 315.

11. Ibid.

12. Ibid., 339–40; Deakin and Storry, *Case of Richard Sorge,* 230. June 20 is the date that Sorge gave to the Japanese police, but a Sorge dispatch recovered from Russian archives fixes the attack date as June 15. See Whymant, *Stalin's Spy,* 167. The importance of this dispatch in the Russian archives is confirmation that Sorge's warning survived Clausen's censorship.

13. Quoted in Andrew and Gordievsky, *KGB,* 264.

14. Ibid. Sorge was one of several sources—including America and Great Britain through codebreaking and Soviet spies in Europe—to warn Stalin of Hitler's treachery. Stalin ignored them all. He believed that the British were scheming to turn him against Hitler and that the others had been suckered in by the British.

15. Whymant, *Stalin's Spy,* 292.

16. Ibid., 233.

17. Ibid., 244.

18. This time, the codebreaking was based not on the theft of cryptosystems but on the efforts of a Soviet team led by Sergei Tolstoy (no relation to the great Russian novelist) in breaking the chief Japanese diplomatic code known in America as "Purple." This outstanding achievement parallels the American solution of Purple a year earlier, but details of the Soviet breakthrough are lacking. See Andrew and Gordievsky, *KGB,* 271–72; Kahn, "Soviet Comint."

19. Deakin and Storry, *Case of Richard Sorge,* 233. Historian Gordon Prange in Prange, Goldstein, and Dillon, *Target Tokyo,* 521, concludes in this thoughtful, well-documented study that the desperate Soviets had no other option and would have transferred the troops no matter what Tokyo decided. One fact supports Prange's view: the Soviet High Command ordered the Sixteenth Army transferred from the Baikal area westward on May 26, more than a month before Japan adopted its southern strategy. Both sides of the argument seem to have merit.

20. Whymant, *Stalin's Spy,* 181.

21. Ibid., 225.

22. Ibid., 179.

23. Prange, Goldstein, and Dillon, *Target Tokyo,* 393.

24. Many observers assume that Miyagi was tortured. Denying it, police officials have said that Miyagi was not the kind to crack under torture. Prange, in ibid., 420, concludes that the Tokko subjected him to tough questioning but probably not torture.

25. Ibid., 462.

26. Ibid., 466.

Chapter 9: "Lucy," Man of Mystery

1. Kesaris, *Rote Kapella,* 165, 174–75.
2. Rado's background is from Tarrant, *Red Orchestra,* 147–51.
3. Kesaris, *Rote Kapella,* 175.
4. Tarrant, *Red Orchestra,* 156, 168. Rado, *Codename Dora,* 54, claims to have sent a radiogram to Moscow as early as June 6, 1940, when France was about to fall. *Codename Dora* was first published in Hungarian as *Dora Jelenti.*
5. Accoce and Quet, *Man Called Lucy,* 17. The French edition was titled *La Guerre a été Gagnee en Suisse (The War Was Won in Switzerland).*
6. Dallin, *Soviet Espionage,* 193.
7. Kesaris, *Rote Kapella,* 184.
8. Dallin, *Soviet Espionage,* 196.
9. Kesaris, *Rote Kapella,* 222.
10. Background on Roessler from Read and Fisher, *Operation Lucy,* 77–81; Tarrant, *Red Orchestra,* 156–61.
11. Kesaris, *Rote Kapella,* 213.
12. Read and Fisher, *Operation Lucy,* 87. The authors do not cite sources, but Roessler's close friend Schnieper was one person interviewed for the book.
13. Rado, *Codename Dora,* 58.
14. Ibid., 137.
15. Ibid., 131.
16. Dallin, *Soviet Espionage,* 195.
17. Mulligan, "Spies, Ciphers and 'Zitadelle,'" 237.
18. Kesaris, *Rote Kapella,* 176–80.
19. Rado, *Codename Dora,* xxiii.
20. Kesaris, *Rote Kapella,* 173–74.
21. Rado, *Codename Dora,* 54–58.
22. Quote from Kesaris, *Rote Kapella,* 176–77.
23. Kesaris, *Rote Kapella,* 199.
24. Rado, *Codename Dora,* 76–81, cites correspondence with the director to support this assertion.
25. Ibid., 151–52.
26. See ibid., 203–07.
27. Ibid., 175–89.
28. Mulligan, "Spies, Ciphers, and 'Zitadelle,'" 237, 240.
29. Kesaris, *Rote Kapella,* 176, 222.
30. Andrew and Gordievsky, *KGB,* 304–05.
31. Ibid., 305–08.
32. Tarrant, *Red Orchestra,* 176.
33. Demise of Die Rote Drei, in ibid., 178–88.
34. Rado, *Codename Dora,* 136.

35. Accoce and Quet, *Man Called Lucy*, 27.

36. Ibid., 42–43.

37. Rado, *Codename Dora*, 140–41.

38. West, *Thread of Deceit*, 59.

39. Tarrant, *Red Orchestra*, 159–62. Nigel West's book is not listed in Tarrant's bibliography.

40. Read and Fisher, *Operation Lucy*, 94–104.

41. Rado, *Codename Dora*, 145–46; West, *Thread of Deceit*, 60.

42. Deacon, *History of British Secret Service*, 363.

43. Rado, *Codename Dora*, 145.

44. West, *Thread of Deceit*, 62.

45. Dallin, *Soviet Espionage*, 227.

46. Kesaris, *Rote Kapella*, 213–17.

47. Hinsley et al., *British Intelligence*, vol. II, 60.

48. Hinsley, "Introduction to Fish," 145.

49. Ibid.

50. Kesaris, *Rote Kapella*, 185.

51. Rado, *Codename Dora*, 138.

52. Ibid., 140.

53. Ibid., 143–44.

Chapter 10: Infamy and Sacred Duty

1. Yoshikawa, "Top Secret Assignment," 30.

2. Ibid., 32.

3. Ibid., 33.

4. The FBI has always claimed no knowledge of Yoshikawa's espionage activities prior to December 7, 1941. But in his meticulously researched book, Stinnett, *Day of Deceit*, 83–118, 338, writes that American agents were waiting for him when he got off the boat and kept him loosely under surveillance during his entire stay in Hawaii. Stinnett builds a familiar conspiracy theory charging that Roosevelt knew the Japanese attack was coming and, to jolt America out of its isolationism and bring it into the war against Hitler, deliberately failed to warn Pearl Harbor. Conspiracy is difficult to prove, but Stinnett deserves respect for the research he put into the effort. The definitive proof is lacking because certain essential documents remain under lock and key. But by filling in the gaps with his own assertions, what comes out is a case for the government's obligation to come clean and bring the issue to closure.

5. Yoshikawa, "Top Secret Assignment," 34.

6. Ibid., 35.

7. See Farago, *Broken Seal*, 24–31, 54–55; Layton, Pineau, and Costello, *"And I Was There,"* 29–30, 41–42; Kahn, *Codebreakers*, 351–69. This provision amounted to

national self-flagellation to atone for a codebreaking scandal that occurred in the early twenties. A team of undercover decoders known as the American Black Chamber under Herbert O. Yardley broke the Japanese diplomatic code at the 1921 Washington Conference on the Limitation of Armaments, allowing the Americans, in effect, to read the Japanese mind during the negotiations. Under American pressure the Japanese acceded to a formula that allowed them only three capital ships to every five for the United States and Great Britain. The Americans knew from codebreaking that the Japanese would cave in to their pressure. Upon learning of the Black Chamber's secrets in 1929, a shocked Henry L. Stimson, newly named Secretary of State in the Hoover Administration, proclaimed, "Gentlemen do not read each other's mail," and withdrew State Department funding for the Yardley operation. Without funds the Black Chamber folded its tent, and Yardley exacted his revenge with a tell-all book in 1931. Not only did the book foreshadow the prohibition of radio intercepts, it was probably one of the Japanese resentments that exploded at Pearl Harbor a decade later.

8. Yoshikawa, "Top Secret Assignment," 36–38; Farago, *Broken Seal,* 245–46. For a different version of how the ninety-seven questions were forwarded to Yoshikawa, see Prados, *Combined Fleet Decoded,* 151–52. Most germane to this narrative is the fact that Yoshikawa received the questionnaire and filled it out.

9. Yoshikawa, "Top Secret Assignment," 38.

10. See Stinnett, *Day of Deceit,* 138–50.

11. Ibid., 105–07. The date is coincidental with the decryption of Yoshikawa's bomb plot message of September 24, but Stinnett reports that Roosevelt was motivated by the fact that Churchill received these reports from MacKay Radio & Telegraph, a British company, when MacKay was in the rotation serving the consulate, and Roosevelt did not like being left out.

12. Ibid., 107–08. To Stinnett these missteps went beyond bungling to conspiracy.

13. Years later during an oral history interview, Rochefort, the officer in charge of Hypo and the hero of Midway six months later, blamed himself for not anticipating the Pearl Harbor raid. When asked what he meant, his answer lacked specificity. "I have often said," he told the interviewer, "that an intelligence officer has one task. . . . This is to tell his commander . . . today what the Japanese are going to do tomorrow. This is his job. If he doesn't do this, then he's failed." See Capt. Joseph J. Rochefort (Ret.), *Oral History,* U.S. Naval Institute, 111. Clearly, something was eating at him, but the world might never know exactly what it was. Stinnett, *Day of Deceit,* 203–23, has no doubt that Rochefort and the Pacific Fleet intelligence officer, then Lt. Cdr. Edwin T. Layton, knew from radio direction finding and other intercepted radio messages that the Japanese carriers were coming and failed, for one reason or another, to notify Admiral Kimmel.

14. Farago, *Broken Seal,* 332.

15. Yoshikawa, "Top Secret Assignment," 39.

Chapter 11: "Our Man in Tokyo"

1. Quoted in Potter, *Nimitz,* 107.
2. Beach, *United States Navy,* 450.
3. Rochefort, *Oral History,* 45.
4. Quoted in Layton, Pineau, and Costello, *"And I Was There,"* 49.
5. Holmes, *Double-Edged Secrets,* 21, 32.
6. Ibid., 64.
7. In direction-finding, a radio beam is received at different locations and the source located where the beams intersect. In traffic analysis information is extracted by noncryptological means such as a ship's identifying call sign, the volume of traffic and the tell-tale touch, or "fist," of the radio operator on the transmitter's keys.
8. Rochefort, *Oral History,* 50.
9. Layton, Pineau, and Costello, *"And I Was There,"* 359.
10. Ibid., 383.
11. Rochefort, *Oral History,* 131.
12. Holmes, *Double-Edged Secrets,* 95–96.
13. Layton, Pineau, and Costello, *"And I Was There,"* 408.
14. Rochefort, *Oral History,* 195.
15. Holmes, *Double-Edged Secrets,* 90.
16. Layton, Pineau, and Costello, *"And I Was There,"* 412.
17. Prados, *Combined Fleet Decoded,* 318.
18. Redman, "Op-20-G File."
19. Layton, Pineau, and Costello, *"And I Was There,"* 451.
20. Rochefort, *Oral History,* 252.
21. Layton, Pineau, and Costello, *"And I Was There,"* 467.
22. Holmes, *Double-Edged Secrets,* 116.
23. Potter, *Nimitz,* 217–18.
24. Rochefort, *Oral History,* 258.
25. Prados, *Combined Fleet Decoded,* 411.
26. Holmes, *Double-Edged Secrets,* 117.

Chapter 12: The Spy Who Knew Everything

1. Bell, "Cambridge Politics," 731, quoted in Page and Knightley, *Philby Conspiracy,* 40. Cambridge probably seemed more radical then than it actually was. Only about 10 percent of roughly five thousand students belonged to communist or socialist organizations. See Newton, *Cambridge Spies,* 35.
2. Newton, *Cambridge Spies,* 74.
3. Ibid., 332.
4. Andrew and Mitrokhin, *Sword and Shield,* 112.
5. Venona, "Report on Information Given by 'Homer.'"

6. A number of American moles in the Roosevelt Administration contributed to Stalin's store of knowledge at Yalta. Harry Dexter White, a high-ranking official in the Treasury Department, was probably the most damaging American in Stalin's service. During his 1944 reelection campaign Roosevelt promised Polish-American voters he would support the London Poles. White advised his Soviet handler that Roosevelt's support was softer than it appeared on the surface. In a message sent by the KGB a few days later from New York to Moscow, partially decrypted after the war, White is quoted as saying that America would offer a "compromise agreement" to exclude "the most hostile [anti-Soviet] elements" from the Polish government. In the same conversation White stated that America would accept the Soviet annexation of the Baltic States—Latvia, Lithuania, and Estonia—and a border settlement with Finland favorable to Moscow. Venona, "KOL'TsOV's Account of Conversation with 'Jurist.'" One caveat: these decrypted messages can be difficult to read because many code groups were not recovered, leaving broken sentences and disrupted thoughts.

7. Venona, "Material from 'H.'"

8. Venona, "Material of 'G.'"

9. For a lengthy account of Maclean's atomic espionage, see Newton, *Cambridge Spies*, 145–85.

10. Ibid., 175.

11. Holloway, *Stalin and the Bomb*, 352–53.

12. Newton, *Cambridge Spies*, 136–37.

13. Ibid., 167.

14. Cecil, *Divided Life*, 83.

15. Newton, *Cambridge Spies*, 87–89.

16. Quoted in Cecil, *Divided Life*, 104.

17. Newton, *Cambridge Spies*, 282.

18. Ibid., 284.

19. Ibid., 297–300.

Chapter 13: The Spy of the Century

1. Holloway, *Stalin and the Bomb*, 82; Andrew and Mitrokhin, *Sword and Shield*, 114.

2. Fuchs's background from Moss, *Klaus Fuchs*, 2–26.

3. Ibid., 134.

4. Rhodes, *Making of Atomic Bomb*, 338–42.

5. Hyde, *Atom Bomb Spies*, 122.

6. Moss, *Klaus Fuchs*, 56.

7. Background on Hall in Albright and Kunstel, *Bombshell*, 10–17, 35–43, 51–61.

8. Weinstein and Vassiliev, *Haunted Wood*, 195–98.

9. Holloway, *Stalin and the Bomb*, 102.

10. Ibid., 107.

11. Ibid., 108. Holloway did not know of Ted Hall when he wrote those words. His book was published in 1994, but the Venona codebreaking decrypts, which exposed Hall, were not released until the following year. Holloway thought David Greenglass must have been the source for the first KGB report. Whether it was Hall or Greenglass his conclusion would be the same.

12. Hyde, *Atom Bomb Spies,* 245.

13. Holloway, *Stalin and the Bomb,* 105.

14. Andrew and Gordievsky, *KGB,* 318.

15. Haynes and Klehr, *Venona,* 311–13; Weinstein and Vassiliev, *Haunted Wood,* 190–92.

16. Holloway, *Stalin and the Bomb,* 108.

17. Ibid., 297, 310–12.

18. Moss, *Klaus Fuchs,* 105–08.

19. Ibid., 139–40.

20. Ibid., 150.

21. Ibid., 151–52.

Chapter 14: Speak, Ciphers!

1. Daniel Patrick Moynihan, *Report of the Commission on Protecting and Reducing Government Secrecy,* 37, quoted in Weinstein and Vassiliev, 340. Senator Moynihan deserves to be honored as Superman in disguise. He moved a mountain of government bureaucracy to declassify many of the Venona decrypts of Soviet World War II messages between Moscow and the United States, thus partially lifting the veil of secrecy that obscured the story of Soviet espionage for half a century.

2. Haynes and Klehr, *Venona,* 9.

3. Ibid., 31.

4. Ibid., 34–35.

5. Albright and Kunstel, *Bombshell,* 204.

6. Cecil James Phillips, "What Made Venona Possible?" in Benson and Warner, *Venona,* xv.

7. Benson and Warner, *Venona,* 452.

8. Albright and Kunstel, *Bombshell,* 205–06.

9. Ibid., 206.

10. Haynes and Klehr, *Venona,* 33.

11. Phillips, "What Made Venona Possible?" xv.

12. Lamphere and Schachtman, *FBI-KGB War,* 78–86; Wright, *Spycatcher,* 180.

13. Benson and Warner, *Venona,* 455.

14. Albright and Kunstel, *Bombshell,* 207.

15. Benson and Warner, *Venona,* 453.

16. Ibid., xxii, 453.

17. Andrew and Mitrokhin, *Sword and Shield,* 144–45; Albright and Kunstel, *Bombshell,* 209. In fact, the CIA had not been penetrated at that time.

18. Lamphere and Schachtman, *FBI-KGB War,* 82.

19. All recovered code names are from Benson and Warner, *Venona,* xxiv–xxvii, unless otherwise specified.

20. Lamphere and Schachtman, *FBI-KGB War,* 100.

21. Haynes and Klehr, *Venona,* 311.

22. Albright and Kunstel, *Bombshell,* 98.

23. Ibid., 226–30.

24. Haynes and Klehr, *Venona,* 311–13.

25. Benson and Warner, *Venona,* 456; Haynes and Klehr, *Venona,* 313–14.

26. See Haynes and Klehr, *Venona,* 339–70.

27. Ibid., 145–50.

28. Haynes and Klehr, *Venona,* 131–37; Weinstein and Vassiliev, *Haunted Wood,* 170.

29. Haynes and Klehr, *Venona,* 123, 129.

30. Benson and Warner, *Venona,* xxviii; Weinstein and Vassiliev, *Haunted Wood,* 291–93; Andrew and Mitrokhin, *Sword and Shield,* 144.

31. Wright, *Spycatcher,* 185.

Chapter 15: Exposing Comrade Bluster

1. Schecter and Deriabin, *Spy Who Saved the World.* The book is particularly helpful because the authors quote and paraphrase extensively from transcripts of Penkovsky's meetings with American and British intelligence.

2. Andrew, *For President's Eyes,* 267.

3. Quoted in ibid., 265.

4. Quoted in Schecter and Deriabin, *Spy Who Saved the World,* 181–82; see also Andrew, *For President's Eyes,* 267.

5. Quoted in Beschloss, *Crisis Years,* 225. See also Schecter and Deriabin, *Spy Who Saved the World,* 183; Andrew, *For President's Eyes,* 267.

6. Schecter and Deriabin, *Spy Who Saved the World,* 1–3.

7. Wynne, *Contact on Gorky Street,* 31.

8. Ibid., 32–33.

9. Ibid., 42.

10. Schecter and Deriabin, *Spy Who Saved the World,* 93.

11. Ibid., 48.

12. Ibid., 56.

13. Ibid.

14. Ibid., 68.

15. Ibid., 195. Interestingly, Penkovsky described the main objective of Soviet intelligence as providing early warning of an enemy attack, the very same rationale that justified the arms race in the West. This suggests that the Cold War, which brought the world so close to nuclear annihilation, was driven by fear based, at least in some measure, on mutual ignorance of the other side's intentions.

16. Quoted in ibid., 154–55; see also Andrew, *For President's Eyes,* 267.

17. Schecter and Deriabin, *Spy Who Saved the World,* 185–87.
18. Beschloss, *Crisis Years,* 278.
19. Schecter and Deriabin, *Spy Who Saved the World,* 278.
20. Ibid., 272.
21. Beschloss, *Crisis Years,* 330.
22. Dino A. Brugioni, *Eyeball to Eyeball,* 181–217.
23. Ibid., 276–77.
24. Andrew, *For President's Eyes,* 290.
25. Beschloss, *Crisis Years,* 499.
26. Quoted in Schecter and Deriabin, *Spy Who Saved the World,* 336.
27. Quoted in Conlin, *Morrow Book of Quotations,* 258.
28. Andrew and Gordievsky, *KGB,* 474.
29. Ibid., 475; Schecter and Deriabin, *Spy Who Saved the World,* 315–37.
30. Schecter and Deriabin, *Spy Who Saved the World,* 376–77.

Chapter 16: Workers against the Workers' State

1. Kuklinski's background from Weiser, "Question of Loyalty."
2. Gates, *From the Shadows,* 238; Rosenberg, *Haunted Land,* 181–82; Weiser, "Question of Loyalty."
3. Gates, *From the Shadows,* 227.
4. Rosenberg, *Haunted Land,* 161.
5. Gates, *From the Shadows,* 167.
6. Bernstein and Politi, *His Holiness,* 258–59.
7. See Kramer, "Colonel Kuklinski."
8. Rosenberg, *Haunted Land,* 188; Bernstein and Politi, *His Holiness,* 255–56.
9. Gates, *From the Shadows,* 228.
10. Ibid., 230.
11. Rosenberg, *Haunted Land,* 191–92.
12. Andrew and Mitrokhin, *Sword and Shield,* 527–28.
13. This quote from one of the few Kuklinski messages released by the CIA, in Kramer, "Colonel Kuklinski."
14. Weiser, "Question of Loyalty"; Rosenberg, *Haunted Land,* 204.
15. Bernstein and Politi, *His Holiness,* 333.
16. Gates, *From the Shadows,* 450–51.
17. Bernstein and Politi, *His Holiness,* 379–80.
18. Kramer, "Colonel Kuklinski."

BIBLIOGRAPHY

Books

Accoce, Pierre, and Pierre Quet. *A Man Called Lucy*. Translated by A. M. Sheridan Smith. New York: Coward-McCann, 1967.

Albright, Joseph, and Marcia Kunstel. *Bombshell: The Secret Story of America's Unknown Atomic Spy Conspiracy*. New York: Times Books, 1997.

Andrew, Christopher. *For the President's Eyes Only: Secret Intelligence and the American Presidency from Washington to Bush*. New York: HarperCollins, 1995.

Andrew, Christopher, and Oleg Gordievsky. *KGB: The Inside Story of Its Foreign Operations from Lenin to Gorbachev*. New York: HarperCollins, 1990.

Andrew, Christopher, and Vasili Mitrokhin. *The Sword and the Shield: The Mitrokhin Archive and the Secret History of the KGB*. New York: Basic Books, 1999.

Barnett, Correlli. *The Desert Generals*. New York: Viking, 1961.

———. *Engage the Enemy More Closely: The Royal Navy in the Second World War*. New York: W. W. Norton, 1991.

Beach, Edward L. *The United States Navy: 200 Years*. New York: Henry Holt, 1986.

Beesly, Patrick. *Room 40: British Naval Intelligence, 1914–1918.* San Diego: Harcourt Brace Jovanovich, 1982.

———. *Very Special Intelligence: The Story of the Admiralty's Operational Intelligence Center.* Garden City, N.Y.: Doubleday, 1978.

Benson, Robert Louis, and Michael Warner, eds. *Venona: Soviet Espionage and the American Response, 1939–1957.* Laguna Hills, Calif.: Aegean Park Press, 1996.

Bernstein, Carl, and Marco Politi. *His Holiness, John Paul II and the Hidden History of Our Time.* New York: Doubleday, 1996.

Beschloss, Michael R. *The Crisis Years: Kennedy and Khrushchev, 1960–1963.* New York: Edward Burlingame Books, 1991.

Blair, Clay, Jr. *Silent Victory: The U.S. Submarine War against Japan.* Philadelphia: Lippincott, 1975.

Boyd, Carl. *Hitler's Japanese Confidant: General Oshima Hiroshi and the Magic Intelligence.* Lawrence: University Press of Kansas, 1993.

Bradley, Omar N. *A Soldier's Story.* New York: Henry Holt, 1951.

Brugioni, Dino A. *Eyeball to Eyeball: The Inside Story of the Cuban Missile Crisis.* New York: Random House, 1990.

Cave Brown, Anthony. *Bodyguard of Lies.* New York: Harper & Row, 1975.

Cecil, Robert. *A Divided Life: A Personal Portrait of the Spy Donald Maclean.* New York: William Morrow, 1989.

Churchill, Winston S. *Great Contemporaries.* Chicago: University of Chicago Press, 1937.

Clark, Ronald. *The Man Who Broke Purple: The Life of Colonel William F. Friedman, Who Deciphered the Japanese Code in World War II.* Boston: Little, Brown, 1977.

Clemens, Diane Shaver. *Yalta.* New York: Oxford University Press, 1970.

Conlin, Joseph R. *The Morrow Book of Quotations in American History.* New York: William Morrow and Company, Inc., 1984.

Cruickshank, Charles. *Deception in World War II.* Oxford: Oxford University Press, 1979.

Dallin, David J. *Soviet Espionage.* New Haven: Yale University Press, 1955.

Deacon, Richard. *A History of the British Secret Service.* Marlboro, N.J.: Taplinger, 1959.

Deakin, F. W., and G. R. Storry. *The Case of Richard Sorge.* New York: Harper & Row, 1966.

Delmer, Sefton. *The Counterfeit Spy.* New York: Harper & Row, 1971.

Drae, Edward J. *MacArthur's Ultra: Codebreaking and the War against Japan, 1942–1945.* Lawrence: University Press of Kansas, 1992.

Farago, Ladislas. *The Broken Seal: The Story of Operation Magic and the Pearl Harbor Disaster.* New York: Random House, 1967.

Gates, Robert M. *From the Shadows: The Ultimate Insider's Story of Five Presidents and How They Won the Cold War.* New York: Simon & Schuster, 1996.

Haynes, John Earl, and Harvey Klehr. *Venona: Decoding Soviet Espionage in America.* New Haven: Yale University Press, 1999.

Hinsley, F. H., and Alan Stripp, eds. *Codebreakers: The Inside Story of Bletchley Park.* Oxford: Oxford University Press, 1993.

Hinsley, F. H., E. E. Thomas, C. F. G. Ransom, and R. C. Knight. *British Intelligence in the Second World War.* Vols. I, II, and III in two parts. London: Her Majesty's Stationery Office, 1979–1988.

Hodges, Andrew. *Alan Turing, the Enigma.* New York: Simon & Schuster, 1983.

Holloway, David. *Stalin and the Bomb: The Soviet Union and Atomic Energy, 1939–1956.* New Haven: Yale University Press, 1994.

Holmes, W. J. *Double-Edged Secrets: U.S. Naval Intelligence Operations in the Pacific during World War II.* Annapolis: Naval Institute Press, 1979.

———. *Undersea Victory: The Influence of Submarine Operations on the War in the Pacific.* Garden City, N.Y.: Doubleday, 1966.

Hyde, H. Montgomery. *The Atom Bomb Spies.* New York: Atheneum, 1980.

Johnson, Chalmers. *An Instance of Treason: Ozaki Hotsumi and the Sorge Spy Ring.* Palo Alto, Calif.: Stanford University Press, 1964.

Kahn, David. *The Codebreakers: The Story of Secret Writing.* New York: Macmillan, 1967.

———. *Kahn on Codes: Secrets of the New Cryptology.* New York: Macmillan, 1983.

———. *Seizing the Enigma: The Race to Break the German U-boat Codes, 1939–1943.* Boston: Houghton Mifflin, 1991.

Kesaris, Paul, ed. *The Rote Kapella: The CIA's History of Soviet Intelligence and Espionage Networks in Western Europe, 1936–1945.* Bethesda, Md.: University Publications of America, 1979.

Kettle, Michael. *Sidney Reilly: The True Story of the World's Greatest Spy.* New York: St. Martin's Press, 1983.

Knightley, Phillip. *The Master Spy: The Story of Kim Philby*. New York: Alfred A. Knopf, 1988.

Kozaczuk, Wladyslaw. *Enigma: How the German Machine Cipher Was Broken, and How It Was Read by the Allies in World War Two*. Translated and edited by Christopher Kasparek. Frederick, Md.: University Publications of America, 1984.

Laloy, Jean. *Yalta: Yesterday, Today and Tomorrow*. Translated by William R. Tyler. New York: Harper & Row, 1988.

Lamphere, Robert J., and Tom Schachtman. *The FBI-KGB War: A Special Agent's Story*. New York: Random House, 1986.

Layton, Rear Adm. Edwin T., Capt. Roger Pineau, and John Costello. *"And I Was There": Pearl Harbor and Midway—Breaking the Secrets*. New York: William Morrow (Quill), 1985.

Lewin, Ronald. *The American Magic: Codes, Ciphers and the Defeat of Japan*. New York: Farrar Straus Giroux, 1982.

———. *Ultra Goes to War: The First Account of World War II's Greatest Secret Based on Official Documents*. New York: McGraw-Hill, 1978.

Marshall, S. L. A. *World War I*. New York: American Heritage Press, 1964.

Masterman, J. C. *The Double-Cross System in the War of 1939 to 1945*. New Haven: Yale University Press, 1972.

Metropolis, N., J. Howlett, and Gian-Carlo Rota, eds. *A History of Computing in the Twentieth Century*. San Diego: Academic Press, 1980.

Miller, Nathan. *War at Sea: A Naval History of World War II*. New York: Scribner, 1995.

Montagu, Ewen. *The Man Who Never Was*. Philadelphia: J. B. Lippincott, 1953.

Moss, Norman. *Klaus Fuchs: The Man Who Stole the Atom Bomb*. New York: St. Martin's Press, 1987.

Neumann, William L. *After Victory: Churchill, Roosevelt, Stalin and the Making of the Peace*. New York: Harper & Row, 1967.

Newton, Verne W. *The Cambridge Spies: The Untold Story of Maclean, Philby and Burgess in America*. Lanham, Md.: Madison Books, 1991.

Page, Bruce, David Leitch, and Phillip Knightley. *The Philby Conspiracy*. Garden City, N.Y.: Doubleday, 1968.

Pipes, Richard. *A Concise History of the Russian Revolution*. New York: Alfred A. Knopf, 1995.

Potter, E. B. *Nimitz*. Annapolis: Naval Institute Press, 1976.

Powers, Thomas. *Heisenberg's War: The Secret History of the German Bomb.* New York: Alfred A. Knopf, 1993.

Prados, John. *Combined Fleet Decoded: The Secret History of American Intelligence and the Japanese Navy in World War II.* New York: Random House, 1995.

Prange, Gordon W., Donald M. Goldstein, and Katherine V. Dillon. *At Dawn We Slept: The Untold Story of Pearl Harbor.* New York: McGraw-Hill, 1981.

———. *Target Tokyo: The Story of the Sorge Spy Ring.* New York: McGraw-Hill, 1984.

Rado, Sandor. *Codename Dora.* Translated from the German by J. A. Underwood. London: Abelard, 1977.

Read, Anthony, and David Fisher. *Operation Lucy: The Most Secret Spy Ring in the Second World War.* New York: Coward, McCann & Geoghegan, 1981.

Rhodes, Richard. *The Making of the Atomic Bomb.* New York: Simon & Schuster, 1986.

Rosenberg, Tina. *The Haunted Land: Facing Europe's Ghosts after Communism.* New York: Random House, 1995.

Rowan, Richard Wilmer, with Robert G. Deindorfer. *Secret Service: Thirty-Three Centuries of Espionage.* New York: Hawthorn Books, 1967.

Rowlett, Frank B. *The Story of Magic: Memoirs of an American Cryptologic Pioneer,* with Foreword and Epilogue by David Kahn. Laguna Hills, Calif.: Aegean Park Press, 1999.

Schecter, Jerrold L., and Peter S. Deriabin. *The Spy Who Saved the World: How a Soviet Colonel Changed the Course of the Cold War.* New York: Charles Scribner's Sons, 1992.

Smith, Bradley F. *The Ultra-Magic Deals and the Most Secret Special Relationship.* Novato, Calif.: Presidio Press, 1993.

Stevenson, William. *A Man Called Intrepid: The Secret War.* New York: Harcourt Brace Jovanovich, 1976.

Stinnett, Robert B. *Day of Deceit: The Truth about FDR and Pearl Harbor.* New York: Free Press, 2000.

Sulzberger, C. L. *Such a Peace: The Roots and Ashes of Yalta.* New York: Continuum, 1982.

Tarrant, V. E. *The Red Orchestra: The Soviet Spy Network inside Nazi Europe.* New York: John Wiley & Sons, 1995.

Tuchman, Barbara. *The Guns of August.* New York: Dell, 1962.

———. *The Zimmermann Telegram.* New York: Macmillan, 1966.

Van der Vat, Dan. *The Atlantic Campaign: World War II's Greatest Struggle at Sea.* New York: Harper & Row, 1988.

Weinstein, Allen. *Perjury: The Hiss-Chambers Case.* New York: Random House, 1997.

Weinstein, Allen, and Alexander Vassiliev. *The Haunted Wood: Soviet Espionage in America—the Stalin Era.* New York: Random House, 1999.

Welchman, Gordon. *The Hut Six Story: Breaking the Enigma Codes.* New York: McGraw-Hill, 1982.

West, Nigel. *The Sigint Secrets: The Signals Intelligence War, 1900 to Today, Including the Persecution of Gordon Welchman.* New York: William Morrow, 1986.

———. *A Thread of Deceit: Espionage Myths of World War II.* New York: Random House, 1985.

Whymant, Robert. *Stalin's Spy: Richard Sorge and the Tokyo Espionage Ring.* New York: St. Martin's Press, 1996.

Williams, Robert Chadwell. *Klaus Fuchs, Atom Spy.* Cambridge, Mass.: Harvard University Press, 1987.

Winterbotham, F. W. *The Ultra Secret.* New York: Harper & Row, 1974.

Wright, Peter, with Paul Greenglass. *Spycatcher: The Candid Autobiography of a Senior Intelligence Officer.* New York: Viking, 1987.

Wynne, Greville. *Contact on Gorky Street.* New York: Atheneum, 1968.

Articles, Interviews, and Studies

Bell, Julian. "Cambridge Politics." *The New Statesman and Nation,* VI, no. 146 (December 9, 1933), 731–732.

Breindel, Eric. "Hiss's Guilt." *The New Republic.* April 15, 1996 18–20.

Brzezinski, Zbigniew. "White House Diary, 1980." *Orbis* (winter 1988) 32–48.

Kahn, David. "Soviet Comint in the Cold War." *Cryptologia* 22, no. 1 (1998) 1–23.

Kramer, Mark. "Jaruzelski, the Soviet Union, and the Imposition of Martial Law in Poland: New Light on the Mystery of December 1981." *Bulletin, Cold War International History Project* (Washington, D.C.: Woodrow Wilson International Center for Scholars) 11 (winter 1998): 5–16.

———. "Colonel Kuklinski and the Polish Crisis, 1980–81." *Bulletin, Cold War International History Project* (Washington, D.C.: Woodrow Wilson International Center for Scholars) 11 (winter 1998): 48–59.

Kuklinski, Ryszard. "The Crushing of Solidarity." *Orbis* (winter 1988): 7–31.

Mulligan, Timothy P. "Spies, Ciphers and 'Zitadelle': Intelligence and the Battle of Kursk, 1943." *Journal of Contemporary History* 22 (1987): 236–260.

Rejewski, Marian. "Remarks on Appendix I to British Intelligence in the Second World War by F. H. Hinsley," tr. by Christopher Kasparek, *Cryptologia* 6, no. 1 (January 1982): 75–83.

Schmidt, Maria. "The Hiss Dossier." *The New Republic* (November 8, 1993) 17–20.

Weiser, Benjamin. "A Question of Loyalty." *Washington Post Magazine* (December 13, 1992). Washington Post Archives: http://newslibrary.krmediastream.com/cgi-bin/do.../wp

Yoshikawa, Takeo, with Lt. Col. Norman Stanford, USMC. "Top Secret Assignment." *United States Naval Institute Proceedings* 86, no. 12 (December 1960): 27–39.

Archives

Friedman, William F. "Preliminary Historical Report on the Solution of the 'B' Machine." SRH-159, National Archives.

"JN40 Cryptographic System, History of Attack." Box 578, NR-1389, National Archives.

Redman, Adm. Joseph R. "Op-20-G File." SRH-268, National Archives (June 1942).

Safford, Captain Laurance F. "A Brief History of Communications Intelligence in the United States." SRH-149, National Archives.

Venona. "Account of a Discussion with 'Albert' [Akhmerov] Concerning 'Robert's' [Silvermaster's] Group," New York to Moscow. Nos. 1388–1389, National Archives (October 1, 1944).

———. "KOL'TsOV's Account of a Conversation with 'Jurist' [White]," New York to Moscow. Nos. 1119–1121, National Archives (August 4–5, 1944).

———. "Material from 'H' [Maclean]," Washington to Moscow. Nos. 1808, 1809, National Archives (March 30, 1945).

———. "Material of 'G' [Maclean]," Washington to Moscow. No. 1788, National Archives (March 29, 1945).

———. "Report on Information Given by 'Homer' [Maclean], 1944," New York to Moscow. Nos. 1271–1274, National Archives (September 7, 1944).

Internet

Tony Sale, *Codes and Ciphers in the Second World War,* "The Lorenz Cipher and How Bletchley Park Broke It," http://www.codesandciphers.org.uk.

Stealing Secrets, Telling Lies, James Gannon's first book, follows his extensive career as a journalist. He has worked as a newspaper reporter and television writer and producer and was on the staff of NBC News for twenty years. From 1982 to 1984, he wrote and produced four one-hour documentaries that won several awards for their elucidation of economic issues and clear writing on technical subjects. As a freelance writer, Gannon has published articles in *The American Legion Magazine, The Nation,* and *Parks and Conservation Magazine.*